Is the Gospel Good News?

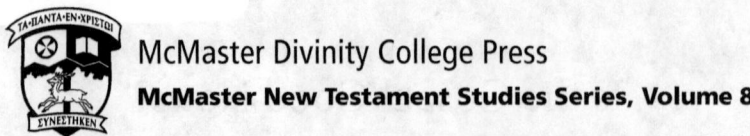

McMaster Divinity College Press
McMaster New Testament Studies Series, Volume 8

Patterns of Discipleship in the New Testament (1996)

The Road from Damascus: The Impact of Paul's Conversion on His Life, Thought and Ministry (1997)

Life in the Face of Death: The Resurrection Message of the New Testament (1998)

The Challenge of Jesus' Parables (2000)

Into God's Presence: Prayer in the New Testament (2001)

Reading the Gospels Today (2004)

Contours of Christology in the New Testament (2005)

Hearing the Old Testament in the New Testament (2006)

The Messiah in the Old and New Testaments (2007)

Translating the New Testament: Text, Translation, Theology (2009)

Christian Mission: Old Testament Foundations and New Testament Developments (2010)

Empire in the New Testament (2011)

The Church, Then and Now (2012)

Rejection: God's Refugees in Biblical and Contemporary Perspective (2015)

Rediscovering Worship: Past, Present, and Future (2015)

The Bible and Social Justice: Old Testament and New Testament Foundations for the Church's Urgent Call (2015)

The Letter to the Romans: Exegesis and Application (2018)

Is the Gospel Good News?

Edited by
STANLEY E. PORTER
and HUGHSON T. ONG

◆PICKWICK *Publications* • Eugene, Oregon

IS THE GOSPEL GOOD NEWS?

McMaster New Testament Studies Series, Volume 8
McMaster Divinity College Press

Copyright © 2019 Wipf and Stock Publishers. All rights reserved. Except for brief quotations in critical publications or reviews, no part of this book may be reproduced in any manner without prior written permission from the publisher. Write: Permissions, Wipf and Stock Publishers, 199 W. 8th Ave., Suite 3, Eugene, OR 97401.

McMaster Divinity College
1280 Main Street West
Hamilton, Ontario, Canada L8S 4K1

Pickwick Publications
An Imprint of Wipf and Stock Publishers
199 W. 8th Ave., Suite 3
Eugene, OR 97401

www.wipfandstock.com

PAPERBACK ISBN: 978-1-5326-1132-2
HARDCOVER ISBN: 978-1-5326-1134-6
EBOOK ISBN: 978-1-5326-1133-9

Cataloguing-in-Publication data:

Names: Porter, Stanley E., editor. | Ong, Hughson T., editor.

Title: Is the gospel good news? / edited by Stanley E. Porter and Hughson T. Ong.

Description: Eugene, OR: Pickwick Publications, 2019. | McMaster New Testament Studies Series 8. | Includes bibliographical references and indexes.

Identifiers: ISBN 978-1-5326-1132-2 (paperback) | ISBN 978-1-5326-1134-6 (hardcover) | ISBN 978-1-5326-1133-9 (ebook)

Subjects: LCSH: Bible—Theology. | Bible—Criticism, interpretation, etc.

Classification: BS543.A1 I7 2019 (paperback) | BS543.A1 (ebook)

Manufactured in the U.S.A. 04/29/19

Contents

Preface / vii

Contributors / ix

Abbreviations / xi

The Gospel as Good News: An Introduction / 1
—*Stanley E. Porter and Hughson T. Ong*

Bible

1 The Gospel According to Nathan:
 The Good News of the Davidic Promises in 2 Samuel 7 / 9
 —*Paul S. Evans*

2 The Signs and Wonders of Salvation:
 Beholding Isaiah and His Children / 31
 —*Mark J. Boda*

3 When Did the Good News Become the Gospel?
 A Corpus and Diachronic Study of Εὐαγγέλιον / 46
 —*Francis G. H. Pang*

4 The Good News of the Gospels:
 Good News as Form and Content / 58
 —*Stanley E. Porter*

5 Jesus' Social Network as Evidence for the Gospel
 as Good News / 83
 —*Hughson T. Ong*

6 In the Making and the Unmasking: Spiritual Formation as
 Paul's Missional "Good News," Then and Now / 97
 —*Matthew Forrest Lowe*

7   We Need the Gospel: A Response to Douglas A. Campbell with
    Regard to Paul's Diagnosis of the Human Predicament / 121
      —*Jae Hyun Lee*

8   The Gospel as God's Gift: Good News from Ephesians
    1:1—3:12 / 154
      —*Lynn H. Cohick*

Theology

9   "*The Word Became Flesh*": Christian Theology and Science
    as Coinherent, Not Conflicted . . . A Post-Intellectual
    Approach / 179
      —*W. Ross Hastings*

10 The Spirit of the Gospel / 223
      —*Steven M. Studebaker*

11 Can I Get a Witness? Proclaiming the Gospel
    in a Post-Everything World / 245
      —*Lee Beach and Nicole Reid*

Crucial Topics

12 Baptism in the Holy Spirit: A Circumcised Heart,
    A New Disposition / 267
      —*Ronald D. Peters*

13 The Gospel as Good News to the Poor:
    God as the King of Justice and Reconciliation / 284
      —*Beth M. Stovell*

14 Is the Gospel Good News for Women? / 314
      —*Cynthia Long Westfall*

   Index of Modern Authors / 355

   Index of Ancient Sources / 361

Preface

THE 2015 H. H. Bingham Colloquium on the New Testament at McMaster Divinity College in Hamilton, Ontario, Canada, held on June 4–5, was entitled "Is the Gospel Good News?" We thought that we already knew the answer to this question, but we were pleasantly surprised to hear the variety of answers proposed by our participants. None of them chose to answer in the negative (or at least leave it at that), but all of them offered their own individual perspectives on a range of topics related to the notion that the gospel is indeed good news. This Colloquium was the nineteenth in a continuing series held here at MDC. This conference continued the general format that we use for such conferences, although we expanded our usual offerings over two days. We were able to invite two scholarly guests to participate in the conference as plenary speakers, one a biblical scholar and the other a theologian (and chemist, and he will say more about that in his paper). They provided a range of helpful perspectives on our topic. In conjunction with other activities at MDC, we were also able to invite a number of our own alumni back to the College to participate in the conference. We were pleased to welcome graduates back from various parts of the world, and their contribution was profound, as is witnessed in this volume.

We have organized the papers around three broad topics: Bible, Theology, and Crucial Topics. The papers in the Bible section are themselves diverse, ranging over both Old and New Testament passages and ideas, and as will be noticed in the introduction and the essays themselves, many if not most of the other papers could well have been placed in this category as well. The Theology section includes papers that address focused theological topics in light of the question of what constitutes the good news. The third and final category, Crucial Topics, is in no way less important than the other two. In our vision for this

Preface

conference, we wanted our participants—including our alumni from around the world—to be able to explore our topic from their particular set of interests, and they have done so. These papers provide some new and different perspectives on ways in which the gospel is good news.

The Bingham Colloquium is named after Dr. Herbert Henry Bingham, who was a noted Baptist leader in Ontario, Canada. His leadership abilities were recognized by Baptists across Canada and around the world. His qualities included his genuine friendship, dedicated leadership, unswerving Christian faith, tireless devotion to duty, insightful service as a preacher and pastor, and visionary direction for congregation and denomination alike. These qualities endeared him both to his own church members and to believers in other denominations. The Colloquium has been endowed by his daughter as an act of appreciation for her father. We are pleased to be able to continue this tradition.

The first volumes of the Bingham Colloquium were published by Eerdmans Publishing, but since 2010 all of the volumes in this series have been published by McMaster Divinity College Press, in conjunction with Wipf & Stock Publishers of Eugene, Oregon, in the McMaster New Testament Studies Series. We appreciate this active and continuing publishing relationship.

I finally would like to thank the individual contributors for accepting their assignments and for all their efforts in the preparation and presentation of papers that make a significant contribution of benefit to those who are captivated by the notion of the gospel as good news, whatever form that may take. I would especially like to thank my New Testament colleague, Hughson Ong, for working together with me to edit this volume for publication. We would like to thank the staff and student helpers and volunteers at McMaster Divinity College, all of whom were integral in creating a pleasant environment and a supportive atmosphere for the Colloquium. I would also like to thank my graduate assistant, Bryan Fletcher, for his work on the indexes.

—Stanley E. Porter

Contributors[1]

LEE BEACH (PhD, McMaster Divinity College), Associate Professor of Christian Ministry, and Garbutt F. Smith Chair in Ministry Formation and Director of Ministry Formation, McMaster Divinity College, Hamilton, Ontario

MARK J. BODA, Professor of Old Testament, McMaster Divinity College, Hamilton, Ontario

LYNN H. COHICK, Provost/Dean, Professor of New Testament, Denver Seminary, Littleton, Colorado

PAUL S. EVANS, Assistant Professor of Old Testament, McMaster Divinity College, Hamilton, Ontario

W. ROSS HASTINGS, Sangwoo Youtong Chee Professor of Theology, Regent College, Vancouver, British Columbia

JAE HYUN LEE (PhD, McMaster Divinity College), University Chaplain, Handong Global University, South Korea

MATTHEW FORREST LOWE (PhD, McMaster Divinity College), Independent Scholar, Writer, and Editor, Hagersville, Ontario

HUGHSON T. ONG (PhD, McMaster Divinity College), Assistant Academic Dean and Registrar, and Associate Professor of Biblical Studies, Emmanuel Bible College, Kitchener, Ontario

---

1. In this list of contributors, we note those who are graduates of McMaster Divinity College, whom we welcomed back to participate in this conference.

Contributors

FRANCIS G. H. PANG (PhD, McMaster Divinity College), Assistant Professor of New Testament and Information Technology Systems Analyst, McMaster Divinity College, Hamilton, Ontario

RONALD D. PETERS (PhD, McMaster Divinity College), Professor of New Testament, Great Lakes Christian College, Michigan

STANLEY E. PORTER, President and Dean, Professor of New Testament, and Roy A. Hope Chair in Christian Worldview, McMaster Divinity College, Hamilton, Ontario

NICOLE A. REID (MTS, McMaster Divinity College), Independent Writer and Community Ministry Leader, Niagara, Ontario

BETH M. STOVELL (PhD, McMaster Divinity College), Associate Professor of Old Testament, Ambrose University, Calgary, Alberta

STEVEN M. STUDEBAKER, Associate Professor of Systematic and Historical Theology, and Howard and Shirley Bentall Chair in Evangelical Thought, McMaster Divinity College, Hamilton, Ontario

CYNTHIA LONG WESTFALL, Associate Professor of New Testament, McMaster Divinity College, Ontario

Abbreviations

AB	Anchor Bible
ABD	Freedman, David Noel, ed. *Anchor Bible Dictionary*. 6 vols. New York: Doubleday, 1992.
ABR	*Australian Biblical Review*
AcBib	Academia Biblica
AnBib	Analectica Biblica
ANEM	Ancient Near East Monographs
ANET	*Ancient Near Eastern Texts Relating to the Old Testament*. Edited by James B. Pritchard. 3rd ed. Princeton: Princeton University Press, 1969.
AOAT	Alter Orient und Altes Testament
BBR	*Bulletin of Biblical Research*
BCOTWP	Baker Commentary on the Old Testament Wisdom and Psalms
BDAG	Bauer, Walter, et al. *Greek-English Lexicon of the New Testament and Other Early Christian Literature*. 3rd ed. Chicago: University of Chicago Press, 2000.
BibInt	Biblical Interpretation
BNTC	Black's New Testament Commentaries
BT	*The Bible Translator*
BTB	*Biblical Theology Bulletin*
BZAW	Beihefte zur Zeitschrift für die alttestamentliche Wissenschaft
CBQ	*Catholic Biblical Quarterly*

Abbreviations

CC	Continental Commentaries
CD	Barth, Karl. *Church Dogmatics*. Edited by T. F. Torrance and G. W. Bromiley. Translated by G. T. Thomson et al. 14 vols. Edinburgh: T. & T. Clark, 1936–1977.
ChrCent	*Christian Century*
CILT	Current Issues in Linguistic Theory
ClQ	*Classical Quarterly*
CTA	*Corpus des tablettes en cunéiformes alphabétiques découvertes à Ras Shamra-Ugarit de 1929 à 1939*. Edited by Andrée Herdner. Paris: Geuthner, 1963.
CTL	Cambridge Textbooks in Linguistics
CTM	*Concordia Theological Monthly*
CTR	*Criswell Theological Review*
ECHC	Early Christianity in Its Hellenistic Context
EDNT	Balz, Horst, and Gerhard Schneider, eds. *Exegetical Dictionary of the New Testament*. 3 vols. Grand Rapids: Eerdmans, 1990–1993.
EKKNT	Evangelisch-katholischer Kommentar zum Neuen Testament
ExpTim	*The Expository Times*
FN	*Filología Neotestamentaria*
FRLANT	Forschungen zur Religion und Literatur des Alten und Neuen Testaments
HBT	*Horizons in Biblical Theology*
HSM	Harvard Semitic Monographs
HTR	*Harvard Theological Review*
IBC	Interpretation: A Bible Commentary for Teaching and Preaching
ICC	International Critical Commentary
IEJ	*Israel Exploration Journal*
Int	*Interpretation*

Abbreviations

IVPNTC	IVP New Testament Commentary
JAOS	*Journal of the American Oriental Society*
JBL	*Journal of Biblical Literature*
JCS	*Journal of Cuneiform Studies*
JETS	*Journal of the Evangelical Theological Society*
JGRChJ	*Journal of Greco-Roman Christianity and Judaism*
JQR	*Jewish Quarterly Review*
JRS	*Journal of Roman Studies*
JSNT	*Journal for the Study of the New Testament*
JSNTSup	Journal for the Study of the New Testament Supplement Series
JSOTSup	Journal for the Study of the Old Testament Supplement Series
JSPL	*Journal for the Study of Paul and His Letters*
JTSA	*Journal of Theology for Southern Africa*
LAPO	Littératures anciennes du Proche-Orient
LBS	Linguistic Biblical Studies
LCC	Library of Christian Classics
L&N	Louw, Johannes P., and Eugene A. Nida. *Greek-English Lexicon of the New Testament: Based on Semantic Domains*. 2 vols. 2nd ed. New York: UBS, 1989.
LNTS	Library of New Testament Studies
LOTS	Library of Old Testament Studies
LSJ	Liddell, Henry George, Robert Scott, Henry Stuart Jones. *A Greek-English Lexicon*. 9th ed. with revised supplement. Oxford: Clarendon, 1996.
MNTS	McMaster New Testament Studies
MRS	Mission de Ras Shamra
NAC	New American Commentary
NCBC	New Century Bible Commentary

Abbreviations

NIVAC	NIV Application Commentary
NICNT	New International Commentary: New Testament
NICOT	New International Commentary: Old Testament
NIDOTTE	*New International Dictionary of Old Testament Theology and Exegesis.* Edited by Willem A. VanGemeren. 5 vols. Grand Rapids: Zondervan, 1997.
NovT	*Novum Testamentum*
NovTSup	*Novum Testamentum Supplements*
NTS	New Testament Studies
Or	*Orientalia*
OTL	Old Testament Library
PNTC	Pillar New Testament Commentaries
RIME	The Royal Inscriptions of Mesopotamia, Early Periods
SBG	Studies in Biblical Greek
SBLSS	SBL Symposium Series
SBT	Studies in Biblical Theology
SJT	*Scottish Journal of Theology*
SNTSMS	Society for New Testament Studies Monograph Series
SP	Sacra Pagina
ST	*Studia Theologica*
StT	Studi e Testi, Biblioteca apostolica vaticana
TDNT	*Theological Dictionary of the New Testament.* Edited by Gerhard Kittel and Gerhard Friedrich. Translated by Geoffrey W. Bromiley. 10 vols. Grand Rapids: Eerdmans, 1964–1976.
TDOT	*Theological Dictionary of the Old Testament.* Edited by G. Johannes Botterweck and Helmer Ringgren. Translated by John T. Willis et al. 8 vols. Grand Rapids: Eerdmans, 1974–2006.
Them	*Themelios*
ThTo	*Theology Today*

Abbreviations

TNTC	Tyndale New Testament Commentaries
TS	*Theological Studies*
VT	*Vetus Testamentum*
VTSup	Vetus Testamentum Supplements
WAW	Writings from the Ancient World
WBC	Word Biblical Commentary
WGRW	Writings from the Greco-Roman World
WUNT	Wissenschaftliche Untersuchungen zum Neuen Testament
ZAW	*Zeitschrift für die alttestamentliche Wissenschaft*

The Gospel as Good News
An Introduction

Stanley E. Porter and Hughson T. Ong

The Greek term that is often translated "good news" or "gospel" was not a creation of early Christianity. In fact, the Greek word that is translated with the English "good news" was used to indicate fortunate events or circumstances before the advent of Christianity. In the ancient Greco-Roman world, significant events, such as the birthday of a Caesar, could be proclaimed as an event of "good news," because the gods had seen fit to bestow upon humanity the good fortune of this person's birth, life, and beneficent activities. With this in mind, it is not surprising that Christianity made use of this term, as listeners and readers who encountered the word would have been prepared to recognize the fact that contained within the appearance of an event or person was good news for those who received it. Early Christians recognized that, in the advent and life and death and resurrection of Jesus Christ, there was indeed something to be celebrated—there was good news in what God had chosen to do through Jesus Christ that was worth noting to the point of claiming that it marked the turning point in all of human history. All of the previous events of good news, as good and as celebratory as they may have been, were seen to pale in comparison with the good news that was brought by Jesus Christ as the minister of God's transformative salvation and life for humanity. As a result, it is not surprising to see how the notion of "good news" became the "gospel," a term that now carries significant theological weight. Speaking of the gospel is a means of referring in encapsulated form to this good news that was proclaimed through the events surrounding the coming of Jesus Christ in fulfillment of God's will for humanity. Christians did not hesitate to proclaim this gospel as the good news for them and for their fellow human beings. Once this proclamation began to spread, it was only a short time before this gospel message took on not just oral but written form, what we now call Gospels. There is some debate among scholars about when it was that the good news became a written Gospel, but we know that the four Gospels are all accounts of this good news found in Jesus Christ, recorded in a gospel-like way so as to be able to deliver this written account to others. From there, one can see that the spreading of the gospel became a matter of not just proclamation but transmission and publication and dissemination far and wide. What began as a singular Greek word, with nothing distinct in its particular formation, was transformed from its simple depiction of an event of merit to a worldwide announcement of the good news of how God had acted on behalf of humans to provide for their redemption. This is a message—the gospel—that we as Christians continue to proclaim, not just on Sundays but through various activities throughout the rest of the week as well. This volume encompasses some accounts of how this good news has been understood through the ages and continues to be understood in relation to some of the major topics and issues of our contemporary world. In order to deal with the topic, we have divided the essays into three categories: Bible, Theology, and Crucial Topics.

In the first section, on the Bible, we include eight chapters. This is the largest section of the book. In some ways, this is entirely appropriate, as the gospel as good news originates in the biblical account of how God has given his good news to humanity. As will be noted below, many of the other papers could legitimately be included in this category also, but we have chosen to divide them into two further categories. Two of the papers of this first section go back even before the good news of Jesus Christ to find the good news, or gospel, in the Old Testament. Paul Evans deals with the Davidic promises in 2 Samuel 7 as an encapsulation of the "good news" in several different ways. These include, but are not limited to, its looking back to the Abrahamic covenant and its looking forward to the messianic fulfillment. This set of promises serves as a foundation that undergirds larger organizational structures in the Old

Testament as well as other fulfillment of Davidic good news throughout the biblical account. As a result, Evans ends his paper, as do several other contributors, in the New Testament, in his case especially in Paul's letter to the Romans. In the second essay, Mark Boda examines the good news from the book of Isaiah in a similar light, especially as Isaiah is the prophetic book that is so clearly re-proclaimed by the New Testament authors and is therefore often referred to as the "Fifth Gospel." Boda concentrates upon Isa 6–12 as the focal point of his examination of Isaianic salvation, but he too ends up making important connections to the New Testament, especially the Matthean birth account.

This first section also includes five papers specifically on the New Testament. Three of these essays concern the Gospels. Francis Pang raises the legitimate question of when it was that the notion of good news became something more than that, something that was seen to represent a developed theological concept regarding God's work in the world. To do this, he provides a corpus linguistics-based study that describes the semantic range of the Greek word for "good news" in its pre-Christian and then its non-Christian use as a means of chronicling how it became a technical Greek term with high theological significance. Stanley Porter focuses upon the Gospels themselves by looking at the notion of good news as both having a message, its content, and being translated into a tangible form. He traces the use of the cognate noun and verb forms of the Greek word translated "good news" or "preach good news" throughout Mark, Matthew, and Luke's Gospels. The third essay in this group, by Hughson Ong, also treats the Gospel accounts and how the "good news" would have been received by those who were hearing it for the first time in the first century. Ong rejects a number of ways that the gospel has been popularized or even distorted as he tries to reconstruct how its first appearance in a Christian context would have been understood. To do so he reconstructs Jesus' social network—in that sense, this is an essay in sociolinguistics—as the environment in which this message would have been shared and received, comparing the results in relation to the women who accompanied Jesus, to religious leaders, and to the crowds. The final three essays in this biblical section are concerned with Paul's letters. The first essay, by Matthew Lowe, takes up a contemporary topic, the notion of mission, and sees how this concept is developed both within Paul's letters and in practical terms within the contemporary church. He responds to several recent books on Paul by taking what he calls a socio-rhetorical perspective, with attention to matters of empire. The second essay, by Jae Hyun Lee, confronts the scholarly work of Douglas Campbell, who has proposed some interpretations, concerned especially with Paul's letter to the Romans, regarding Paul's view of the human situation that Lee simply finds indefensible. Lee provides arguments for why he thinks that the foundation of Campbell's argument, his reconstruction of the early chapters of Romans, cannot be defended in the text. The final essay of this first section is by Lynn Cohick, the first essay of the volume by one of our invited conference speakers. This essay is specifically focused upon Paul's letter to the Ephesians, especially 1:1—3:12 and in particular 2:8–10. This essay first explores the implications of this passage from the New Perspective on Paul, but finds that such an approach cannot answer all of the questions raised. Cohick then examines the passage in light of recent discussion of benefaction in the ancient world. She finds that this is a passage reflecting unsurpassed divine beneficence in the giving of salvation through Christ apart from the worthiness of those receiving it.

The second group of essays has been given the label Theology, by which we mean theology broadly defined to encompass a number of the implications of discussion of the good news for the church as the people of God. Within this section, there are three essays. The first of this group is by Ross Hastings, the second of our invited speakers, who has offered a major treatment of a timely and pressing subject. Hastings, having a background in both science (chemistry, in particular) and theology, discusses the relationship of theology to science. Rather than finding them opposed to or at odds with each other, he reframes the discussion in light of recent research and uses the term "coinherent" to describe their compatibility. By this he means that both science and theology coinhere in the same source, God. He teases out some of the significant implications of this perspective in this essay. The second essay, by Steve Studebaker, involves a conscious play upon the use of the word "Spirit" in the essay's title to explore the role of the Holy Spirit in Christian theology with regard to the meaning of the gospel and the attitude we take toward this good news. Studebaker rejects the notion that the good news is about escaping from this earthly life (which he characterizes as emerging out of cruciform or Christocentric views) and instead offers a sketch of the role of the Spirit in Christian theology. He grounds this in both the Old and New Testaments as a means of responding to recent theological positions that do not endorse a fuller view of the Spirit's work in the gospel. The third essay, by Lee Beach and Nicole Reid, addresses one of the most trenchant issues of our time, how it is that the gospel as good news can be seen to be relevant in a world that is, as the authors characterize it, post-everything. We live in what is often facilely characterized as a postmodern world, but this terminology often masks deeper-seated issues that have direct relevance for the timeliness of the gospel witness to people who live what are, to them, moral, happy lives in a vaguely deistic universe. Therefore, the question of whether the gospel is good news extends to the question of whether evangelism is relevant in our day. Beach and Reid argue that it is—but it must be re-conceptualized and reinvigorated in a way that first affects those who are emboldened to proclaim it.

The third group of essays has been given the inelegant title Crucial Topics. We must explain that this does not in any way mean that these essays do not fit within the scope of this volume or that they are considered inferior to the other essays (and there was nowhere else for them to be placed). Nothing could be further from the truth. The reason for this title is that we simply could not find a more suitable descriptor to capture the diversity of the three papers included within this section and recognized that they raise crucial issues that merit consideration in light of the topic of our entire volume. If we had been so inclined, we could have placed each of these essays within one of the other two categories (in fact, probably the biblical section), but we did not want unnecessarily to force these categories and run the risk of some of the important things they have to say being overlooked. The first essay, by Ronald Peters, addresses the question of the meaning of the baptism of the Holy Spirit. At first glance, it may appear strange to include this essay in the third section, as much of the essay is devoted to examination of Greek passages and is concerned in particular with the presence or absence of the article and its implications for defining instances of the Holy Spirit. Nevertheless, we have placed it here because of the implications of the essay. Peters is concerned especially with those instances without the article, which he posits indicate "holy disposition." This understanding has implications for not only how we understand the Holy Spirit, but how we understand what it means to have a holy spirit within us as humans. This has major practical implications. The last two essays address topics of indisputably contentious Christian relevance. The first of these, by Beth Stovell, raises the question of how the good news is good news for the poor, whether they are in spiritual, economic, or relational poverty. Stovell's essay is an exercise in biblical theology, but with acute practical relevance. Stovell takes a thorough look at the ancient world and the full range of biblical testimony before she turns to the contemporary social context to address this residual societal problem. In order to do so, she uses Conceptual Metaphor Theory to explore the notion of divine kingship and its implications for God's work of restoring people to himself and eliminating inequity. In other words, Stovell wishes to encourage evangelicals to have greater social consciousness and greater social engagement. The final essay, by Cynthia Westfall, tackles the question of how the gospel is good news for women. The church has often, even into the twenty-first century, been seen not as a promoter of good news for women but as a place of restriction of women on a number of different fronts and in a number of different ways. Westfall marshals plenty of evidence that this has been and continues to be the case. In this essay, Westfall goes back to the biblical texts and then describes how it is possible to see the gospel as good news for women, even within the church, and in fact how, rightly understood, the gospel can be the source of eminently good news for women (and men) of any age and especially in contemporary society.

There is much more that could be said about each of the essays within this volume. Those who are examining the list of contributors will notice the mix of MDC faculty, visiting speakers, and alumni included in the roster. We believe that the mix of scholars from various locations and in different stages of their academic careers has led to a stimulating environment that resulted in the addressing of our topic of the gospel as good news in invigorating and vibrant ways. This intellectual engagement was often reflected in the time for questions that we reserved at the end of each paper presentation. We are unable to present those questions and answers here in this volume, but the presentations themselves offer insight into the type of provocation of and the kinds of questions raised by the original hearers. We hope that the essays in this volume will have an equivalent effect upon readers as well.

Bible

1

The Gospel According to Nathan

The Good News of the Davidic Promises in 2 Samuel 7

Paul S. Evans

INTRODUCTION

THE IMPORTANCE OF DAVID in Old Testament theology and in the rise of messianism in Judaism and Christianity is well known. Many prophetic texts center their expectations on a future Davidic king who will deliver Israel and put things to rights (e.g., Isa 9:2–7; 11; Ezek 34), and many psalms focus on the special relationship of the Davidic king to Yahweh (e.g., Pss 2; 72) and the promises made to David (Pss 18:50; 84:9; 89:3–4; 132:10, 17). Even in the face of their apparent failure, Psalmists continue to invoke Yahweh's promises to David and call for Yahweh to be faithful to them (e.g., Ps 89:46–51).

The hopes and expectations that center around David stem from Nathan's famous oracle to David in 2 Sam 7. In this passage David himself responds to the gracious words of Nathan and describes them as "speaking good things" (ותדבר את־הטובה) (2 Sam 7:28), which is quite close to the definition of "gospel." In light of David's characterization of this prophetic word as nothing less than gospel, and in light of the central importance of 2 Sam 7 for messianic expectations, this paper will examine this prophecy as the gospel according to Nathan and, in light of the theme of this volume, will explore the ways in which this gospel is indeed good news. It will be seen that the radical nature of

Yahweh's unconditional commitment to David became the basis for future hope in Israel despite difficult historical conditions or Israel's sinful past. However, this gospel also created a tension between the demands of the Mosaic law and the free gift of the Davidic covenant. In the Old Testament both are affirmed, but it is the gospel of Nathan that provided ongoing hope to those in exile and beyond. Furthermore, Yahweh's gracious commitment to David became the seedbed not only for messianism, but also for the gospel of grace proclaimed in the New Testament. In fact, it still has implications for understanding the gospel today.

THE GOSPEL OF NATHAN AS PART OF THE DEUTERONOMISTIC HISTORY

The study of the books of Joshua—2 Kings has varied throughout the history of interpretation, with some treating each book separately as its own discrete and independent literary work and others treating them as a connected, grand literary work of Israel's history from their entrance into the land to their departure into Babylonian exile.[1] Martin Noth was the first to put forward a theory of the unity of these books, which he explained as the product of one author living during the time of the Babylonian exile.[2] Noth labeled the historical work the "Deuteronomistic History" (hereafter DH) due to the obvious influence of Deuteronomy on the work. Noth argued that the historian, labeled the Deuteronomist (hereafter Dtr), incorporated Deuteronomy as the introduction to his historical work, framing the original Deuteronomic core with the speeches of Moses in Deuteronomy (thought to be his own creative compositions) and added other sources (conquest tales, prophetic narratives, annals, etc.) that he organized and shaped into a coherent story. Situated at integral junctures throughout the history were his own summarizing reflections or speeches that he placed on the lips of key characters, which spelled out the course of events in his history

---

1. The influence of Deuteronomy on these books was noted in many early studies, even if their unity as one lengthy history was not explained in this way. For example, Julius Wellhausen (*Prolegomena*, 280) argued that Judges, Samuel, and Kings were impressed by religious ideals of the exile typified in Deuteronomy, writing, "It came into existence under the influence of Deuteronomy which pervaded the whole century of the exile."

2. Noth, *Überlieferungsgeschichtliche Studien*. The first part of this work was translated into English as *The Deuteronomistic History*.

and demarcated major sections within his work.[3] Dtr shaped his source material, imposing unity on chronology, themes, and literary style. In many respects Noth accepted the literary judgments of his predecessors but was novel in stressing the unity of the work as a whole.[4]

One aspect of Noth's conclusions that has been vigorously disputed is the theme(s) of the history. Noth maintained a purely negative view of Dtr's purposes. The guiding principle in Dtr's narrative was the Deuteronomic law of Moses, which he used to judge the entire history of Israel and present it as a history of disobedience to Yahweh's law. According to Noth, the history was written to show the consequences of such disobedience, climaxing as it does in the destruction of Jerusalem and the end of the Davidic monarchy. Thus, the emphasis of the history was on law, judgment, and curse as well as on disobedience. As Cross has summed it up, "the theme running through the framework of the Deuteronomistic history, according to Noth, is a proclamation of unrelieved and irreversible doom."[5]

However, there have been numerous responses to Noth's position in this area that draw attention to the presence of other themes in the DH as well. Von Rad and Wolff pointed to a hopeful theme that existed alongside the pessimistic theme highlighted by Noth.[6] Von Rad rejected the pessimistic interpretation and instead saw the history as not simply a reflection on the past, but one that looked forward and spoke to its exilic audience about how to live in the present. Instead of purely stressing that in the past Israel was disobedient, von Rad saw an emphasis on obedience and a hopeful outlook. Wolff similarly saw in the history a word that addressed the present audience rather than simply reflecting on the tragic circumstances of the past. Wolff discerned in the history a call to repentance and renewal, which affirmed that Israel could still be Yahweh's covenant people even after 587 BCE.[7]

---

3. The speeches Noth (*Deuteronomistic History*, 5–6) isolated were Deut 31 (Moses); Josh 1:11–15; 23 (Joshua); 1 Sam 12 (Samuel); and 1 Kgs 8:14–61 (Solomon). Noth's summarizing narratives are: Josh 12; Judg 2:11–23; and 2 Kgs 17:7–23.

4. For further discussion of the composition of the DH, see Evans, *Invasion of Sennacherib*, 21–27.

5. Cross, "Themes of the Book of Kings," 275.

6. Von Rad, *Studies in Deuteronomy*, 84; Wolff, "Das Kerygma," 171–86; Wolff, "Kerygma," 83–100. Cf. Smend, "Das Gesetz und die Völker," 494–509; Cross, "Themes of the Book of Kings," 274–89; Dietrich, *Prophetie und Geschichte*, 108.

7. Based on the recognition of contrasting positive and negative themes in the

Adding to these positive motifs in the DH, Brueggemann detected a counter-theme to "repentance," that of "good/goodness" (טוב) in the history. He observes that the positive themes outlined by von Rad and Wolff presuppose Yahweh's "goodness" to Israel and that "the graciousness of Yahweh ... stands as the foundation of Dtr theology."[8] It is only Yahweh's goodness that is the basis for repentance and any attempt to find meaning in the midst of exile. Brueggemann notes that, without the theme of "goodness," one might, like Noth, see Dtr theology as purely "legalistic, judgmental, retribution theology."[9]

Adding to this recognition of a positive viewpoint in Dtr was McCarthy's suggestion that Nathan's oracle to David in 2 Sam 7 was structurally important to the DH.[10] While Noth did not consider this chapter as the work of Dtr or as vital to the history, McCarthy pointed out that the chapter seemed to have ideas important to Dtr and asserted that Nathan's oracle should be added to Noth's list of Dtr speeches, as it "fills the same function as the key passages picked out by Noth."[11] This chapter is clearly pivotal in the history, anticipated by what goes before[12]

---

history, F. M. Cross offered an alternative to Noth's exilic Dtr by postulating both a pre-exilic (Josianic) Dtr1 and an exilic Dtr2. Cross suggested that the hopeful theme contained in the promises to David would not have flourished during the exile, necessitating a pre-exilic edition of the DH (see Cross, "Themes of the Book of Kings"). He notes how Josiah fulfills the Davidic ideal in the DH and how Josiah is prophesied about by name centuries before his arrival on the scene. This prophecy shows how Josiah was central to the book and fulfilled the hopes of the writers. In fact, when his regnal résumé is read, it seems to resemble the eulogy of Moses himself in Deut 34, with reference to the fact that there was never a king like Josiah before who "turned to Yahweh with all his heart, soul and might according to Moses' law" and that there was no king like him afterward (2 Kgs 23:25).

8. Brueggemann, "Kerygma," 388.

9. Ibid., 389.

10. McCarthy, "II Samuel 7," 131–38.

11. Ibid., 131.

12. There are anticipatory references to this chapter throughout the story. For example, in 1 Sam 13:13–14 Samuel declares to Saul, "Yahweh would have established your kingdom forever" (which sounds exactly like the dynastic oracle of 2 Sam 7) "... but Yahweh has sought a man after his heart" (clearly David). In 1 Sam 25:28 Abigail says to David, "Yahweh will make my lord a sure house," clearly anticipating the oracle regarding David's "house" in 2 Sam 7. In 2 Sam 3:18 it is predicted that "through my [Yahweh's] servant David I will save my people from the Philistines," and it is in 2 Sam 7 that David has "rest" from all enemies (2 Sam 7:1). Cf. ibid., 133–34.

and alluded to by what follows.[13] What is more, at 197 words, it is the longest speech by Yahweh in the history since the days of Moses.[14] Clearly this chapter and its promises to David are of central importance to Dtr.[15]

In support of his recognition of a hopeful aspect to Dtr, von Rad further underscored the role of Yahweh's reliable word in the DH.[16] Several places in the larger narrative affirm the infallible fulfillment of Yahweh's word. For example, in the book of Joshua, following the taking of the land, the narrator sums up: "Not one word of Yahweh's good word to the house of Israel failed; all was fulfilled" (Josh 21:45; similarly, Josh 23:14–15). As Brueggemann points out, this emphasis on Yahweh's word is not only looking to the past, but it also encourages hope for the future.[17] In 1 Kgs 8:56, the past is again invoked as an example of the faithfulness of Yahweh's word: "Praise be to Yahweh, who has given rest to his people Israel just like he promised. Not one word of all the good words given through Moses, his servant, has failed" (1 Kgs 8:56), but this past is leveraged to encourage hope in the present—and beyond—as the next verse continues, "May Yahweh our God be with us like he was with our fathers. May he never leave us or forsake us" (1 Kgs 8:57). Due to the reliability of Yahweh's word, evidenced in the past, Israel can trust in his word for the future.[18]

This Deuteronomistic emphasis on the importance and reliability of Yahweh's word again underscores the importance of Nathan's oracle to David in 2 Sam 7, as David characterizes Yahweh's words here as "good" (2 Sam 7:28). From this point on in the history, hope for the

---

13. E.g., 1 Kgs 2:3–4 (similar to 2 Sam 7) states, "You will not fail to have a successor on the throne of Israel." Similarly, 1 Kgs 8:17 alludes to the chapter, when it states, "My father David had in mind to build a house for Yahweh." Cf. ibid., 134.

14. Bergen, *Samuel*, 336.

15. As has been the conclusion of many studies. See Veijola, *Die ewige Dynastie*, 193:32–48; Van Seters, *In Search of History*, 271–77; McCarter, *II Samuel*, 217–31; Kruse, "David's Covenant," 148–55; Knoppers, *Two Nations Under God*, 1.61–71; Römer, *The So-Called Deuteronomistic History*, 146–47.

16. Von Rad, *Studies in Deuteronomy*, 78; von Rad, *Theology of Israel's Historical Traditions*, 340.

17. Brueggemann, "Kerygma," 396.

18. Weippert ("Geschichten und Geschichte," 116–31) has argued that the promise and fulfillment of Yahweh's word is a key to understanding the DH. Through an examination of texts from Judges, Samuel, and Kings, Weippert has demonstrated that this promise-fulfillment schema is found throughout the DH both in long stretches of text and in minute examples.

future is tied to David and Yahweh's good word to David's descendants. As Brueggemann notes, "The Davidic house is the visible manifestation of the reliability of Yahweh's good word to Israel."[19]

THE LITERARY CONTEXT OF THE GOSPEL OF NATHAN: HUMAN EFFORTS AT KINGDOM BUILDING

The literary context of Nathan's oracle is one of David's consolidating his power and further establishing himself as king of Israel. David's predecessor, Saul, has been killed (not by David's hand), and the people of Israel have crowned David as Israel's sole king (2 Sam 5:1–3). Immediately following his coronation, David has captured and renovated his new capital city of Jerusalem (2 Sam 5:6–9). David has secured the longevity of his dynasty with the birth of multiple sons in Jerusalem (2 Sam 5:13–16), in addition to those born to him previously in Hebron (2 Sam 3:2–5). Foreign rulers have even acknowledged David's legitimacy (2 Sam 5:11), and his military success has been thorough and widespread, with consistent suppression of the threats of Israel's archenemy, the Philistines (2 Sam 5:17–25). What is more, David's house (palace) of cedar has been built, due in part to the generous donations of cedar by a Phoenician king (2 Sam 5:11).

Finally, after a failed attempt (2 Sam 6:1–11), David managed to bring the ark to his new capital city, Jerusalem (2 Sam 6:17). To understand the importance of this, the significance of the ark in ancient Israel must be understood. The ark represented God's presence in Israel, and the narrative of 1–2 Samuel spends considerable time chronicling the loss (1 Sam 4–5) and recovery (1 Sam 6–7) of Yahweh's ark. These narratives reveal the anxiety concerning God's presence, or lack of thereof, in ancient Israel. David's success in bringing the ark to Jerusalem would have alleviated such anxiety and led David to feel confirmed that Yahweh really was with him.

In sum, the chapters preceding Nathan's oracle to David in 2 Sam 7 present a context of human effort at establishing a dynasty, which is that of David's own works contributing to his establishment and consolidation as king of Israel. Now, in the ancient world, one of the key moments for a king establishing his legitimacy was to build a temple to the patron

---

19. Brueggemann, "Kerygma," 397.

deity.[20] It is therefore not surprising that, having done all he can to establish himself as king, David then approaches a prophet with his idea of building a house (temple) for his God (2 Sam 7:2). The prophet Nathan (appearing for the first time in the story) initially replies in the affirmative, telling David, "Go, do all that you have in mind; for Yahweh is with you" (2 Sam 7:3). However, shortly after this (2 Sam 7:4), God speaks to Nathan and disagrees. David is *not* to build a temple for him.

Several reasons for this withdrawal of the temple building permit are given. First, God did not ask for David to build the temple (2 Sam 7:7).[21] That is, the initiative for such a move should be from God, not the king. Secondly, unlike David, God has no desire for "a house of cedar" (2 Sam 7:7) or posh palace in which to reside. It is presumptuous to think God is in need of such a structure, as are human kings. Furthermore, God has historically been on the move (as the ark and tent of meeting are portable shrines) (2 Sam 7:6). Yahweh is a free God; he will not be confined to one place.[22]

Perhaps the most important reason for denying David's request is Yahweh's concern that it should be clear that *he*, not David's human efforts, is the one who is building David's kingdom. Yahweh's response seems to be cognizant of David's somewhat selfish motivations for building the temple (that it would further legitimize him in the eyes of the people). Yahweh emphatically states that he himself, not David's actions—including any building of a temple—will establish David. Here we can see God's concern that the temple does not become a means to a selfish, human end.

Nathan's oracle narrates Yahweh's history with David, how he took him from shepherds' fields to become the king of the nation (2 Sam 7:8–9a). God emphasizes that *he* will make David's name great—not David himself (2 Sam 7:9). This is stated somewhat explicitly in v. 11, where God counters David's suggestion that he build God a house by saying, "Yahweh declares to you that Yahweh himself will establish a house for you" (2 Sam 7:11).

---

20. As Brueggemann (*First and Second Samuel*, 254) writes, "The obvious answer to the problem of legitimacy characteristic of every ruler in the ancient world is to build a temple." Cf. Hurowitz, *I Have Built You an Exalted House*, 171–223.

21. Avioz (*Nathan's Oracle*, 16) suggests that this is the main problem, since from an ancient Near Eastern perspective, the god must first ask for a temple to be built.

22. Brueggemann, *First and Second Samuel*, 254; Eslinger, *House of God*, 64.

In sum, in a context of human effort to establish a kingdom, Yahweh counters with an emphasis that he is in need of no such efforts. Not only is God not in need of a temple, there is actually no role for David's good works to play here. David's kingdom will actually be established apart from David's own good works. It will be established on the basis of God's gracious gift: a covenant of pure grace given to David.

THE GOSPEL OF NATHAN AS COVENANT

There is a fairly broad consensus that Nathan's oracle is setting out a new covenant in this chapter, though the term covenant (*berit*) is not used.[23] The oracle clearly speaks of David's son in covenantal terms when it states that "I will be his father, and he will be my son" (2 Sam 7:14), which is language akin to the classic covenant formula, "You will be my people, and I will be your God" (cf. Jer 31:33; Ezek 37:23, 27; cf. Isa 54:5–10; ironically in Hosea).[24] Furthermore, 2 Sam 7:15 uses covenant terminology when it states, "My steadfast love (חסד) will never be taken away from him." In the OT חסד is a standard technical term for Yahweh's steadfast love that makes covenants possible. Yahweh's חסד is "the essence of the covenant itself," and the use of this terminology seems to imply a covenant between Yahweh and David.[25] Furthermore, later in the narrative of 2 Samuel, David himself refers to Yahweh's promise as a covenant, saying, "Is not my house like this with God? For he has made with me an everlasting covenant" (2 Sam 23:5).[26] Adding to this evidence of covenant, later biblical texts clearly understand Nathan's oracle as a covenant (e.g., Ps 89:3, 28, 34, 39 [HB vv. 4, 29, 35, 40]); 2 Chr 13:5; 21:7). For example, Ps 89:3–4 (HB vv. 4–5) reads:

> You said, "I have made a covenant with my chosen one, I have sworn to my servant David: 'I will establish your descendants forever, and build your throne for all generations.'"[27]

---

23. E.g., Weinfeld, "Davidic Covenant," 189; Mendenhall and Herion, "Covenant," 1189–90. Cf. Fensham, "Covenant, Alliance," 236; Arnold, *1 & 2 Samuel*, 479.

24. Cf. Weinfeld, "Covenant of Grant," 190; Fensham, "Father and Son," 121–28; McCarthy, "Notes on the Love of God," 144–47.

25. Arnold, *1 & 2 Samuel*, 479. See also Williamson, "Covenant," 419–29; Kalluveettil, *Declaration and Covenant*, 34–51; Weinfeld, "Covenant of Grant," 185.

26. Arnold, *1 & 2 Samuel*, 480.

27. The word "covenant" also occurs later in the chapter (Ps 89:28, 34, 39)

Thus, most view Nathan's oracle to David in 2 Sam 7 as establishing a new covenant, the so-called Davidic covenant.

Relationship to the Abrahamic Covenant

Many have compared the promises to David in 2 Sam 7 to the Abrahamic covenant and have found significant similarities.[28] Indeed, in both instances God makes promises to individuals and binds himself by an oath.[29] Furthermore, both covenants promise their recipient a "great name" (Gen 12:2; 2 Sam 7:9), a victory over their enemies (Gen 22:17; 2 Sam 7:11), and a distinctive relationship with God (Gen 17:7; 2 Sam 7:14). Both also refer to the recipients' "seed" through whom their name will be preserved (Gen 21:12; 2 Sam 7:12, 16).[30] Finally, the Davidic and Abrahamic covenants are also similar in their promissory nature, as initially the Abrahamic covenant is offered to Abram with no stipulations (Gen 12), and in Nathan's oracle no stipulations are mentioned in regards to the Davidic covenant (2 Sam 7).[31] Based on these similarities, some conclude that the Davidic and Abrahamic covenants are related, with the promises made to Abraham becoming "more focused" in the Davidic covenant (or perhaps the latter "inherits" the promises of the former).[32]

THE UNCONDITIONAL NATURE OF THE GOSPEL OF NATHAN

The most striking aspect of the gospel of Nathan is its unconditional nature. This is especially brought into relief by the prominence of Deuteronomic law in the history and Dtr's emphasis on legalistic demands of obedience to Mosaic law. Contrary to the Mosaic covenant, with its clear bilateral nature (with obligations for both parties to the

---

28. E.g., Clements, *Abraham and David*, 47–60; Gordon, *I & II Samuel*, 236; Weinfeld, "Covenant of Grant," 190.

29. Mendenhall and Herion, "Covenant," 1188.

30. Williamson, "Covenant," 419–29.

31. Weinfeld, "Covenant of Grant," 190.

32. For example, while the Abrahamic covenant promised royal descendants (Gen 17:6, 16), the Davidic covenant actually identifies the specific royal dynasty in view. Cf. ibid., 419–29.

agreement),[33] Nathan's oracle to David involves only obligations on God's behalf toward the recipient, without any explicit reciprocal obligations.

Significantly, the promissory nature of the Davidic promises in 2 Sam 7 are not without historical analogues, as some interpreters have observed close parallels in Hittite treaties that describe the pledge of a suzerain to support his vassal's dynasty.[34] Still others have found analogues in ancient Near Eastern royal land grants which bestow land as a gift on loyal subjects without subjecting the recipient to any conditions.[35] A promissory covenant was not without precedent in the ancient Near East.

As noted above, the promissory nature of the Davidic covenant is one of its perceived similarities with the Abrahamic covenant.[36] Yet the promises to David in 2 Sam 7 even surpass the Abrahamic covenant in terms of lack of stipulations. Initially, the Abrahamic covenant hinges only on Abram's willingness to leave his homeland and go to a land God will give him (Gen 12). Similarly, when God ratifies his covenant with Abram in Gen 15, again the promises appear to be purely promissory, with no stipulations mentioned and Abram's only contribution being "faith" (Gen 15:6). However, in a later iteration or restatement of the covenant, Abraham is called to "walk before me, and be blameless" (Gen 17:1), which suggests a contingent requirement of the covenant. Further on in the same chapter, an explicit stipulation for being in this covenant is given—that of circumcision (Gen 17:10–14). While many would still

---

33. In a bilateral covenant (or bilateral suzerainty covenant), the faithfulness of the vassal/weaker party to the terms of the covenant is paramount. If the vassal defaults on required duties, action would be taken against the violating party, which could result in the covenant's termination. However, in a promissory covenant the reliability of the one granting the gifts and making the promises is paramount. A promissory covenant emphasizes the certainty of the promise rather than the necessity of the faithfulness of the vassal. Cf. ibid., 419–29.

34. E.g., Calderone, *Dynastic Oracle*, 41–71; de Vaux, "Le roi d'Israël, vassal de Yahvé," 119–33. However, some have argued against seeing ancient Near Eastern treaties as parallels to the Davidic covenant. E.g. Clements, *Abraham and David*, 47–60; Kruse, "David's Covenant," 148–49.

35. E.g., Weinfeld, "Covenant of Grant," 184–203. Though Knoppers ("Ancient Near Eastern Royal Grants," 670–97) has disputed this association and instead argued that ancient Near Eastern treaties are a better parallel.

36. E.g., Weinfeld ("Davidic Covenant," 189) asserts, "Both covenants are diametrically opposed to the Mosaic covenant, in which the people pledge loyalty to God. The Abrahamic and Davidic covenants are then a promissory type while the Mosaic covenant is an obligatory type."

call the Abrahamic covenant promissory, these stipulations do contrast with the Davidic promises in 2 Sam 7, which do not contain *any* stipulations whatsoever.[37]

The lack of stipulations for these promises is most clearly seen in 2 Sam 7:14–16, where an unequivocal commitment to David's descendant is made:

> When he commits iniquity, I will punish him with the rod of humans, with floggings inflicted by people. But my love (חסד) will never be taken away from him, as I took it away from Saul, whom I removed from before you (2 Sam 7:14–16).

Though David's descendants may be punished for their wickedness, they will not be rejected—*ever*. In fact, "forever" (עולם) is used twice in this good word to David: "Your house and your kingdom will endure *forever* before me; your throne will be established *forever*" (2 Sam 7:16). This is a remarkable statement. It explicitly presents a contrast with David's predecessor, Saul, whom Yahweh did reject and from whom he withdrew his חסד and his spirit (cf. 1 Sam 16:14). Not so with David's house. Yahweh makes a startling unconditional commitment to David—forever. This eternal commitment to David became the seedbed of messianism, as Nathan's oracle in 2 Sam 7 was clearly not only for David, but also for a future descendant of David. It explicitly mentioned his son, but clearly has in mind future "Davids" as well.[38] Of course, the later history of Israel problematized the gospel of Nathan, as most of David's descendants were faithless and failed to live up to the standard of their namesake, with only a few Davidic kings being assessed positively by Dtr—and only Hezekiah (2 Kgs 18:3–5) and Josiah (2 Kgs 22:2) being said to meet this standard without reservation.[39] Yet the failure of Davidides did not squelch the hope of Nathan's gospel. Israel continued to look to the future for a faithful David who would put things to rights. Despite what has become of the monarchy and the bleak current situation, Nathan's oracle reminds Israel of Yahweh's unconditional promise.

---

37. As McCarthy (*Old Testament Covenant*, 47) asserts, the Davidic covenant "was a kind of covenant which was simply a promise of God and was valid despite anything Israel might do."

38. As Brueggemann (*Theology of the Old Testament*, 604) asserts, "the Davidic Dynasty became in principle . . . a nonnegotiable fixture in Israel's life."

39. E.g., Asa is positively compared, but fails in regards to high places (1 Kgs 15:11–14).

In spite of the fact that no stipulations are mentioned in 2 Sam 7, there continues to be some debate concerning whether the Davidic promises in 2 Sam 7 were *really* unconditional in nature. For example, Arnold writes:

> For 2 Samuel 7, it is incorrect to assume that because there are no conditions mentioned, it must be an unconditional covenant. Later biblical references make it painfully clear that continued succession of Davidic kings was contingent upon obedience . . . Nothing in 2 Samuel 7 . . . implies that the king is somehow exempt from the stipulations of the Mosaic covenant. Indeed, any such concept would be anathema to ancient Israelites. On the contrary, the reverse should be assumed: David and his descendants are all committed to keep the Mosaic covenant as part of their responsibility as kings, and certainly as a citizen of Israel. In this way, the Davidic covenant is built on the earlier covenants and assumes their continuing validity.[40]

In my judgment, such a position is partly right. Surely Davidic monarchs, as Israelites, were *not* exempt from obedience to stipulations of Mosaic law in that they, like all Israel, were expected to follow the law. However, in my judgment, it is incorrect to argue from this that the new covenant with David as proclaimed in 2 Sam 7 was contingent on the Davidides' obedience to Mosaic stipulations.[41] To be sure, later in the DH narrative the Davidic monarchy was removed from power due to their violations of the Mosaic covenant (2 Kgs 24–25), but this temporary punishment did *not* revoke the Davidic covenant. The Davidic covenant as stated by Nathan in 2 Sam 7 allowed for temporary punishment of the sins of the Davidides, but the covenant could not be broken as it *was* unconditional. It clearly states that even if David's descendants sin, God will not remove his covenant חסד from them (2 Sam 7:14).

However, it seems clear that objections to understanding 2 Sam 7 as proclaiming an unconditional covenant are not actually based on the text of 2 Sam 7. Instead, such objections are actually based on other factors: (1) other iterations of the Davidic covenant in the Old Testament, (2) the ten-

---

40. Arnold, *1 & 2 Samuel*, 481–82.

41. As Knoppers ("Ancient Near Eastern Royal Grants," 680) explains, Dtr "reinterprets and reapplies Nathan's dynastic oracle. Associating the divine bequest of an everlasting dynasty to David with David's loyalty to the deity is an important feature of the Deuteronomist's introduction to the northern monarchy." But he notes that this "is not a constituent feature of the Davidic promises themselves."

sion between the Mosaic law and the Davidic promises, and (3) concerns about the relationship between faith and works in biblical faith.

The Davidic Covenant Elsewhere in the Old Testament

One of the main reasons for assertions regarding the conditional nature of Nathan's oracle in 2 Sam 7 is not so much based on 2 Sam 7 as on other iterations of the Davidic promises found in other Old Testament passages. Besides 2 Sam 7, the main passages that discuss the promises to David are 1 Chr 17, Ps 89, and Ps 132. A brief survey of these passages will reveal the distinctives of these different presentations of the Davidic promises and will help explain why some interpreters have read conditionality into 2 Sam 7.

1 Chronicles 17

As is well known, Chronicles used the books of 1–2 Samuel and 1–2 Kings as the main source for its history of Israel.[42] Since we have access to the Chronicler's[43] main source text, a comparison of his reworking of the material with his source text often reveals his theological goal for a specific passage. In this case, the Chronicler's reworking of 2 Sam 7 emphasizes the unconditionality of the Davidic promises, as the Chronicler has removed the notice that David's descendant would be punished when he commits iniquity. This can be seen clearly in the table below (with the section deleted in Chronicles presented in italics).

1 Chr 17:13–14	2 Sam 7:14–15
I will be his father, and he will be my son. I will never take my love away from him, as I took it away from your predecessor.	I will be his father, and he will be my son. *When he commits iniquity, I will punish him with the rod of humans, with floggings inflicted by people.* But my love will never be taken away from him, as I took it away from Saul, whom I removed from before you.

---

42. Against this broad consensus, Auld and Ho argue for a common source behind both Chronicles and the DH rather than a theory of dependence of the former on the latter. Cf. Auld, *Kings Without Privilege*; Auld, "What Was the Main Source?" 91–135; Ho, "Conjectures," 82–106. However, their view has not been influential, with the majority still holding to the theory of Chronicles' reliance on the DH. Cf. Childs, *Introduction*, 645.

43. By the Chronicler I mean the author(s) of the books of Chronicles.

Thus, the Chronicler's presentation of Nathan's oracle not only continues the emphasis on its unconditional nature but also accents it even further.[44]

Psalm 89

The second of these passages also presents the gospel of Nathan as unconditional, similarly to 2 Sam 7. This can be clearly seen in Ps 89:31–34:

> If they violate my statutes and do not keep my commandments, then I will punish their transgression with the rod and their iniquity with scourges; but I will not remove from him my steadfast love, or be false to my faithfulness. I will not violate my covenant, or alter the word that went forth from my lips.

However, despite the unconditional nature of the covenant presented in this psalm, the second half of the psalm declares that Yahweh has actually repudiated this covenant (e.g., Ps 89:38–39) and calls on God to be faithful to his promises (Ps 89:46–51). However, despite its lament of the present situation, it is an appeal to the unconditional nature of the covenant that undergirds the complaint and request in the second half of this psalm.

Psalm 132

Finally, unlike other iterations of the Davidic promises already examined, the third passage, Ps 132, *does* present the Davidic covenant as conditional. This is clearly seen in Ps 132:11–12:

> Yahweh swore a sure oath to David which he will not revoke: "One of your own descendants I will place on your throne—if your sons keep my covenant and my decrees I teach them, then their sons, forever and ever, will sit on your throne."

---

44. This emphasis is understandable in its historical context, as the Chronicler addressed a post-exilic audience. Unlike the exilic audience of the DH, which needed to be told that their present circumstance of exile was due to the nation's disobedience, the Chronicler's audience, having already survived the temporary punishment by "the rod of men," had returned to the land and needed to see hope for the future. The Chronicler's treatment of this text is consistent with his approach to Judah's history elsewhere, as he chose not to narrate the sins of David (e.g., the sin with Bathsheba) and of Solomon (e.g., his sins with foreign women and their gods), but instead focused on the positive aspects of their reigns and legacies for the postexilic community. Cf. Evans, "Let the Crime Fit the Punishment," 66.

Most commentators understand this text to be a later revision of the Davidic covenant, such as that we find in 2 Sam 7.[45] It seems likely that Ps 132 is a post-exilic work that seeks to explain the exile as due to the disobedience of the Davidic kings.[46] In this way the psalm represents a faithful reading of the DH as a whole, which clearly explains the exile as due to the sins of Judah's kings (2 Kgs 21:11–15; 24:19–20). However, the psalm is not pessimistic regarding the future of the Davidides. To be sure, the psalmist has repositioned the "forever" expressed to David and his dynasty in 2 Sam 7:16 to a "forever" associated with Jerusalem, as can be seen in Ps 132:13–14: "For Yahweh has chosen Zion, he has desired it for his dwelling place: 'This is my resting place forever and ever; here I will dwell, for I have desired it.'" However, this commitment to Zion still has a future with David in view, as the psalm continues, "Here [i.e., Jerusalem] I will make a horn grow up for David and I have prepared a lamp for my anointed one. I will clothe his enemies with shame, but on him his crown will sparkle" (Ps 132:17–18). Further, it is striking that, even though the psalm explicitly notes the responsibility of Davidic monarchs to obey (Ps 132:11–12), it still envisions Yahweh's commitment "forever" and a future for the Davidic throne, *without* any reference to the future obedience of the Davidides.

In sum, these different iterations of the Davidic promises display different emphases. In Chronicles, the unconditionality is underscored with even the possibility of Davidic disobedience being edited out of its presentation. In Ps 89, the psalmist laments the current situation, which does *not* see the Davidic promises being fulfilled, yet appeals to Yahweh to live up to his promises on the basis that they were unconditional in nature. In Ps 132, the promises of Davidic succession are presented as conditional, yet a Davidic future is envisioned without a corresponding reference to future Davidic obedience.

So what are the implications of this diversity within Old Testament iterations of the Davidic covenant? First, perhaps it is inaccurate to talk about *the* Davidic covenant in the Old Testament as if it were presented

---

45. Veijola (*Die ewige Dynastie*) seems to be alone in suggesting that the unconditional nature of the Davidic covenant only had its origins in the exile.

46. A post-exilic date is held by many scholars. E.g., Patton, "Psalm 132," 653–54; Hossfeld and Zenger, *Psalms 3*, 458–60; Briggs and Briggs, *Book of Psalms*, 2:468–69. However, some have argued for a pre-exilic date. E.g., Kraus, *Psalms 60—150*, 475; Laato, "Psalm 132 and the Development," 49–66; Laato, "Psalm 132," 24–33. Regardless of the dating argued for, most still hold to the priority of 2 Sam 7.

uniformly throughout. As Knoppers has observed, "None of the principal passages [2 Sam 7, 1 Chr 17, Pss 89 and 132] is strictly juridical in nature. If the Davidic covenant ever existed as a legal document, it is no longer extant."[47] Secondly, realizing the diversity present in each of the major iterations of the Davidic promises should caution against attempts at harmonizing the data from each passage or reading the distinctives from one passage into another. In other words, while conditionality is clearly a part of Ps 132, it is *not* found in 2 Sam 7. Our interpretation must allow 2 Sam 7 to have its own distinctive voice in its own literary context.

Mosaic and Davidic Covenants in Tension

Another impetus for interpreters to soften the unconditional nature of the Davidic promises in 2 Sam 7 is likely due to the perception of a tension in the narrative of the DH between the requirements of the Mosaic law and the grace of the Davidic promises.[48] This tension is not just a modern imposition onto the text.[49] Given the primacy of Deuteronomy for the author of the DH and its emphasis on law, Nathan's promises clearly introduced a new tension into the narrative. How do the Mosaic and Davidic covenants relate?[50] As von Rad observed, "the Deuteronomist sees the main problem of the history of Israel as lying in the question of the correct correlation of Moses and David."[51]

However, acknowledging the tension between these covenants does not necessitate an approach that would somehow amalgamate these covenants or assert that the Davidic covenant assumed the stipulations of the Mosaic.[52] These two themes addressed the history's exilic audience in different ways. The Deuteronomistic focus on Mosaic law explained the audience's current situation of exile as due to the implementation of the covenant curses of Deuteronomy. Jerusalem and her

---

47. Knoppers, "Ancient Near Eastern Royal Grants," 695.

48. Cf. Bright, *History*, 227; von Rad, *Theology of Israel's Historical Traditions*, 339–41; Knoppers, "Ancient Near Eastern Royal Grants," 117–18.

49. Knoppers, "David's Relation to Moses," 118.

50. Bright, *History*, 227.

51. Von Rad, *Theology of Israel's Historical Traditions*, 339–41.

52. As does Arnold (*1 & 2 Samuel*, 482) when he asserts that, even in 2 Sam 7 and the Davidic covenant, "I believe the Bible assumes the Mosaic covenant, with its stipulations and conditions."

temple were destroyed due to Judah's covenant violations, not because of Babylonian might or the superiority of Babylonian gods. Yahweh was behind the destruction of Jerusalem and the deportation of the bulk of the population into exile (2 Kgs 24:20). However, the Deuteronomistic focus on the promises to David offered hope for the future to the exilic audience.[53] Through these gracious promises to David, hope could be seen beyond the loss of land, beyond the hardships of exile, to a future that is grounded in God's good word. Davidic hope thrived in the exilic period and beyond, as the Davidic promises were the well from which prophetic proclamations of hope sprang and the "nucleus around which messages of hope proclaimed by Hebrew prophets of later generations were built."[54]

Both foci are found in the narrative, but neither focus negated nor subsumed the other. Both were necessary for Dtr's message to his exilic audience. While Mosaic law explained the necessity of the exile, its covenant curses did *not* negate the Davidic promises. Likewise, though the Davidic promises looked to God's unconditional commitment, these promises did *not* negate the Mosaic law, as Jerusalem was destroyed and its inhabitants exiled.[55] Perhaps it is better to talk of the covenant being unconditional but its recipient still being accountable. These are both seen in the broader narrative, as Solomon's kingdom is to be torn apart due to his sin but one tribe will remain under the Davidic kings due to the promises made to David (cf. 1 Kgs 11:13, 32, 34–36; 12:15).[56]

---

53. As Mendenhall and Herion ("Covenant," 1:192) write, "the metaphor of covenant did shift decisively during the monarchic period, so much so that from that time on any attempt to envision the relationship between God and his people in some way had to accommodate the new synthesis incorporating some (usually vaguely defined) Davidic figure (cf. Jer 30:8–33; 33:14)."

54. Bergen, *Samuel*, 337.

55. Knoppers ("Ancient Near Eastern Royal Grants," 679 n. 46) has further suggested that the tension between Moses and David was partly dealt with by Dtr using David's example as a paradigm of "loyal conduct" by which other kings were measured. He writes, "By upholding both the Davidic promises and David as a paradigm of loyal conduct, the Deuteronomist balances two concerns—legitimating the Davidic monarchy and exhorting his audience to observe YHWH's commands." However, as Provan has shown, the Davidic promises also served a promissory function that restrained Yahweh's judgment on Judah. Provan, *Hezekiah*, 93–99.

56. Cf. Knoppers, "David's Relation to Moses," 99–100.

The Relationship between Grace and Works in Biblical Faith

In many ways, the Davidic promises are foundational for an evangelical faith based not on works, but on God's gracious promise. They are a covenant offered with no stipulations, with right standing in the covenant dependent only upon Yahweh's gracious initiative, that is, something very much like salvation through faith alone.[57]

However, as we have seen, the gospel of Nathan created its own tensions. Given the obvious emphasis on good works elsewhere in the DH, this emphasis on grace opens up the question of the relationship between works and faith. The difficulties of living with this tension may lead some to harmonize passages like 2 Sam 7 and Ps 132 or to assume Mosaic stipulations as part of the Davidic promises. Yet this same tension exists not only in the DH but more broadly in Old Testament theology and biblical theology in general.[58] While the Mosaic covenant emphasized the role of good works in God's salvation, the Davidic covenant emphasized God's unconditional grace. Yet both are part of Scripture. In the New Testament Paul vehemently asserts that salvation is through faith and unrelated to a believer's good works (Eph 2:8–9). However, the author of James is quick to point out that good works have an important role even in New Testament faith (Jas 2:23). This is a tension inherent in New Testament faith as well.[59] Attempts to harmonize 2 Sam 7 and Ps 132 are only the beginning. Such a program has many more Scriptures to contend with in order to alleviate such tension in the Scripture.

CONCLUSION

In conclusion, it must be noted that a concern to read conditionality into 2 Sam 7 acknowledges the legitimate dangers of a gospel of pure grace. In fact, it is a similar concern to those expressed of Paul's gospel—that it might promote antinomianism—causing the apostle to address this twice in one passage:

---

57. Brueggemann (*First and Second Samuel*, 257) calls this "a powerful, clear articulation of 'justification by grace.'"

58. Bright, *History*, 227.

59. As Brueggemann (*First and Second Samuel*, 259) writes, "God's conditional requirement and God's unconditional promise [both] belong to biblical faith . . . Both belong to God's character . . . Both are crucial to the fullness of our human life. Both matter to our life with God and with each other."

> What then are we to say? Should we continue in sin in order that grace may abound? (Rom 6:1)
>
> What then? Should we sin because we are not under law but under grace? By no means! (Rom 6:15)

While Paul vehemently denies that the gospel would promote the idea of continuing in sin, the nature of the gospel opens itself up to such misunderstanding. Not too long ago Martyn Lloyd-Jones addressed this issue. He wrote,

> The true preaching of the gospel of salvation by grace alone always leads to the possibility of this charge being brought against it. There is no better test as to whether a man [sic] is really preaching the New Testament gospel of salvation than this, that some people might misunderstand it and misinterpret it to mean that it really amounts to this, that because you are saved by grace alone it does not matter at all what you do; you can go on sinning as much as you like because it will redound all the more to the glory of grace. That is a very good test of gospel preaching. If my preaching and presentation of the gospel of salvation does not expose it to that misunderstanding, then it is not the gospel.[60]

Despite the dangers of a gospel of grace, the gospel according to Nathan would actually speak against an antinomian understanding of the gospel. Though Yahweh offered an unconditional covenant to David in 2 Sam 7, this did not mean Israel could sin with impunity. The conclusion to the DH taught that this was not the case, as the harsh realities of exile drove home the reality of judgment.[61]

Furthermore, the gospel according to Nathan would speak against an approach that would resolve the works-grace tension by emphasizing the latter and thereby concluding that *all* people are therefore justified and all will be saved (universalism). The specificity of the gospel of Nathan militates against such universalism. The covenant is offered *only* through David and his descendant/Son. It is *not* a universal covenant with all of humanity. David's descendant is given a unique relationship with Yahweh that will facilitate divine blessing (Ps 72:17). Yahweh himself will be this Son's father (2 Sam 7:14; Ps 2:7), and God's unmerited, unconditional favor is offered through the Son of David and through no

---

60. Lloyd-Jones, *Romans*, 8–9.
61. Cf. Brueggemann, *First and Second Samuel*, 259.

other. For "there is salvation in no one else, for there is no other name under heaven given to humans by which we must be saved" (Acts 4:12).

BIBLIOGRAPHY

Arnold, Bill T. *1 & 2 Samuel*. NIVAC. Grand Rapids: Zondervan, 2003.

Auld, A. Graeme. *Kings Without Privilege: David and Moses in the Story of the Bible's Kings*. Edinburgh: T. & T. Clark, 1994.

———. "What Was the Main Source of the Books of Chronicles?" In *The Chronicler as Author*, edited by M. P. Graham and S. L. McKenzie, 91–135. JSOTSup 263. Sheffield: Sheffield Academic, 1999.

Avioz, Michael. *Nathan's Oracle (2 Samuel 7) and Its Interpreters*. Bible in History. Bern: Peter Lang, 2005.

Bergen, Robert D. *1, 2 Samuel*. NAC. Nashville: Broadman & Holman, 1996.

Briggs, Charles A., and Emilie G. Briggs. *The Book of Psalms. A Critical and Exegetical Commentary*. 2 vols. ICC. New York: Charles Scribner's Sons, 1907.

Bright, John. *A History of Israel*. 3rd ed. Philadelphia: Westminster, 1981.

Brueggemann, Walter. *First and Second Samuel*. IBC. Louisville: John Knox, 1990.

———. "Kerygma of the Deuteronomistic Historian." *Int* 22 (1968) 387–402.

———. *Theology of the Old Testament: Testimony, Dispute, Advocacy*. Minneapolis: Fortress, 1997.

Calderone, Philip J. *Dynastic Oracle and Suzerainty Treaty, 2 Samuel 7, 8–16*. Logos 1. Manila, Philippines: Ateneo University Publications, 1966.

Childs, Brevard S. *Introduction to the Old Testament as Scripture*. Philadelphia: Fortress, 1979.

Clements, R. E. *Abraham and David: Genesis XV and Its Meaning for Israelite Tradition*. SBT. London: SCM, 1967.

Cross, Frank Moore. "The Themes of the Book of Kings and the Structure of the Deuteronomistic History." In *Canaanite Myth and Hebrew Epic*, 274–89. Cambridge, MA: Harvard University Press, 1973.

Dietrich, Walter. *Prophetie und Geschichte; Eine redaktionsgeschichtliche Untersuchung zum deuteronomistischen Geschichtswerk*. FRLANT. Göttingen: Vandenhoeck & Ruprecht, 1972.

Eslinger, Lyle M. *House of God or House of David? The Rhetoric of 2 Samuel 7*. JSOTSup 164. Sheffield: Sheffield Academic, 1994.

Evans, Paul S. *The Invasion of Sennacherib in the Book of Kings: A Source-Critical and Rhetorical Study of 2 Kings 18—19*. VTSup 125. Leiden: Brill, 2009.

———. "Let the Crime Fit the Punishment: The Chronicler's Explication of David's 'Sin' in 1 Chronicles 21." In *Chronicling the Chronicler: The Book of Chronicles and Early Second Temple Historiography*, edited by Paul S. Evans and Tyler F. Williams, 65–80. Winona Lake, IL: Eisenbrauns, 2013.

Fensham, F. Charles. "Covenant, Alliance." In *New Bible Dictionary*, edited by J. D. Douglas, 234–38. Downers Grove, IL: InterVarsity, 1996.

———. "Father and Son as Terminology for Treaty and Covenant." In *Near Eastern Studies in Honor of William Foxwell Albright*, edited by Hans Goedicke, 121–35. Baltimore: Johns Hopkins University Press, 1971.

Gordon, R. P. *I & II Samuel: A Commentary*. Library of Biblical Interpretation. Grand Rapids: Regency Reference Library, 1986.

Ho, C. Y. S. "Conjectures and Refutations: Is 1 Samuel XXXI 1–13 Really the Source of 1 Chronicles X 1–12?" *VT* 45 (1995) 82–106.
Hossfeld, F.-L., and E. Zenger. *Psalms 3: A Commentary on Psalms 101–150*. Hermeneia. Minneapolis: Fortress, 2011.
Hurowitz, Victor. *I Have Built You an Exalted House: Temple Building in the Bible in Light of Mesopotamian and Northwest Semitic Writings*. JSOTSup 115. Sheffield: JSOT Press, 1992.
Kalluveettil, Paul. *Declaration and Covenant: A Comprehensive Review of Covenant Formulae from the Old Testament and the Ancient Near East*. AnBib 88. Rome: Pontificio Instituto Biblico, 1982.
Knoppers, Gary N. "Ancient Near Eastern Royal Grants and the Davidic Covenant: A Parallel?" *JAOS* 116 (2006) 670–97.
———. "David's Relation to Moses: The Contexts, Content and Conditions of the Davidic Promises." In *King and Messiah in Israel and the Ancient Near East: Proceedings of the Oxford Old Testament Seminar*, edited by John Day, 91–118. JSOTSup 270. Sheffield: Sheffield Academic, 1998.
———. *Two Nations Under God: The Deuteronomistic History of Solomon and the Dual Monarchies*. HSM 52–53. Atlanta: Scholars, 1993.
Kraus, Hans-Joachim. *Psalms 60–150: A Commentary*. CC. Minneapolis: Augsburg Fortress, 1989.
Kruse, Heinz. "David's Covenant." *VT* 35 (1985) 139–64.
Laato, Antti. "Psalm 132 and the Development of the Jerusalemite/Israelite Royal Ideology." *CBQ* 54 (1992) 49–66.
———. "Psalm 132: A Case Study in Methodology." *CBQ* 61 (1999) 24–33.
Lloyd-Jones, Martyn. *Romans: The New Man, An Exposition of Chapter 6*. Grand Rapids: Zondervan, 1973.
McCarter, P. Kyle. *II Samuel*. AB 9. Garden City, NY: Doubleday, 1984.
McCarthy, Dennis J. "II Samuel 7 and the Structure of the Deuteronomic History." *JBL* 84 (1965) 131–38.
———. "Notes on the Love of God in Deuteronomy and the Father-Son Relationship Between Yahweh and Israel." *CBQ* 27 (1965) 144–47.
———. *Old Testament Covenant: A Survey of Current Opinions*. Growing Points in Theology. Richmond: John Knox, 1972.
Mendenhall, George E., and Gary A. Herion. "Covenant." In *ABD* 1:1179–203.
Noth, Martin. *The Deuteronomistic History*. JSOTSup 15. Sheffield: JSOT Press, 1981.
———. *Überlieferungsgeschichtliche Studien: Die sammelnden und bearbeitenden Geschichtswerke im Alten Testament*. Schriften der Königsberger Gelehrten Gesellschaft, Geisteswissenschaftliche Klasse 18. Jh. H. 2. Bd. 1. Tübingen: Niemeyer, 1943.
Patton, Corinne L. "Psalm 132: A Methodological Inquiry." *CBQ* 57 (1995) 643–54.
Provan, Iain W. *Hezekiah and the Books of Kings: A Contribution to the Debate about the Composition of the Deuteronomistic History*. BZAW 172. Berlin: de Gruyter, 1988.
Rad, Gerhard von. *The Theology of Israel's Historical Traditions*. Vol. 1 of *Old Testament Theology*. Translated by D. M. G. Stalker. New York: Harper & Row, 1962.
———. *Studies in Deuteronomy*. Translated by D. M. G. Stalker. SBT 9. London: SCM, 1953.
Römer, Thomas. *The So-Called Deuteronomistic History: A Sociological, Historical, and Literary Introduction*. London: T. & T. Clark, 2006.

Smend, Rudolf. "Das Gesetz und die Völker: Ein Beitrag zur deuteronomistischen Redaktionsgeschichte." In *Probleme biblischer Theologie: Festschrift Gerhard von Rad*, edited by Hans Walter Wolff, 494–509. Munich: Chr. Kaiser, 1971.

Van Seters, John. *In Search of History: Historiography in the Ancient World and the Origins of Biblical History*. New Haven: Yale University Press, 1983.

Vaux, Roland de. "Le roi d'Israël, vassal de Yahvé." In *Melanges Eugène Tisserant: Écriture Sainte Ancien Orient*, 119–33. StT 231. Vatican City: Biblioteca Apostolica Vaticana, 1964.

Veijola, Timo. *Die ewige Dynastie: David und die Entstehung seiner Dynastie nach der deuteronomistischen Darstellung*. Annalae Academiae Scientiarum Fennica 193. Helsinki: Suomalainen Tiedeakatemia, 1975.

Weinfeld, Moshe. "The Covenant of Grant in the Old Testament and in the Ancient Near East." *JAOS* 90 (1970) 184–203.

———. "The Davidic Covenant." In *Interpreter's Dictionary of the Bible: Supplementary Volume*, edited by K. Crim, 189. Nashville: Abingdon, 1976.

Weippert, Helga. "Geschichten und Geschichte: Verheissung und Erfüllung im deuteronomistischen Geschichtswerk." In *Congress Volume: Leuven*, edited by J. A. Emerton, 116–31. VTSup 43. Leiden: Brill, 1991.

Wellhausen, Julius. *Prolegomena to the History of Israel*. Edinburgh: A. & C. Black, 1885.

Williamson, Paul R. "Covenant." In *New Dictionary of Biblical Theology*, edited by T. D. Alexander and B. Rosner, 419–29. Downers Grove, IL: InterVarsity, 2000.

Wolff, Hans Walter. "Das Kerygma des deuteronomistischen Geschichtswerk." *ZAW* 73 (1961) 171–86.

———. "The Kerygma of the Deuteronomic Historical Work." In *The Vitality of Old Testament Traditions*, edited by Hans Walter Wolff and Walter Brueggemann, 83–100. Atlanta: John Knox, 1975.

2

The Signs and Wonders of Salvation
Beholding Isaiah and His Children

Mark J. Boda

Many Christians have called Isaiah the "Fifth Gospel," reflecting the evaluation of Isaiah by Jerome: "he should be called an evangelist rather than a prophet."[1] Such an embrace of Isaiah by Christian interpreters cannot only be traced to the meaning of the prophet's name (salvation of Yahweh), but also to the fact that this prophetic book contains two of the most important texts in Christian gospel proclamation, one pointing to the final phase of Jesus Christ's life, the Suffering Servant of Isa 52–53, and the other to the initial phase of Jesus Christ's life, the Immanuel figure of Isa 7. It is to the section in which this Immanuel figure is encountered in the book of Isaiah that we will turn for our consideration of the nature of salvation in Isaiah, and Isa 6–12 will provide insight into the severity of God's salvation. Is the gospel good news? Yes, indeed, but the divine enactment of salvation comes at great cost not only for the one who grants salvation, but also for the ones who would receive it.

LITERARY INTEGRITY OF ISAIAH 7–12: HISTORICAL CONTEXTS

Isaiah 7–12 begins, at the outset of ch. 7, by alerting the reader to the historical context of the attack of the Syro-Ephraimite coalition against the

---

1. Sawyer, *Fifth Gospel*, 1–2; Weber, *Biblia Sacra Iuxta Vulgatam Versionem*, 2:1096.

kingdom of Judah. Threatened by the increasing power of Assyria to the north and east, the two kingdoms immediately north of Judah, Aram-Damascus (Syria) and Israel (Ephraim), sought support from Judah to strengthen their military capability against Assyria while eliminating vulnerability on their southern flank. Diplomatic gestures from Aram-Damascus and Israel soon turned to military and political threats when Judah rebuffed plans aimed against Assyria. The prophetic message in Isa 7–12 is directed at both the royal house and the people of Judah, as seen in the references to "his heart and the hearts of his people" in 7:2 and to "you, your people, your father's house" in 7:17. Isaiah 7 emphasizes the "house of David" (7:2, 13), while Isa 8 emphasizes "this people" (8:6, 11, 12). In Isa 7 the prophet confronts the fear of Ahaz, who is understandably concerned about the strategy of the kingdoms to his north to replace him with "the son of Tabeel" (7:6). The prophet calls Ahaz to trust in Yahweh (7:9b). In Isa 8 the prophet confronts the fear of Ahaz's people who have embraced these northern conspiracy theories (8:12), which have drawn their affections towards the leaders of these northern kingdoms rather than trust in Yahweh (8:6). After Isa 7 (see throughout, but especially as anticipated in 7:17) the context of the Syro-Ephraimite threat can be discerned in the several references to Ephraim:

- 9:8 [ET 9:9]: " . . . all the people know it, that is, Ephraim and the inhabitants of Samaria . . . "[2]
- 9:21 [ET 9:20]: "Manasseh [devours] Ephraim, and Ephraim Manasseh, and together they are against Judah . . . "
- 11:13–14: "Then the jealousy of Ephraim will depart,
And those who harass Judah will be cut off
Ephraim will not be jealous of Judah, And Judah will not harass Ephraim
They will swoop down on the slopes of the Philistines on the west
Together they will plunder the sons of the east

They will possess Edom and Moab, and the sons of Ammon will be subject to them."

Isaiah 9:8 looks to Ephraim in the wake of its defeat, arrogantly seeking to rebuild yet judged through a divinely sponsored attack from their former coalition partner Aram (9:11). Isaiah 9:21 looks to the po-

2. Biblical citations drawn from NASB, at times with modification.

litical turmoil within the Northern Kingdom between the Joseph tribes Ephraim and Manasseh and their common attack against Judah. Isaiah 11:13 looks to the future restoration when Ephraim and Judah will experience reconciliation.

At the same time, it is difficult to ignore historical references to the Assyrian crisis experienced by Ahaz's son Hezekiah a generation later.[3] This begins in 8:7–8 as the king of Assyria is pictured as a flooding Euphrates that sweeps in to Judah and covers it with water up to its neck, an allusion to Jerusalem, its royal capital. So also 10:8–14, 32 alludes to the boast of Sennacherib in Isa 36, and 10:15–16, 24–26 to the divine punishment he suffered in Isa 37.

But there is one other historical context in view as these chapters end. Isaiah 11:11—12:6 looks to "a second time," which occurs "on that day" (11:11) as a remnant of the dispersed exiles of both Israel and Judah is assembled by Yahweh from throughout the world (11:11b) with special emphasis on those exiled to Assyria (11:16).

While often such variety in historical references is used to argue against the integrity of a literary unit, the variety of historical contexts reflects the literary integrity now represented by the book of Isaiah in its final form. Nearly all scholars working on the book of Isaiah today affirm its literary integrity, even if many of these do not link this integrity to the influence of a single individual named Isaiah.[4] John Oswalt, for instance, has shown the importance of the narratives related to the two royal figures in Isa 7–39, father Ahaz in Isa 7–12 and son Hezekiah in Isa 36–39, who are interlinked and juxtaposed in order to challenge the readers of the book to embrace faith in Yahweh.[5] Christopher Seitz shows how Isa 36–39 is designed to prepare the way for Isa 40–66 and the message directed towards an audience living after the fall of Jerusalem.[6] The variety of historical contexts noted for Isa 7–12 (Ahaz's Syro-Ephraimite crisis, Hezekiah's Assyrian crisis, the exilic crisis) reflects the three events that are key to the integration of the book as a whole.

---

3. See Seitz, *Isaiah 1–39*, 30.

4. Webb, "Zion in Transformation," 65–84; Schultz, "How Many Isaiahs," 150–70; Tull, "One Book, Many Voices," 279–314.

5. See Oswalt, *Isaiah 1–39*; cf. Seitz, *Isaiah 1–39*, 64, drawing on Ackroyd, "Isaiah 36–39," 3–21, and Clements, "The Immanuel Prophecy," 225–40.

6. Seitz, *Zion's Final Destiny*.

Bible

LITERARY INTEGRITY OF ISAIAH 7–12: LEXICAL STOCK

Even without orientation to the integrity of the book of Isaiah, one can discern from the lexical stock of Isa 7–12 its literary integrity.[7] Repeated words and phrases draw together key sections:

- 8:22/8:23—9:1 [ET 9:1–2]: "darkness (חֲשֵׁכָה) . . . gloom (מְעוּף) . . . anguish (צוּקָה)"/"gloom (מוּעָף) . . . anguish (מוּצָק) . . . darkness (חֹשֶׁךְ)"
- 10:1/10:5: "Woe (הוֹי)"/"Woe (הוֹי)"
- 8:16/8:20: "testimony (תְּעוּדָה) . . . law (תּוֹרָה)"/"law (תּוֹרָה) . . . testimony (תְּעוּדָה)"
- 9:11 [ET 9:12]/9:16 [ET 9:17]/9:20 [ET 9:21]; 10:4: "In spite of all this, his anger does not turn away and his hand is still stretched out (בְּכָל־זֹאת לֹא־שָׁב אַפּוֹ וְעוֹד יָדוֹ נְטוּיָה)"
- 11:10/11:12: "standard (נֵס)"/"standard (נֵס)"
- 7:2/9:17 [ET 9:18]/10:18/10:19/10:34: "trees of the forest (עֲצֵי־יַעַר)"/"thickets of the forest (סִבְכֵי הַיַּעַר)"/"glory of his forest (כְּבוֹד יַעְרוֹ)"/"trees of his forest (עֵץ יַעְרוֹ)"/"thickets of the forest (סִבְכֵי הַיַּעַר)"
- 7:11/8:18: "sign (אוֹת)"/"signs (אֹתוֹת)"
- 7:23–24/9:17 [ET 18]/10:17: "briars and thorns (לַשָּׁמִיר וְלַשָּׁיִת)"/"briars and thorns (שָׁמִיר וָשַׁיִת)"/"his thorns and his briars (שִׁיתוֹ וּשְׁמִירוֹ)"
- 9:3 [ET 9:4]/10:26: "day of Midian (יוֹם מִדְיָן)"/"slaughter of Midian (מַכַּת מִדְיָן)"
- 9:11, 16, 20 [ET 9:12, 17, 21]; 10:4/12:1: "his anger . . . turn away (שָׁב אַפּוֹ)"/"your anger . . . is turned away (יָשֹׁב אַפְּךָ)"

The first five repetitions link together adjacent pericopae, either by placement at the end of one pericope and the beginning of the next (8:22/8:23—9:1 [ET 9:1–2]; 11:10/11:12), placement at the beginning (10:1/10:5) or end (9:11 [ET 9:12]/9:16 [ET 9:17]/9:20 [ET 9:21]; 10:4) of successive pericopae, placement at the beginning of one pericope and the middle of the next (8:16/8:20) or at the end of one pericope and the middle of the next (11:10/11:12). The final five repetitions link more distant

---

7. On the integrity of Isa 7–12, see Oswalt, "The Significance of the Calmah Prophecy," 223–35, who also draws on the child motif.

pericopae within the collection (7:2/9:17 [ET 9:18]/10:18/10:19/10:34; 7:11/8:18; 9:3 [ET 9:4]/10:26; 9:11, 16, 20 [ET 9:12, 17, 21]; 10:4/12:1).

LITERARY INTEGRITY OF ISAIAH 7–12: MOTIFS

These lexical repetitions provide key indications of the literary integrity of this unit of Isaiah. To this evidence should be added three key motifs: children, vegetation, and burning.

The Motif of Children

The agenda for the motif of children is evident in the programmatic verse 8:18:[8]

> Behold, I and the children whom the Lord has given me are for signs and wonders in Israel from the Lord of hosts, who dwells on Mount Zion.

Three children are presented prior to this verse in Isa 7–8.[9] Shear-jashub (שְׁאָר יָשׁוּב) comes first, accompanying his father Isaiah to challenge Ahaz in 7:3. While the name is not explained explicitly, reference to a remnant returning is simultaneously encouraging and ominous.[10] A remnant will survive, but the fact that it is remnant assumes a painful transition in the future. Maher-shalal-hash-baz (מַהֵר שָׁלָל חָשׁ בַּז) is the focus of Isa 8, his name meaning "Swift is the spoil, speedy is the plunder." At first this appears to be an encouraging sign for the kingdom, since the child is linked to the carrying away of the wealth of Damascus and spoil of Samaria, the enemies of Judah (8:4). However, the immediately following pericope shows that the Assyrian action to carry away the spoil and plunder has serious implications for Judah as well, as the king of Assyria sweeps on into Judah (8:7).

The third child appears initially in Isa 7, the Immanuel (עִמָּנוּ אֵל) figure promised to the young woman in 7:14. This child at first is clearly

---

8. See, e.g., the key work of Clements, *Isaiah 1–39*, 78–81; Roberts, *First Isaiah*, 107.

9. See Seitz, *Isaiah 1–39*, 62–63, on the role of the three children in these chapters, and see Brodie, "Children and the Prince," 27–31, for their impact on the literary structure.

10. Day, "Shear-Jashub," 76, drawing on Clements, *Isaiah 1–39*, 83. However, I disagree with the interpretation that connects the remnant to the opposing Syro-Ephraimite armies. The Isaianic tradition clearly links this name to a series of events set in motion in the time of Ahaz and continued with Hezekiah and the exilic community (see further below on Isa 6).

a sign of salvation, typified by the defeat of the two kings who opposed Judah and the child eating curds and honey (7:15–16). But as with the other children, there is a contrastive dimension, as seen in 7:17, where Isaiah warns, "The Lord will bring on you, on your people, and on your father's house such days as have never come since the day that Ephraim separated from Judah, the king of Assyria." A reference to this Immanuel child appears again following mention of Isaiah's second child, Maher-shalal-hash-baz, again indicating the salvation of Judah from the threat of the northern kingdoms (8:7) but also the threat that Assyria represents for Judah (8:8).

The precise identity of the Immanuel figure has been hotly debated, with the majority favoring either a child of Ahaz or a child of Isaiah.[11] Nevertheless, there is no question that the other two children, Shear-jashub and Maher-shalal-hash-baz are Isaiah's children and thus fulfil the programmatic verse of Isa 8:18, serving as signs and wonders in Israel from Yahweh of hosts. It must be noted, however, that Isa 8:18 refers not only to *children* as signs and wonders but also to Isaiah as fulfilling that same role. The testimony of Isaiah in the previous verse, 8:17, highlights one aspect of Isaiah's role as a sign and wonder, his stance of trust expressed in the declaration "I will wait for Yahweh who is hiding his face from the house of Jacob; I will even look eagerly for him." Such trust is what was expected of the royal house according to 7:9b: "If you will not believe, you surely shall not last." Since Isaiah's name means "salvation of Yahweh," his testimony emphasizes the importance of trust to such salvation. The names of the children, however, point to the ominous character of salvation, which some might call a severe mercy that ensures the survival of the nation but through much suffering.[12]

---

11. There are those who connect this Immanuel child to Hezekiah, who is depicted in contrast to Ahaz (at least in part) in Isa 36–39 as one who (at least initially) trusted in Yahweh when threatened by a foreign enemy. Verbal similarities between the Immanuel prophecy in Isa 7 and the prophecy concerning Maher-shalal-hash-baz in Isa 8 suggest to others that Immanuel is Isaiah's child. See the discussion in Oswalt, *Isaiah 1–39*, 213, 220; Roberts, *First Isaiah*, 119.

12. The negative character of Isaiah's "salvation" name will become evident in Isa 12, where praise is given when God's anger is finally turned away. Such salvation assumes previous judgment. Roberts, *First Isaiah*, 140, sees the negative tone of the names referring to the Northern Kingdom (Israel) and the positive tone to the Southern Kingdom (Judah), but this is mostly because he restricts his interpretation to the "original" connection of the names to Ahaz's Syro-Ephraimite crisis. In light of the historical introduction above, these names are connected to the three eras of Ahaz, Hezekiah, and the

Boda—*The Signs and Wonders of Salvation*

Echoes of these names, those of Isaiah and his children, can be discerned in the material which follows in chs. 9–12. Shear-jashub (שְׁאָר יָשׁוּב) is explicitly mentioned two times:[13]

- 10:21: "A remnant will return (שְׁאָר יָשׁוּב), the remnant of Jacob, to the mighty God."
- 10:22: "For though your people, O Israel, may be like the sand of the sea, a remnant within them will return (שְׁאָר יָשׁוּב)."

On three other occasions reference is made to the restoration of the remnant, suggestive of Shear-jashub:[14]

- 10:20: "Now in that day the remnant (שְׁאָר) of Israel, and those of the house of Jacob who have escaped will never again rely on the one who struck them, but will truly rely on Yahweh, the Holy One of Israel."
- 11:11: "Then it will happen on that day that Yahweh will again recover the second time with his hand the remnant (שְׁאָר) of his people, who will remain, from Assyria, Egypt, Pathros, Cush, Elam, Shinar, Hamath, and from the islands of the sea."
- 11:16: "And there will be a highway from Assyria for the remnant (שְׁאָר) of his people who will be left, just as there was for Israel in the day that they came up out of the land of Egypt."

The name of Isaiah's other child, Maher-shalal-hash-baz (מַהֵר שָׁלָל חָשׁ בַּז) can also be discerned in the two woe oracles that lie at the center of chs. 9–12:

- 10:1–2
 "Woe to those who enact evil statutes
 And to those who constantly record unjust decisions,
 So as to deprive the needy of justice
 And rob the poor of my people of their rights,
 So that widows may be their spoil (שָׁלָל)
 And that they may plunder (בזז) the orphans."

Judean exilic community.

13. See further Roberts, *First Isaiah*, 170. Brueggemann, *Isaiah 1–39*, 65, focuses on the negative dimension of this name, restricting meaning to the immediate context of Ahaz's reign, admitting that "in a later context, the 'remnant' might be taken as assurance." Better is his claim, "The bad news is *only* a remnant. The good news is *a remnant*" (73).

14. See further Roberts, *First Isaiah*, 186.

- 10:5–6

"Woe to Assyria, the rod of my anger
And the staff in whose hands is my indignation,
I send it against a godless nation
And commission it against the people of my fury
To capture (שלל) booty (שָׁלָל) and to seize (בזז) plunder (בַּז),
And to trample them down like mud in the streets."

These allusions to Maher-shalal-hash-baz make clear that the object of discipline is the people of God (whether Israel and/or Judah), who will bear the brunt of Assyrian abuse based on the abuse of the vulnerable within Israelite and/or Judean society.[15]

Two other children are showcased in chs. 9–12, both connected with the royal household: the child born and given in 9:5–6 [ET 9:6–7] and the shoot from the root of Jesse in 11:1–5. Possibly this (or these) royal child(ren) relate(s) to the Immanuel (God with us) promise, which appears intermixed with Isaiah's children in Isa 7–8, especially considering the employment of the names of deity in the child's name in 9:6 (A wonderful counselor is the Mighty God, An Everlasting Father is the Prince of Peace) and the infusion with the spirit of the deity for the second offspring in 11:1–5.[16]

These allusions to children can be found in all the major pericopae in Isa 9–11, leaving Isa 12 without an allusion. However, this final chapter of Isa 7–12 contains two liturgical responses to the climactic salvation of Yahweh pictured in ch. 11. Key is the declaration in 12:1–2, words offered to those who survive the wrathful discipline of Yahweh depicted in chs. 9–10:

> I will give thanks to you, O Lord;
> For although you were angry with me,
> Your anger is turned away,
> And you comfort me.
> Behold (הִנֵּה), God (אל) is my salvation (יְשׁוּעָה),
> I will trust and not be afraid;

---

15. See Seitz, *Isaiah 1–39*, 91, who sees 10:1–4 as singling "out Judah's leaders for special indictment." See further Childs, *Isaiah*, 83–87, for the extension of the indictment from Israel to Judah, seeing 10:1–4 as "directed against those in Judah, who have learned nothing from Ephraim's folly but rather use their special position to pervert justice" (86).

16. See Roberts, "Whose Child Is This?" 115–29, for the connection between deity and royal figure in Isa 9 and Ps 2.

> For Yah (יָה) Yahweh is my strength and song,
> And he has become my salvation (יְשׁוּעָה)
> Therefore you will joyously draw water
> From the springs of salvation (יְשׁוּעָה).

This declaration of thanksgiving begins with the particle הִנֵּה, the same particle that was used to introduce the programmatic verse in 8:18. Furthermore, this thanksgiving is focused on the lexical stock of "salvation," employing יְשׁוּעָה three times and linking this not only to God and Yahweh (יהוה), but to the shortened version of Yahweh יָה as one finds in the prophet's name (יְשַׁעְיָהוּ) and the shorter version of the common name for deity (God, אֵל). In this way, the final allusion to Isaiah and his children is found in the declaration of salvation provided for the community. This declaration of thanksgiving brings closure to this section with the words: "although you were angry with me, your anger [אַף] is turned away [שׁוּב], and you comfort me," which echo the earlier refrain, "In spite of all this, his anger [אַף] does not turn away [שׁוּב], and his hand is still stretched out," which punctuated the text at 9:11, 16, 20 [ET 9:12, 17, 21]; 10:4.[17]

The Motif of Vegetation

There is a second motif that can be discerned throughout Isa 7–12, and it is the motif of vegetation.[18] Two of the key lexical repetitions have already highlighted the key role of this motif: the word pair "briars and thorns" appearing in 7:23, 24; 9:18; 10:17 and "the thickets of the forest" occurring in 9:17 [ET 9:18] and 10:34. But vegetation images are ubiquitous within this section of Isaiah:

- 7:1–2: "the trees of the forest shaking with the wind"
- 7:23: a vineyard of a thousand vines transformed into briars and thorns

---

17. The reference to the reception of comfort in place of divine wrath is reminiscent of the beginning of Isa 40, as the divine council or company of prophets is called to comfort God's people. This is further evidence that shows that Isa 7–12 has been shaped in line with the message of later sections in the book.

18. See also Wieringen, "Jesaja 6–12," 203–7, who demonstrates the importance of vegetation language for the structure and integrity of this section of Isaiah, noting especially links between Isa 7–10 and Isa 11–12 (see below on links between Isa 6 and Isa 11–12).

- 9:9 [ET 9:10]: Samaria's infrastructure compared to sycamores being cut down to be replaced by cedars
- 9:13 [ET 9:14]: divine judgment on elder/honorable man and prophet compared to cutting off palm branch and bulrush
- 9:17 [ET 9:18]: people pictured as briars and thorns, thickets of forest that are burned
- 10:15: Assyria compared to various implements used with lumber (axe, saw, club, rod)
- 10:18: destruction of the glory of his forest and his fruitful garden
- 10:19: small remnant of trees in his forest after destruction
- 10:33–34: divine judgment of lopping off tree boughs, felling tall trees, cutting down forest thickets with an axe with focus on the Lebanon forests
- 11:1, 10: a shoot and sprig growing from a root as image of a new royal descendant anointed for service and serving as a rallying point for people from the nations

As can be seen, the imagery of vegetation is largely focused on judgment, but in its last occurrence in this section of Isaiah, judgment shifts to salvation. Of course, the fact that only a shoot/sprig emerges from the root system of a tree suggests that this salvation is pictured against the dark backdrop of a cataclysmic judgment.

The Motif of Destruction

The final motif is one that is nearly always intertwined with the motif of vegetation in Isa 7–12, and it is the motif of destruction.[19] At times the vocabulary of cutting is used:

- 9:9 [ET 9:10]: "The sycamores have been cut down, but we will replace them with cedars."
- 9:13 [ET 9:14]: "So the Lord cuts off head and tail from Israel, both palm branch and bulrush in a single day."
- 10:15: "Is the axe to boast itself over the one who chops with it? Is the saw to exalt itself over the one who wields it? That would be like a club wielding those who lift it, or like a rod lifting him who is not wood."

19. See Seitz, *Isaiah 1–39*, 88–89.

- 10:33–34: "Behold, the Lord, the God of hosts, will lop off the boughs with a terrible crash; those also who are tall in stature will be cut down, and those who are lofty will be abased. He will cut down the thickets of the forest with an iron axe, and Lebanon will fall by the Mighty One."

At other times, however, the destruction is more extensive and involves fire. Possibly this is the final stage of destruction, which begins with felling trees:

- 9:17 [ET 9:18]: The fire caused by wickedness (and God's judgment of that wickedness) burns the briars and thorns, setting aflame the thickets of the forest to produce a column of smoke as the land and its people are burned up.
- 10:16–18: A similar fire is pictured as consuming forest and garden alike.
- 7:4: Judah's two enemies are depicted as merely "stubs of smoldering firebrands," leftover charred remains from a cooling fire.

Intertwining the Motifs

The vegetation and destruction motifs intertwined in Isa 7–12 are finally connected with the child motif in Isa 11:1, 8. These two verses employ vegetation imagery to depict a new generation emerging from the nearly destroyed root of Jesse (the royal family). The emergence of a royal figure through new vegetation growth is key to the future hope for the community, as this growth from the root of Jesse is used by Yahweh as the rallying point for the remnant that returns/repents.

LITERARY INTEGRITY OF ISAIAH 7–12: SUMMARY

Close attention to the historical and especially recurring lexical stock and motifs highlights not only the literary integrity of Isa 7–12 but, more importantly, the key message of this section of Isaiah. Salvation is announced by this prophet in keeping with his name, but this salvation is accomplished without compromising divine justice enacted through redemptive history at three key moments: Ahaz's reign, Hezekiah's reign, and the exilic crisis.[20]

---

20. Note especially the superb review of Oswalt, *The Holy One of Israel*, 28–40, in a chapter entitled "Judgment and Hope: The Full-Orbed Gospel," in which he speaks of

ISAIAH 6 AS INTRODUCTION TO ISAIAH 7–12

While our focus so far has been on the literary integrity and imagery of Isa 7–12 and the message that results from attention to these aspects of this key text, no reference has been made to Isa 6, which immediately precedes this section. At least from the time of Budde, most scholars have highlighted the similarities between Isa 6 and Isa 8, particularly in their common use of autobiographical style, which has suggested to many the existence of a *Denkschrift*, or memoir, that underlies this section of Isaiah.[21] While there are significant problems with Budde's theory, further reflection on these literary motifs from Isa 7–12 highlights the introductory role played by Isa 6 for reading Isa 7–12.

First of all, Isa 6 depicts the experience of the prophet Isaiah in the divine court. This experience is often linked to his commissioning as a prophet, and rightly so due to the clear allusions to the call of Moses with the use of the verbs "send" (שלח) and "go" (הלך) in 6:8–9a.[22] But what is often not appreciated is the close association forged between the prophet and the people as Isaiah encounters the presence of Yahweh, declaring:

> "Woe is me, for I am ruined!
> Because I am a man of unclean lips,
> And I live among a people of unclean lips;
> For my eyes have seen the King, the Lord of hosts."

Here the prophet turns the prophetic "woe" upon himself, echoing the woes directed towards the people in Isa 5:8–25 and preparing the way for the woes yet to be directed towards people and enemy alike in Isa 7–12 (10:1, 5). More explicitly, the prophet embeds himself among the people, identifying himself and his people as those possessing "unclean lips" who stand before the thrice holy King, Yahweh of hosts. This link between prophet and people suggests that Isaiah is not only a sign and wonder related to the royal house through the theme of trust, as argued

---

the "inseparability of judgment and hope" (35) and describes Isa 7–12 in the following way: "Back and forth the pendulum swings, between hope on the one hand, and judgment on the other" (37).

21. For a superb review of this issue, see, for example, Williamson, *Variations on a Theme*, 73–112; cf. Budde, *Jesaja's Erleben*.

22. Cf. Clements, *Isaiah 1–39*, 72–73; Watts, *Isaiah 1–33*, 104–5; Seitz, *Isaiah 1–39*, 54.

above, but also a sign and wonder related to the entire community through the theme of uncleanness.

Second, Isa 6 goes on to depict multiple waves of divine discipline and does so in a way that echoes the latter two phrases that we have discovered in Isa 7–12: those associated with the reign of Hezekiah and the exilic crisis.[23] The first wave in Isa 6 results in a destruction of infrastructure and population that literally decimates the land, leaving only a tenth behind. This wave is most likely referring to the destruction and conquest of the land by the Assyrians against Hezekiah (6:11–13a). But there is another wave depicted in the closing verse (6:13b), one that will result in complete devastation.

Interestingly, the images used in this final verse are reminiscent of the literary motifs highlighted above for Isa 7–12.[24] The devastation is pictured in terms of vegetation, with a focus on great trees (terebinth, oak) that are destroyed by burning. What remains is but a "seed," an apt image after a devastating forest fire and an image that has the advantage of bridging two imagistic domains: that of the offspring of vegetation and that of humans. This seed would be the survivors of Judah (and possibly Israel), whether royal or not, as expected in the transition from the end of Isa 39 to Isa 40.[25]

This fusion of the two imagistic domains, vegetation and humans, also appears in 11:1, 8 (a shoot/sprig growing from the root of Jesse) in the transition to the climax of salvation in Isa 7–12. The adjective "holy" at the conclusion of Isa 6 highlights the alignment between the thrice holy Yahweh (6:3) and the seed that emerges from divine judgment and salvation, overcoming the earlier uncleanness voiced by the prophet in 6:5. The antidote for the uncleanness in 6:5 is a burning coal plucked from the incense altar, that is, fire in the cultic setting of the temple precincts.

Isaiah 6, then, prepares the way for Isa 7–12 and highlights once again the picture of salvation that is developed in this section of Isaiah. Salvation does not come cheaply, nor does it overlook sin, turning a blind eye to humanity's rebellion against God and abuse of one another.

---

23. See further Seitz, *Isaiah 1–39*, 58, on "graded judgment" in Isaiah.

24. See Wieringen, "Jesaja 6–12," 203–7 who shows connectivity between vegetation vocabulary in Isa 6 and Isa 7–12, noting especially links between Isa 6 and Isa 11–12.

25. Clements, *Isaiah 1–39*, 78, favors "the survivors of Judah in general, rather than . . . the royal seed of the house of David."

NEW TESTAMENT

Lest anyone think this understanding of salvation is merely the fixation of an Old Testament scholar, it is important to end this article with a quick glance at the New Testament. The hope of Immanuel connected to Jesus by Matthew in Matt 1:21 is related to saving "his people from their sins." But John the Baptist makes clear as he appears in Matt 3 that the salvation that comes from this Immanuel is a salvation that demands fruit aligned with repentance, employing imagery reminiscent of what we have encountered in Isa 6–12. John the Baptist declares:

> The axe is already laid at the root of the trees; therefore every tree that does not bear good fruit is cut down and thrown into the fire. As for me, I baptize you with water for repentance, but he who is coming after me is mightier than I, and I am not fit to remove His sandals; he will baptize you with the Holy Spirit and fire. His winnowing fork is in his hand, and he will thoroughly clear his threshing floor; and he will gather his wheat into the barn, but he will burn up the chaff with unquenchable fire. (Matt 3:10–12)

Hope is rooted in the baptism with the Holy Spirit and fire, and this baptism entails a burning of all that offends the Lord. These are not contrastive visions of salvation: if Immanuel comes into our lives individually and communally, we must remember that this is the "holy, holy, holy One among us" and that his salvation will not stop short of transforming the lives and communities of those who dare to take up the cross and follow this Immanuel.

BIBLIOGRAPHY

Ackroyd, Peter R. "Isaiah 36–39: Structure and Function." In *Von Kanaan bis Kerala: Festschrift, Professor Mag. Dr. J. P. M. van der Pleog, O. P. zur Vollendung des Siebzigsten Lebensjahres am 4, Juli 1979*, edited by W. C. Delsman et al., 3–21. AOAT 211. Kevelaer, Germany: Butzon und Bercker, 1982.

Brodie, Louis T. "Children and the Prince: The Structure, Nature and Date of Isaiah 6–12." *BTB* 9 (1979) 27–31.

Brueggemann, Walter. *Isaiah 1–39*. Westminster Bible Companion. Louisville: Westminster John Knox, 1998.

Budde, Karl. *Jesaja's Erleben: Eine Gemeinverständliche Auslegung der Denkschrift des Propheten (Kap. 6, 1—9, 6)*. Gotha: L. Klotz, 1928.

Childs, Brevard S. *Isaiah*. OTL. Louisville: Westminster John Knox, 2001.

Clements, Ronald E. "The Immanuel Prophecy of Isa 7:10–17 and Its Messianic Interpretation." In *Die Hebräische Bibel und ihre Zweifache Nachgeschichte:*

Festschrift für Rolf Rendtorff zum 65 Geburtstag, edited by Erhard Blum et al., 225–40. Neukirchen-Vluyn: Neukirchener, 1990.

———. *Isaiah 1–39*. NCBC. Grand Rapids: Eerdmans, 1980.

Day, John. "Shear–Jashub (Isaiah 7:3) and 'the Remnant of Wrath' (Psalm 76:11)." *VT* 31 (1981) 76–78.

Oswalt, John N. *The Book of Isaiah, Chapters 1–39*. NICOT. Grand Rapids: Eerdmans, 1986.

———. *The Holy One of Israel: Studies in the Book of Isaiah*. Eugene, OR: Cascade, 2014.

———. "The Significance of the Calmah Prophecy in the Context of Isaiah 7–12." *CTR* 6 (1993) 223–35.

Roberts, J. J. M. *First Isaiah: A Commentary*. Hermeneia. Minneapolis: Fortress, 2015.

———. "Whose Child Is This? Reflections on the Speaking Voice in Isaiah 9:5." *HTR* 90 (1997) 115–29.

Sawyer, John F. A. *The Fifth Gospel: Isaiah in the History of Christianity*. New York: Cambridge University Press, 1996.

Schultz, Richard L. "How Many Isaiahs Were There and What Does It Matter?" In *Evangelicals & Scripture: Tradition, Authority, and Hermeneutics*, edited by Vincent Bacote, Laura C. Miguélez et al., 150–70. Downers Grove, IL: InterVarsity, 2004.

Seitz, Christopher R. *Isaiah 1–39*. IBC. Louisville: John Knox, 1993.

———. *Zion's Final Destiny: The Development of the Book of Isaiah—a Reassessment of Isaiah 36–39*. Minneapolis: Fortress, 1991.

Tull, Patricia K. "One Book, Many Voices: Conceiving of Isaiah's Polyphonic Message." In *"As Those Who Are Taught": The Interpretation of Isaiah from the LXX to the SBL*, edited by Claire Mathews McGinnis and Patricia K. Tull, 279–314. SBLSS 27. Atlanta: Society of Biblical Literature, 2006.

Watts, John D. W. *Isaiah 1–33*. Rev. ed. WBC 24. Waco, TX: Word, 2005.

Webb, Barry G. "Zion in Transformation: A Literary Approach to Isaiah." In *The Bible in Three Dimensions*, edited by David J. A. Clines et al., 65–84. JSOTSup 87. Sheffield: JSOT Press, 1990.

Weber, Robert. *Biblia Sacra Iuxta Vulgatam Versionem*. 2nd ed. Stuttgart: Deutsche Bibelgesellschaft, 1975.

Wieringen, A. L. H. M. van. "Jesaja 6–12: Die Vegetationsbildsprache und die Prophetische Struktur." In *The Book of Isaiah—Le livre d'Isaïe: Les oracles et leurs relecteurs: Unité et complexité de l'ouvrage*, edited by Jacques Vermeylen, 203–7. Leuven: Leuven University Press, 1989.

Williamson, H. G. M. *Variations on a Theme: King, Messiah and Servant in the Book of Isaiah*. Didsbury Lectures 1997. Carlisle: Paternoster, 1998.

3

When Did the Good News Become the Gospel?

A Corpus and Diachronic Study of Εὐαγγέλιον

Francis G. H. Pang

INTRODUCTION

MOST PEOPLE WOULD AGREE that the English word "gospel" is a religious or, more particularly, a Christian term that refers to the message or the core content of the Christian faith. In fact, most standard English dictionaries share a similar list of glosses or definitions. An entry usually starts with the more common definitions, both of which pertain to the Christian faith. The first two definitions from the Oxford dictionary, for example, are "the teaching or revelation of Christ," and "the record of Jesus' life and teaching in the first four books of the New Testament."[1] From Merriam-Webster, we have "the message concerning Christ, the kingdom of God, and salvation," and "one of the first four New Testament books telling of the life, death, and resurrection of Jesus Christ."[2] In either case, the meaning of the word "gospel" has to do with the core message of Christianity, the life of Christ, or the records of Christ's life and work, which are the written Gospels.

---

1. *Oxford English Living Dictionaries*, "Gospel," https://en.oxforddictionaries.com/definition/gospel.

2. *Merriam-Webster*, "Gospel," https://www.merriam-webster.com/dictionary/gospel.

In fact, if we look into the etymology of this word, most English dictionaries would say that it is derived from an old English word *gōdspel*, meaning "good"+"news/story." This is also a gloss of the Ecclesiastical Latin word *evangelium*, which translates the Greek word εὐαγγέλιον,³ the word that the New Testament authors used to refer to the salvific work of Jesus.

What is interesting linguistically is that if we go back to the English dictionary and look at the entry for the word "gospel" again, we find another sense of the word, possibly an extension of the meaning of the gospel truth: the word can be used to describe anything that is believed to be definitely true.⁴ Apparently the word "gospel" has developed a generalized meaning from the original, more restricted sense. So today if you search the phrase "the gospel according to . . ." or "the gospel of . . ." on the Internet, the list of results you get is mostly related to non-religious or non-Christian subject matters, for example, "the gospel according to ESPN" and "the gospel according to Peanuts."⁵ Therefore, what we have is a word that arguably originated as part of the technical vocabulary of Christianity and gradually took on a more generalized meaning. This particular kind of semantic shift is called "semantic extending" or "semantic broadening," which, formally, is "the process by which the meaning of a word becomes more general or more inclusive than its earlier meaning."⁶

Interestingly, we see a similar process of semantic shift at work in the Greek εὐαγγέλιον word group. However, instead of starting from a specialized meaning and taking on a more generalized sense, in this case "the meaning of the word becomes less inclusive or less general than the historically earlier meaning."⁷ If we look at the Greek literature spanning the period of five centuries on both sides of the time of Jesus, we

---

3. *Oxford English Living Dictionaries*, "Gospel," https://en.oxforddictionaries.com/definition/gospel.

4. So, the fourth gloss in Merriam-Webster reads "something accepted or promoted as infallible truth or as a guiding principle or doctrine" (*Merriam-Webster*, "Gospel," https://www.merriam-webster.com/dictionary/gospel).

5. An Internet search in May 2015 yielded a list of links including subject matter such as TV shows, celebrities, comic strips, and movies.

6. Pavlou, "Semantic Adaptation," 444. For a discussion of semantic change in general (by way of synchronic processes of meaning extension), see Cruse, *Meaning in Language*, 214–15.

7. Pavlou, "Semantic Adaptation," 444.

find that the εὐαγγέλιον word group went through this reverse process of semantic shift, starting from a generalized meaning (good news or good tidings) and developing into a more restricted or less inclusive sense (*the* good news of Jesus). Eventually, this specialized sense took over as the core meaning and became the most common definition of the word, at least as seen in the limited surviving literature of the time. This kind of semantic shift is called semantic narrowing.

The objective of this study is to probe how the general εὐαγγέλιον word group became a more specific part of the standard Christian vocabulary. By way of a diachronic investigation of the word in Greek texts spanning the pre-Hellenistic period to the early medieval period, I want to look at how and when the specialized meaning of the word emerged in Christian literature. This is how this paper is organized: I will first examine the definitions given by various Greek lexicons based on different corpora. I will then describe the semantic range of εὐαγγέλιον and εὐαγγελίζομαι in two groups of texts: (1) the pre-Christian Greek literature and (2) the non-Christian literature contemporary with the time of the early church. I will identify the common features in these occurrences in terms of context and common word collocations. I will demonstrate, albeit only in a handful of examples, how the specialized or highly religious sense took over as the core meaning of the word in the later period. And finally, I will offer a few suggestions as to how and when this semantic shift happened and what the implications are for exegetes of the New Testament.

THE SEMANTIC RANGE OF ΕΥΑΓΓΕΛΙΟΝ

Before moving on, let me briefly go through the corpus of this study. Instead of focusing on the occurrences of the εὐαγγέλιον word group in the New Testament and the patristic literature, I will focus on the non-biblical Greek literature from the fifth century BCE to the second century CE. In an ideal world, there would be enough instances of the word in non-biblical literature before and after the first century to compare and determine how the word use changed after it was taken over by the early Christian communities. However, the samples of Greek literature we have that are annotated and searchable are extremely rare. I will have to settle for the body of searchable and tokenized texts and see if a reasonable conclusion can be drawn from them. I need to express one caveat before moving on: my objective in this study is not so much to locate the precise point in time when the semantic shift occurred, but rather to focus on the process of semantic narrowing of the εὐαγγέλιον/ εὐαγγελίζομαι word group.[8]

First, let us briefly look at the lexicons. I will start with lexicons that cover the Greek Bible, later Christian writings, and extrabiblical material. The entry of εὐαγγέλιον in E. A. Sophocles' *Greek Lexicon of the Roman and Byzantine Periods* lists eight senses.[9] These can be grouped into three general usages. The first usage is a general sense of good news (and good tidings) that has nothing to do with Jesus and his salvific work (category 1). References for this sense are from ancient documents that predate the New Testament. The second usage (category 2) is the more specialized meaning of good tidings or gospel that "applied to the revelation by Christ."[10] The rest of the entry (categories 3–8) is a third general usage that refers to documents that bear the title εὐαγγέλιον. Most of these documents are related to the life and work of Jesus, the written Gospels; however, there are a few documents that bear the name of a gospel without making any reference to the life of Jesus.[11] Most of the references listed under these usages (3–8) are from patristic sources.

The entry for εὐαγγέλιον in the Liddell, Scott, and Jones lexicon, which covers the ancient Greek texts from the eleventh century BCE to the Byzantine Period, focuses mostly on the more general sense of "good tidings, good news," citing both non-biblical and biblical (mainly Septuagint) sources. Εὐαγγέλιον is also used to signify the reward of good tidings that is given to the one who delivers the news.[12] The Christian sense is only briefly mentioned under the general heading of good news with only one reference (Gal 1:11).

---

8. For those who are interested in a detailed discussion of the instances of εὐαγγέλιον in the New Testament, please refer to the article by Stanley E. Porter in this volume, "The Good News of the Gospels," 54–78.

9. Sophocles, *Greek Lexicon*, 1:529–30.

10. All of the references for this use are from the New Testament. Ibid., 529.

11. This list includes: (3) the canonical Gospels and the apocryphal Gospel, (4) the written Gospels in a collective sense, (5) the four canonical Gospels bound together in one volume, (6) and (7) the Gospel of the day or the lectionary; and finally (8) a book of faith "without any reference to the life or doctrine of Christ" (ibid., 530).

12. LSJ, "εὐαγγέλιον," A.1. This is apparently the oldest sense of the word, which is also found, as the only definition, in the Homeric Dictionary. See, for example, Auenrieth, *A Homeric Dictionary*.

Turning to the standard lexicons for the study of the Greek New Testament, the change in emphasis is rather obvious. Bauer's lexicon has the following three definitions for εὐαγγέλιον:[13]

1. God's good news to humans, good news as proclamation

2. Details relating to the life and ministry of Jesus, good news of Jesus

3. A book dealing with the life and teaching of Jesus, a gospel account

It is rather obvious that all three definitions have a religious or Christian connotation. Even the more generalized definition of the three, the first one, is religious in tone. In fact, if we look at the references listed under the first definition, a majority of the instances of the words refer to the εὐαγγέλιον of Jesus, not good news in general. One example of this is Gal 1:6–7, in which Paul compares τὸ εὐαγγέλιον τοῦ Χριστοῦ with ἕτερον εὐαγγέλιον. In this instance εὐαγγέλιον is used in a more restricted sense, referring to the εὐαγγέλιον of Christ.

Finally, Louw and Nida have only one entry for εὐαγγέλιον under domain 33 (Communication: Inform, Announce). Their definition covers both the general sense "the content of good news," and a qualification that in the New Testament this content (of the good news) is "a reference to the gospel of Jesus."[14]

Let me summarize this brief survey by means of two observations. First, it is rather obvious that the Christian sense of the word εὐαγγέλιον is less prominent in the lexicons that cover both biblical and non-biblical sources. It is rather the general sense of the word that occupies the central position. Second, the distinctions among the different glosses given by the biblical Greek lexicons are not clear. Louw and Nida, for example, give both "the good news" and "the gospel" as glosses. At times, it seems like they are using one gloss to define another gloss for εὐαγγέλιον. This seems to suggest that the two terms can be used interchangeably in the translation of the New Testament. The same can be said regarding the

---

13. BDAG, 402. For a brief discussion of the usages in non-literary sources, see Moulton and Milligan, *Vocabulary of the Greek Testament*, 259.

14. There is also a note on alternative phrases that translators should consider when translating to other languages. The change of wording in these phrases is used to further elaborate the adjective "good" ("makes one happy," "causes one joy," "bring smiles," etc.). See L&N 33.217.

verb εὐαγγελίζομαι. Although both Bauer and Louw and Nida define the term as "communicating or announcing good news," both are quick to qualify that in the New Testament it is a particular reference to the gospel message about Jesus. In Liddell-Scott-Jones, however, the Christian sense "proclaiming the gospel" is listed as only one of the definitions in a sub-category.

EXTRABIBLICAL USAGES OF ΕΥΑΓΓΕΛΙΟΝ

Turning to the instances of εὐαγγέλιον in non-Christian literature that pre-dated or was contemporary with the New Testament, we see that the word is used in quite a wide variety of contexts. Quite often it is used in a military context, particularly for the announcement of news of victory. For example, in the *Library of History* by Diodorus Siculus, εὐαγγέλια is tied to a victory, the announcement of the victory, and the reward of the messenger who announces a victory:[15]

> Now Dionysius ... had won the victory, and one of those who sang in the chorus, supposing that he would be rewarded handsomely if he were the first to give news [ἀπαγγείλη] of the victory ... Dionysius did reward him, and was himself so overjoyed that he sacrificed to the gods for the εὐαγγέλια ...

The good news is also associated in this context with sacrificing to the gods and feasting. However, note that the verb that is used to announce or deliver the news of victory is actually not εὐαγγελίζομαι or εὐαγγελίζω but ἀπαγγέλλω ("report, proclaim, declare, etc."). I will come back to this verb later in our discussion.

Similarly, in other non-biblical (pre-New Testament) instances we see the collocation of the theme of victory, the announcement of the victory, the victor (often described as the savior), the messenger who brings the good news, the reward at the announcement, and the sacrifice to the gods.[16] The Priene Inscription, for example, includes all these elements. This text is often compared to the beginning of the gospel of Mark (1:1) due to the collocation of similar lexical stock (εὐαγγέλιον, θεός, ἀρχή, and also σωτήρ).[17] Note that these instances are not limited to a single

---

15. Diodorus Siculus, *Library* 15.74 (first century BCE).

16. For example, Plutarchus, *Agesilaus* 33.5 (first century CE); Xenophon, *Hellenica* 1.6.37 (fifth to fourth century BCE); and Josephus, *Wars* 4.618 (first century CE).

17. For a discussion of the Priene Inscription, see Evans, "Priene Calendar

author or a collection of texts written over a particular period of time. By my estimate, of the extrabiblical instances that I studied (around one hundred), more than one-third involve a military context.

We can also see different nuances of the lexis when we take a closer look at these instances involving a military context. Quite often the news does not have to correspond to the facts; that is, we see in quite a few instances that false stories of victory are circulated to boost the morale of tired soldiers. Sometimes the communication of this "good" news was quite elaborate. Not only would the messenger spread the news of victory, but he would also dress like a victor and perform a public sacrificial act so that the soldiers would more readily believe it.[18]

In other instances the news of victory may not necessarily be perceived as "good" by the recipient(s). For example, quite a few instances of εὐαγγέλιον and εὐαγγελίζομαι in the Old Testament are from two episodes involving King David (2 Sam 4:10; 18:20).[19] In both cases, the messenger thought he had brought good news regarding victory and the demise of the king's enemy, but in both instances the king did not consider the death of the enemy (Saul and Absalom) as any reason for reward or celebration.

In fact, in a rare instance, εὐαγγελίζομαι is used to talk about luring others into sin. In Philo's *On Courage*, εὐαγγελίζομαι is used to refer to idolatry:[20]

> And when they had accomplished their purpose [idolatry], they sent the glad tidings [εὐαγγελίζονται] to the men of their nation; and they would have been likely to draw over others also of the firmer and stronger-minded sort if the bountiful and merciful God had not taken compassion upon their unhappy state, and by the prompt punishment of those who had gone astray and wrought folly . . .

The ironic use of a word here that is normally used to describe positive news somehow highlights the depravity of those who lure others to join them in sin. They actually think that they have "good" news for others.

Inscription," 67–81; and Porter's chapter, "The Good News of the Gospels," below.

18. See Xenophon, *Hellencia* 4.3.14 and Plutarchus, *Agesilaus* 17.3.6.

19. In both instances, both the verb εὐαγγελίζω and the noun εὐαγγέλιον are used. In 2 Sam 4:10, ἀπαγγείλω is used to refer to the reporting of the death of Saul, but εὐαγγελίζω for the act of bringing good news (the victory).

20. Philo, *Virt.* 41.

Obviously not all the non-biblical instances are used in a military context. There are other instances that have nothing to do with war or victory but rather with good news in general. One of the oft-cited examples is from a play by Aristophanes. In a council meeting, a group of sausage merchants responds to the "good news" that the price of anchovies is at an all-time low.[21] Another example is from Chariton's *Callirhoe*. It involes a servant, Leonas, who wants to tell his master the good news that he has purchased a girl for him to console him for the loss of his wife.[22]

ΕΥΑΓΓΕΛΙΟΝ AND SEMANTIC NARROWING

It is undeniable that the semantic range of εὐαγγέλιον and εὐαγγελίζομαι in non-biblical Greek texts is quite wide and nuanced. What we know for certain is that a semantic shift did occur in the early church. The instances in the New Testament and in the fathers did in fact lose all the previous nuances due to the narrowing of the semantic range. The questions that we need to ask are why and when this semantic shift took place within the early Christian circle. Regarding the reason for the semantic shift, recent studies, particularly in the area of social-scientific criticism, suggest that some of the early church communities were sectarian in nature and that, as a result, these communities developed an insider language for in-group communication.[23] Many believe that an in-group or insider language that can be identified in John is typical of the kind of language used in alternate or fringe societies.[24] This seems to fit the early church setting, where the εὐαγγέλιον word group seems to be taken over or monopolized by the early Christian communities. One may argue that the common collocated words (such as savior, vic-

21. Aristophanes, *The Knights* 643–56.

22. Chariton, *Callirhoe* 2.1.3.

23. For example, the works of Wayne Meeks, Jerome Neyrey, and David Rensberger. Meeks, "The Man from Heaven in Johannine Sectarianism," 44–72; Neyrey, *An Ideology of Revolt*; and Rensberger, "Sectarianism and Theological Interpretation in John," 139–56.

24. See, for example, the works by Bruce Malina and Norman Petersen on anti-language. Malina mainly draws the idea from the work of the linguist Michael Halliday. He argues that the ideas of anti-language and anti-society can help the modern reader better understand the Johannine community by means of the text of John. See Malina, "Maverick Christian Group," 167–82, and Malina and Rohrbaugh, *Social Science Commentary*. See also Petersen, *Sociology of Light*, for a similar line of argument.

tory, and good news) in the εὐαγγέλιον texts surveyed above all went through a similar process of technicalization. All these collocated lexical items took on a more technical or specialized meaning. Εὐαγγέλιον and εὐαγγελίζομαι have indeed become part of the specialized vocabularies of the Christian community, designating the good news of Jesus. However, semantic narrowing is not considered in the linguistic literature to be a trait of an insider language, or "anti-language," in sociolinguistic terms, for the use of a sectarian society. Although the specialization or technicalization of terms such as εὐαγγέλιον and σωτήρ seems to set up a reality in opposition to an established norm—i.e., Jesus, not Caesar, is the victor, the source of the good news, and the savior of the people—most would consider that this kind of semantic change does not constitute an anti-language.[25] An anti-language, instead, is formed through language relexicalization and overlexicalization, where new words are used for old words.[26] I do not think that in this instance the semantic shift of the εὐαγγέλιον word group can be considered as relexicalization and thus as evidence of an anti-language. However, this does not mean that I do not think the social setting of the early church plays a part in the specialization of the vocabularies. On the contrary, I think it does contribute to the development of semantic narrowing of the εὐαγγέλιον word group. However, I am not sure whether the anti-language hypothesis is the right tool for making such a connection.[27]

We now turn from the question of why to the question of when the semantic narrowing took place. We see hints of semantic narrowing of the εὐαγγέλιον word group as early as the beginning of Jesus' ministry. Obviously, I am not suggesting that when Jesus reads the scroll of Isaiah (61:1–3) in Luke 4:18, he is referring to "good news to the poor" as a fully fledged and developed idea of the Christian gospel, that is, his

---

25. Malina, "Maverick Christian Group," 176.

26. In the communication among prisoners in a prison community, for example, one expects to find new words for types of criminal acts and classes of criminals and victims, for tools of the trade, for police and other representatives of law enforcement, for penalties, etc. created in place of the old words. See Halliday, "Anti-Languages," 572.

27. The use of anti-language to support the sectarian Johannine community hypothesis have been heavily criticized recently. See, for example, Phillips, *Prologue of the Fourth Gospel*, 59–64; Lamb, *Text, Context and the Johannine Community*, 103–44. I want to thank Zachary Dawson for the insightful conversations on this topic. For a review of Lamb's work, see Dawson, Review of *Text, Context, and the Johannine Community*, R1–R4.

own salvific life and ministry on earth. However, one cannot deny that his understanding of the "good news" has to do with his ministry on earth. In fact, when we examine New Testament quotations of the "good news" passages from Isaiah,[28] most would agree that these passages had taken on, to a certain extent, an eschatological or messianic connotation. However, this does not mean that any eschatological re-interpretation of an Old Testament text that has the word εὐαγγέλιον indicates semantic narrowing.

Take Amos 4:13 as an example. Most scholars would agree that in the Masoretic Text this verse is a simple description of the power of the Lord that has little eschatological or messianic connotation: "He who forms the mountains, who creates the wind, and who reveals his thoughts to humankind, who turns dawn to darkness, and treads on the heights of the earth—the Lord God Almighty is his name" (Amos 4:13 NIV). However, in the Septuagint, the third participial phrase ("reveals his thoughts to humankind") was changed to "declares to humans his Messiah."[29] The main discussion point here is: how did the Septuagint end up with τὸν Χριστὸν? There are several possible explanations, ranging from a different *Vorlage,* a misreading, or a result of a messianic re-interpretation. However, what is interesting for this study is not the τὸν Χριστόν reading *per se,* but the use of the participle ἀπαγγέλλων. If the LXX translators saw this as a messianic passage, the fact that ἀπαγγέλλω is used instead of εὐαγγλίζομαι may suggest that at this point the semantic narrowing of εὐαγγελίζομαι had not yet completely taken hold. I understand that my interpretation here involves an argument from silence, but given the limitation of the size of my corpus, this may be the best evidence at this point in my study.

I would like to close this section by way of a call to Bible translators to reconsider the translation of the εὐαγγέλιον word group. As I mentioned above, the process of semantic narrowing could not happen overnight. The shift was probably developing gradually between the time of Jesus to the time of the beginning of the second century, that is, anywhere from 30–130 CE. If this assumption is correct, the New Testament documents were written in a period where the meaning of εὐαγγέλιον and εὐαγγελίζομαι was still in a state of flux, gradually moving from the general sense to a more restricted Christian sense. If this

---

28. Such as Isa 61:1 in Matt 11:5 and Luke 4:19; and Isa 52:7 in Rom 10:15–16.

29. Amos 4:13 (my translation of the LXX).

was the case, Bible translators should reconsider whether they should use the same gloss to translate every instance of the εὐαγγέλιον word group in the New Testament, whether it is "good news" or "gospel."[30] It is, of course, anachronistic to translate the Isaiah passages (Isa 40:9; 52:7; 61:1, etc.) with "the gospel," but what about the quotations of this text in the New Testament? If we can safely assume that the word εὐαγγέλιον did not have the status of technical language until well into the second century (in the fathers), should we argue that at least some of the occurrences (such as Matt 11:5; Luke 4:18; and Rom 10:15–16, etc.) in the NT would better be rendered as the "good news" instead of the "gospel?"[31]

CONCLUSION

In this brief study I documented the development of a specialized meaning of the εὐαγγέλιον word group in the early church. The word εὐαγγέλιον (and its cognates) originally signified the reward of good tidings given to the messenger or, in Greek literature (such as LXX 2 Sam 4:10) predating the time of Jesus, good tidings/news more generally. New Testament writers use this word in a more restricted sense, narrowing the content of the good news to the salvific life, teaching, and ministry of Jesus. It is further developed in the writings of the church fathers into an even more technical sense, signifying largely the written accounts of Christ's words and deeds, that is, the (canonical and non-canonical) Gospels. By means of a diachronic investigation of the word in a corpus of Greek texts spanning the pre-Hellenistic period to the early medieval period, I looked at why and when the specialized meaning of the word emerged in Christian literature and what the implications are for Bible translation.

BIBLIOGRAPHY

Autenrieth, Georg. *A Homeric Dictionary for Schools and Colleges*. New York: Harper, 1891.

30. CEV, for example, uses "the good news" for all occurrences of εὐαγγέλιον in the New Testament, while NASB uses "gospel" for all instances except 10:15–16.

31. While many English versions translate εὐαγγελίσασθαι in Luke 4:18 (Isa 61:1) as "to preach the good news," there are a few translations with "to preach the gospel/Gospel" (NASB, KJV, and ironically, the Good News Bible). Virtually no modern translation translates the original text from Isaiah (Isa 61:1) with "gospel." Likewise, while most versions use "good news" for εὐαγγελιζομένων and εὐαγγελίῳ in Rom 10:15 and 10:16, a few versions have "gospel" or "Gospel" (HCSB, KJV, etc.) while no translation uses it for the original text (Isa 52:7).

Cruse, Alan. *Meaning in Language: An Introduction to Semantics and Pragmatics*. Oxford: Oxford University Press, 2000.

Dawson, Zachary K. Review of *Text, Context and The Johannine Community: A Sociolinguistic Analysis of the Johannine Writings*, by David A. Lamb. *Dialogismos* 1 (2016) R1–R4.

Evans, Craig A. "Mark's Incipit and the Priene Calendar Inscription: From Jewish Gospel to Greco-Roman Gospel." *JGRChJ* 1 (2000) 67–81.

Halliday, M. A. K. "Anti-Languages." *American Anthropologist* 78 (1976) 570–84.

Lamb, David A. *Text, Context and the Johannine Community: A Sociolinguistic Analysis of the Johannine Writings*. LNTS 477. New York: T. & T. Clark, 2014.

Malina, B. J. "John's: The Maverick Christian Group: The Evidence of Sociolinguistics." *BTB* 24 (1994) 167–82.

Malina, B. J., and Richard L. Rohrbaugh. *Social-Science Commentary on the Gospel of John*. Minneapolis: Fortress, 1998.

Meeks, Wayne. "The Man from Heaven in Johannine Sectarianism." *JBL* 91 (1972) 44–72.

Moulton, James Hope, and George Milligan. *The Vocabulary of the Greek Testament: Illustrated from the Papyri and Other Non-Literary Sources*. London: Hodder and Stoughton, 1929.

Neyrey, J. H. *An Ideology of Revolt*. Philadelphia: Fortress, 1988.

Pavlou, Pavlos. "The Semantic Adaptation of Turkish Loan-Words in the Greek Cypriotic Dialect." In *Themes in Greek Linguistics: Papers from the First International Conference on Greek Linguistics, Reading, September 1993*, edited by Irene Phillippaki-Warburton et al., 443–48. CILT 117. Amsterdam: Benjamins, 1994.

Petersen, Norman R. *The Gospel of John and the Sociology of Light: Language and Characterization in the Fourth Gospel*. 1993. Reprint, Eugene, OR: Wipf and Stock, 2008.

Phillips, Peter M. *The Prologue of the Fourth Gospel: A Sequential Reading*. LNTS 332. New York: T. & T. Clark, 2006.

Rensberger, David. "Sectarianism and Theological Interpretation in John." In *"What is John?" Vol. 2: Literary and Social Readings of the Fourth Gospel*, edited by Fernando F. Segovia, 139–56. Atlanta: Scholars, 1998.

Sophocles, E. A. *Greek Lexicon of the Roman and Byzantine Periods (From B.C. 146 to A.D. 1100)*. Vol. 1. New York: Frederick Ungar, 1900.

4

The Good News of the Gospels
Good News as Form and Content

Stanley E. Porter

INTRODUCTION

THE TITLE OF THIS volume is "Is the gospel good news?" Those with knowledge of the Bible, and more particularly of ancient Greek, will realize the play on words indicated by such a title. The English word "gospel" is a translation of the Greek word εὐαγγέλιον. The Greek word εὐαγγέλιον is a transparent word in Greek—as are many Greek words[1]— that indicates a "good" (εὐ) "announcement" or "proclamation" (neuter form of ἀγγελία; verb, ἀγγέλλω), to which analysis I will return below. The translation in Old English was *gōdspell* or "good spell," which in Middle English became *go(d)spell*, and then in modern English "gospel." For most Christian theologians, the gospel is "the proclaimed message about Christ's death and resurrection,"[2] a meaning clearly found in Paul's writings on the basis of his use of the neuter noun form (εὐαγγέλιον). The term "gospel" has also come to be identified with a particular form of writing found in the New Testament, of which there are four examples.

---

1. Transparency is not to be confused with etymologizing. Unwarranted basing the meaning of a lexeme upon a tracing of its history back to some original meaning—etymologizing—is not the same as the transparent meanings of the components of a lexeme.

2. Koester, *Ancient Gospels*, 9.

The four Gospels are Matthew, Mark, Luke, and John. These books are called Gospels purportedly on the basis of several features: the use of the noun in the opening verse of Mark's Gospel (1:1), "beginning of the gospel/good news of Jesus Christ, Son of God," and the fact that they use both noun and verb forms of this word and depict, if not overtly proclaim, the message about Christ's death and resurrection. I will return to both of these issues as well.

Thus, the title of this volume itself is ambiguous in two ways. In the first way, the title asks whether the Christian proclamation, the good news, is in fact good news. This is a topic that is being directly addressed in a number of the papers of this volume. There have been many who have questioned whether, in fact, the Christian proclamation of Christ's death and resurrection is good news for any number of different people and groups, both inside and outside of the church. That is not the direct topic of my paper, but is addressed by others. The title is ambiguous in a second way as well. In this second way, the term "gospel" refers to those four books that are labeled the Gospels, Matthew, Mark, Luke, and John, and asks what the relationship of the "good news" is to these individual books. This is a more approximate representation of the topic of my paper.

In order to attempt to get close to an answer to such a question, I will undertake an examination of the use of the noun and verb forms of the word that is often translated "good news" or "gospel" (εὐαγγέλιον) or "to proclaim the gospel" (εὐαγγελλίζομαι). I will examine the usage within the Gospels wherever such instances occur, to determine the sense in which they are used within the Gospels. On the basis of this, I wish to make two types of observations. The first concerns what the Gospels say about the "good news," that is, what the content of that good news is within the Gospels. The second observation concerns the possible designation of the Gospels as "good news" books. I will examine how language of the "good news" is used as an indicator of the type of literature that we find within the books that are designated Gospels, that is, what the form of that good news takes in relation to the books called Gospels.

Before I proceed to this task, I wish to say that a fuller study would want to explore all of the lexemes within Louw and Nida's semantic domain 33, sub-section O, "Inform, Announce" (L&N 33.189–33.217). However, I believe that the more limited study of the two lexemes that

I have identified provides a basis for making some observations on the gospel and whether it is good news as it is found within the Gospels themselves, especially as these lexemes, and particularly the noun form, seem to be used in theologically significant ways within the Gospels.

THE EVIDENCE OF THE GOOD NEWS IN THE GOSPELS

This part considers the evidence of the good news in the Gospels and is divided into two major parts, with the first discussing the content of the good news and the second the form of the good news.

The Content of the Good News

In the first part of this section, I wish to examine the use of the noun "good news" (εὐαγγέλιον) and the verb "proclaim good news" (εὐαγγελίζομαι). I will concentrate upon the noun form, as that is the one most widely used in the Gospels.

Before I say more about the use of these words in the New Testament, I wish to say something about the history of the use of these words. As important as the words for "good news" are in the New Testament, it may come as a surprise to discover that both the noun and the verb forms of this word are relatively infrequent in extrabiblical Greek. The verb form apparently occurs initially in the comic author Aristophanes. In classical times, the noun had the general sense of "reward for good news" and appeared often in the plural with the sense of "thankoffering for good news."[3] The plural form is used in a number of Roman inscriptions. The most famous of these is the so-called Priene inscription, erected probably in 9 BCE to commemorate the birth of Caesar Augustus.[4] The inscription lauds the beneficence to the world of Augustus, who is characterized as the world's savior who has brought peace and an end to war. The inscription says the following regarding Caesar: "the birthday of our God signaled the beginning of Good News for the world because of him" (lines 40–41).[5] Helmut Koester admits that, in Roman impe-

---

3. Koester, *Ancient Gospels*, 1. The discussion of the lexemes for "good news" is based upon Koester.

4. The inscription is conveniently found in Ehrenberg and Jones, *Documents*, 81–83.

5. Danker, *Benefactor*, 217 (216–18 for the entire inscription). Cf. Koester, *Ancient Gospels*, 3–4, who cites lines 36–40, but does not indicate that two of the crucial words for his argument, "appear" and the first instance of "good news," are completely

rial usage, the noun was "used to designate the good news itself,"[6] but doubts this usage in what he calls "ordinary Greek usage," the kind of Greek presumably found in the New Testament. He acknowledges that the noun and verb forms are construed with the prefixed morpheme "good" (εὐ), which usually adds a "positive connotation," but says that "there is little reason to assume that the meaning '"good" news' was felt strongly in ordinary usage," even though he also says that he believes that "the early Christian missionaries were influenced by the imperial propaganda in their employment of the word."[7] Instead, Koester says that the "noun normally means simply 'news,' 'message' and particularly in Christian usage 'preaching'; the verb should then be translated as 'to bring a message,' or 'to preach.'" His support for this is the supposed use of similar Greek words. The two words in the New Testament that he cites are "thanksgiving" (εὐχαριστία) and "blessing" (εὐλογία). These are unfortunate choices, as they do nothing to support his case. The word "thanksgiving," used especially of the Lord's Supper, in fact does have the positive connotation that Koester sees in the Roman imperial use. The term may have a different referent (that seems to be Koester's point of confusion), but the sense has a positive one (or perhaps better, a more positive one) over the sense of the un-prefixed lexeme "grace" or "thanks" itself (χάρις). The same is true of "blessing," where the positive connotation is clear over the use of the un-prefixed "words, messages" (λογία).

There is no reason to doubt that "good news" retains its positive sense in the New Testament, as there is no evidence otherwise from the evidence cited by Koester. A similar sense is found in the Greek Old Testament, where the author of Isaiah uses the verb form in a theological sense. He speaks of "proclaiming good news (εὐαγγελιζόμενος) to Zion

---

missing from the now fragmentary inscription and are provided by the editors. The latter use of "good news," cited above, is present, except for the neuter genitive plural ending. He translates the passage as "the birthday of the god was the beginning of his good messages" (Koester, *Ancient Gospels*, 4).

6. Koester, *Ancient Gospels*, 1–2. This is confirmed by further examination of the Priene Inscription itself. The relatively bombastic and highly rhetorical opening (lines 1–30) contains seven uses of "good" prefixed lexemes, each one having its positive "good" sense.

7. Ibid., 4. This is an odd statement, as Koester also admits that "the Christian usage is eschatological, as the missionaries proclaim the beginning of a new age and call this proclamation their 'gospel.'"

and Jerusalem (Isa 40:9), of the feet of the one proclaiming good news (εὐαγγελιζομένου) of a report of peace, or of one proclaiming good news (εὐαγγελιζόμενος) of good things (Isa 52:7). Isaiah 61:1 speaks of proclaiming good news (εὐαγγελίσασθαι) to the poor. Many of these verses are taken up in the New Testament, in both Paul and the Gospels. This makes it surprising that Koester claims that "there is no evidence that the earliest Christian use of εὐαγγέλιον and εὐαγγελίζεσθαι in its formative stage is in any way influenced by these prophetic passages from the Old Testament," as he claims they are products of "secondary redaction."[8] I will discuss the key passages in the Gospels below, where it is clear that in fact the positive sense is retained.

As I have argued elsewhere, especially with reference to Paul, I believe that early Christians may well have been influenced in some way by the Roman imperial usage of "good news,"[9] as well as Septuagint usage, as I will show below. However, I also think that the evidence suggests that the term indicated the sense of the advent of "good news," used with positive connotations.

Mark

I begin with Mark's usage—not because I necessarily think that Mark's was the first Gospel or that the others used Mark (this may have been the case, but that is not the argument that I wish to engage in here), but because of his usage itself. Mark is the primary Gospel to use the noun form of the word. Apart from four uses in Matthew—these are admittedly important, as I will discuss below—all of the other instances of the noun "good news" appear in Mark's Gospel (seven instances, as well as once in Mark 16:15, part of the long ending, which I will not discuss). Mark's Gospel does not have any instances of the verb form, which appears once in Matthew and ten times in Luke (which has no instance of the noun).

Mark 1:1: "beginning of the good news of Jesus Christ Son of God." I return now to what is probably the most difficult and controversial uses of "good news" (εὐαγγέλιον) in the New Testament. I thankfully do not need here to deal at length with the question of whether "Son of God" is original to the text. It is highly disputed, as there is a range of evidence on either side. However, just because a reading is popular in

---

8. Ibid., 3.
9. Porter, "Paul Confronts Caesar."

the later Byzantine tradition, as "Son of God" is, does not mean that it is a later reading. In this case, the early evidence is divided, but I think that the weight of the manuscript evidence is stronger for inclusion (early Alexandrian and Western readings) than it is for deletion (with the original hand of Sinaiticus, although corrected to "Son of God," and the early church fathers, who are not necessarily reliable).[10]

Mark's Gospel, nevertheless, opens with a verbless clause. There are many interpretive questions connected to this clause: Is it a title for the entire book or only for a portion of the book? If only for a portion of the book, what is the extent of that portion? What is the relationship between use of the lexeme "good news" and the literary type that we have come to call "Gospel"? In response to the last question, I simply note here that I believe that the reason that the term "Gospel" was given to the Gospels is because of this use in Mark 1:1, on the basis of the fortuitous correlation between the meaning of the lexeme and how it was developed in early Christian writing. I will return to this question and its implications in the second part, below.

As for the first set of questions, most scholars today interpret the verbless clause as a heading for a portion of the book, perhaps down to Mark 1:8 or possibly v. 13 (although there are other options).[11] If the ending of the section is v. 8, then the verbless clause is an introductory heading for the story of the background of John the Baptist. If the ending is v. 13, then the verbless clause is an introductory heading for a slightly longer preliminary section including Jesus' baptism and temptation before he begins his ministry in v. 14. Either of these, as well as others, might be a possibility. However, I think that there are difficulties with proposals that the verbless clause is a subheading for only a portion of the Gospel. Some of these difficulties include the following: there is no other subheading to begin the next section, leaving this one to stand on its own; if the new section begins with v. 9, this section begins with "and," a common connective in Mark, but not one parallel with the verbless clause in v. 1; and there is no clear division that is without problems, as v. 8 arguably divides the episode with John the Baptist from Jesus' baptism and v. 13 places several events concerning Jesus (his baptism and his temptation) with John and separates Jesus' temptation from the beginning of his ministry.

10. Contra Collins, *Mark*, 130–32, esp. 130.
11. See Guelich, *Mark*, 3–4.

There are, to the contrary, several positive arguments for this verbless clause constituting the heading for the entire Gospel. One includes the fact that it is the only heading of this sort in Mark's Gospel at any type of major division. Another is that it is a verbless clause that is not only unusual in Mark in such a position, but marks a major transition. A third is that the verbless clause itself has no connecting word (there is asyndeton) and therefore clearly marks the beginning of something. Fourth and finally, the verbless clause is lexically intense, with a number of important lexemes in syntactical configuration: "beginning," "good news," "Jesus Christ," and "Son of God." The construction is relatively unusual, consisting of a single complex word group with a noun as head-term, with three serially elaborating dependent genitive word groups. There have been many attempts to parse the genitive relationships involved in the use of these word groups. The restrictive semantics of the genitive case can be appropriately captured by the expansive paraphrase as follows: "this is the beginning that is restricted to good news [i.e., a beginning of good news], that is restricted to Jesus Christ [i.e., good news of Jesus Christ], that is restricted to Son of God [i.e., Jesus Christ as Son of God]." I do not think that anyone can dispute that the relationship of the genitive word groups, whether or not one uses the same terminology that I have used, is something akin to what I have outlined, with each one serving to restrict further the meaning of the element upon which it is dependent. The problem seems to be in what sense the entire Gospel can be said to be a "beginning." This may be more of a problem with English than with Greek. The word translated "beginning" (ἀρχή), like its cognate verb form (ἄρχομαι), indicates the beginning or origins of something. This is how it is used in the Priene inscription that I discussed above. Caesar is said to be the origin of peace and prosperity. Similarly, Mark says that his Gospel describes the origins of the good news that is specifically concerning Jesus Christ. The entire Gospel can readily be seen as an exposition of the origins of the good news, that is, the good news brought to humanity (note similarities to the imperial usage) by Jesus Christ as Son of God.

Mark 1:14, 15: "Jesus came into Galilee proclaiming the good news of God and saying, 'The time is fulfilled and the kingdom of God is near; repent and believe in the good news.'" Those who argue that the heading of Mark 1:1 only extends to v. 13 have a reasonable argument that, even if Mark does not offer another subheading, he does introduce Jesus' ministry by outlining Jesus' message regarding the good news. This is indeed what we find in Mark 1:14, 15. After John has been arrested, Jesus launches his own ministry. Whereas there are some clear similarities between the messages of John and Jesus (e.g., on repentance) to the point that some think that Jesus' earliest followers may well have originally been followers of John,[12] this is understandable in light of their respective roles: John, as the forerunner of the Messiah, might well be expected to have a similar message to that Messiah himself. Nevertheless, the use of language of bringing the good news is restricted to Jesus. At the advent of Jesus' ministry in Galilee, Mark encapsulates Jesus' message in a twofold statement, the first a summary and the second a quotation of what Jesus proclaimed.

The content of Jesus' proclamation is summarized as "the good news of God" (Mark 1:14). I note that the previous use of "good news" restricts its meaning to the "good news of Jesus Christ Son of God." In Mark 1:14, this good news is said to be the "good news of God." In the Priene inscription, I quickly passed over several places where the inscription says not only that Caesar Augustus is the bringer of good news, but that the "birthday of god" is the occasion for the bringing of this good news (lines 40–41). This inscription is often referred to as a "son of god" inscription, as it indicates that those who erected it wished to make clear their divinization of Caesar. I believe that something similar may be occurring in Mark's Gospel, although perhaps in a slightly different way. Mark opens the Gospel by referring to the "good news of Jesus Christ," with the good news defined as pertaining to Jesus Christ. Jesus' message, however, is "the good news of God." By use of the second phrasing, I believe that there is an implicit indication being made by the Gospel author that Jesus is God. This is in noticeable ways similar to the kind of statement being made of Caesar, and it quite possibly contains an anti-imperial claim within it, especially as Mark's Gospel was probably written down by Mark in Rome.[13] The logic of substitution is that the good news is about Jesus Christ, but when Jesus himself refers to it, at least in the words of the author of the Gospel, this good news has become the good news of God. The use of "God" in the encapsulation is ambiguous, indicating that the good news of Jesus Christ and the good

---

12. See, e.g., Robinson, *Priority of John*, 168–72.

13. This is the traditional view, first attributed to Papias regarding Mark and Peter, as cited in Eusebius, *Hist. eccl.* 3.39.15.

news of God are perhaps to be equated to the point of Jesus Christ and God being in some way equated or related to each other. Jesus himself is quoted as saying that the time for the good news to be made manifest is fulfilled—note the use of the stative aspect of the perfect tense-form to describe the fulfillment as a state of affairs represented by the process—and the kingdom of God stands near (another use of stative aspect). The "kingdom of God" is a loaded term based on the Old Testament indicating God's eschatological fulfillment of his purposes through his Messiah. Jesus is announcing the fulfillment of this mission in his own ministry. The Greek verb often translated "has come near," but that I have translated "stands near," is in the perfect tense-form with stative aspect. This lexeme, contrary to the usual thought, indicates not motion, as if we were heading toward the time of the kingdom, but location.[14] This is a verb of location. The kingdom stands near. As a result, repentance and belief in this good news of the work of God in fulfilling his kingdom work through his Messiah are the appropriate response. Belief in the good news is the appropriate response of allegiance to the good news represented in God's kingdom program. This is the message proclaimed and realized by Jesus Christ, Son of God.

Mark 8:35: "whoever desires to save his/her soul can expect to lose (or destroy) it; and whoever can expect to lose (or destroy) his/her soul on account of me and (or even) the good news can expect to save it." After Peter's confession or declaration of who Jesus is, Jesus begins to teach his disciples about his coming suffering, arrest, and death. His disciples of course do not want to hear this, and Peter reacts most strongly, prompting his rebuke by Jesus (Mark 8:31–33). This prompts Jesus to tell the disciples and his other followers of the cost of discipleship. If one wants to follow Jesus, that person must deny him- or herself and take up his/her cross and follow him. If one instead wishes to save him- or herself, that person can expect destruction. Instead, one who denies self for Jesus and, or even, the good news can expect salvation of the soul.

I note several important features about this passage. The first is that this is the next use in Mark's Gospel of the noun "good news" after the opening announcement of his ministry. This instance is recorded as being used by Jesus once his identity with his disciples is firmly established and he turns towards his own death. The second feature is how Jesus refers to the good news. He in some ways links himself to the good news.

---

14. Porter, *Studies*, 125–38.

The Greek construction is not entirely clear. Jesus may be speaking of losing one's soul on account of two things, him and the good news, or he may use "good news" to define who he is: one loses one's soul on account of him, the good news (the Greek is ἕνεκεν ἐμοῦ καὶ τοῦ εὐαγγελίου, but note that there is a textual variant indicating "on account of my good news"). In either case, Jesus is closely linked to the good news, just as he was in the opening heading of Mark's Gospel. The good news is the good news of Jesus Christ (Mark 1:1), but it is also the good news that either is one of two causes for which it is worth losing one's life or is the only cause, especially as it is embodied in Jesus Christ, for whom it is worth losing one's life. The first is the more likely understanding, but the result is much the same in either case: the singular cause for losing one's life is Jesus and the good news, that is, his message of bringing God's kingdom in his messianic mission.

Mark 10:29: "Truly I say to you, no one exists who leaves house or brothers or sisters or mother or father or children or fields on account of me and on account of the good news," who will not receive much more in the present age, especially persecutions, and eternal life in the age to come. In the continuing journey to Jerusalem, Jesus encounters a rich man who is not able to make the choice to follow Jesus. The disciples are realizing the difficulties inherent in following him. Peter even expresses it by saying that they have left everything to follow Jesus. Jesus responds by telling Peter that those who leave everything—and he provides a list of such things—can expect two results. One of these is to receive the things of this world, including persecutions, but the other is to receive eternal life in the coming age. These people must, however, give up the things of this age on account of Jesus and on account of the good news. The wording here is similar to the example in Mark 8:35, except that the construction is clarified by the repetition of the preposition "on account of" (ἕνεκεν ἐμοῦ καὶ ἕνεκεν τοῦ εὐαγγελίου). Here Jesus makes clear that one must leave the things of this world on account of two reasons: himself and the good news. Even if these two causes are separated, they are still closely linked together as having both this-worldly and other-worldly consequences. Here the consequences are explicitly stated in their eschatological and even apocalyptic dimensions as providing eternal life (using a word group that is often associated with Jesus in John's Gospel) in the age to come. The good news is again linked directly to

Jesus and his messianic ministry of fulfilling God's kingdom work in both its present and future dimensions.

Mark 13:10: "and it is necessary first for the good news to be proclaimed to all the nations." In Jesus' Olivet Discourse, after saying that the temple will be destroyed, Jesus tells his disciples when these events will come about. He recounts a number of events that can be expected and that they need to watch out for. But before all of the events can be culminated, Jesus says that it is necessary for the good news to be proclaimed to all nations. There are several observations to be made about this statement embedded within the larger discourse regarding Jesus' vision for what his disciples can expect. The first is that Jesus sees that his original message, the proclamation of the good news, is constant throughout not just his immediate but his long-term ministry. He depicts events that the disciples can expect, but he puts them in terms of all of these events happening as a means of facilitating and enabling the good news being proclaimed to all nations. The second observation is that Jesus envisions even from this point in his ministry that the audience of his good news extends beyond the Jewish people. The persecution of his followers is to become a means whereby all of the nations are to become recipients of the proclamation of the good news. In other words, whereas Jesus' mission has, to this point, concentrated upon the Jewish people, from the outset there is a conception of his mission also being addressed to all nations, with both aspects of this mission being focused upon the message of proclamation of the good news. Jesus, as God's messianic agent for his kingdom, delivers one and only one message, and that is that the good news is to be proclaimed and made available to all people of all nations everywhere.

Mark 14:9: "Truly I say to you, wherever the good news might be proclaimed in the entire world, indeed what this woman has done can be expected to be spoken of as her memorial." This last use of "good news" in Mark's Gospel extends and re-enforces the previous reference. Jesus has just been anointed in Bethany by the nameless woman who is looked at askance by some of his followers. However, Jesus commends and commemorates her actions by endorsing them, because she had, perhaps unknowingly, acknowledged his destiny with the cross and had anointed his body in advance of his death. As a result, Jesus says that wherever the good news is proclaimed—and that is the message and mission of Jesus' followers, to proclaim the good news—this woman will be remembered. There is perhaps an indication in this instance of the further recognition that Jesus' message is not restricted to one group but it is to be extended not only to all peoples (as in Mark 13:10) but to all types of people, including the woman who anointed him in anticipation of his death.

These are the instances of the use of "good news" language in Mark's Gospel. These uses show that the "good news" indicates the message and mission of Jesus as God's messianic agent for the promotion of his kingdom to those present and those future, those here and those everywhere.

Matthew

I turn now to Matthew's Gospel. The noun "good news" (εὐαγγέλιον) appears in Matthew's Gospel in four places. The interesting fact that emerges from an examination of these instances is that there are several that do not have parallels in Mark's Gospel (the only other Gospel that uses the noun form). Koester claims that the lack of parallels may indicate that use of "good news" (εὐαγγέλιον) was not found in Mark, but was added later, after Matthew had used Mark as a source.[15] There is no textual evidence for Koester's claim. This reveals a supposition (of Markan priority and Matthean dependence) in search of (lacking) evidence, when other theories of Synoptic relations might prove more plausible on the basis of the lack of parallels (such as that Matthew is not dependent upon a literary Mark).

Matthew 4:23: "and he went about in all of Galilee, teaching in their synagogues and proclaiming the good news of the kingdom and healing every disease and every malady in the people." This passage is the first instance in Matthew's Gospel of "good news" language. In some ways, it is the equivalent of Mark 1:14, 15, although it is not as focused an introduction to Jesus' Galilean ministry as is the passage in Mark's Gospel. The sequence of events in Matthew's Gospel includes the infancy narrative, the trip to Egypt, the killing of the infants by Herod, the return from Egypt, the events with John the Baptist, the temptation of Jesus, and then the beginning of the Galilean ministry (in Matt 4:12–14), followed by the calling of some disciples. The closest equivalent to Mark 1:14, 15 is Matt 4:12–17, not Matt 4:23–25, where the first "good news" saying appears. Nevertheless, there are some rough equivalences. The first is that there are clear markers that this is early in Jesus' ministry, in particular

---

15. Koester, *Ancient Gospels*, 10–12.

his Galilean ministry. Matthew indicates here that Jesus not only lived in Galilee (Matt 4:12–13), but that he was going about the region teaching and proclaiming a message. The second is that whereas in Mark's Gospel Jesus' message regarding the good news is linked with his message regarding the kingdom of God and the need for repentance, these ideas are found in two separate places in Matthew's Gospel. Matthew 4:17 says that Jesus began to proclaim and to say, "Repent, for the kingdom of heaven stands near," very similar to what is found in Mark 1:15. However, the statement regarding the good news is not found until Matt 4:23. When the Galilean ministry of Jesus is resumed in Matthew after the recounting of the calling of four fishermen, Matthew then gives the proclamation regarding the "good news."

Matthew's description of the good news, however, has several distinctives to it. The first is that he refers only to "proclaiming the good news of the kingdom," without calling it the kingdom of God or of heaven. This is probably because he has already introduced the kingdom as being the kingdom of heaven and can now refer to it in an abbreviated form due to proximity with the earlier usage. Nevertheless, it is important to note that the good news in Matthew is restricted to (note use of the genitive) the kingdom of heaven (or of God, with Matthew preferring the heaven language to the God language). The second distinctive is that Matthew's description of the good news as a proclamation of the good news of the kingdom of God/heaven is accompanied and further defined by actions that Jesus performs. Jesus was healing various diseases and maladies. For Matthew's accounting of the kingdom, there is both an explicit proclamation and a realization of the power of that proclamation in Jesus' healings. Matthew does not explicitly say that the "good news of the kingdom" had power attendant to it, but such appears to be the case. For Matthew, Jesus' proclamation of the good news of the kingdom means that he is God's messianic emissary to bring God's presence and power to humanity. Considering that there is a variety of actions and other exceptional deeds that Jesus could have performed, I think that it is telling that he performs healings. Jesus does not just perform personal miracles or events that benefit only himself or his close followers. He performs actions that show that the good news of the kingdom has a real and tangible manifestation in the lives of more than just Jesus and his disciples. Jesus is bringing a message of God's power through himself to all people, as demonstrated by his healing of their diseases.

Matthew 9:35: "and Jesus went around all the cities and the villages, teaching in their synagogues and proclaiming the good news of the kingdom and healing every disease and every malady." This statement, again unparalleled in Mark's Gospel, is virtually identical to the one found in Matt 4:23. The only significant comment I wish to make is that this repetition of Jesus' message and mission occurs near the end of the period when Jesus ministered primarily in the region of Galilee. In Matt 10, Jesus commissions and sends the disciples out to extend his ministry in other places. In so doing, he gives them authority over unclean spirits so that they are able to cast them out and heal every disease and every malady, using language very similar to that used to describe Jesus' message and mission. Matthew seems to be indicating that Jesus' disciples are being given the same message and mission as Jesus—that is, they are given their own extensions of his work. Even though the specific statement regarding proclaiming the good news is not made, the implication is that they are proclaiming this same message as the basis of their healing ministry.

Matthew 24:14: "and this good news of the kingdom can expect to be proclaimed in the entire inhabited world as testimony to all nations, and then the end will come." This passage is parallel to the statement in Mark 13:10, but with some variations. Jesus is speaking of the events that his followers can expect, including various trials and tribulations to be endured. Matthew then speaks of the good news using language we have seen previously in Matthew's Gospel. He speaks of the good news as good news of the kingdom, using the phrasing that he has used elsewhere. However, I note that Matthew's wording is also similar in some ways to that of Mark, with reference to the entire world (see Mark 14:9). This statement extends Matthew's previous statements regarding the good news while also being consonant with Mark's statements. The extension is made in several ways. Jesus says in both that proclamation of the good news is imperative as an indication of God's timing in future events. Before other things can happen, or while other things transpire, the proclamation of the good news is crucial. For Matthew, this good news is explicitly good news of the kingdom, but we saw above that for Mark too the good news is of the kingdom. Matthew brings good news and kingdom together into a single word group, whereas Mark explicates each separately, even though they are clearly related—the kingdom is part of the content of the good news. For both Matthew and Mark, the scope of the proclamation must reach the entire inhabited world (or all the nations for Mark). For both, the good news is extended beyond the confines of Jesus and his disciples or even those in the immediate vicinity and is to reach to all people everywhere. Matthew adds that the proclamation of the good news of the kingdom to all the world is meant as a testimony to all nations, perhaps offering a more expansive view of the similar statement in Mark regarding all nations. In any case, for Matthew the good news involves its proclamation to all people of all nations throughout the world.

Matthew 26:13: "Truly I say to you, wherever this good news might be proclaimed in the whole world, it can be expected to be said regarding what this woman has done as her memorial." Apart from a small difference in the grammar, this is the same statement as is found in Mark 14:9. I note that for Matthew also this is the last of the "good news" statements, and this statement includes both the entire world in its scope and people of all types, including the unnamed and suspect woman at Bethany who performed the action.

The verb appears in Matthew's Gospel once. Matthew 11:5: "poor are proclaimed good news." When John's followers approach Jesus with the question of whether he is the one who is to come, that is, the Messiah, or whether they should be expecting another, Jesus answers that they should tell John what they have seen and heard: "the blind are receiving their sight, the lame are walking, the lepers are being cleansed, the deaf are hearing, the dead are being raised, and the poor are being proclaimed the good news (πτωχοὶ εὐαγγελίζονται)." There is much in this passage that bears examination in these six statements that Jesus makes. Whereas the first five are concerned with physical transformation, similar to those found in Isa 35:5–6 and 42:18, the last one is not a physical transformation. The last transformation, found in Isa 61:1 (already noted above) but in different grammatical construction, concerns not physical malady but an *apparently* socioeconomic misfortune. Whereas the first five are also concerned with a direct remedy that counters or negates the physical condition, the last one does not directly address the malady at all. If the parallelism were exact, we would expect Jesus to say that the poor are made rich. This raises the question of whether Jesus is in fact addressing socioeconomic misfortune. He may be, in which case

Jesus is saying that the solution to poverty is not money but acceptance and response to the good news that Jesus proclaims. There is also the possibility—and perhaps even the likelihood—that Jesus is not speaking of socioeconomic misfortune at all but the kind of poverty that he addresses in the beatitudes: poverty of spirit (Matt 5:3). The solution to poverty of spirit, that is, spiritual destitution (Matt 5:3), is acceptance of God's good news, which brings such people into God's kingdom. That is in fact what Jesus has said earlier in his beatitudes: "Blessed are the poor in spirit, because of them is the kingdom of heaven" (Matt 5:13). In this passage, the proclamation of the good news is implicitly linked to the kingdom of God/heaven. Those who recognize their destitute spiritual condition have only one means of remedying their situation, and that is the good news of God's kingdom brought by the ministry and mission of Jesus.

There are a number of ways in which Matthew expresses the content of the good news in a manner that is slightly different from that of Mark. However, we see that the essence of the good news is the same: Jesus is bringing a proclamation of good news that involves the coming of God's kingdom, which is extended beyond the immediate time or place to all people everywhere. For both Matthew and Mark, the basis of this content is mostly established by the use of the noun form of the word.

Luke

The third and final Gospel is that of Luke. As I mentioned before, the noun form does not appear in Luke's Gospel. However, the verb form appears in ten places. Not all of the instances of the verb add to our knowledge of the "good news" in the theological sense that we are primarily concerned with in this paper, even if they reflect usage found in other Greek writers. To avoid lexical confusion, I will not discuss such minimalist examples at length.

Luke 1:19: "the angel said to him [Zechariah], 'I am Gabriel who stands before God, and I am sent to speak to you and to proclaim this good news to you.'" This use of the verb appears to reflect the wider kind of usage of the time, in which the message involves good news, in this instance the birth of a son to Zechariah and Elizabeth.

Luke 2:10: "the angel said to them, 'Don't fear, for behold, I am proclaiming good news to you of great joy that shall be to every people.'"

This instance of the verb appears to reflect the wider usage of the time as well, in which the angels proclaim good news to the shepherds, good news that involves great joy. This good news is, of course, the birth of Jesus, whose message and mission will extend to the entire world, a theme that we have already seen is clearly attached, not to the notion of good news in and of itself, but to Jesus' bringing of good news to all people.

Luke 3:18: "comforting many others, he proclaimed good news for the people." This use of the verb has been over-interpreted by some commentators. The NIV2011 renders the verse: "John exhorted the people and proclaimed the good news to them." This rendering makes the notion of proclaiming the good news into a technical term regarding proclamation of a specific good news. There is a possible hint of this in John's previous reference to the coming of Jesus as the Messiah rather than himself being the Messiah. However, there is little in the context to link the coming of Jesus specifically with the proclamation of the good news, at least as that news is depicted by John as one of judgment, as witnessed by burning and destruction. I think that a better explanation might be to see the wider and non-technical use of the verb in this verse as well, with John at best seeing the coming of Jesus as good news, which he is announcing to his hearers.

Luke 4:18: "Spirit of the Lord is upon me, on account of which he has anointed me to proclaim good news to the poor (εὐαγγελίσασθαι πτωχοῖς). He has sent me to proclaim release to the captives and sight to the blind, to send out the oppressed in release, to proclaim the acceptable year of the Lord." In his important and initiatory sermon in the Nazareth synagogue, which sets the tone for the entire Gospel,[16] Jesus, having taken the biblical text in hand, reads this passage from Isa 61:1–2 (note comments above) and 58:6 and announces that today this Scripture stands fulfilled in their ears. At first his hearers accept this, until he offers two examples of gentiles who received God's favor, indicating that they are examples to be included within the redemptive work of God. At that point, the crowd attempts to kill him.

If we examine more closely what Jesus has said, we can see that Jesus has made a number of claims in his endorsed citation of the Isaianic passages. First, he claims that God's spirit or being is upon him. Second, he claims to be anointed by God. Third, he claims to be anointed for the

---

16. See Porter, "Messiah," 150.

purpose of proclaiming good news to the poor. He claims, fourth, that he has been sent on a particular mission: to proclaim freedom to captives and sight to the blind, to send out the oppressed in freedom, and to proclaim the acceptable year of the Lord. There are several more particular observations to make about this passage. The first is that there are several indications of Jesus appropriating for himself the role of the Old Testament prophet by the invocation of this passage. More particularly, he claims to be more than just the prophet, but the one who fulfills the prophecy when he declares that the passage has been fulfilled in their hearing. The second observation is that the citation divides into two types of proclamation. The first is the calling and anointing to proclaim good news to the poor, and the second is being sent on a mission of redemption and restoration. Since all of the maladies that are depicted appear to be physically related, there is good reason to consider all of them, including poverty, being thought of in this physical sense. However, I think that exegetes have perhaps been too quick to embrace this particular interpretation, with the result that they often see Luke's Gospel as the one addressed to the physically oppressed. All of the conditions that are described in this passage may be physical in nature, but they may also be more than physical, that is, spiritual, in nature. These would include spiritual poverty (similar to Matthew's poor in spirit), captivity or any kind of being controlled, blindness of spirit, and oppression of any sort. That would appear to be the way that Jesus' audience took the passage upon hearing it. If he had been referring simply to physical release, one might have expected the crowd to react at his claiming fulfillment. That they see it as in some way involving spiritual oppression is made more acute by the inclusion of non-Jews in the equation. More particularly related to the good news of this passage, I note that the proclamation of good news to the poor is the direct task of the one who is imbued with the Lord's spirit and anointed by him for a purpose. In that sense, this statement is very similar to the statement that we previously examined, though admittedly formulated in another way (by use of the noun) in both Mark and Matthew, regarding the fundamental proclamation of Jesus' ministry and mission: Jesus' ministry involves proclamation of the good news to those in spiritual need.

Luke 4:43: "in every city it is necessary to proclaim the good news of the kingdom of God." Early in Jesus' ministry, he is already overwhelmed by the crowds. In this episode, he is diligently pursued by such crowds, and cannot escape them. As a result, he speaks to them regarding his message and mission. This statement in Luke 4:43 has similarities to a number of the statements found in Mark and Matthew. In both accounts of Jesus' Olivet Discourse, he speaks of the necessity of proclaiming the good news, as he does here. Whereas in the other Gospels this proclamation is to be to all nations, here it is in the other cities. Jesus says in Luke that he has been sent specifically for this purpose. In Matthew's Gospel the good news is directly said to be of the kingdom, and in Mark's Gospel the kingdom is part of the message of the good news. In Luke, similar to both but not identical with either in formulation, the object of the proclamation of good news is the kingdom of God. Thus, in this concise statement, Jesus states that the good news has in its focus the proclamation of the kingdom of God.

Luke 7:22: "the poor are proclaimed good news (πτωχοὶ εὐαγγελίζονται)." This statement appears in a similar context and has similar content and form to the statement found in Matt 11:5. Whereas many interpreters wish to see Luke as the Gospel for the physically disenfranchised, the lack of parallelism in Luke's Gospel, as in Matthew's, indicates that Jesus here is not speaking of physical poverty but poverty of spirit, something that is addressed by the proclamation of the good news that he brings.

Luke 8:1: "he himself was traveling around in each city and village, preaching and proclaiming good news regarding the kingdom of God." This statement, which records the mission and ministry of Jesus, is like other statements found in Mark and Matthew's Gospels. The statement specifies that Jesus was preaching (or proclaiming), that he was proclaiming a message of good news, and that that good news consisted of the kingdom of God. This statement has some of the features of other statements in the other Gospels that link the proclamation of good news to the kingdom of God, with the added feature of the repeated verb of proclamation.

Luke 9:6: "they were passing through each village, proclaiming good news and healing everywhere." This statement summarizes the work of the twelve when they are sent out by Jesus to proclaim the kingdom of God and to heal the sick (Luke 9:2). This summary statement recapitulates both their message and their mission. They were proclaiming the good news as the message they brought to each village, and they were healing those with physical ailments everywhere as well. As noted above, in Mark's Gospel, the combination of the message and mission seems to be an integral part of understanding the proclamation of the good news. It is good news that results in clear displays of its power and ability to extend beyond Jesus and the twelve to those in need of physical restoration.

Luke 16:16: "the law and the prophets until John; from then the kingdom of God is proclaimed as good news, and everyone is entered into it by force." This statement is part of Jesus' description of the kingdom to the Pharisees. He says that God knows the wicked hearts of individuals. Until the time of John, they were governed by the law and the prophets, but now the kingdom of God, that is, God's new order brought by Jesus, is proclaimed. This is indeed good news, so far as Jesus and his followers are concerned, as it has power to compel obedience. This passage is similar to other passages that link the kingdom of God with proclamation of the good news. However, there are two differences. One is in the formulation, in which the kingdom becomes the subject of the verb and not its object. This is not the usual formulation. The second is that there is an added dimension to the nature of this kingdom that is proclaimed as good news, and that is the compelling force that it has. In other usage, it appears that the good news is something proclaimed, and a few times it is said to be believed, but here Jesus speaks of the kingdom as something that compels obedience.

Luke 20:1: "and it came about on one of the days that he was teaching the people in the temple and proclaiming good news that the chief priests and the scribes stood around him." Whereas in usage by others at the beginning of Luke's Gospel the notion of proclaiming good news does not have a particular theological sense, in this case it does on the basis of Jesus being the one who uses the verb. In light of what we have seen in the Gospel regarding Jesus and the proclamation of the good news, even though the kingdom of God is not mentioned, it seems appropriate to infer that Jesus' proclamation that drew the attention of the chief priests and scribes was his proclaiming the good news of the kingdom.

Luke's Gospel differs in some ways from the other Gospels in his exclusive use of the verb form "proclaim good news." However, despite some differences in expression, there are also a number of similarities. These include the link between proclaiming the good news and the kingdom of God ("heaven" in Matthew) and the wider scope envisioned.

This concludes my treatment of the content of the good news. From this evidence, we can see that within the Gospels there is a notion of the good news being something proclaimed by Jesus, in some way an outworking of God's guidance or inspiration, and concerned with the kingdom of God/heaven. It is proclaimed to all people, including the Jews, but is also extended to all people in every nation, and its proclamation to the world is a vital element of God's plan for humanity.

The Form of the Good News

In the second part, on the basis of the evidence examined above, I wish to examine the form of the good news within the Gospels. Above, I have examined the good news as content. Now I wish to see if we can see the good news as in any way related to form.

The standard view of the Gospel as a literary form is that the use of "good news" in the Gospels does not indicate a literary type or genre but a label for content, much as has been discussed above. The standard view instead argues that the evidence from the church fathers is that the term "Gospel" did not come to indicate a literary type or genre until possibly the mid-second century or so. This is seen in the early church work *2 Clement*, which mentions Jesus speaking in "the gospel" (8.5).[17] Confirmation of the third century as the time in which "Gospel" came to indicate more than the content of the good news and specifically referred to a literary type or genre is found in the titles of the Gospels. The earliest form of the Gospel titles is "According to . . . ," as found in a few manuscripts, such as P72, which has the ending of Luke's Gospel and the beginning of John's. By the third century, however, the title "Gospel according to . . . " is found in manuscripts.

This is in fact a plausible explanation of the timing of the transformation of the word "good news" from a designation of particular early Christian content into a fully institutionalized designation of a literary type or genre, a transformation reached at some point in the third century and accompanied by the attaching of this word to each of the Gospel documents, to which the title has been attached ever since. However, this description of the timing of the movement from use of the word to full attribution as a literary type or genre does not account for how this transformation occurred and the process by which the acceptance of

---

17. See Koester, *Ancient Gospels*, 18, for discussion, though he is skeptical.

such a designation took place. An observation of the major points along the timeline is not to be equated with determining the causes of such a semantic shift in referent.

There is another explanation of the transformation that preserves the major contours of the timeline noted above, but determines the causes of such a transformation. The major issue at stake is how it is that the word "good news," translated "gospel" once it is attributed to a literary work, became a designation of a form of literature and not just its content. I believe that such a transformation must be attributed to the use of "good news" at the beginning of Mark's Gospel. By this, I do not necessarily think that Mark used the term "good news" as a technical term to indicate a literary type, what we would now call a gospel. However, there must have been some kind of a mechanism or process of thought by which the use of the term "good news" was transformed from a characterization of a message, first primarily of Jesus, into a more widespread encapsulation of that message in a particular literary form. Most scholars are hesitant to want to find such a connection because they wish to keep the content and the form of the gospel separate. Much of this desire seems to stem from the wish to avoid equating the gospel with a particular type of literature, especially that of the biography. There are two major responses to the biographical hypothesis for the Gospels. One is to reject it and opt instead for some other characterization of the literary type of the Gospels. The traditional twentieth-century explanation, endorsed by form criticism, is that the Gospels are not historical documents but are records of the transmuted oral tradition attributed to Jesus but shaped within the context of the early church. In this regard, the Gospels are neither *Hochliteratur* nor *Kleinliteratur*, but a type of *Zwischenliteratur*—which leads to the now-well-known explanation of the Gospels as a unique type of literature (*sui generis*), what later came to be characterized as a Gospel. The Gospels in this regard were not seen to be historical documents but rather reflective of the developing situation of the early church. The alternative, and more recently renewed, hypothesis is that the Gospels are a type of ancient biography. The biographical hypothesis was, in fact, a widely held explanation of the Gospels before the rise of modern criticism, and especially of form criticism, as ancient biographies of various types seemed to provide the most convincing comparative literature. With the revaluation of Christian literature in the nineteenth and, especially, twentieth centuries, this theory fell on hard times, until revived by a number of recent scholars who are arguing for both a literary genre, the biography, and a chastened view of the influence of the early church on the development of tradition. The traditional view of the "good news" taking the form of a Gospel, however, has continued to suffer under the influence of the form-critical hypothesis.

Neither of these explanations adequately addresses the question of how the content of the good news became the form of the good news as found in the Gospels. As noted above, I believe that the opening clause of Mark's Gospel is a heading for the entire book and that the statement is meant to indicate the origins of the "good news" of Jesus Christ, Son of God. This good news is attributed especially to Jesus as constituting the content of his message. The work that we call Mark's Gospel is, thereby, the vehicle by which this good news, as depicted and recorded in the proclamation of Jesus, is conveyed and hence is in some sense the embodied display of this good news. This is not to say that the author is identifying his heading with a particular literary genre. I do think, however, that the use of the term "good news" in the heading had the effect of identifying the content of the Gospel with the "good news" and hence with the type of literature found within the Gospel, whatever one wishes to call it, that is, whether it is biography or something else.

I think that this explanation may well account for the transformation from the "good news" as the content of Jesus' preaching into the "good news" as the form in which this is contained. Mark's Gospel is probably the primary vehicle for this transformation.

This does not explain how it is that, at least according to the standard resolution of the Synoptic Problem, Mark's Gospel may well be indicating both the form and content of the good news, while Matthew and Luke do not. There are several assumptions here. The first is that, if Mark's Gospel is first, Matthew and Luke as subsequent must recognize and enshrine the same perspective. This does not necessarily follow. However, I note that Matthew's Gospel does begin with the words "Book of genesis of Jesus Christ son of David son of Abraham." This verbless clause is similar to the opening of Mark's Gospel. In fact, one might argue that it is the equivalent, but with Matthew using the word "book" (βίβλος), sometimes translated "record" or "account." Matthew may well indicate that he is about to offer a book—a form—that accounts for the lineage of Jesus Christ, beginning with his actual genealogy but extending through to all of his work, including his final commissioning. Luke's

Gospel does not begin with an opening verbless clause, but does have an opening prologue that seems to indicate that Luke knew of "narratives" (διήγησις) regarding the deeds fulfilled in the actions of Jesus. Thus, even by the traditional Synoptic account, there may be more indication that Mark was seen as writing both of the content and in the form of the good news.

There are, however, other explanations worth brief exploration, including those that do not follow the traditional solution to the Synoptic Problem. If Matthew's Gospel is first, then we have Mark choosing to describe his "book" as a "good news" or Gospel. If a theory of independent oral tradition is followed, then there is no literary dependence among the Gospels. Each of the Gospels draws upon various types of apostolic tradition, probably associated with various locations. As a result, regardless of their relative order of composition, there is no need for another Gospel to refer to itself as a "good news" book, even if one, such as Mark's Gospel, does so.

CONCLUSION

In this paper, I have examined the use of the cognate forms of the word for "good news" or "proclaim good news" in the Synoptic Gospels (the words are not used in John's Gospel). The uses are not nearly as frequent within the Gospels as one might expect, especially when Paul uses such terminology more frequently. Nevertheless, the uses are significant. The uses of the term, especially by and about Jesus, help to define the content of the preaching of Jesus. Jesus' preaching is the good news regarding God's work in the world. This is proclaimed by Jesus and responded to by others in the course of his ministry. There is more to the use of the terminology, however, than merely to indicate the content of the "good news." I would contend that the content of the term has an influence upon the term becoming a designation of the form in which it appears. This is especially seen in Mark's Gospel, where, in the introductory verbless clause, Mark states that his entire work concerns the origins of the good news, seen as both the content and (in some way) the form in which it is presented—as embodied within the ministry of Jesus.

BIBLIOGRAPHY

Collins, Adela Yarbro. *Mark*. Hermeneia. Minneapolis: Fortress, 2007.

Danker, Frederick W. *Benefactor: Epigraphic Study of a Graeco-Roman and New Testament Semantic Field*. St. Louis: Clayton, 1982.

Ehrenberg, Victor H., and A. H. M. Jones. *Documents Illustrating the Reigns of Augustus and Tiberius*. 2nd ed. Oxford: Clarendon, 1955.

Guelich, Robert A. *Mark 1—8:26*. WBC 34A. Dallas: Word, 1989.

Koester, Helmut, *Ancient Christian Gospels: Their History and Development*. London: SPCK, 1990.

Porter, Stanley E. "The Messiah in Luke and Acts: Forgiveness for the Captives." In *The Messiah in the Old and New Testaments*, edited by Stanley E. Porter, 144–64. MNTS 7. Grand Rapids: Eerdmans, 2007.

———. "Paul Confronts Caesar with the Good News." In *Empire in the New Testament*, edited by Stanley E. Porter and Cynthia Long Westfall, 164–96. MNTS 10. Eugene, OR: Pickwick, 2011.

———. *Studies in the Greek New Testament*. SBG 6. New York: Peter Lang, 1996.

Robinson, John A. T. *The Priority of John*. Edited by J. F. Coakley. Oak Park, IL: Meyer Stone, 1987.

5

Jesus' Social Network as Evidence for the Gospel as Good News

Hughson T. Ong

WHAT IS THE GOSPEL AS GOOD NEWS?

THIS VOLUME SEEKS TO address the question of whether the gospel delivers good news to a bad-news world. This is a good and profound question, but it is also one that needs to be asked appropriately. I say "appropriately" because not all people today would say that they live in a bad-news world[1] and because people, including churches and scholars, have different conceptions and interpretations of the New Testament's use of the term "gospel." While our contemporary world may still refer to the kingdom of God as good news, its general use of the term "gospel" usually refers either to the person Jesus or to his teachings and actions (but cf. Mark 1:1 TNIV).[2] Jesus preached about the coming kingdom of God—that was his gospel; that was his good news (see Matt 4:17; Mark 1:14–15; Luke 4:43). The gospel for the later church, however, is not about that "kingdom of God" gospel any more than it is about the person Jesus Christ and his redemptive work on the cross or

---

1. Cf. Beach and Reid's essay, "Can I Get a Witness?" 239–57, in this volume.

2. The translation "the good news about Jesus the Messiah" by the TNIV might not clearly reflect the intended meaning in the original Greek, which reads, τοῦ εὐαγγελίου Ἰησοῦ Χριστοῦ. The genitive construction simply restricts the meaning of τοῦ εὐαγγελίου, indicating that the τοῦ εὐαγγελίου is one that is *of* or *relates to* Jesus the Messiah.

about the particular gospel theology derived from the New Testament (or the Bible).³ These conceptions of the term "gospel" are, of course, validly considered good news.

In this essay, I ask the question "Was Jesus' gospel good news to the people of his time?" and from this I show that the evidence for whether a person or an audience *receives* (i.e., accepts, trusts, and embraces) the gospel as good news can be seen in how they *respond* to the proclamation of the gospel. The question of whether the gospel is good news to us, or whether Jesus' gospel was good news to the people of his time is a question that can only be answered by an individual's personal response. I will explain more about my claim below and will then present my justification for it, after noting briefly a few (overgeneralized) observations on how some churches today differ in their conception or understanding of the term "gospel." Their conceptions of the gospel seem to deviate from the New Testament notion of εὐαγγέλιον and the historical and theological narrative that depicts it,⁴ and they raise the question of whether people who listen to these types of gospel can be said to have actually heard, let alone received, the good news.

WHAT IS NOT THE GOSPEL AS GOOD NEWS?

I observe that many churches today proclaim the gospel as good news because they believe that the gospel gives hope, comfort, and prosperity to a hopeless and degenerating world or to a suffering person; hence, we have the term "prosperity gospel" on the extreme end of the gospel proclamation. As one popular pastor often says in his sermons, "Happy, successful, fulfilled individuals have learned how to live their best lives *now*."⁵ Unsurprisingly, many Christians today are being drawn to it because this kind of gospel only dwells on and displays the positive and bright side of life—"As Christians, you are the head and not the tail," "You need to be at the top and not at the bottom," "You need to be rich and not poor," "You're a winner and not a loser," and so on are some

---

3. I will say, however, that the kingdom of God should still be central to our preaching of the gospel (Rom 8:19–22).

4. For more information on the term εὐαγγέλιον, see Porter's essay "The Good News of the Gospels," 52–76, in this volume.

5. Osteen, *Your Best Life Now*, ix (emphasis original); see also Osteen, *Become a Better You*. I am very hesitant to quote this pastor here, but I have found no better exemplar who seems to believe in such a gospel.

common refrains I hear in Sunday sermons. It even almost has become today's trend (for some congregations, to say the least) to include or mix this kind of material into a preacher's sermon for all sorts of pragmatic reasons. But can this really be true in real life? Is this the teaching of Scripture? Was this Jesus' intention when he preached his message to the people of his time (Mark 8:35; 10:28)? I note that all the women and men that God commissioned to service from Old Testament to New Testament times, and throughout church history, had their own share and experience of trouble or suffering during their lifetime (Ps 34:19; Rom 5:3–5; Phil 1:29–30; Jas 1:2–4; 1 Pet 1:6–7).[6]

Some churches offer the gospel as a kind of membership ticket to their community; hence, we have the term "friendship evangelism." Brian McLaren in fact believes that "Christians are 'converted' first in authentic spiritual friendships."[7] I am not sure whether the Bible teaches about conversion through friendship evangelism or spiritual friendship. I believe in being a true spiritual friend and showing authentic spiritual friendship to my non-Christian friends with the hope of sharing the gospel with them or inviting them to church or our small group, but this spiritual gesture is far from thinking that that spiritual friendship is equivalent to spiritual conversion. Salvation is costly—it was bought for a price (1 Cor 6:20)—and conversion thus requires a personal decision and commitment on the part of the person to choose to trust in Christ (e.g., Rom 10:8–10) and to follow in the footsteps of Christianity (e.g., Phil 2:12).

There are also churches that are drawn towards making the gospel offer appear more or less like "an exclusive thing" for a certain group of people; hence, we have the theological notions of "election" and "predestination" perhaps on the other extreme end of the gospel proclamation. People who belong to this camp see a theology in Scripture, especially in the New Testament, that God selects within his divine providence those whom he wants to see in heaven (but see John 3:16; 1 Tim 2:4). Of course, it needs to be mentioned that churches who embrace this theology come in various types and forms, and their teaching on it has

---

6. Our salvation and peace with God also entails our own share of suffering for the sake of the gospel as we await our future hope of heaven (see Ong, "Suffering, Reconciliation, and Eschatological Hope," 39–55).

7. McLaren, *More Ready Than You Realize*, 58. See also Henderson, *Evangelism Additives*.

become more complex than what the churches during the Reformation period believed and taught.

It is not my purpose in this paper to enter into a debate over these various interpretations or expressions of the term "gospel," nor is it my intention to argue for my own theological view of it. I only mention them to highlight the complexity and difficulty in answering the question "Is the gospel good news?" For people who do not like to hear about sin, punishment, and suffering, the gospel is not good news. For others who are unaware of the fact that the gospel is costly because it was purchased by Jesus' blood, their understanding of the gospel being good news becomes naturally superficial—that is, "good news" means being in good, caring Christian company. For still others, the good news is (ultimately) probably only for a selected group, as they have been preselected from the very beginning. Keeping these differing gospels in mind, I would now like to turn to my earlier claim that the evidence for whether a person or an audience receives the gospel as good news can be seen in their response to the proclamation of the gospel.

JESUS' SOCIAL NETWORK AS EVIDENCE FOR THE GOSPEL AS GOOD NEWS OR AS NOT GOOD NEWS

The four canonical Gospels show that Jesus interacted (and conversed) with various individuals and social groups in the course of his public and private ministry on earth. These various individuals and social groups with whom he interacted constitute his social network.[8] A person's social network can be analyzed using what is known in sociolinguistics as social network theory.[9] This theory is used to determine the "pattern of informal [or formal] relationships people are involved in on a regular basis."[10] The idea is that an instance of social interaction between individuals or groups is also at the same time a type of social relationship between them. So, when two people begin to communicate with each other, they are actually creating and establishing a social relationship. A

---

8. Cf. Ong, *Multilingual Jesus*, 227–40, where I outline Jesus' social network in the Gospel of Matthew.

9. First developed by John Barnes ("Class and Committees," 39–58), sociolinguists today use social network theory to analyze patterns of social relationships among groups and individuals in organizations and the implications of these relationships (see Vetter, "Social Network," 208–18; and Mitchell, "Network Procedures," 73–92).

10. Holmes, *Introduction to Sociolinguistics*, 194.

social interaction (so also a social relationship) always happens within a specific social domain.

A social domain is a particular social situation or institution in which a social interaction takes place. There are more or less six social domains that are universally recognized, as these domains can be found in virtually all societies.[11] The two well-known private ones are the family and friendship domains, and the four public domains are the religion, government, education, and business domains. A social interaction can be classified as either unidirectional (called a transaction) or inter-directional (called a dialogue).[12] Whereas Jesus' dialogue with Nicodemus (John 3:1–21) happened in a private, friendship social domain, his transaction with the crowds that gathered in his Sermon on the Mount (Matt 5–7) was in a public, religion or education social domain.

Examining Jesus' social interactions in the Gospels allows us to determine the plexity and density of his social network.[13] The density of a person's social network indicates the structure of his or her social relationships. For example, if Jesus knew Mary, Martha, and Lazarus and his disciples also knew these three people, then the social network would be said to be denser than that of the disciples not knowing these three people. A denser social network signals uniformity of norms and values within one's social network, and this happens because members in the social network interact frequently with each other and in multiple social domains. It also signals, more importantly, that people within a network know each other in multiplex relationships rather than in a simply uniplex relationship.

The plexity of a person's social network refers to the types of relationships an individual has with another person or group. If a person is related to another in more than one area or capacity, then their relationship is called a multiplex relationship. Otherwise, it is called a uniplex relationship. For instance, Jesus was a teacher, mentor, and friend to his twelve disciples, and they thus have a multiplex type of social relationship. By contrast, Jesus' relationship with the many individuals to whom he ministered, like the two blind men and the demon-possessed man in Matt 9:27–31, was probably a uniplex one, since these men would

---

11. See Fishman, "Relationship Between Micro- and Macro-Sociolinguistics," esp. 22.

12. Milroy, *Language and Social Networks*, 148.

13. My discussion here follows Milroy, *Language and Social Networks*.

have considered him only as a teacher or prophet or even as simply a miracle worker or healer. A multiplex relationship between individuals or groups creates greater accessibility to each other, which, in turn, breeds greater familiarity.

Based on these concepts, we can see that a multiplex relationship and a denser social network are produced only when people *respond* well to each other; they accept and embrace the ideas and stories they communicate with one another, because they believe in and trust each other. This type of response, therefore, is what I would call a positive response, and it is indicated by a multiplex relationship and a denser social network between them. A negative response means that parties only hear or listen to each other without actually accepting, trusting, or embracing what they say to each other,[14] and such a response is indicated by a uniplex relationship and a less dense social network between them. Such a response is also often characterized by a transaction, instead of a dialogue-type of social interaction.

It is evident from the Gospels that Jesus interacted with three major groups of people—his disciples, including the women he encountered; the religious leaders; and the crowds (ὄχλοι). Aside from these three major groups of people, Jesus also had conversations with a large number of particular individuals. The Gospels show the differing responses of these groups of people and individuals to Jesus' proclamation of the gospel of the kingdom of God, and their responses indicate and exemplify, in turn, whether they truly receive the message about the kingdom of God as good news. What happened back then can serve as an appropriate comparison for our contemporary situation and, at the same time, a lens by which we can see whether a person has received the gospel as good news; like Jesus, Christians and churches today proclaim the gospel, and the evidence for whether their audience *receives* it as good news can be seen in their response to the gospel message. More specifically, their positive response can be seen in whether they have become members of a congregation in which people actively and intentionally seek to grow in their Christian life.

---

14. Of course, it should go without saying that, given the absence of adequate information in the Gospels, there are many cases in the Gospel accounts where we cannot be certain whether a person actually did accept, trust, and embrace Jesus' gospel.

Jesus' Disciples and the Women

We notice in the Gospels that Jesus most frequently interacted with his disciples. It is even arguably true that Jesus would have interacted the most with "the three"—Peter, James, and John—as they were the only ones with him on some special occasions, such as the transfiguration (Matt 17:1–9; Mark 9:2–8; Luke 9:28–36), the prayer at Gethsemane (Matt 26:37–38; Mark 14:33–34), and the healing of the daughter of Jairus (Mark 5:37–43; Luke 8:51–57). There were also women who were included in Jesus' circle of friends and disciples. Some interactions with these women were brief and casual, such as when he healed Simon's mother-in-law (Matt 8:14–15; Mark 1:29–31; Luke 4:38–39), the synagogue ruler's daughter (Matt 9:18–19, 22–26; Mark 5:21–24, 35–43; Luke 8:40–42, 49–56), the bleeding woman (Matt 9:20–22; Mark 5:25–34; Luke 8:43–48), and the Canaanite woman's daughter (Matt 15:21–28; Mark 7:24–30). Others were longer, more intimate, and familial in nature, such as his anointing by the woman with the alabaster jar of perfume (Matt 26:6–13; Mark 14:3–9; Luke 7:36–50; John 12:1–8) and his visitation by the "many women" (γυναῖκες πολλαί), including Mary Magdalene, Mary the mother of James and Joseph, and the mother of the Zebedee brothers during his crucifixion (Matt 27:55–56; Mark 15:40–41; Luke 23:49; John 19:25b–27), his burial (Matt 27:61; Mark 15:47; Luke 23:55–56), his resurrection (Matt 28:1–8; Mark 16:1–8; Luke 24:1–11; John 20:1–2, 11–13), and some postresurrection events (Matt 28:9–10; [Mark 16:9–11]; Luke 24:10–11; John 20:14–18).

It is very likely that wherever Jesus was in his public ministry, especially in the regions of Galilee and Judea, his disciples (including some of these women) were also with him. They were his companions and friends. Their social interactions range from short, casual conversation to occasions of serious, intimate teaching and instruction. Thus, Jesus would have spent most of his time with his disciples and these women in many social domains, particularly in the family, friendship, and religion domains. In addition, because they were with him wherever Jesus went, their social interactions include those that happen beyond these three domains. For example, Jesus' dining at Matthew's house (Matt 9:9–13; Mark 2:14–17; Luke 5:27–32), an event that seemingly transpired in a friendship-religion domain, could also probably be considered an event that would have occurred in the government domain, since their conversations in Matthew's house might have included non-personal, business-related matters—Matthew was a tax collector, and his decision to trust Jesus would have included a confession of his deeds as a tax collector (or sinner). Similarly, Jesus often taught the people in the synagogues and the temple courts (see Matt 26:55; Luke 19:47; cf. 21:37), and on many of these occasions, the disciples were also with him. Given the nature and function of the synagogues during Jesus' time, it is accurate to say that these teaching incidents should belong to the education domain.[15] The point here is that Jesus' interactions with his disciples were more frequent and took place in more social domains than his interactions with other individuals and social groups. This high frequency of interaction was possible because the disciples were related to him in more than one area or capacity. Jesus was their teacher and master, but he was also their close friend and companion.

The account of the resurrection of Lazarus (see John 11:1–44) is strong evidence of Jesus' intimate network ties with this social group. Jesus and his disciples, including Mary, Martha, and some other Jews, were present in this event. All of them knew each other, and they truly loved and cared for Lazarus, who was dead. Jesus was "deeply moved in spirit and was troubled," and he wept after sensing their grief (vv. 5, 33–36). The disciples placed their physical safety after their devotion to their master and their love for their friend Lazarus (vv. 8–16); Thomas even declared that he wanted to go with Jesus so that he might die with him (v. 16).[16] This event shows the strong network structure of Jesus with this social group, that is, his disciples and these women.[17] More importantly, it highlights Jesus' multiple, complex relationships with them, as they see him as their teacher, master, and close friend. The many occasions this group of people spent with Jesus in the past culminated in this special event where genuine friendship, and belief in Jesus' teaching, would finally be tested. Mary and Martha not only believed in Jesus and his authority (vv. 21–22, 27, 32), but also in his teaching—Martha says,

15. Rainer Riesner says that the synagogue functioned as a kind of popular educational system in small villages like Nazareth in Galilee (see "Jesus as Preacher and Teacher," 185–210; cf. Hezser, "Private and Public Education," esp. 468).

16. The translation of the TNIV here is ambiguous, since the participants in the verse are not explicitly stated and the phrase "with him" would seem to refer to Lazarus (so the disciples will die with Lazarus). However, it is better to translate "with him" as "with Jesus" instead, as the context seems to make clear.

17. Of course, Judas Iscariot's relationship with them has always been questionable (see John 12:4–8).

"I know he will rise again in the resurrection at the last day" (v. 24; cf. Matt 22:23; Acts 23:8; 1 Cor 15:3). The sisters' act of running in haste to meet their friend and Lord even before his arrival in Bethany further demonstrates their love and longing for each other (vv. 20, 28–30). Their actions and Jesus' responses to them raise the question of whether the faith of these sisters even surpasses that of the Twelve; it is therefore unsurprising to learn later on that Jesus appeared to the women first on resurrection day. Their faith is embodied in their social relationship with Jesus. However, this is not the case with Jesus' relationship with the religious leaders of his day.

The Religious Leaders

Jesus also frequently interacted with the religious leaders of his time, his most frequent interactions being with the Pharisees (e.g., Matt 9:11, 34; 12:2, 14, 24; 15:12; 22:15, 34, 41). In some instances in Matthew's Gospel, the Pharisees are mentioned with the Sadducees (Matt 3:7; 15:39; 16:21; cf. Mark 8:11–21) and with the scribes (Matt 5:20; 23:2, 13, 15). The relationship between Jesus and the Pharisees was almost always antagonistic, especially since the Pharisees were always searching for ways to trap him. To be sure, these religious leaders would often challenge Jesus, either demanding a sign (Matt 12:38) or questioning him on breaking Sabbath laws (Matt 12:1–8; Mark 2:23–28; Luke 6:1–5). The chief priests constituted another religious group that Jesus encountered, and they were the ones who plotted the arrest and trial of Jesus that eventually delivered him to the cross (Matt 16:21; 20:18; 21:15, 23; 27:1, 3, 12, 20, 41; Mark 8:31; 10:33; 11:18, 27; 14:1, 43, 53; 15:1, 31; Luke 9:22; 20:1, 19; 22:2, 66; 23:10).

It is apparent from the conversations between Jesus and these religious leaders that their social interactions mostly happened only in one social domain—the religion domain. The religious leaders were mostly concerned with looking for specific situations where Jesus might have violated their religious laws, rites, and traditions. Jesus' dealings with the Sanhedrin assembly and the chief priests, however, would have transpired in the government domain, especially during the events of his arrest and trial. That Jesus' social interactions with these religious leaders only took place in these two public domains should tell us about the nature of their social relationship. These religious leaders were only socially related to Jesus in a single capacity—they were Jesus' detractors and even his enemies, and they perhaps would have seen and treated Jesus as a religious rabbi only. These religious leaders were neither his friends nor his frequent companions; they did not acknowledge Jesus' authority (Matt 21:23; Mark 11:28; Luke 20:2) and did not trust him (Matt 12; John 12:37–43). They might have showed up frequently when Jesus taught the people, but they never became his followers and friends. Thus, Jesus and these religious leaders did not share common goals, ideals, and beliefs even though they might have observed a number of similar Jewish laws and practices (e.g., the Passover). Moreover, the network structure between Jesus and this religious group is clearly less dense than that between him and his disciples and the women.

In fact, Matt 23 provides us with perhaps the clearest example in the Gospels of their actual social relationship. Jesus' warning against and teaching about hypocrisy was addressed "to the crowds" (τοῖς ὄχλοις) and his disciples, but his intention was also to mock and rebuke the Pharisees who were with them (Matt 22:41–46). Jesus' move was swift, changing from a dialogue with the Pharisees that shut their mouth—"No one could say a word in reply, and from that day on no one dared to ask him any more questions" (Matt 22:46; cf. Mark 12:34; Luke 20:40)—to a sarcastic transaction (i.e., a monologue) that pronounces seven woes against them. It is hard to miss the differing, non-intimate tone of Jesus' words here when compared with that towards his disciples and the women. Furthermore, this transaction transpired in a strictly public religion domain, where we see clearly from Jesus' words that, even though the religious leaders knew him and his teaching about the good news, they still refused to trust and accept him. Accordingly, Jesus told his disciples to follow the Pharisees' teachings, though not their works (Matt 23:3, 13–14; cf. 5:20).

It is easy to draw a contrast between the idea, on the one hand, of the Pharisees as a strict religious sect that imposed their traditions and practices on the people and, on the other hand, Jesus' ethical and more practical teaching about the good news. However, as is clear in Jesus' own teaching to his audience and disciples that they are to surpass the righteousness of the Pharisees (Matt 5:20) and to obey the Pharisees' teaching (Matt 23:3), this comparison does not really show that the Pharisees did not receive the gospel about the kingdom of heaven as good news, especially since they themselves were awaiting it. The evidence is only provided in their social relationship with Jesus, who is the

Messiah and who preaches about the gospel of God's kingdom. In other words, their antagonistic relationship betrays and exposes their unbelief.

The Crowds and Other Individuals

The last group of people that Jesus interacted with is the various groups of "crowds" mentioned in the Gospels, and included in this group would have been the various individuals to whom Jesus had ministered. Like Jesus' disciples, the women, and the religious leaders, the various groups of "crowds" (ὄχλοι) mentioned in the Gospels also played a significant role in Jesus' social network. The use of the term ὄχλοι in the Gospels could refer to a large group of people that gathered together for a specific common purpose (e.g., Matt 9:23, 25; 15:35; Mark 2:4; 3:9; Luke 5:1; John 5:13; 6:22), such as to listen to a sermon or to attend a trial, but ὄχλοι could also refer to the "common people" in contrast to those of the upper echelons of society (e.g., Matt 14:5; 15:10; 21:26, 46; 26:5; Mark 6:34; 11:18, 32; John 7:49).[18] As mentioned in the Gospels, the large crowds that convened on various occasions came from various geographical places (Matt 5:1; 7:28; 8:1; 12:15; 13:2; 15:30; 19:2; Mark 10:1; Luke 5:15; 14:25), and they appear to have been the target of Jesus' teaching and social ministry. Jesus often encountered the various individuals who might have been members of the various groups of ὄχλοι in the public, friendship-religion domain during those instances when he healed them, performed signs for them, and ministered to them. However, during those instances when he taught them things about the kingdom of God, such as the event of the Sermon on the Mount (Matt 5–7) or the Sermon on the Plain (Luke 6:1–49), their social interactions would have happened in the religion domain. It is difficult to say whether Jesus had more than a single social interaction with these groups of crowds, but it is certainly fair to say that some of them might have become members of Jesus' circle of disciples and friends after their initial encounter with Jesus. To be sure, some crowds seemed attentive to his teaching (e.g., Matt 13:1–3a; Luke 5:1), but others were quite hostile to him (e.g., Matt 27:20, 22).

Like Jesus' social interactions with the religious leaders, an important thing to highlight here is that Jesus' social relationship with the crowds appears to be, based on the Gospel accounts, more of a uniplex relationship. Also worth noting is that it is unlikely that the people in

---

18. See L&N 1:119, 739.

these large crowds, numbering in the thousands (see Matt 14:21; Mark 6:44; 8:9; Luke 9:14) and coming from various geographical places, knew each other. The several hundred thousands of residents that composed the population of Judea, Samaria, and Galilee could further discredit the theory that everyone apparently knew each other in the first-century community.[19] For this reason, whereas the people who individually encountered Jesus might have seen him as a prophet, healer, or miracle worker on account of the fact that these social situations occurred mostly in the friendship or religion domain, the large crowds that gathered together on different occasions to listen to his sermons and teachings would naturally have seen him as a religious teacher. In other words, the people who belonged to these large crowds would only have limited access to Jesus because of their uniplex relationship. Similarly, because we cannot readily assume that these people knew each other, it is likely that Jesus' social network with them was less dense than was his social network with his disciples and friends.

A comparison of Jesus' extended back-and-forth conversation with James and John in Mark 10:35–45 with his pithy, straightforward question-and-answer dialogue with Bartimaeus in the remainder of Mark 10 highlights his multiplex relationship with James and John and his uniplex relationship with Bartimaeus. When James and John asked Jesus to do what they wanted (v. 35), and when Bartimaeus came to Jesus for help (v. 50), Jesus gave exactly the same response in both cases: "What do you want me to do for you?" (vv. 36, 51).[20] However, after Bartimaeus called him "Rabbi" and told him that he wanted to see, Jesus simply replied, "Go, your faith has healed you" (vv. 51–52). By contrast, Jesus gave James and John a long explanation about their ignorance as to what they had asked for, about their agreement regarding drinking the cup and being baptized with Jesus' baptism, and about what it means to be a servant lord (vv. 37–45). While one could argue that Bartimaeus's desire and request to see does not require further explanation by Jesus, Jesus' reply to him could actually go either way—simply to heal him or to tell him more about what he needs to do after his healing. The short response to Bartimaeus signals the kind of social relationship that they

---

19. See my discussion of the estimated population of these regions in Ong, *Multilingual Jesus*, 163–67 (Judea), 171 (Samaria), 180–83 (Galilee).

20. Mark 10:36 reads, Τί θέλετέ [με] ποιήσω ὑμῖν, and 10:51 reads, Τί σοι θέλεις ποιήσω.

have, and whether Bartimaeus has actually received the healing (and the kingdom of God for that matter), as good news depends on whether he actually became one of Jesus' disciples and part of Jesus' strong, intimate network structure with them.

CONCLUSION

Returning now to my claim in this paper, we can see from the Gospels that the only group that considered the gospel of the kingdom of God to be good news was Jesus' disciples and friends, which, of course, included the previously discussed women he encountered and the people from the various crowds who followed him. We cannot be certain whether the religious leaders and the large crowds that followed him understood the gospel as good news, since neither of these groups demonstrated close and frequent social interactions with Jesus. In fact, for these two groups of people, they were socially related to Jesus in only one area or capacity, and they interacted with him mostly in the public religion domain. They did not establish a real, intimate relationship with him, as we have seen on the basis of Jesus' social network with them. By contrast, Jesus' interaction with his disciples happened in the family, friendship, religion, and other public domains (on a few occasions), and his disciples treated him as their teacher, master, and close friend. This scenario during Jesus' time is not much different from our contemporary situation. We perhaps can only say that a person understands and receives the gospel as good news if we can see that the person has a dense social network with other believers and a multiplex relationship with them.

BIBLIOGRAPHY

Barnes, J. A. "Class and Committees in a Norwegian Island Parish." *Human Relations* 7 (1954) 39–58.

Fishman, Joshua A. "The Relationship Between Micro- and Macro-Sociolinguistics in the Study of Who Speaks What Language to Whom and When." In *Sociolinguistics: Selected Readings*, edited by J. B. Pride and Janet Holmes, 15–32. Harmondsworth: Penguin, 1972.

Henderson, Jim. *Evangelism Additives: What If Sharing Your Faith Meant Just Being Yourself?* Colorado Springs: Waterbrook, 2007.

Hezser, Catherine. "Private and Public Education." In *The Oxford Handbook of Jewish Daily Life in Roman Palestine*, edited by Catherine Hezser, 465–81. Oxford: Oxford University Press, 2010.

Holmes, Janet. *An Introduction to Sociolinguistics*. 3rd ed. Learning about Language. New York: Pearson & Longman, 2008.

McLaren, Brian D. *More Ready Than You Realize: The Power of Everyday Conversations.* Grand Rapids: Zondervan, 2006.

Milroy, Lesley. *Language and Social Networks.* Oxford: Blackwell, 1980.

Mitchell, J. C. "Network Procedures." In *The Quality of Urban Life*, edited by D. Frick et al., 73–92. Berlin: de Gruyter, 1986.

Ong, Hughson T. *The Multilingual Jesus and the Sociolinguistic World of the New Testament.* LBS 12. Leiden: Brill, 2015.

———. "Suffering, Reconciliation, and Eschatological Hope in Rom 5.1–11: A Linguistic Analysis." *FN* 28–29 (2014–2015) 39–55.

Osteen, Joel. *Become a Better You: 7 Keys to Improving Your Life Everyday.* New York: Free Press, 2007.

———. *Your Best Life Now: 7 Steps to Living at Your Full Potential.* New York: Warner Faith, 2004.

Riesner, Rainer. "Jesus as Preacher and Teacher." In *Jesus and the Oral Gospel Tradition*, edited by Henry Wansbrough, 185–210. London: T. & T. Clark, 2004.

Vetter, Eva. "Social Network." In *The Sage Handbook of Sociolinguistics*, edited by Ruth Wodak et al., 208–18. Thousand Oaks, CA: Sage, 2011.

6

In the Making and the Unmasking
Spiritual Formation as Paul's Missional "Good News," Then and Now

MATTHEW FORREST LOWE

THE PAPERS PRESENTED IN this volume offer various (and essentially affirmative) answers to our generative question, "Is the Gospel Good News?" A glance at the contents shows contributors speaking to this question from the Old and New Testaments—demonstrating, once again, the thematic biblical theology implicit in this volume's structure[1]—and from several theological vantage points. At issue, of course, is our answer not just to the initial question, but to the implied follow-up question: *if* the gospel is the "good news" it claims to be, then *how* is that news expressed? How did those who first proclaimed and heard the gospel experience it as good news, and in what comparable ways do we do so today?

I propose that one way the apostle Paul found the gospel "good news" was in what we might today call the spiritual formation of his church communities—that is, the way believers were shaped toward greater conformity with the (cruciform) life of Christ. I will focus here on two cases where Paul links the gospel to his followers' spiritual for-

---

1. As I commented in my 2007 Bingham paper, published as "'This Was Not an Ordinary Death,'" 198–200. Each year, the Colloquium papers tend collectively to imply a biblical theology, or at least a New Testament theology, of the given theme, e.g., resurrection, discipleship, empire, etc.

mation. First, in Philippians, we will see that Paul expects that his joy, while he is in chains for the gospel's advancement, will encourage the Philippian church to "live together in a manner worthy" (Phil 1:27) of the gospel. Second, in 1 Thessalonians, we will note that the Thessalonian believers' hospitality, as a reflection of their combined decision to turn "to God from idols" (1 Thess 1:9) encourages other churches as well as Paul's own further investment in them.

So, we suspect that Paul's gospel bore fruit in the lives of his congregants. So far, so good—or at least, so far, so uncontroversial. This intersection of Pauline studies, missiology, and spiritual formation has received welcome, recent, and ongoing attention, including Rodney Reeves's *Spirituality According to Paul*, portions of Jason Hood's *Imitating God in Christ*, Tom Wright's ever-so-slightly larger work *Paul and the Faithfulness of God*, and my friend Mike Gorman's recent book *Becoming the Gospel*.[2] Somewhat more controversial is the second component of what I will argue here, as I have done elsewhere—that there is an extent to which, for Paul, "spiritual formation constitutes a living response to the presence of empire" and other powers that be.[3] There is not (nor should there be!) sufficient space in this chapter to unpack all of Paul's varied engagements with the Roman Empire or other potential opponents any more than there is space to consider everything he wrote concerning spiritual formation. And admittedly, my attempts to place the study of spiritual formation alongside socio-rhetorical criticism might be dismissed as autobiographical; perhaps this is simply what you get when a biblical theologian and imperial critic marries a Baptist pastor and spiritual director, as I have! Nonetheless, as I will argue, in both the *making* of disciples (that is, their spiritual formation) and the *unmasking* of forces and situations that hamper this process, the gospel is worked out as "good news" in missional relationship with God and neighbor, in

---

2. See Reeves, *Spirituality*; Hood, *Imitating God*; Wright, *Paul*; and Gorman, *Becoming the Gospel*. For a follow-up interview with Gorman on his book, see "Five *(or Six)* Questions with Michael Gorman."

3. Lowe, "Being Conformed to His Death," 1. What I go on to say on the same page, specific to the practicing of justice, and what is worth repeating here, is, "This is not to say that the formative practices of Christian spirituality are necessarily empire-contingent, but that the practices themselves—living as though crucified, buried and raised with Christ—should inform what the doing of justice looks like in today's imperially shaped world."

Paul's settings, and in Canada today. Let us begin unpacking that process with Philippians.

PHILIPPIANS: ENCOURAGEMENT, CITIZENSHIP, AND IMITATION

Writing under some form of arrest, probably from Rome, Paul feels the need to show his Philippian friends that, as Stephen Fowl puts it, being "in chains" is not inconsistent with being "in Christ."[4] Evidently, the Christians in Rome already understand this and act upon it: as Paul reports, "Most [though, interestingly, not *all*] of the brothers and sisters have had more confidence through the Lord to speak the word boldly and bravely because of my jail time" (Phil 1:14 CEB).[5] Barth notes that Paul's imprisonment has been "publicized in Christ" to the Romans (whether Christian or not; see 1:13!), becoming "a Word from the Lord" to a church that Paul did *not* found.[6] But in "publicizing" the same word to the Philippians, alerting them that "the things that have happened to me have actually advanced the gospel" (1:12), Paul risks drawing too much attention to his own situation: ironically, in communicating encouragement and his "affection for all of you with the compassion of Jesus Christ" (1:8), he could easily look selfish in his preaching like those he critiques (1:15-18) and could be violating his later teaching in anticipation of the Christ-hymn (2:1-5). No wonder he effectively "displaces himself" as the subject of the letter, even though he will later ask the Philippians to imitate him and his company (3:17); as Fowl says, he is trying to alter their entire "pattern of perception," with *Christ's* imitability, not his own, taking center stage.[7]

Even in his *apologia* for the gospel, Paul is unapologetic about the political context of the state he is in—and here, too, he implies that the Philippians should follow his example. As Peter Oakes observes, Paul's emphasis on his own Roman context is likely to encourage his corre-

---

4. Fowl, *Philippians*, 39.
5. Unless otherwise noted, all biblical citations are from the CEB.
6. Barth, *Epistle to the Philippians*, 28.
7. Fowl, *Philippians*, 37 (cf. 154); so too Oakes, *Philippians*, 122, contra Bloomquist's *Function*: Paul is not trying to "reinforce an image of himself" but "to persuade the Philippians to action" (and, as I argue below, beyond "action," to spiritual formation via practice and imitation).

spondents in theirs.⁸ Anticipating the political language Paul uses in 1:27, Ben Witherington says that the apostle's opening *narratio* (1:12–26) provides a pilot example for their behavior: "the narratio not only prepares for the persuasion that follows but participates in it in a preliminary kind of way."⁹ Once there, the public, political character of ἀξίως τοῦ εὐαγγελίου τοῦ Χριστοῦ πολιτεύεσθε has drawn frequent scholarly comment, though it is often underemphasized in English translations. For example, compare the NIV and NASB's identical phrasing, "conduct yourselves in a manner worthy of the gospel," or the CEB's slight improvement, "live together in a manner . . . " with Witherington's "live *as citizens* worthy of the good news," Fowl's "order your common life," Gordon Zerbe's deliberately provocative choice, "politicize," or Barth's clever wording, "your state must be worthy."¹⁰ Barth—no stranger to imperial politics, his preaching and theology having been shaped in opposition to them¹¹—sees πολιτεύεσθε indicating (together with πολίτευμα in 3:20) the kingdom of heaven, of which Christians, "amid the homeless anarchy of this aeon, are secretly now already citizens. Their state, their 'form,' their bearing must therefore here and now already be under the invisible discipline of that kingdom."¹² I might argue against Barth that this gospel citizenship is hardly a "secret," but it is certainly one that the rest of Philippi would not have acknowledged as worthwhile.¹³ That, in

8. Oakes, *Philippians*, 113.

9. Witherington, *Paul's Letter*, 72; so too Oakes, *Philippians*, 110.

10. Witherington, *Paul's Letter*, 96, 98 (italics mine); Fowl, *Philippians*, 59; Zerbe, *Citizenship*, 4, and later 20 ("Singularly, be a citizen body and practice your citizenship in a manner worthy of the good tidings of Messiah") and n. 16 in support; Barth, *Epistle to the Philippians*, 44. Oakes (*Philippians*, 177–78) opts for a combination of "'Live as citizens of heaven' and 'Live in community'"—showing a caution against over-anticipating Paul's use of πολίτευμα in 3:20. Such caution should perhaps be applied as well when reading Barth's comments (45–46), notwithstanding the translator's note that the German *Verfassung* (like the English "state") "can mean both '(political) constitution' and also 'frame of mind,' 'attitude,' etc." (45 n. 2).

11. Grenz and Olson, *Twentieth-Century Theology*, 66–67: even before Barth's wartime writing of his commentary on Romans, his surprise that "nearly all of his theological teachers" publicly endorsed Kaiser Wilhelm's imperialism "led Barth to believe that something must be terribly wrong with their theology, if it could be so quickly compromised in the face of the ideology of war."

12. Barth, *Epistle to the Philippians*, 45–46 (cf. 114–15); as Paul chafes under Rome, he has told the Philippians "tacitly what his 'state' is in his struggle."

13. Following Smit, *Paradigms*, 81: to use the gospel as the "measure" of citizenship is rhetorically risky for Paul and perhaps personally risky for the Philippians, as it

turn, raises the question of whether the early Christians—whether in Philippi, Thessalonica, or elsewhere—would have sought recognition from their cities had the option been open to them.[14]

Perhaps questions like these are not entirely answerable. We must be cautious about over-interpreting Paul's political language here and elsewhere, but neither should we ignore it. As Young-Ho Park surmises, the notable absence of ἐκκλησία (conventionally translated as "church") from the prescript of Philippians, as well as from much of the rest of the letter, may relate to the term's absence in Romans and to the "strong 'Romanness' of Philippi." The ἐκκλησία would have been "a totally foreign institution" on Roman soil and at least somewhat alien in a colony with a heavy cultural, linguistic (Latin), and imperial affiliation with Rome.[15] And Witherington is right, first, to commend Markus Bockmuehl's comment—with "the coveted citizenship of Rome" in view, Paul reminds the church that "Philippi may be a colony enjoying the imperial patronage of Lord Caesar, but the church at Philippi is a personal colony of Christ the Lord above all"—and, second, to add that Paul has a more inclusive, "higher and prior" citizenship in mind, superseding Roman citizenship, not being in direct competition with it.[16] Rome is not, Witherington adds, an "evil empire"; but there is "probably" a critique of the imperial cult in Philippi here (a note that Wright sounds considerably louder concerning the empire-reminiscent acclamation of Christ as Lord in 2:9–11).[17] *Right in the midst of encouraging his correspondents and mak-*

---

is an "inner-Christian criterion."

14. Park, *Paul's Ekklesia*, 211, working from Phil 1:27; 3:20; and 1 Cor 6:3: "For Paul, an ἐκκλησία was not a group striving to be recognized by the civic authority . . . [it] claimed that its constituents were above any civic authority . . . The early Christians were equipped with a self-understanding higher than that members of any voluntary association would have imagined for themselves. In this respect, Paul used the civic term ἐκκλησία not because the civic scale perfectly depicted the glorious status of the people of God but because there was hardly any other option available."

15. As Park (*Paul's Ekklesia*, 141–42) also notes, "Philippi is the only city labeled as 'a colony of Rome' in the New Testament (Acts 16:12) . . . If the letter to the Philippians was written during Paul's time in custody in Rome, Paul's political consideration in avoiding such a heavily political Greek term became more plausible." Also see Zerbe's evocative description (*Citizenship*, 18): "Philippi holds status as a mini-Rome."

16. Bockmuehl, *The Epistle to the Philippians*, 98, quoted in Witherington, *Paul's Letter*, 99.

17. Witherington, *Paul's Letter*, 100, 102; Wright, *Paul*, 279–347, 1271–319, and especially 1294 (italics his): "Though it may be doubted whether [Phil 2:]6–8, the story of incarnation, servanthood and death, would remind anyone of the stories of people

ing them into people who can practice joy even in the course of suffering, Paul is unmasking a rival claim on their allegiance.

Imperial allegiance is not Paul's only target here. In ch. 3, he warns, "Watch out for the dogs. Watch out for people who do evil things," followed closely by his discussion of the "assets" that he wrote off "as a loss for the sake of Christ" (3:2–11). There is, predictably, debate about how we should read βλέπετε: whether as "look out for," "beware," "consider" (so Robertson, Witherington), "observe . . . with the aim of avoiding" (Fowl), or "the dual sense of 'observe' and 'danger'" (Zerbe).[18] The "dogs" themselves—usually, though not universally, understood as a Judaizing element, consistent with Paul's incisive comments about circumcision—sharpen the "beware" image. Paul twists the conventional Latin warning sign, *CAVE CANEM*, alerting the Philippians to dogs *outside*, rather than those that guard homes from within.[19] Dogs, unclean scavengers in both Jewish and Greco-Roman eyes, are the perfect insult here: as Barth notes, the epithet comes "like the lash of a whip," for the opponents are "unclean, *precisely* in [their] cleanness," mutilating in their attention to circumcising, undone in the core of their industry.[20] They are unmasked as "bad dogs," and thus bad examples, in their very attempts to do good.

---

coming to imperial power by means of great trials, there should be no question about the force of the 'therefore' in verse 9: this is a narrative of imperial legitimation, and would be readily recognized as such. *This* is how Jesus has attained the position of *kyrios*."

18. Robertson (*Paul's Joy*, 176–78) uses "beware" and *cave canem* but finds "to look out for" more precise; Witherington (*Paul's Letter*, 185, 188–89) also considers "consider," following Kilpatrick's "Βλέπετε," 145–48. Fowl (*Philippians*, 145) argues for "avoid" because "context makes it clear that Paul is calling the Philippians to observe . . . with the aim of avoiding" the "dogs" in question. Zerbe (*Citizenship*, 171 and n. 12) notes a helpful parallel for his dual suggestion in the French usage of "*attention!*"

19. Witherington, *Paul's Letter*, 185, 188–89, as noted immediately above, and 191; Martin (*Philippians*, 141) remarks on the reversal of the insult's *application*, such that "the enemies of God are now those Jewish Christian emissaries who misrepresent the gospel" rather than "Gentile nations who were treated as Israel's enemies and therefore God's (1 Enoch 89:42)," with 2 Cor 11:3–4, 13–15, *Didache* 9:5, and Ignatius' *To the Ephesians* 7:1 all cited in support. One exception to the "Judaizing" reading is Zerbe, *Citizenship*, 22–24, who interprets the attack as a carefully veiled deconstruction of Roman allegiance/citizenship, discussed in more detail below.

20. On the depiction of dogs, see, e.g., Robertson, *Paul's Joy*, 177; Fowl, *Philippians*, 145; Barth, *Epistle to the Philippians*, 93 (italics his), 95. Worth noting, in anticipation of Barth's comments on Paul's invective, is the Geneva Bible, on Paul's warning (Phil 3:1) against false apostles "who beat into men's heads the ceremonies which are abolished instead of true exercises of godliness and charity. And he calls them dogs, as profane

But stopping with "beware the dogs" leaves Paul's verbal picture incomplete. It is no coincidence that Paul intensifies what he now considers his "losses" in 3:8 by calling them σκύβαλα, variously rendered as "rubbish" (NIV, NASB; so too Cohick), "sewer trash" (CEB), "muck" (Martin), "dung" (KJV; so too Witherington, Barth, and others) and even "shit" (Luther, of course).[21] Richard Hays has suggested a slightly less profane option, "crap," describing the reference as "a burst of retrospective candor" (adding the welcome observation that Paul has suffered the loss not only of accomplishments but a "network of trusts and observances to which he was once passionately committed"—that is, there is an underappreciated *social* and *ritual cost* to leaving these losses behind).[22] A link back to the "dogs" here has been theorized before: for Witherington, "If the 'dog' theme is still in play here, then the implication would be that these 'dogs' are being contentious about things that Paul would consider just 'scraps' . . . compared to what he has in Christ"; similarly, Fowl endorses Hays's suggestion of "crap" because it acknowledges the range of "discarded food and even human excrement."[23] But

---

barkers, and evil workmen, because they neglected true works and did not teach the true use of them. To be short, he calls them concision, because in urging circumcision, they cut off themselves and others from the church." Cited in Tomlin, ed., *Philippians, Colossians*, 71.

21. "Rubbish" (so Cohick, *Philippians*, 56); "muck," but in agreement with "rubbish" (Martin, *Philippians*, 150); "dung" (Witherington, *Paul's Letter*, 185; Barth, *Epistle to the Philippians*, 98; and Robertson, *Paul's Joy*, 189 n. 4 [an either/or reference to dung/refuse thrown to dogs]). Luther's rendering refers back (at 3:17—4:1) to "'shit' or excrement and a complete obstacle to eternal life," in "Summer Postil (1544), Twenty-Third Sunday after Trinity" (found in *WA* 22:365–66); as editor Graham Tomlin explains in *Philippians, Colossians*, 90, and in the † note following n. 18: "Luther uses the word *Kot* to translate Paul's *skybala* in Phil 3:8, which is in context a shockingly vivid reference to (human) waste—Luther's language was always colorful, earthy and sometimes rude."

22. So Hays (*Echoes*, 122) as he introduces the opening "New Covenant Hermeneutics?" section of his chapter "A Letter from Christ." One wonders how fully the Paul of, say, Acts 9:5–9 understood the extent of these costs that he would pay! But in relation to Hays's translation choice, as I presented the paper that became the present chapter, my friend and co-contributor Cindy Westfall noted that "crap" was seriously discussed as a translation option here for the CEB (for which she is New Testament Associate Editor).

23. Witherington, *Paul's Letter*, 202; cf. Robertson, *Paul's Joy*, 189, and n. 4 again. Fowl (*Philippians*, 153 and n. 35) says that Hays's "crap" "may be most appropriate" (citing *Echoes*, 122), adding that if, "as was thought in the Middle Ages," σκύβαλα derived from a contraction of "*to tois kysi ballomenon*, 'that which is thrown to the dogs,' then we may have a further play on v. 2."

even these comments seem to miss what we might call a more natural process in Paul's thought, one I have tried *not* to arrive at by elimination, as it were. As a relative few—Melanchthon and Eugene Peterson among them—have hinted, what if the "crap" in question is not (exclusively) human, but (perhaps even more unclean) canine excrement?[24] Are not Paul's "physical advantages" (3:4b) and accomplishments largely "crap" he has produced rather than "scraps" that have been thrown to him?

At the risk of appearing immature (precisely in my attempts at maturity, Barth might say), I elaborate here on an idea recently hinted at by Peter-Ben Smit, who calls Paul the "Superdog"—that is, he was once a better "dog" than these opponents.[25] Without wishing to wipe anyone's nose in anything, when Barth says that "dung" is "never touched again or even looked at,"[26] he is—however briefly—wrong. For Paul *does* look at it and wants his audience to see it too, to see it for what it is. *I was once a dog,* he is saying, *a superdog; I left crap like this. Look closely. Learn from it. Beware of those who leave it. And then leave it behind, as I did—to* "gain Christ and be found in him."[27] Noting, with Smit, that there are identifications in this letter not just between Paul, Christ, and the Philippians, but *also* between Paul, the Philippians, and the dogs, we cannot ignore the repeated emphasis Paul places on βλέπετε: the politics of the Philippians' discipleship demand that they *see, be aware,* and *recognize* both the good examples and the bad—and that they *co-*imitate the good, collectively, as citizens of the gospel.[28]

---

24. Melanchthon: "σκύβαλα means excrement . . . a heaping pile, as coming from a dog" (cited in Tomlin, ed., *Philippians, Colossians,* 79). As Peterson puts Paul's words in the MSG, "everything I once thought I had going for me is insignificant—dog dung." Martin (*Philippians,* 150) calls an attempt to connect σκύβαλα back to the dogs "rather fanciful," though he too notes some support for it.

25. Smit (*Paradigms,* 121–24) also links an underappreciated political element, namely, Paul's concern for the Philippians' *asphales* (3:1, cf. 1 Thess 5:3) to other political elements of Philippians, as the safety of the *polis* was a *topos* "frequented by political, or in other words, deliberative, rhetoric."

26. Barth, *Epistle to the Philippians,* 98.

27. To complete the thought, I have borrowed, of course, from 3:8–9, where Fowl (*Philippians,* 153–54) helpfully notes the shift from an active to a passive verb, from "gain" to "found": "he does not find Christ; Christ finds him."

28. Smit, *Paradigms,* 121–23; and with an eye toward Zerbe's comment (*Citizenship,* 2) that where "discipleship (or 'following,' German *Nachfolge*) has been the core watchword in my own Anabaptist-Mennonite tradition, I find that word easily susceptible to an individualist interpretation or practice."

As we begin to conclude the portion of this study specific to Philippians, asking what this co-imitation might have looked like, I would like to take a moment to consider (though not, in light of the various translations of Paul's βλέπετε, with the aim of avoiding!) Zerbe's argument about this passage. In keeping with his earlier argument that Paul's warning against the "Judaizing" element is part of a veiled deconstruction of the value of Roman citizenship, Zerbe finds that

> a good case can be made that the referent of Paul's verbal outburst and warning is the . . . Roman imperium and elite Roman culture in general, not "judaizing" nor "Judaic" rivals . . . Recent scholarship has increasingly recognized that there are no "judaizing" elements in the city of Philippi, and that 3:2–11 is hortatory and paradigmatic, not polemical or apologetic . . . [W]hat is astonishing is the glee with which the anti-Judaic or anti-judaizing interpretation is often propounded in mainstream Christian commentaries, with hardly a nod as to how this might affect contemporary social dynamics . . . [U]ncritically repeated is the notion that Paul is . . . throwing back the cursing invective of "dogs" from its (supposed Judaic) source, thereby somehow exonerating it, but not admitting that this very retaliatory verbal assault would not measure up against Paul's own ethical standards (Rom 12:14; 1 Cor 4:13).[29]

As Zerbe rightly notes, even if the question of the invective's referent is left open, *the question itself still matters*—not just because the violence in the text reads differently if it suggests "engaging in an act of resistance and naming imperial violence" instead of "slanderously attacking sibling rivals," but also because of Paul's own physical trauma, psychological trauma, and (comparatively) marginal position, among other reasons.[30] Then, too, there is the matter of how (if this interpretation is correct) Paul masks his critique of empire, and not just of imperial power as such, but of "elite Roman culture in general," as Zerbe puts it here. Does Paul's polemic—and it *is* a polemic, though the surrounding passage may be

---

29. Zerbe, *Citizenship*, 22–24 and 171–74, particularly 172–73 (from which the excerpt is taken) and nn. 15–21; as he indicates in *Philippians*, 172 n. 15, his then-forthcoming commentary on Philippians has since expanded this argument. Oddly, Zerbe—if I am reading his notes correctly—highlights Fee (*Paul's Letter*, 293–96) as his leading example of (favorable) recent scholarship here, *and* of "the glee with which the anti-Judaic or anti-judaizing interpretation is often propounded"; Nanos ("Paul's Reversal," 448–82) is also cited with respect to the "(supposed Judaic) source."

30. Zerbe, *Citizenship*, 171.

"hortatory and paradigmatic," as Zerbe says above—participate in the ways of the powers that be by helping them to remain masked?

Yes—and no. It may not be locally safe for Paul (or for his congregants) to name the dangerous referents outright,[31] regardless of whether they are Judaizers, members of (or clients with connections to) the Roman cultural elite, or an actual or potential amalgamation of the two; but Paul wants the Philippian Christians to be able to *identify, avoid,* and *avoid the imitation of* their *tactics,* their *practices.* Paul is modeling theopolitical discernment.[32] Obvious though it may seem, his readers are to learn to recognize "people who do evil things" (3:2b) *by their evil things,* seeing them for what they are and refusing to follow such examples. Not that it does not matter who the potentially influential enemy is; it may matter a great deal. But by allowing them to *appear* to remain masked, Paul is teaching his readers to identify potential influences by their actions, not their names or claims—or what Zerbe rightly calls the "preoccupation" that these produce.[33] So yes, the referents remain mostly masked. But as Billy Crystal's character "Miracle Max" says in the film *The Princess Bride,* "There's a big difference between *mostly* dead and *all* dead"; so, too, there is a big difference between *mostly* masked and *all* masked.

How then, finally, does Paul want the Philippians' life to be shaped? That is, of course, what he spends much of the rest of the letter unpacking—and much more so about the rejoicing co-imitation of good examples than what we might call the co-rejection of negative ones, though

---

31. Zerbe, *Citizenship,* 24: "While the logic of his argument is that he is renouncing any serious identification with his own Roman citizenship (just as Messiah renounced claims to his status by birthright), he can hardly say so specifically here, without serious risk to his life. His nominal Roman citizenship, even though it really meant nothing to him, is what is keeping him alive by a thread." If the referents are Judaizers, as has been traditionally assumed, then we can imagine that the issue of safety may be less immediately one of life and death, but with real social and theopolitical repercussions.

32. For his readers today, that discernment should probably admit a degree of postcolonial hybridity—certainly with regard to Paul's (rhetorically powerful) self-marginalization in Philippians, as noted earlier, but also concerning his (often simultaneous) renunciation or redefinition of, and participation in, Roman elite cultural values. One example would be patronage, as explored in 1 Cor 1 by Punt, "Pauline Agency," 60–61.

33. Zerbe, *Citizenship,* 172, speaking primarily of "the preoccupation with the status, the questing for, or the practice of Roman citizenship and its values."

discernment comprises both.[34] And Paul takes pains to note that what *he* thinks of as a good example is not the same as what the rest of his world thinks. Rather, he, Timothy, Epaphroditus, and (increasingly, they hope) the Philippians are "being conformed to [Christ's] death so that [they all] may perhaps reach the goal of the resurrection of the dead" (3:10b–11, with 3:12–17 in mind as well). They are to live together as citizens of heaven rather than following the example of "enemies of the cross" (3:18, 20). *If* they can be "glad in the Lord always," show "gentleness" to everyone, remember that the Lord is near, and bring their requests to God in prayer and thanksgiving rather than being anxious, *then* "the peace of God that exceeds all understanding will keep [their] hearts and minds safe in Christ Jesus" (4:4–7). And so on (an understatement!) from there to the end of the letter, before closing not just with greetings from Paul and his company, but from "[a]ll God's people here, especially those in Caesar's household," too (4:21–22, remembering 1:13).

All of that said, "greetings" are effectively all that Paul can send, whether in the letter itself or through the interpersonal agency of those who bear and present the letter. Paul and Timothy can only ask that the Philippians "use us as models" (3:17), encourage the imitation of Christ as the foundation of their joy, and suggest ways in which their friends' cruciform life might be lived out—leaving it to the Philippians as a community to figure out what that practice will look like in their context, in their city.

1 THESSALONIANS: THEOPOLITICS AND THE RESHAPING OF HOPE

Like the Philippians, Paul's Thessalonian correspondents are learning to follow his example as a reflection of Christ's example. So Paul gladly affirms, early in his first letter to them, what they began to do when they "accepted the message that came from the Holy Spirit with joy in spite of

---

34. I use "co-rejection" here because I have yet to find a suitable opposite for "imitation"; "unimitating" is occasionally recognized as a word, but not "unimitation" (and "co-unimitation" seems a few bridges too far). Recalling the problems of translating Paul's βλέπετε with words like "avoid," "co-avoidance" seems (to me) to commend a *disengagement*, when I think Paul means quite the opposite, a deliberate engagement (without preoccupation). Related problems arise with describing the imitability of Christ, over against negative examples: "inimitable" (not to be confused with "inimical" or its alternate, "inimicable"!) means that the subject *cannot* be imitated, not that it *should not* be.

great suffering"; fittingly, they have become an example to others (1 Thess 1:6–7). In other words, as Ann Jervis has demonstrated, their suffering is integral to the examples that they follow and those that they set: "The circumstances of this imitation were, Paul says, their receiving of the word in much θλῖψις (affliction), with joy from the Holy Spirit (1:6)."[35] And much the same as when he writes to Philippi—in 1 Thessalonians' first thanksgiving passage, no less—Paul explains that "the *fundamental* shape of the affliction involved in the gospel is the shape of Christ's afflictions."[36] The similarity to Philippians should not surprise us. Both letters convey a strong link between suffering and exemplary discipleship: *the mere existence of such an example means that suffering is shared.* "Paul does not conceive of solitary suffering 'in' Christ. The connectedness Paul affirms among believers extends beyond their suffering to their response to their suffering."[37] And even in 1 Thessalonians alone, before Philippians was written, we will see substantial hints about what Park and others have called the "translocal" character of the church: "In the translocal network, a local ἐκκλησία, modeled after the civic assembly, existed as a distinctive unit. At the same time, each ἐκκλησία was expected to participate in the translocal relationship, modeled after the diplomatic relationship between states."[38]

The exemplary Thessalonians are already growing in their practice of the good news of the gospel. The part that they have played in Paul's story (and Paul's part in theirs) has evidently become so well known among believers in their province and (translocal) neighboring ones that Paul's company hears it told back *to them*, so Paul returns the rhetorical favor: "People tell us about what sort of welcome we had from you and how you turned to God from idols. As a result, you are serving the living and true God, and you are waiting for his Son from heaven." The "welcome" or "visit" Paul enjoyed in Thessalonica, the unlimited mutual

---

35. Jervis, *At the Heart*, 15 (transliteration mine). She continues (15–16): "Paul here signals that he understands suffering to be part of the warp and woof of the gospel, that acceptance of the gospel is at the same time acceptance of suffering. Suffering is not an accidental by-product of believing in Jesus Christ. Rather, suffering is intrinsic to the good news."

36. Jervis, *At the Heart*, 18 (italics hers).

37. Jervis, *At the Heart*, 62, here describing Philippians; as she continues, "For Paul, joy is the fitting response to suffering 'in' Christ, and he considers this joy not an individual experience but a shared one (2:17–18)."

38. Park, *Paul's Ekklesia*, 115.

access and vulnerability he implies, is not expressed here as "hospitality" as such (φιλοξενία, the showing of love to strangers), as it is, for example, in Rom 12:13.[39] Nonetheless, the Thessalonians' hospitable practice of welcome is a vital component of the story, a local expression of the "good news," which Paul naturally wants to encourage them to continue. As Bruce Longenecker explains it, Paul

> imagined the gospel itself to be compromised when economic relationships were skewed in unhealthy configurations ... the whole socio-rhetorical situation for Paul's Thessalonian letter/letters is one in which care for the needy was assumed to be a fundamental feature of the very character of that community, whose practical "love" (i.e. burden bearing) was proclaimed throughout the region.[40]

Also part of this regional story, however, are forces working *against* the Thessalonians' continued spiritual formation. Behind 1 Thess 1, we can glimpse something of the context to which Paul wrote. Regarding Paul's statement that "the message about the Lord rang out from you, not only in Macedonia and Achaia but in every place" (1:8), Witherington agrees that the news of the converts would have traveled easily along the Via Egnatia, a principal Roman road, on which Thessalonica was located.[41] This was a prosperous, (relatively) free city in a prime location.[42] From the perspective of Christians in other cities, the story of the converts amounted to *good news about good news*—not unlike Paul's words in Phil 1:12, "I want you to know that the things that have hap-

---

[39]. First Thessalonians 1:9–10a; "welcome" (or "reception," NIV/NASB) is εἴσοδον, which, when repeated in 2:1, is rendered as "visit with" (CEB), "visit to" (NIV), or "coming to" (NASB)—variously reflecting the construction with *pros*, connoting access to a given person, as discussed by Michaelis, "ὁδός, κ.τ.λ.," 106–7. I thank Lois Dow for graciously supplementing my explanation of this term during the initial presentation of this paper. Concerning the comparison with Rom 12:13, Barth's closing comment (*Epistle to the Romans*, 459) on that text is worth remembering: "By charity the tension between self and others is overcome; and, for this reason, charity is a demonstration of the recognition of the 'One' in the others. It is this recognition which makes of charity an ethical action. Consequently, the range of what is strange and foreign is capable of unlimited expansion." This point, in turn, suggests some strong connections to Beth Stovell's chapter in this volume, "The Gospel as Good News for the Poor," 278–307.

[40]. Longenecker, *Remember the Poor*, 155–56, citing 1 Thess 1:2–10.

[41]. Witherington, *1 and 2 Thessalonians*, 73.

[42]. Donfried, *Paul, Thessalonica*, 35, noting how Thessalonica's extensive numismatic evidence underscores its prosperity.

pened to me have actually advanced the gospel." But from *outside* the Christian assembly, this was *not* good news. As David deSilva observes, even under Rome, the new Macedonian capital "was not restructured as a Roman colony." Yet it maintained "a strong commitment to Roman imperial ideology" as well as the cults of Dionysus, Isis, Osiris, Kabiros, and Sarapis[43]—whose cult demonstrated multilayered imperial politics, promoted first by the Ptolemies (as a unifier of Greeks and Egyptians), then by Rome.[44] So when Paul highlights that the Thessalonian believers' conversion involved not just turning *to* a living God but also turning *from* idols, it is no casual reference.[45] As deSilva says,

> As solid citizens of Thessalonica began to withdraw from all contact with the gods whose favor cradled society and ensured the common good . . . to await the coming of a new order that would replace Roman rule, their family, friends and associates would try to amend their deviant ways. Pressure of all kinds—reproach, shunning, economic distress—would be applied to "help" the converts decide to return to a suitable way of life.

Turning to a living God and from idols, then, was more than just a one-time decision, but a daily recommitment, with consequences on multiple fronts. Not unlike our earlier extrapolation from Hays, concerning the *social and ritual costs* of Paul's own change of commitments when he began to follow Christ, the Thessalonians' conversion had left them in a liminal situation, with strained ties to their neighbors and devoid of familiar ritual practices.[46]

As in Philippi, Paul engages *theopolitical* structures quite deliberately in Thessalonica, as I have argued previously and will do again only

---

43. So deSilva, *An Introduction*, 527–28; he also notes here that Thessalonica, along with nearby Philippi, allied itself with Antony and Octavian against Brutus and Cassius and subsequently, in the conflict between Antony and Octavian, first sided with Antony but "quickly"(!) expressed loyalty to Octavian after Actium.

44. Wikipedia, "Serapis," accessed June 4, 2015, http://www.wikipedia.org/wiki/Serapis.

45. Witherington (*1 and 2 Thessalonians*, 73) notes that Paul "appears to be using a traditional formula here for conversion, perhaps taken from early missionary preaching," and observes (74) that the LXX uses *eidolon* for both the carving and the deity it represents, with a nod to 1 Cor 8. But when he argues that "here alone in Paul's letters does he speak of the 'living' God," he is simply wrong: see 2 Cor 3:3; 6:16; Rom 9:25–26, and, focusing on all of these texts, Goodwin, *Paul: Apostle*.

46. Witherington, *1 and 2 Thessalonians*, 76: "Paul seems not to have left them with much liturgy for them to identify as religious behavior."

briefly here.⁴⁷ Karl Donfried has found "elements in the proclamation of Paul and his co-workers in Thessalonica" that could have been perceived as "politically inflammatory." The "unusually strong civic cult" there created "an environment particularly hostile to early Christian proclamation and language"—especially when Paul pointedly deploys terms like παρουσία ("presence," or "arrival," i.e., of the emperor or his representative), ἀπάντησις (the public reception for such an arrival) and κύριος ("lord," but ultimately Caesar).⁴⁸ Paul also describes Jesus, as the Thessalonians assemble and "wait" for him (1:10), as the Son of God, suggesting some competition for Caesar as *divi filius*.⁴⁹ Donfried argues that even the opening address, τῇ ἐκκλησίᾳ Θεσσαλονικέων ("To the Thessalonians' church," rather than Paul's usual opening, "To the church of God in Corinth," for example), is a (theo)political choice, as the residents' *nomen gentilicium* was also employed in coinage linked to the imperial cult. He further contends that the selection of ἐκκλησία itself, in this early letter, is used with "an actual assembly in mind," allowing a glimpse of Paul's ecclesiology taking shape in opposition to Thessalonica's royal theology.⁵⁰ Perhaps all this informs Paul's phrasing in 1:5, "*our* good news didn't come to you just in speech but also with power and the Holy Spirit and with deep conviction."⁵¹ The apostle

---

47. See Lowe, "'This Was Not an Ordinary Death,'" 215–19, and the sources noted there.

48. Donfried, *Paul, Thessalonica*, 34, 144–45.

49. Donfried, *Paul, Thessalonica*, 144: "That Paul is intentionally engaging and challenging the political, civic and religious structures of pagan Thessalonica is suggested at several points in the letter and it is in dialogue with such an environment that he advances his ecclesiology"—a point to which 1:10 is brought in immediate support.

50. As we began to observe, following Park, above. Donfried, *Paul, Thessalonica*, 140–41: against Thessalonica's "royal theology," ἐκκλησία is "used in such a general, civic manner rather than in a way suggesting a developed Christian understanding of ecclesiology"; and 143, where believers pointedly assemble not in the name of the goddess Roma, or Rome's leaders as just any θεός or *divi filius*, but in the name of God the Father and the Lord Jesus Christ. Of these "two types of assemblies," one has a "christological character" (145; cf. 154–56). It is tempting to see, in this deconstructed (or not-yet-constructed) image, a picture of the post-Christendom, "emergent," "missional" church as it stands today, but this risks anachronism and is beyond the scope of this chapter. For a critical refinement of Donfried's argument here, see Park (*Paul's Ekklesia*, 104), who concludes that "it is certain that the later letters of Paul did not exit this political world to enter the theological realm but rather developed the theological understanding of the church around the political world" of the ἐκκλησία.

51. Italics mine; cf. 1 Cor 2:4.

hardly needs to mention how "news about your faithfulness has spread" in 1:8. Neither does he need to mention that another gospel—Rome's imperial "good news"—is one possible source of the Thessalonians' difficulties, at least indirectly. Rome's gospel is devoid of the Holy Spirit, but it operates with a different power, one that must be treated carefully.[52]

Judging from Paul's letter, how is this theopolitically loaded social context affecting the Thessalonian Christian assembly's spiritual formation? Once more, Donfried's analysis is astute and worth exploring a little further. He finds Paul speaking in 1 Thess 1:3 and 5:8 of a familiar triad of "faith, love, and hope," but in 3:6, Timothy's report is only "good news about your faithfulness and love." If "hope is absent," then it is understandable that Paul adds again that he is praying constantly for them, that his desire is to see them in person and to "complete whatever you still need for your faith."[53] Thus, hope is emphasized at several key points, not least at the παρουσία, which "gives meaning and encouragement to the suffering and hopeless Thessalonians ... a desolate and discouraged people."[54] I suggest that *a people surrounded by reminders of the ways of empire may be desperately in need, first, to be encouraged to hope and, second, to be reminded that (appearances aside) the powers that be are not the only powers at work.* No less than in Thessalonica, in our own time and place this point is all the more essential, especially given how thoroughly the hope of Christ's return has been hijacked by "Left Behind" theology. Although it is beyond the scope of this chapter, I hope

---

52. What N. T. Wright has recently said of Galatians is perhaps also true here, at a similar stage in 1 Thessalonians: "Galatians does not emphasize Jesus as *kyrios*. But it does warn against 'another gospel' (1:6). The only 'other gospel' for which we have any evidence in the world of first-century Anatolia was the gospel of Caesar and Rome." See Wright, "Messiahship," 23, and sources cited there. But as with Philippians above, we should be careful not to overemphasize Rome's role in Paul's missional approach to Thessalonica, even if *under*-emphasis has traditionally been the more common problem. In response to points made by Wright in *Paul*, Rabens ("Paul's Mission Strategy," 6) strikes a good balance, with our principal text here in 1 Thess 1 in view: "Wright's suggestion gives Caesar too much credit for Paul's movements. Paul was less concerned about the emperor than about 'all people' and 'all Gentiles' (1 Cor 9:22; Rom 1:5; 15:11) who needed to hear the gospel, turn away from whatever Greek, Roman, Egyptian, or local deity people worshiped, in order to believe in Jesus and serve the living and true God (cf. 1 Thess 1:1–10)."

53. Donfried, *Paul, Thessalonica*, 39–40, also noting the frequent emphasis on ἐλπίς, "hope," throughout the letter (1:10; 2:19; 3:13) and the correspondingly significant accent on the παρουσία.

54. Donfried, *Paul, Thessalonica*, 161.

(so to speak) that many of us will take up the challenge issued by Richard Middleton of re-envisioning how the return of Christ should shape our hope in ways more faithful to the biblical metanarrative.[55] And more generally, when faced with so much bad news today, as noted in the initial description of this conference that gave rise to its main question, we can find ourselves in a place comparable to the first-century Thessalonians, badly in need of encouragement in order to *sustain*, to *practice*, our well-founded hope. In such places, we need to remind one another that Christ is indeed returning, but we need to recall, as well, what difference that hope makes here and now, not just at his return.

CONCLUSION: EMBODYING MISSION AND ENCOURAGING SUCH PRACTICES AS JOY AND HOPE

I have noted, in this chapter, how Paul helped his correspondents in Philippi and Thessalonica to recognize the theopolitical realities around them—to unmask some of the powers that be. I have noted, too, that this unmasking is closely connected to the ways in which he encouraged his friends in these cities, exhorting the Philippians especially to joy and the Thessalonians especially to hope. In the *unmasking* of opposition and the continued *making* of these disciples, we see them imitating Paul's example, as he imitates Christ, and we see them being asked to imitate these examples even more closely and consistently—more joyfully, more hopefully—thus becoming expressions, embodiments, of the gospel as good news. As I hinted at the outset, in agreement with Gorman, they are to *become* the good news.[56]

So Paul encourages these two congregations in their spiritual formation—the Philippian ἐκκλησία especially in living together as citizens of heaven (which, I would argue, *comprises* Paul's subsequent commen-

---

55. Middleton, *A New Heaven and a New Earth*. This is not to imply that the Left Behind books and films represent, or should be equated with, empire or the powers—though I, for one, have some concerns with a Christian eschatological project that becomes a multi-million-dollar entertainment franchise while ignoring the real, historical, imperially charged contexts from which Scripture's apocalyptic texts emerged.

56. As I have done at the outset of this chapter and again here, Rabens has also (independently) affirmed the significance of Gorman's approach in *Becoming the Gospel*, concluding that Paul "wanted to reach the unreached, and it is this focus on people that drove him. He didn't just want to win people for the Gospel, but he wanted them to Become the Gospel, to use the title of Michael Gorman's new book" ("Paul's Mission Strategy," 9).

dation of the disciplines of showing gentleness, remembering that the Lord is near, bringing their requests to God in prayer, and practicing joy) and the ἐκκλησία of the Thessalonians principally in continuing their practice of hospitality and reclaiming their practice of hope. But what do these forms of spiritual formation have to do with *mission*?

To attempt at least a partial answer to this question, I turn to a paper given by Volker Rabens at a recent conference assessing early Christian engagement with the urban environments of the ancient world. For his discussion of Paul's mission strategy, Rabens makes a crucial point in support of a provisional definition of mission that, I believe, will be helpful to develop here: "Paul entered into an *intensive relationship* with those whom he wanted to reach with the gospel. He identified himself as their servant . . . 'Mission' is therefore understood in this article as the multi-dimensional engagement of an individual or of a faith community, with the goal of winning others to the message of faith and to the lifestyle related to it."[57] At the risk of (over)stating what Rabens has already explained, *mission is relational and multi-dimensional*. Paul's missional practice is not limited to the co-writing of letters any more than his missional partnerships are limited to his co-writers. Mission in Paul's letters is not (just) a matter of senders and addressees. Rather, as Rabens goes on to point out, it is reciprocal and involves "working and eating together, theological reflection and discussion, ethical instruction, and the experience of spiritual gifts and wonders"[58]—much of which is worked out, I would suggest, in spiritual disciplines or practices through which mission and spiritual formation become difficult to distinguish, let alone to separate, from one another.

With Rabens, we can affirm that Pauline "mission" meant a relational, "reciprocal process in which Paul shared his life," expressed not just "with his coworkers with whom he traveled to the cities," but also

---

57. Rabens, "Paul's Mission Strategy," 2 n. 7 (italics mine), citing 2 Cor 4:5; 12:14-15; and Col 1:25 in support of δοῦλος ("servant"). Before continuing, for Paul, "'multi-dimensional' means that engagement was not limited to verbal proclamation, but encompassed *an integrated and reciprocal participation in the lives of others*" (italics mine).

58. Ibid., and elaborated on p. 3: Paul's work "is embedded in a wide-ranging co-operation with various co-workers in the context of their common missionary activity (e.g. 1 Cor 3:6; 2 Cor 8:23; Phil 2:25; Ro[m] 16:3, 9, 21). This praxis is based on Paul's theological understanding of the church as the body of Christ, in which the individual members complement one another (1 Corinthians 12)."

"*in the work of urban industry* as well as in the synagogues and houses in which Paul worked. With the values [and, I would add, the practices] which Paul communicated in this lifestyle, his congregations had a solid basis from which to lead a life attractive to outsiders in the city."[59] Part and parcel with this lifestyle-transmission—and reflected in Paul's letters, as we have noticed—was a respect for specific urban contexts. Even as they began to build "translocal" ties between each city's ἐκκλησία, Paul and his partners in mission were out to demonstrate how to "lead a life attractive to outsiders in the city," and not just *any* city, but the city that they and/or their correspondents called home. As we have seen, there are certainly points of comparison between Philippians and 1 Thessalonians, but it is noteworthy that Paul does not "reverse his directions," as we might say today when finding our way from unfamiliar surroundings to more familiar ones. That is, he does not tell the Thessalonians that they are citizens of heaven, nor commend the Philippians for turning away from idols. He knows the geographic and cultural contexts where (and the people with whom) he speaks and engages in mission.

This lesson is worth remembering as we consider what Paul's missional good news looks like for us today. One temptation for churches—and certainly for writers!—in North America, I think, is to lean too far toward the "translocal," seeking ideas and initiatives that can be readily "transplanted" from one context to another. What I hope I have suggested here, among other things, is *a respect for reciprocal, and contextual, missional praxis, without losing sight of the translocal aspect*. Rather than focusing on bad examples (not that this makes them "dogs" or "people who do evil things"!), I will briefly highlight one series of what I generally find to be good examples of balance between local and translocal mission, with an emphasis on spiritual formation and/or practices—the New Monastic Library series, from which we might single out Tim Dickau's book, *Plunging into the Kingdom Way*. In relating his story of the ongoing transformation of his church (and its neighborhood) through a deep investment in shared practices of community, hospitality, justice-seeking, and confession, Dickau allows a window into ways of doing mission and spiritual formation that *could* be transplanted elsewhere, but only with great sensitivity to each reader's own context.[60]

---

59. Ibid., 16 (italics and brackets mine).
60. See Dickau, *Plunging*.

Of course, a related sensitivity is called for as we continue to discern biblical resources for missional practice today: we should beware of assuming that what Paul wrote to a specific cultural place and a specific time automatically applies to our own situations today. For example, given the imperial context of the Thessalonians whom Paul commended for turning away from idols, we might be tempted to deploy this and other Pauline texts when speaking out against contemporary iterations of empire, whether political, commercial, military-industrial, etc. But if this chapter—orienting, as it has, around the three-way intersection between the fields of biblical (and specifically Pauline) studies, mission, and spiritual formation—also has a contribution to make toward confessionally grounded imperial criticism as a sub-discipline of biblical studies, perhaps it is this: it is essential that we recall (and imitate!) Paul's own example in such politically tempting situations, carefully and prayerfully discerning when, where, under what circumstances, in what way, with what motives, how much, and to whom to speak out in prophetic protest. The making of disciples and the unmasking of the powers that be are parts of the same mission in embodying the good news together; one should not come at the expense of the other.

By way of conclusion, I will focus briefly on how we might live out Paul's good news today with regard to the practices he commended most often and emphatically to the Philippians and Thessalonians. Concerning the practice of joy, I turn to John Chrysostom's reading of Philippians. When he comments on Phil 1:30 ("You are having the same struggle that you saw me face and now hear that I'm still facing"), he says that Paul demonstrates "that they are engaged in the same conflict as he is on all sides, engaged in the same struggles, both in private by themselves and through enduring temptations with him. He didn't say, 'You heard,' but [said], 'you *saw*,' because it was there in Philippi that he struggled."[61] Chrysostom helpfully stresses here, in 1:30, the same point as we did above with 3:2—examples, positive and negative, demand careful attention. Though Paul himself has surely struggled to remain joyful, he is able to trust that the Philippians have seen a *consistent practice* of joy in him, both in their first encounters with him and again as he writes to them here. I suggest that *we need more embodied reminders, like this, of the consistent practice of joy today.*

---

61. Chrysostom, *Homilies*, 89 (Homily 5); italics and brackets are the translator's.

With respect to hope, I turn to Jacques Ellul's *Hope in Time of Abandonment*, a book that I think is as frighteningly on target in its appraisal of culture today as it was when it was written, over forty years ago. Ellul admits that for years he had intended to write on the "age of abandonment": he found then-current society reminiscent "of what the Bible says happens when God turns his back and is silent." But, he goes on, it was "borne in upon me forcibly" that he could not write on abandonment alone; instead, "the word now given me, as well as the power dwelling within me, were those of hope."[62] Ellul himself clearly struggles with hope, as Paul must also have done; certainly, there are moments when Ellul's prophetic critique of the age of abandonment drowns out his hopeful solutions. But his words are all the more important *because* of this struggle. If hope is a response to God's silence, then perhaps, he imagines, the "sin against the Holy Spirit" in a "despairing age" is the "rejection of hope, or the inability to live by it," characterized by an anguish—or even a gloomy, or resignedly cheerful, "acceptance"—of God's turning away.[63] "Surely hope is a theological virtue," he concludes,[64] desperately needed in his day—and, I suggest, in our own as well. As Chrysostom urged his congregants concerning the practice of joy, may we do the same with Ellul's urgings toward hope, encouraging one another to become embodied practitioners of hope even in moments when a personal or corporate sense of hope seems lost.

To return, once more, to Philippians and 1 Thessalonians, we must remind one another, too, that what we read here is not the end of the story of how the good news shaped these two churches. That story was lived out in their individual and collective spiritual practices, as well as (somewhat differently, again with respect for context) in the beliefs and practices of those who read these letters in other communities, in the first century and ever since. The essence of this point has often been noted concerning the narratives of the canonical Gospels and Acts—as when, for example, deSilva points out that an advantage of Mark's shorter ending is that it leaves readers "with the expectation that Jesus is to be met 'out there,' not in the end of the story but in the ongoing life of

---

62. Ellul, *Hope*, vi; also very much worth noting, in light of the discussion of idols in Thessalonica above, is his connection of idol worship and the worship of (and hope for) the living God (172–73).

63. Ibid., 209–10.

64. Ibid., 222.

the church and its mission to the world."[65] But this is less often argued (in my experience) for Paul's epistles, which should perhaps be taken up—joyfully and hopefully!—as an encouraging challenge to those who would still affirm and share the gospel as good news today.

BIBLIOGRAPHY

Barth, Karl. *The Epistle to the Philippians*. Translated by James W. Leitch. London: SCM, 1962.

———. *The Epistle to the Romans*. Translated by Edwyn C. Hoskins. 1933. Reprint, New York: Oxford University Press, 1968.

Bloomquist, L. Gregory. *The Function of Suffering in Philippians*. JSNTSup 78. Sheffield: JSOT Press, 1993.

Bockmuehl, Markus. *The Epistle to the Philippians*. BNTC 11. Peabody, MA: Hendrickson, 1998.

Chrysostom, John. *Homilies on Paul's Letter to the Philippians*. Translated by Pauline Allen. WGRW 36. Atlanta: SBL, 2013.

Cohick, Lynn H. *Philippians*. The Story of God Bible Commentary. Grand Rapids: Zondervan, 2013.

deSilva, David A. *An Introduction to the New Testament: Contexts, Methods and Ministry Formation*. Downers Grove, IL: IVP, 2004.

Dickau, Tim. *Plunging into the Kingdom Way: Practicing the Shared Strokes of Community, Hospitality, Justice, and Confession*. New Monastic Library 7. Eugene, OR: Cascade, 2011.

Donfried, Karl Paul. *Paul, Thessalonica, and Early Christianity*. Grand Rapids: Eerdmans, 2002.

Ellul, Jacques. *Hope in Time of Abandonment*. Translated by C. Edward Hopkin. New York: Seabury, 1973.

Fee, Gordon D. *Paul's Letter to the Philippians*. NICNT. Grand Rapids: Eerdmans, 1995.

"Five *(Or Six)* Questions with Michael Gorman." *Eerdword: The Eerdmans Blog*, 13 May 2015. http://eerdword.com/2015/05/13/five-or-six-questions-with-michael-gorman.

Fowl, Stephen E. *Philippians*. Two Horizons Commentary. Grand Rapids: Eerdmans, 2005.

Goodwin, Mark J. *Paul: Apostle of the Living God*. Harrisburg, PA: Trinity Press International, 2001.

Gorman, Michael J. *Becoming the Gospel: Paul, Participation, and Mission*. The Gospel and Our Culture Series. Grand Rapids: Eerdmans, 2015.

Grenz, Stanley J., and Roger E. Olson. *Twentieth-Century Theology: God and the World in a Transitional Age*. Downers Grove, IL: IVP, 1992.

Hays, Richard B. *Echoes of Scripture in the Letters of Paul*. New Haven: Yale University Press, 1989.

Hood, Jason B. *Imitating God in Christ: Recapturing a Biblical Pattern*. Downers Grove, IL: IVP, 2013.

Jervis, L. Ann. *At the Heart of the Gospel: Suffering in the Earliest Christian Message*. Grand Rapids: Eerdmans, 2007.

---

65. deSilva, *An Introduction*, 226.

Kilpatrick, G. D. "Βλέπετε, Philippians 3.2." In *In Memoriam Paul Kahle*, edited by Matthew Black and Georg Fohrer, 145–48. BZAW 103. Berlin: Töpelmann, 1968.

Longenecker, Bruce W. *Remember the Poor: Paul, Poverty and the Greco-Roman World*. Grand Rapids: Eerdmans, 2010.

Lowe, Matthew Forrest. "Being Conformed to His Death: Cruciform Spiritual Formation as a Response to Empire." Paper presented at the St. Ambrose Conference on Bible and Justice, St. Ambrose University, Davenport, Iowa, May 2013.

———. "'This Was Not an Ordinary Death': Empire and Atonement in the Minor Pauline Epistles." In *Empire in the New Testament*, edited by Stanley E. Porter and Cynthia Long Westfall, 197–229. MNTS 10. Eugene, OR: Pickwick, 2011.

Martin, Ralph P. *Philippians: An Introduction and Commentary*. 1959. Reprint, TNTC 11. Downers Grove, IL: IVP, 2007.

Michaelis, Wilhelm. "ὁδός, κ.τ.λ." In *TDNT* 5:42–114.

Middleton, J. Richard. *A New Heaven and a New Earth: Reclaiming Biblical Eschatology*. Grand Rapids: Baker, 2014.

Nanos, Mark D. "Paul's Reversal of Jews Calling Gentiles 'Dogs' (Philippians 3:2): 1600 Years of an Ideological Tale Wagging an Exegetical Dog?" *BibInt* 17 (2009) 448–82.

Oakes, Peter. *Philippians: From People to Letter*. SNTSMS 110. New York: Cambridge University Press, 2001.

Park, Young-Ho. *Paul's Ekklesia as a Civic Assembly: Understanding the People of God in Their Politico-Social World*. WUNT 2.393. Tübingen: Mohr Siebeck, 2015.

Punt, Jeremy. "Pauline Agency in Postcolonial Perspective: Subverter of or Agent for Empire?" In *The Colonized Apostle: Paul through Postcolonial Eyes*, edited by Christopher D. Stanley, 53–61. Minneapolis: Fortress, 2011.

Rabens, Volker. "Paul's Mission Strategy in the Urban Landscape of the First-Century Roman Empire." Paper presented at the conference "Cities of God? An Interdisciplinary Assessment of Early Christian Engagement with the Ancient Urban Environment(s)." Centre for the Social-Scientific Study of the Bible, St. Mary's University, Twickenham, May 2015. Subsequently published in *The Urban World and the First Christians*, edited by Steve Walton, Paul R. Trebilco, and David W. J. Gill, 99–122. Grand Rapids: Eerdmans, 2017. Pagination is from the presentation draft.

Reeves, Rodney. *Spirituality According to Paul: Imitating the Apostle of Christ*. Downers Grove, IL: IVP, 2011.

Robertson, A. T. *Paul's Joy in Christ: Studies in Philippians*. 1917. Reprint, Grand Rapids: Baker, 1979.

Smit, Peter-Ben. *Paradigms of Being in Christ: A Study of the Epistle to the Philippians*. LNTS 476. New York: Bloomsbury T. & T. Clark, 2013.

Stambaugh, John E. *Sarapis under the Early Ptolemies*. Leiden: Brill, 1972.

Tomlin, Graham, ed. *Philippians, Colossians*. Reformation Commentary on Scripture, New Testament 11. Downers Grove, IL: IVP, 2013.

Witherington, Ben, III. *1 and 2 Thessalonians: A Socio-Rhetorical Commentary*. Grand Rapids: Eerdmans, 2006.

———. *Paul's Letter to the Philippians: A Socio-Rhetorical Commentary*. Grand Rapids: Eerdmans, 2011.

Wright, N. T. "Messiahship in Galatians." In *Galatians and Christian Theology*, edited by Mark W. Elliott et al., 3–23. Grand Rapids: Baker, 2014.

Bible

———. *Paul and the Faithfulness of God*. 2 vols. Christian Origins and the Question of God 4. Minneapolis: Fortress, 2013.

Zerbe, Gordon Mark. *Citizenship: Paul on Peace and Politics*. Winnipeg: CMU Press, 2012.

———. *Philippians*. Believer's Church Bible Commentary. Harrisonburg, VA: Herald Press, 2016.

7

We Need the Gospel

A Response to Douglas A. Campbell with Regard to Paul's Diagnosis of the Human Predicament

JAE HYUN LEE

INTRODUCTION

IS THE GOSPEL GOOD news? This question is not new, since it is one of the typical inquiries that evangelists have been asked by outsiders of the church. Even in the Christian community, this question has been frequently raised in order to establish the basis of Christian faith and life. The central issues related to this question are the necessity and effectiveness of the gospel with regard to the human situation. The issue of necessity is connected to how one diagnoses the human condition, and that of effectiveness is concerned with how well the gospel deals with the human condition. Throughout history Christians have unanimously provided a positive response to this question and have considered Paul's letter to the Romans to be the best source to convince others of the validity of the gospel. They have read and believed that Romans contains the gospel, which gives not only insightful knowledge on the human predicament (e.g., Rom 1:18—3:20), but also the divine solution to the problem.

However, a recent publication by Douglas A. Campbell throws a bomb into this field of tradition. He suggests a provocative reading of Rom 1:18—3:20 with a surprising reconstruction of the situation of the letter.[1] Traditionally, Christians have considered this text, especially 1:18–32, as depicting the negative situation of all humans and God's response to it. Contrastingly, Campbell insists that 1:18–32 is just a citation of Paul's opponent and that 2:1—3:20 is Paul's critique and correction of the false teaching. According to Campbell, 1:18—3:20 is not about the human predicament or the necessity of the gospel. Consequently, if one accepts Campbell's view, he or she ought to renounce using Rom 1:18—3:20, especially 1:18–32, as the source for proving the necessity and effectiveness of the gospel with respect to the human problem. It also means that instead of using a two-thousand-year-old rationale for the necessity of the gospel, Christians need to find another foundation for the positive answers to the question above. Indeed, this is a highly important issue, and Christians should respond to Campbell's proposal whether they agree with it or not.

Is his reading legitimate? After the publication of Campbell's book in 2009 many scholars have penned responses to him, pointing out the difficulties in his interpretation and methodology.[2] This paper will be one of such responses, but its focus is mainly on the evaluation of his attack on the so-called traditional reading of Rom 1:18–3:20. Although one should also check the effectiveness of the gospel in order to answer the question properly, this paper will concentrate on the necessity of the gospel, because proper diagnosis of an illness leads one to rely on the help of the doctor. With this purpose in mind, this essay will examine Campbell's argument and then evaluate it based on the textual evidence.

---

1. Campbell, *The Deliverance of God*.

2. E.g., Cayzer, Review of *The Deliverance of God*; Perry, Review of *The Deliverance of God*; Campbell, "Apocalyptic Rereading of 'Justification' in Paul," 382–93; Campbell, "An Attempt to be Understood," 162–208; Campbell, "What Is at Stake in the Reading of Romans 1–3?" 113–37; Gorman, "Douglas Campbell's *The Deliverance of God*," 99–107; de Boer, Review of *The Deliverance of God*; Macaskill, Review of *The Deliverance of God*; Matlock, "Zeal for Paul but Not According to Knowledge," 115–49; Brown, *The Deliverance of God*; Fiore, Review of *The Deliverance of God*; Gaventa, "Rescue Mission," 36–37; Jipp, "Douglas Campbell's Apocalyptic, Rhetorical Paul," 183–97; Moo, Review of *The Deliverance of God*; Schreiner, Review of *The Deliverance of God*; Cousar, Review of *The Deliverance of God*; Seifrid, Review of *The Deliverance of God*; the articles in Tilling, ed., *Beyond Old and New Perspectives*.

CAMPBELL'S REREADING OF ROM 1:18—3:20

Campbell's Reconstructed "Justification Theory" and His Critique

Campbell's attack consists of two parts. One is to point out the problems of the so-called traditional "Justification Theory" (JT) derived from the reading of Rom 1:18—4:25. The other is to suggest an alternative reading based on both his reconstructed situation of Paul's ministry and his apocalyptic understanding of God's salvation depicted in Rom 5-8. Let us begin with his analysis of JT.

THE PREMISES OF ANALYZING JT

Campbell assumes a set of premises in analyzing JT. First, there are two antithetical theological streams in Christian theology. On the basis of J. B. Torrance's analysis of the theological milieu in seventeenth century Scotland,[3] Campbell believes that there have been two different approaches to doing theology in church history. One is the human-initiated way, which traces the truth about God through "criteria and analogies derived by human beings from within the human situation."[4] The other is the divine-initiative approach, which begins its theological thinking with the revelation of God in and through Jesus. These two contrasting theological frameworks produce very different pictures of God's salvation. According to the former approach, salvation refers to a contract between God and humans. God and humans make a deal with conditions, and salvation is only achieved and sustained by human obligation. The latter approach depicts salvation with the concept of covenant. In it God inaugurates the salvific process with his unconditional grace, and the relationship between God and humans is maintained only through the divine initiative and his sustaining work.

Second, the traditional JT is an outcome of the human-initiative theological framework. Campbell believes that JT consists of two kinds of contracts.[5] One is a rigorous contract between God and humans (Rom 1:18-3:20). In this framework, each person appears as the rational and self-interested one, and God acts as a judge who performs his retributive justice against individual human actions. The other kind is

---

3. Torrance, "Covenant or Contract?" 51–76; Torrance, "The Contribution of McLeod Campbell," 295–311.

4. Campbell, "An Apocalyptic Rereading of 'Justification' in Paul," 385.

5. Campbell, *The Deliverance of God*, 15–28.

a generous contract (Rom 3:21—4:25). In this contract, God is the one who satisfies his justice by redirecting to Christ the punishment due sinners, and each person acts as the one who makes a contract with God via a different sort of action, that is, faith. Even though the second one has a gracious aspect with regard to God, it still has the nature of a legal contract, since it still requires human action. Campbell speaks of this aspect in this way:

> Finally, we should emphasize once again the contractual nature of the new soteriological arrangement. After a series of important realizations, the generic subject has to do something in order to be saved, namely, to exercise the criterion of faith (and he or she must continue to exercise it). If faith is exercised, then salvation takes place. If not, however, then this contract is not activated and its obligations not honored by God.[6]

Third, the core issue in the first contract (Rom 1:18—3:20) is ethics. God reveals his existence and power through his creation and makes known to humans both his "ethical concerns" and attributes as "a cosmic lawgiver and judge."[7] Consequently, what God requires from all humans is their ethical response.[8] God also gives each person his retributive justice in response to his or her actions. Unfortunately, in this first contract everyone will be condemned due to his or her ethical incapacity. Because of this premise, Campbell does not hesitate to say that "[in JT] . . . there is considerable overlap with numerous ethical and political systems, not to mention with other religions."[9]

Fourth, Paul's prime theological framework is apocalyptic. This premise is reflected in the subtitle of his book, *An Apocalyptic Rereading of Justification in Paul*. This framework is derived from his reading of Rom 5–8, which has several features:[10] (1) Paul's gospel has an eschatological nature in which there is a conflict between the kingdom associated with Adam and that associated with Christ (Rom 5:12–21); (2) salvation is only through God's initiative and loving action revealed in and through Christ, which Campbell calls God's unconditional rescue

---

6. Campbell, *The Deliverance of God*, 27.
7. Ibid., 15.
8. Ibid., 358–59.
9. Ibid., 19.
10. Campbell, "Christ and the Church in Paul," 113–43; Campbell, *The Deliverance of God*, 62–73.

or deliverance; (3) salvation means the transition of humans from the Adamic kingdom to Christ's kingdom and is typically depicted as freedom from the evil dominion of sin and death and as the state of being enslaved in the Spirit; and (4) the characteristics of salvation in this framework are communal, interpersonal, and relational. The saved are no longer depicted as individual persons but as "brothers," who "are all shaped by the image of the Son and are all beholden to the one Father, crying 'Abba, Father' by the shared Spirit."[11]

With this understanding, Campbell identifies this apocalyptic framework with the covenant framework and makes two important claims about the interpretation of Paul's discussion of justification in relation to JT. One is that JT is inferior to the apocalyptic and God-initiative theology, since JT is not only a rationalistic, moralistic, and individualized model,[12] but is also an outcome of the human-initiative theology, "contract." The other claim is that because Rom 5–8 provides the prime theological framework in Pauline soteriology, one should read Romans backwardly from chs. 5–8 to chs. 1–4 in order to acquire a right understanding of Paul's thought. Accordingly, it is unnecessary to trace Paul's soteriology from Rom 1–4 and onward.[13] Moreover, for him, JT is incompatible with the apocalyptic framework. While the former is based on human initiative and is conditional, the latter is based on divine initiative and is unconditional.[14] Thus, Campbell insists that "a contractual reading of this particular text in Paul is the root of the entire problem" and that "if this text in particular can be reread in unconditional terms then the contractual account of Paul's gospel is undone."[15]

The Reading of Rom 1:18—3:20 in Campbell's JT

Based on the premises above, Campbell explains the textual ground for the so-called JT.[16] Naming Rom 1–4 "the textual citadel," he begins with providing the general structure of it. According to him, Rom 1–4

---

11. Campbell, *The Deliverance of God*, 69.

12. Campbell, "Douglas Campbell's Response to Brittany E. Wilson," 196.

13. In this sense, in his 2011 article he calls the conventional JT "Forward Theory" (FT) (Campbell, "An Attempt to be Understood," 180).

14. Campbell, *The Deliverance of God*, 183–86.

15. Campbell, "An Apocalyptic Rereading of 'Justification' in Paul," 388.

16. Campbell, *The Deliverance of God*, 313–37. Since the focus of this paper is on the problem part, I just examine his reading of Rom 1:18—3:20.

consists of a tripartite argument: (1) problem (1:18—3:20); (2) solution (1:6-17; 3:21-31 [and 4:23-25]); and (3) scriptural attestation to the solution (4:1-25). Since the flow of the argument is from human plight to solution, he understands JT as a prospective or forward-moving model of salvation.[17]

As far as the problem is concerned, Campbell calls it a rigorous contract and divides it into three parts, Rom 1:18—2:8; 2:9—3:9a; and 3:9b-20.[18] As the first stage of the argument, 1:18—2:8 deals with the human inability to satisfy God's retributive justice. It begins, in 1:18-32, with the sinfulness of pagans and God's wrath on them. Then 2:1-5 mentions the Jewish critiques of the preceding pagan sinfulness. Romans 2:6-8 deals with the universal principle of God's retributive justice: "For he will repay according to each one's deeds" (2:6 NRSV). This part functions to lay the foundation of the argument in 1:18-32 that God's wrath on sinful pagans is based on their evil deeds.

Romans 2:9—3:9 describes the failure of the Jews to gain God's salvation in spite of their privilege with regard to law and circumcision. This part "levels the playing field between Jews and pagans, so that Jews as well as pagans seem to be in this sorry pass."[19] In order to draw this conclusion, JT begins to read Rom 2:9-16 as saying that both Jews and pagans can be saved equally on the basis of their deeds, which is relevant to the universal knowledge of God's ethical law. Especially notable is 2:14-15, which contains the idea that "pagans *can* presumably be saved in accordance with desert and hence independently of Jewish privilege."[20] Romans 2:17-24 points out the sinfulness of Jews who live inconsistently with their knowledge of God's will in the law. Romans 2:25-29 denies the importance of circumcision in relation to salvation. Circumcision is meaningless without proper deeds prescribed in the law. Lastly, with a diatribal interaction, 3:1-9a accepts Jewish privilege in the sense that they are entrusted with the oracles of God but rejects an advantage in salvation based on their privilege.

The last argument in the problem is Rom 3:9b-20. Through a scriptural quotation, it affirms the sinfulness of all humans and their

---

17. Ibid., 315.
18. Ibid., 316.
19. Ibid., 319.
20. Ibid.

inability to escape from God's retribution. This part is a reiteration of what 1:18–32 states.

The Criticism of JT's reading of Rom 1:18—3:20

In chapter 11, Campbell presents a two-part criticism of JT's reading of Romans. The first part consists of pointing out how the text of Romans gives less information than is necessary to establish JT. He calls these absences "textual underdeterminations." The other part of the criticism consists of pointing out instances in which the text provides more information than JT needs, instances he calls "textual overdeterminations."

Textual Underdeterminations

As for the textual underdeterminations in Rom 1:18—3:20, Campbell lists four difficulties.

First, the text does not show "the scene-setting strategy."[21] While JT insists that the problem part (Rom 1:18—3:20) functions to anticipate the Christian solution in 3:21—4:25, Campbell contends that there is no textual evidence for this assumption. Relying on the belief that Paul never preaches the gospel in the order of "problem-solution," Campbell boldly says, "We conclude, then: the all-important assumption that [Rom] 1:18—3:20 is an argument that prepares systematically, in an a priori fashion, for the later proclamation of the gospel is not stated by the text at any point."[22]

Second, the text *never* demonstrates a rational, moralistic, and "philosophical man" nor the retributive justice of God.[23] These are merely some of JT's presuppositions with regard to the nature of human beings and God's attributes.

Third, in the conventional JT, the second-person references in Rom 2:1–5 refer to a Jew who hypocritically judges the sinful pagans in 1:18–32. This person represents typical Jews, including Paul himself at an earlier time, who share the general perspective of Judaism on sinful pagans. In contrast, Campbell insists that this figure is a Jewish teacher and judge who is probably a Christian.[24] He suggests the connection

---

21. Ibid., 340–41.
22. Ibid.
23. Ibid., 341.
24. Ibid., 345–46.

between Rom 2:1–8 and 2:17–24a as its rationale. The second-person-singular reference in both passages refers to a learned and hypocritical Jew. This person knows God's ethical standard through the law but does not obey it. In addition, he thinks that this character also reappears as the Jewish interlocutor in Rom 3:1–9. Thus, even though Campbell and JT have in common the supposed identity of the participants in Rom 1:18–32, they differ about the character in 2:1–5. Campbell even complains that in relation to JT the text elucidates neither the Jewishness of a Jew in 2:1–5 nor Paul's own understanding of his contemporary Judaism.[25]

Fourth, JT's axiom is problematic. For Campbell, JT believes that the core problem of humans in Rom 1:18—3:20 is their lack of perfect obedience to the law. This belief is connected to the understanding that first-century Judaism taught that perfect law observance was necessary in order to be saved.[26] In line with the New Perspective on Paul, however, Campbell contends that the text does not support JT. The main reason is that the passage referring to the need of law observance is very brief and bland. For him, only 2:5b-6 mentions God's righteous judgment according to one's deeds, and in 2:7–10 the issues are changed to present a contrast between the good and the bad in relation to God's judgment. Even though Paul criticizes Jewish sinfulness in 2:21–22, it is not about perfectionism. Moreover, the depiction of sinful humans in 3:10–18 does not function to show that no one can obey the law perfectly. It just states that there is nobody who is righteous and that all are corrupt in every aspect. Campbell concludes that "Romans 1:18—3:20 never states clearly that perfect law observance is necessary for all—but especially for Jews."[27] Consequently, for him, it is illogical to say that all need to embrace God's way of salvation in Rom 3:21–31 just because of God's retributive judgment caused by humans' imperfect obedience.

Textual Overdeterminations

As far as the textual overdeterminations in Rom 1:18—3:20 are concerned, Campbell lists eleven cases.

---

25. Ibid., 346.
26. Ibid., 347–49.
27. Ibid., 348.

First, the distinctive style in Rom 1:18–32 is unnecessary for the argument. Following predecessors,[28] he doubts the authenticity of Paul's voice in 1:18–32 for five reasons: (1) this part is well constructed in its own right; (2) there are many α-privatives, (3) following Calvin Porter,[29] he thinks the high density of third-person-plural references is a unique feature; (4) this part has numerous word plays in relation to pagan sinfulness and God's wrath; and (5) the vice lists in Rom 1:29–31 are also unique. He asserts that, since such unique information is unnecessary for the flow of JT's argument, Rom 1:18–32 does not originate from Paul's mind.

Second, there is a temporal conflict between Rom 1:18 and 1:19–32. According to him, while v. 18 describes God's wrath with the present tense verb (ἀποκαλύπτεται, "is revealed"), vv. 19–32, especially v. 32, deal with its futuristic nature. The text does not give a proper explanation of this conflict.

Third, pagan sinfulness has a collective nature. For Campbell, in order to explain God's retributive justice toward each sinful pagan, JT assumes the capacity of an individual 'philosophical man' to acknowledge divine attributes and ethical standards. However, Campbell insists that the use of third-person-plural references in Rom 1:18–32 does not indicate the individual aspect of pagan sinfulness. He even understands the sexual immorality in vv. 24–27 as a collective case. That is, the disobedient pagans overwhelmed by internal lusts express their depraved behavior and "generate an entire culture of idolatry and sexual immorality (so vv. 23–27)."[30] Moreover, since pagans' lustful hearts cause them to produce evil deeds, they are no longer rational beings. Hence, Campbell thinks that "it is difficult to imagine how subsequent generations can fairly be expected either to perceive a transcendent God or to act in accordance with that God's wishes."[31] He concludes that the text does not support JT's assumption regarding the rationality of individual human beings, but merely demonstrates the collective situation of humans who are enslaved by their sinful lusts.

Fourth, intertextuality with Wis 1–16 is unnecessary in JT. He lists at least ten possible connections between Rom 1–3 and the Wisdom of

---

28. Ibid., 1026 n. 47.
29. Porter, "Rom 1.18–32," 210–23.
30. Campbell, *The Deliverance of God*, 360.
31. Ibid.

Solomon.³² He conjectures that Paul seems to use them not to accommodate the theological thought in the Wisdom of Solomon, but to rebut or correct it. Pointing out that the traditional JT is not interested in these connections or does not explain why Paul uses such extensive interactions with the Wisdom of Solomon, Campbell puts this feature into the category of textual overdetermination.

Fifth, the function of Rom 2:1 in the flow of the argument in JT is unnatural. According to Campbell, the traditional JT believes that Rom 2:1 functions to blame the hypocritical judge who criticizes the pagans in 1:18–32 but does the same things. Campbell objects to this view and insists that the core problem Paul points out in Rom 2:1 is "the judge's lack of self-awareness of transgression."³³ Even though the Jewish judge is in the same situation as the pagans with respect to God's retributive justice, he does not realize it. As a result, he accumulates God's future wrath. This analysis gives Campbell assurance that the focus of this part of the argument does not go well with the flow of Paul's argument in JT. If the person in 2:1 is aware of his sinful condition and stops judging pagans, his situation and fate would be different from the case of pagans (cf. Rom 1:32). This reality makes Paul's argument in 2:1 directionless.³⁴ Why, then, does Paul put this contingent case in the flow of his argument at the risk of breaking his solid argument? Campbell claims that JT cannot answer this question and that it is therefore another case of textual overdetermination for JT.

Sixth, the reference to repentance in Rom 2:4–5b is unnecessary. According to JT, the idea that no one can be saved through his/her deeds is found in 1:18—3:30, which Campbell designates as the non-Christian phase. Only from Rom 3:21 can humans experience salvation through faith. However, Campbell argues that even though the function of Rom 2:4–5b is to indicate the foolishness of the judge, the reference to repentance is unnecessary in the flow of the argument. This situation may give an impression that *"Romans 2 views repentance as a possibility in the non-Christian phase."*³⁵ If this is so, the whole flow of the argument becomes messy. Contrary to Paul's proclamation that, owing to their lack of perfect deeds, all humans cannot be saved, the reader may construct a

32. Ibid., 360–62.
33. Ibid., 363, 365.
34. Ibid., 365.
35. Ibid., 367. Italics his.

possible scenario in which humans, without the divine salvation process and without faith, can escape God's wrath by way of repentance. Thus, Campbell designates the reference to repentance in 2:4–5b as a textual overdetermination.

Seventh, it is superfluous to mention a contrast between the salvation of the righteous and the condemnation of the wicked in Rom 2:6–10. This is an embarrassing place in the flow of JT. Although the focus in the problem part of JT is on the incapability of humans and their doom under God's wrath, 2:6–10 states the salvation of the righteous as well as the damnation of the sinner. Campbell also asks whether the purely righteous or purely wicked person can exist. According to him, the text shows an absolute dichotomy, and there is no gray zone between them. The good are entirely seeking after eternal life through their good works, and the wicked keep pursuing disobedience to the truth. It is almost impossible. Why, then, does Paul include this part in unfolding his argument? In light of JT, this question has never been raised or answered. So, Campbell regards the contrast in 2:6–10 as another instance of textual overdetermination.

Eighth, Campbell lists several difficulties in the expression κατὰ τὸ εὐαγγέλιόν μου διὰ Χριστοῦ Ἰησοῦ ("[God will judge] according to my gospel through Christ Jesus") in 2:16b. First, he questions the role of the phrase "my gospel" in this verse. It is redundant, and it also has the danger of implying that "the surrounding material is not according to [Paul's] gospel."[36] Second, the reference to Christ Jesus as the criterion of God's judgment in 2:16b lacks precedent in the context. Paul never mentions Jesus as the criterion until 2:16; before that he speaks only of human deeds as an important element that God evaluates. Third, there is no evidence of Christ's punitive function in the Pauline corpus with regard to the non-Christian condition. Even in Romans, Christ's image as a judge does not go well with the other parts of the letter. In addition, since Campbell rejects other passages, such as 2 Thess 1:6–10 and Eph 1:9–10, 22–23, and so on as the secondary and later legacy of Pauline teaching, he still asserts that there is no direct evidence of Christ's eschatological judging position in the Pauline letters.[37] Because of these reasons, Campbell concludes that Rom 2:16b contains very awkward expressions that do not match with JT's reading.

36. Ibid., 368.
37. Ibid., 370.

Ninth, Paul's attack on the Jews in Rom 2:21-23 does not fit with JT. This part tells about the hypocritical sinfulness of the Jews, such as theft, adultery, and temple robbery (ἱεροσυλέω). Campbell points out that it is inappropriate to think that all Jews commit such sinful behavior, although this list can refer to the sinfulness of specific Jews. Using temple robbery is an especially poor choice because, according to Campbell, it was not a typical sin in Judaism. The presentation of temple robbery as the counterpart to idolatry is also not readily understandable. It would be simpler to say, "You who abhor idols, do you commit idolatry?" Why, then, does Paul use an inappropriate case in order to criticize Jews? Campbell insists that the content of 2:21-23 does not help the reader to follow JT's reading.

Tenth, the presence of a righteous pagan in Rom 2:14-16 is problematic. JT understands 1:18-32 to assert that all pagans are under God's wrath due to their lack of righteous deeds. According to Campbell's reading of 2:14-16, however, the text shows the possibility of the salvation of pagans. These two passages contradict each other, so JT's argument loses its credibility. With this reasoning, Campbell insists that 2:14-16 provides unnecessary information in establishing JT.[38]

Eleventh, JT's reading of Rom 2:25-29 is incorrect. According to JT's reading, Paul here redefines the identity of the Jews and pagans in relation to circumcision. Those who are circumcised can be regarded as the uncircumcised, and the uncircumcised pagans can be regarded as the circumcised, on account of their respective not keeping and keeping of the law. Campbell considers that this understanding makes JT's argumentation shaky. Basically, for him, JT's Paul moves forward his argument with an assumption that pagans have a minimal law leading them to discern God's ethical norm but Jews have the full version. However, such redefinition in 2:25-29 can break the traditional concept of the boundary between Jews and pagans, making Paul's logic inconsistent. Campbell therefore asserts that JT's reading of 2:25-29 is wrong.[39]

Campbell's Alternative Reading of Rom 1:18—3:20

Based on the premises and criticisms of the so-called traditional JT described above, Campbell suggests a brand-new reading of Rom

---

38. Ibid., 372-75; Campbell, "Rereading Romans 1-3," 146.
39. Campbell, *The Deliverance of God*, 376.

1:18—3:20. His reading progresses with a hypothetical situation in Paul's ministry that involves an individual opponent of Paul. As a learned Jew originating from Jerusalem, this opponent visited Paul's churches in Antioch, Galatians, and Philippi, causing trouble with a different soteriology based on Torah observance. Campbell conjectures that Paul knew that the Jewish Teacher would go to the Roman churches and spread false teaching since the Teacher knew Paul's interest in Roman churches. With this reconstructed situation, Campbell insists that Paul wrote a letter to the churches in Rome in order to warn the readers about the coming Jewish Teacher. Romans 1–4 is the outcome of Paul's imaginary debate with the Teacher, which contains the theological propaganda of the Teacher and Paul's attack on it.[40]

With attention to a supposed rhetorical "speech-in-character" and the vivid use of diatribal interactions, Campbell delineates the voice of the Jewish Teacher and of Paul and divides Rom 1:18—3:20 into four parts: 1:18–32; 2:1–8; 2:9–29; and 3:1–20.[41]

The first part is Rom 1:18–32. He argues that Paul is not writing the first phase of his theological concept here, but is just recapitulating the voice of the Teacher. The Teacher says that the sinful pagans are destined to see God's wrathful judgment in the future. Even though they acknowledge God's truth through the universal revelation of divine attributes, they willfully reject such revelation. As a result, they worship idols (v. 23) and indulge in homosexuality (vv. 26, 27) and in various evil deeds (vv. 28–31). They know of God's rule of judgment but do not repent of their evil deeds (v. 32).

The second part is Rom 2:1–8. Restoring his own voice in 2:1, Paul attacks the hypocrisy of the Teacher (2:1–5). Then he deduces from the Teacher's argument in 1:18–32 a universal principle about God's retributive justice in relation to human deeds: God will repay every person according to his/her deeds. This principle, then, is not an original part of Paul's theology.

---

40. Ibid., 459–518. He claims that Rom 1–3 resembles a Socratic teaching method, "which can be defined broadly as 'any rigorous examination or refutation, any testing of the interlocutor's beliefs in which these beliefs are shown to be false or incoherent . . .' with the further critical proviso that this is achieved strictly in their own terms" (cited from Kahn, *Plato and the Socratic Dialogue*, 110; Campbell, "Rereading Romans 1–3," 145).

41. Campbell, *The Deliverance of God*, 542–93.

The third part is Rom 2:9–29. With the universal principle of retributive justice above, Paul attacks the Teacher's theory by demonstrating its inconsistency and awkward implications. In 2:9–16, he nullifies the privileged state of the Jews over pagans by mentioning the cases of righteous pagans and unrighteous Jews. They will be saved and condemned respectively according to the universalized principle. Paul also challenges the Jewish Christian Teacher at Rome in 2:17–29. While the Teacher insists on the benefits of the possession of the law and the information from it, the case of a hypocritical Jewish sage who committed theft, adultery, and temple robbery in 19 CE weakens his claim.[42] Moreover, the boasting of circumcision is useless because it is possible for the righteous uncircumcised pagans to condemn the unrighteous Jews. Thus, what Paul does in 2:9–29 is to break the Teacher's conviction that Jews and pagans are ontologically different on account of circumcision and the law.[43]

The fourth part is Rom 3:1–20. In the diatribal interaction in vv. 1–9a, Paul devalues the advantage of Jewishness in relation to God's judgment. After reaffirming the universal sinfulness of all humans by a long scriptural citation in vv. 9b–18, he concludes in vv. 19–20 that no one, including Jews and pagans, can escape from God's judgment. Campbell summarizes this reading:

> By this point in Romans it is apparent that the Teacher's gospel is incoherent. Its opening—a definition of "the problem" facing all pagans (1)—leads to a set of contradictions in relation to its continuation (2 & 3)—its purported solution in terms of circumcision and law-observance—that ultimately overrule and undermine it (4). Properly understood, this gospel—understood in its own terms—saves no one, not even its proclaimer![44]

---

42. Ibid., 561.
43. Ibid.
44. Ibid., 593.

CRITICAL RESPONSES TO CAMPBELL'S REREADING OF ROMANS

Responses to Campbell's Justification Theory

AGAINST CAMPBELL'S PREMISES OF ANALYZING JT

Are the Contract and Covenant Mutually Exclusive?

The foundation of Campbell's whole argument is the clash between the two exclusive theological approaches, Methodological Arianism (contract) and Athanasian Apocalypticism (covenant). However, many reviewers point out several problems with this issue. For example, his methodology is unsound, since the premise is not derived from Scripture but from a theoretical designation of the situation in seventeenth-century Scotland.[45] J. W. Smith also criticizes Campbell's lack of knowledge in making his contrast between Arianism and Athanasianism.[46]

I will offer two additional criticisms. One is that his use of the contrast between contract and covenant is misleading. His understanding of covenant is especially problematic. Following James Torrance's argument, he believes that a covenant related to God is always unconditional. He even insists that "a (biblical and theological) covenant is *not* a contract!"[47] It is true that a covenant is not a negotiated contract, but an absolute dichotomy between contract and covenant is questionable. There are overlapping aspects between them. Basically, a covenant is defined as "a solemn pact or agreement between two or more parties."[48] Although a covenant has several characteristics,[49] the most fundamental is that it is established only through mutual agreement or interaction between the participants, whether it is a matter of promise and fulfillment, promise and acceptance, or command and obedience. This characteristic appears in the cases of the Old Testament covenants between God and his people. These covenants consistently begin with God's unconditional self-obligation. But God's initiative itself is not everything

---

45. E.g., Seifrid, Review of *The Deliverance of God*, 308; Matlock, "Zeal for Paul but Not According to Knowledge," 124; Tilling, "Campbell's Apocalyptic Gospel and Pauline Athanasianism," 65.

46. Smith, "'Arian' Foundationalism or 'Athanasian' Apocalypticism," 78–92.

47. Campbell, "The Current Crisis," 45 n. 21. Italics his.

48. Scott, "Covenant," 491.

49. As for the characteristics, see Weinfeld, "$b^e rît$," 2:253–79; Mendenhall and Herion, "Covenant," 1:1179–1202.

involved in making a covenant relationship. Human response, whether it is expressed by verbal or nonverbal actions, is indispensable in order for a person to enter and experience the covenantal relationship.[50] For example, in the Abrahamic covenant (Gen 15:18), Abraham responds to God's unconditional initiative with faith (Gen 15:6), and after this God makes a covenant with him.[51] If Abraham keeps rejecting God's offer, it is questionable whether the covenant relationship could be established. I do not mean that God needs human help in establishing a covenant, but that the process of covenant making has some kind of mutual interaction between the participants. Thus, a covenant should not be understood as just God's unconditional promise or salvific activities, which comprise, in reality, the initial and/or final process of the covenant making. Covenant refers to the relationship between the participants from which there are promises and demands.[52] Also, various covenants in the Old Testament have the contractual nature of mutuality and legal agreement, so a clear-cut dichotomy between contract and covenant is not warranted.[53]

Moreover, not every covenant in the Old Testament is unconditional. It is true that the Noahic covenant has an unconditional nature in the sense that it is God who promises and has an obligation to perform. But the Sinai covenant is apparently conditional, because a person maintains the covenantal relationship only through fulfilling the obligations that God gives to humans.[54] Also, this covenant has a renewable character. Unlike an unconditional covenant, the Old Testament shows that this covenant not only was broken by the Israelites, but was also renewed and restored by God or Israel's leaders (e.g., Deut 29–30; Josh 24:1–28;

---

50. McConville, "בְּרִית," 1:752; Dumbrell, *Covenant and Creation*, 2. A unique case is the Noahic covenant in Gen 6:18 and 9:8–17. It does not seem to require human response in establishing the covenant. However, considering that the participants of this covenant are not just humans but all creatures, the absence of the response process is understandable.

51. Freedman and Miano, "People of the New Covenant," 9.

52. Dumbrell, *Covenant and Creation*, 97.

53. Buchanan, "The Covenant in Legal Context," 27–52. In contrast to Campbell's understanding, G. W. Buchanan points out that "the legal dimension of our faith has been overshadowed and overlooked by giving all of these legal treaties and contracts the sixteenth-century term of 'covenant,' which has seemed more mysterious to twenty-first century Christians and Jews than legal" (27).

54. Freedman and Miano, "People of the New Covenant," 7–8.

1 Sam 12; 2 Kgs 23:1–3). The same is also true of the Davidic covenant (e.g., Pss 89; 32:12; Isa 55:3–4; Zech 11:4–17), so it, too, can be viewed as conditional.[55] Additionally, there is no scholarly consensus on the nature of the seemingly unconditional Abrahamic covenant. While some biblical scholars view it as an unconditional covenant, others do not.[56] Consequently, it is totally inadequate to assert, relying on a theological designation, that biblical covenant between God and humans has only an unconditional aspect.

Is JT in Rom 1–4 Purely Contractual?

It is also untenable to maintain a strict dichotomy between JT's reading as only contractual and Campbell's alternative reading as covenantal. There are several reasons. First, the dichotomy between contract and covenant is not supported by Scripture.

Second, contrary to Campbell's argument, Rom 1:18—3:20 also contains covenantal concepts. A good example is in 3:1–8. In the course of diatribal interaction, Paul points out the sinfulness of the Jews and defends God's righteous judgment. God will also be a judge to Jews who have the privilege of being entrusted with God's oracles but are not faithful to them. Here, to be entrusted with God's oracles means to enter into a covenantal relationship. God's judgment to the unfaithful refers to his covenantal faithfulness, because in establishing the covenant, he has already announced the curse to those who are unfaithful to the covenant relationship (e.g., Deut 28:15–68).[57] All are against the backdrop of covenant. Thus, the notion that Rom 1:18—3:20 only deals with a contract is wrong.

Third, the interactions in Rom 1:18—4:25 always begin with God. Romans 1:18 mentions God's wrath on sinful humans, but this wrath is the last phase in the interaction between God and humans. The first phase is God's revelation of his divine attributes as the Creator, and this phase is positive in nature. Likewise, in the interaction between God

---

55. Freedman and Miano, "People of the New Covenant," 13–18.

56. For example, T. D. Alexander and Paul R. Williamson distinguish the covenants in Gen 15 and 17 and argue that the former is unconditional and the latter conditional (Alexander, "Abraham Re-Assessed Theologically"; Williamson, "Covenant," 147). H. Hegermann also states that "in the theology of $b^e r\hat{\imath}t$ sayings of the OT a bilateral commitment is established along with the one-sided obligatory actions, as in the pattern of relationship to a sovereign" ("διαθήκη," 1:299).

57. Cf. Moo, *Romans*, 185; Osborne, *Romans*, 82.

and believers in Rom 3:21–26, it is God who begins the process with the cross of Christ. Thus, to regard Rom 1:18—4:25 as a human-initiated contract is wrong.

Fourth, Campbell's understanding of faith in JT is not convincing. He believes that faith in JT is another kind of work that makes a contract between God and humans. As I mentioned above, however, human response to God's initiative is indispensable for a person to participate in the covenantal relationship. In the Old Testament, faith appears as the key element of human response. Moreover, considering the connection between the blood of Jesus and the promised new covenant (e.g., Luke 22:20; 1 Cor 11:25; Heb 9:15; 12:24), faith in Rom 3:21–26 should be viewed as an element of the covenantal relationship. Therefore, unlike Campbell's JT, the nature of Rom 1:18—4:25 is not purely contractual. Rather, the text shows that it also has a covenantal nature.

Is Ethics the Main Concern of Rom 1:18—3:20 in JT?

Campbell also believes that the main thrust of Rom 1:18—3:20 in JT is ethics. However, there are two problems in this assumption.

The first problem is his dichotomous view of the relationship between contract and covenant. This assumption comes from his understanding that JT's reading of Rom 1:18—3:20 is contractual. Since this section of the letter is about the contract between God and humans, the main issue is ethics. However, such a clear dichotomy does not exist, so his argument is groundless.

The second one is his view of sin. According to Campbell, the fundamental human problem is moral or ethical incapacity. But the text diagnoses the human situation differently. Let me provide some examples. The first comes from Rom 1:18–23. Verses 20–23 describe human sinfulness as having two aspects. One is the internal cognitive aspect, such as foolishness and ignorance (vv. 21b–22), and the other is the external behavioral and attitudinal aspect, such as dishonoring God and worshiping creatures (vv. 21a, 23). This sinfulness is not just related to moral issues, because it is mentioned as the human response to the revelation of the Creator (1:19–20). Moreover, this sinfulness is none other than human oppression of God's truth (1:18).[58] Thus, what 1:18–23 deals with is human reactions to God, and the sinfulness addressed in this part

---

58. Lee, *Paul's Gospel in Romans*, 150.

of the letter consists of negative responses to God, the Creator, and his covenantal relationship with humans.[59]

The second example comes from Rom 2:6–11. The issue in this passage is not just one of human ethical practice. Verse 8 says that God will inflict wrath on those who obey unrighteousness and not the truth. This depiction is very similar to 1:18 in that both mention "truth," "unrighteousness," and God's judgment. Accordingly, the truth here refers to God and his attributes revealed through the creatures. Thus, what God wants to see from human beings in 2:6–11 is not just morality but their fulfillment of the obligations derived from their relationship with God, the Creator.

Furthermore, Rom 1:28–31 shows the nature of human sin very clearly. This part explains God's wrath in relation to the internal cognitive aspect of human sinfulness mentioned in 1:21–22. The text states two kinds of human sin. One, addressed in 1:28a, is humans' willful rejection of God in spite of their knowledge (ἐπίγνωσις). This is the core of human sinfulness. The other, addressed in vv. 29–31, consists of various moral vices. It is significant to take notice of the relations between the two. Moral vices do not come first. They are derived from the core of human sinfulness as a result of God's wrath (v. 28b).[60] Therefore, the heart of the human problem is not moral incapacity but humans' rejection of their God and their relationship with the Creator. In relation to the core of the human problem, the assumption of Campbell's JT is misleading.

Problems in Campbell's Apocalyptic Reading of Rom 5–8

I agree that Rom 5–8 has an apocalyptic nature,[61] but there are several problems with Campbell's understanding. I will here address two such problems that are related to one another.[62]

---

59. Dumbrell links human ethical issues to the covenant relationship with the Creator: "Moral legislation in the Bible always takes place within a framework of relationship established by covenant. We may instance the Decalogue (cf. Exod. 20:1–17) and Jesus' new covenant admonition of John (14:15): 'If you love me, you will keep my commandments.' Within divine biblical relationships, obedience follows, and is enabled by, covenant grace. We may suppose that the same order of creation—grace and then demand (cf. Gen. 2:17)—underlines the known moral demands inherent for humanity by the act of creation" (Dumbrell, *Covenant and Creation*, 12).

60. Lee, *Paul's Gospel in Romans*, 125–26.

61. Ibid., 435–39. However, unlike Campbell, I view Rom 5:12 as the beginning of the apocalyptic framework.

62. As for the critique of Campbell's understanding of Rom 5–8, see the articles in

The first one concerns the individual aspect of sin. For Campbell, Rom 5–8 does not deal with personal sinfulness. The target of God's future wrath (e.g., Rom 5:9) is personalized universal sin and death. However, the text shows a different picture. The verb ἁμαρτάνω ("to sin") appears four times (5:12, 14, 16; 6:15), and all instances indicate personal sinful acts. Among them, the instances in 5:14 and 16 refer to Adam's disobedience, and those in 5:12 and 6:15 are about personal sinfulness. I will focus on the latter two. Romans 5:12 explains the beginning of the Adamic realm, where sin and death rule over all humans. Death entered into the world on account of Adam's disobedience, and it spread to all human beings, because all have sinned (ἐφ' ᾧ πάντες ἥμαρτον). Apparently, the third-person-plural verb ἥμαρτον indicates the personal and actual sins of individual humans. Romans 6:15 features a diatribal question, "Are we to sin (ἁμαρτήσωμεν) because we are not under law but under grace?" (ESV). Even though Paul answers this question in the negative, he still admits the possibility of Christians committing sins. This case also appears to be concerned with personal sinful acts, as the text clearly demonstrates that, under the dominion of sin, each person still commits personal sins. Thus, Campbell's view is incorrect.

The second problem is his denial of God's retributive justice. This denial is derived from his disavowal of individual sinfulness in Rom 5–8 and his emphasis on God's unconditional and universal love. As I have mentioned above, however, individual sin appears in this part of the letter. Other passages in Paul's letters also mention God's wrathful judgment upon those who sin personally against God (e.g., Phil 1:28; 1 Thess 1:9–10; 2:16; cf. Gal 6:7). Moreover, God's grace and wrath go hand in hand in the covenantal relationship. If human participants reject God's graceful initiation and are unfaithful in their relationship with God, God responds to them with his justice, which is his faithfulness to the covenantal relationship. If there is no response from God to the sinners, God's initial grace becomes universalism. Actually, several scholars feel uncomfortable with Campbell's argument because his excessive emphasis on God's unconditional grace seems to be similar to the view of universal salvation, which the Bible does not support.[63]

Schreiner et al., eds., *Four Views on the Apostle Paul*, esp. 144–58.

63. Hilborn, "A Response to Campbell's 'Connecting the Dots,'" 121–22; Moo, Review of *The Deliverance of God*," 149.

In sum, Campbell's assertions regarding JT are the foundation of his whole argument. However, these assertions are not very solid, making his argument unstable.

Against Campbell's Reconstructed JT and Its Reading of Rom 1:18—3:20

Many reviewers have criticized Campbell's understanding of JT. To these criticisms I would like to address just one more point: the division of Rom 1:18—3:20 in JT. In his book *The Deliverance of God*, he says that JT divides Rom 1:18—3:20 into three parts, 1:18—2:8, 2:9—3:9a, and 3:9b–20. But in an article, he states that JT divides the same text into Rom 1:18–32, 2:1—3:9a, and 3:9b–20.[64] Which is the *real* division according to JT? More serious is the fact that, as far as I know, no such division is maintained by those whom he regards as traditional JT supporters. It seems to be *his* reading or *his* hypothetical division. R. B. Matlock's questions are appropriate: "Just whose theory of salvation is this, this 'Justification theory'? *Who reads Paul like that?*"[65]

Against Campbell's Criticism of JT's Reading of Rom 1:18—3:20

Against Textual Underdeterminations

Campbell lists four difficulties in relation to the textual underdeterminations of JT's reading of Romans. I will present and examine them one by one.

First, Campbell claims that there is no textual evidence for reading Rom 1:18—3:20 as involving a progression from plight to solution. According to him, it may be possible for Paul to present the true meaning of the gospel by moving from solution to plight. However, such a scenario does not mean that Paul will always write a letter following the pattern of "solution-plight." His aim in Rom 1:18—4:25 is not to articulate how he was converted from Judaism to Christianity or how he received the knowledge of the gospel, but to explain the contents of the gospel, namely that God saves sinners through Jesus. With this aim, the best way is to begin with the human problem that needs God's salvation, just as a doctor prescribes medicine to the patient only after diagnosing his/her disease. The same order also appears in Rom 5–8. Even though

---

64. Campbell, "An Attempt to be Understood," 182–83.
65. Matlock, "Zeal for Paul but Not According to Knowledge," 123. Italics his.

Campbell believes that this section of the letter is the center of Paul's soteriology, Paul does not describe his gospel with the structure of solution-plight. On the contrary, Paul unfolds his argument with Adam's sin and its result (5:12–14) and then introduces Christ's work as a counterpart (5:15–21). This indicates that the fundamental order in explaining God's salvation in the gospel is plight-solution. If the order of the "real gospel" is plight-solution, it is fully possible that Rom 1:18—4:25 also has the same order.

Second, Campbell believes that the text never shows a rational man or God's retributive justice. However, he misunderstands the nature of human sin in Rom 1:18–32. The depiction of human sin in vv. 21–23 is not about ethical incapacity; sin here is a willful resistance to the truth that God revealed and made known to humans through his creation. In this passage human beings are depicted as rational. The same appears to be true of the humans in v. 28. They can think and determine (ἐδοκίμασαν) whether it is good for them to include God as an important element in their cognitive systems. Their sinfulness comes from their unworthy thinking (ἀδόκιμον νοῦν). Basically, God's retributive response is toward their willful determination to deny God as God and to reject their relationship with him. In this sense, the text clearly presents humans as rational beings who can interact with God in spite of their limited knowledge of him. Thus, Campbell's reading is incorrect.

Third, Campbell agrees with JT about whom Paul is talking about in Rom 1:18–32, that is, gentiles,[66] but he disagrees with JT about who is in view in 2:1, that is, in Campbell's opinion, Jews. However, he and his understanding of JT take no heed of the textual evidence. One piece of evidence is διό ("therefore") in 2:1. If the people in 1:18–32 and 2:1 are different, it would be illogical for Paul to use such an inferential conjunction. It would mean that as a result of the interaction between the sinfulness of gentiles and God's wrath, the Jews, who judge gentiles, are also without excuse. The most logical way to connect 1:18–32 and 2:1 in Campbell's interpretation would be with "in the same way also" (ὡς or ὥσπερ), not "therefore." However, there is no textual variant for this. It is better to interpret 1:18–32 and 2:1 as dealing with the same group, both Jews and gentiles. If this is the case, Paul first shows the overall description of the human sinful situation with a third-person-

---

66. Instead of pagans, I will use gentiles, which is more focused on the racial distinction between Jews and non-Jews.

plural reference in 1:18–32. Then he provides a more vivid depiction of human sinfulness by narrowing down the focus to the second person in the hypothetical dialogue.[67]

Moreover, there is no need to suppose that the third-person references in 1:18–32 are only related to gentiles, for several reasons. First, when Paul refers to the beneficiary of God's wrath, he uses ἀνθρώπων ("men"; 1:18), not Ἕλληνι ("Greek"; 1:16) or ἔθνη ("gentiles"; 2:14). Second, the use of "all" in 1:16 and 18 indicate that there is no distinction between Jews and gentiles with regard to both God's salvation and wrath. Third, it is unlikely that the mention of the revelation of God's attributes (1:19–20) and the description of human suppression of divine truth (1:21–23) only apply to gentiles. Fourth, it is nonsense to think that the vice lists in 1:29–31 are only about the sinfulness of gentiles. They happen in every society in every generation. Thus, it is not very convincing to interpret the person in Rom 2:1 as different from those in Rom 1:18–32.[68]

Lastly, Campbell criticizes the issue of perfect obedience to the law in JT. However, there are several things to consider in his argument. First, the NPP's view does not yet persuade every New Testament scholar. Many people still maintain the traditional perspective.[69] Second, he does not consider the nature of sin. The core of sin is not just the breaking of ethical norms, but the rejection of God as the center of one's worldview (Rom 1:21–23, 28). This issue has the nature of "all or nothing." There is no gray area about the fact that two masters cannot sit on the same throne in one's heart and mind (cf. Matt 6:24). It is on the basis of this core sin that God inflicts his wrath against humans (Rom 1:28). Accordingly, every sinful activity in Rom 1:18—3:20 is fundamentally related to humans' lack of "perfectness" with regard to their relationship with God. There is no sin that does not break the relationship between God the Creator and humans, nor is there a sin that does not deserve God's wrath. Thus, Campbell's conclusion that there is no perfectionism in Rom 1:18—3:20 is misleading.

---

67. Lee, *Paul's Gospel in Romans*, 131–37.

68. For a more detailed explanation, see ibid., 109–10.

69. E.g., Carson et al., *Justification and Variegated Nomism*; Kim, *Paul and the New Perspective*; Westerholm, *Perspectives Old and New on Paul*.

Bible

Against Textual Overdeterminations

Campbell lists eleven textual overdeterminations, but his criticsms also have difficulties. First, the theory of interpolation regarding Rom 1:18-32 is the least convincing. Is this part not Pauline because of its sophisticated expressions? Is it unfit for the logical flow of the letter because of its well-articulated structure? That is nonsense! Paul is a highly competent letter writer, and he uses manifold stylistic features in composing his letters with Greek and Jewish material and various communication methods.[70] Contrary to Campbell's belief, the well-structured argument can be good evidence for Pauline authorship.[71] Moreover, the order in which Campbell reads Romans is problematic. It is Paul who is writing a letter to his intended audience with his own purpose. He has the authority over his writing and controls the overall logical flow of his text. We should seek to understand Paul's intention only from his expression in the text, not from our presupposed framework or theological agenda. Therefore, it is unwarranted to suggest that Rom 1:18-32 is unnecessary to Paul's argument.

Second, Campbell's understanding of the temporal conflict between Rom 1:18 and 19-32 is also problematic. The structure of Rom 1:18-32 does not allow it to break into the two separate sections of vv. 18 and 19-32. Thematically, v. 18 provides three components, God's truth, human suppression of that truth with unrighteousness, and God's wrath, and the following material gives additional explanation of them. The first element is explained in vv. 19-20 as the revealed attributes of God, the Creator. The second one is expounded in vv. 21-23, which addresses internal and external aspects of human sinfulness. The third element is articulated in vv. 24-32, in which God appears as the subject of παραδίδωμι ("hand over") in relation to the two aspects of human sinfulness. Verses 24-27 refer to God's wrath on the external sin of "exchange," and vv. 28-32 are about his judgment on the internal sinfulness, their cognitive rejection of God. The whole of 1:18-32 explains one interactive process between God and humans: God's revelation (truth)—human rejection—God's response to humans with wrath.[72] Thus, contrary to what Campbell thinks, there is no temporal difference in this part.

---

70. For discussion of Paul's communicative techniques, see McDonald and Porter, *Early Christianity and Its Sacred Literature*, 342-52; Porter, "Paul of Tarsus," 567-84.

71. Kruse, *Paul's Letter to the Romans*, 83 nn. 3, 4.

72. For the structure, see Lee, *Paul's Gospel in Romans*, 101-2.

Third, Campbell thinks that the sinfulness of the gentiles is collective because of the third-person-plural references. This is very unlikely. There is no rule dictating that the third-person-plural references should be viewed as collective.

Fourth, Campbell comments that the intertextual relationship with Wisdom of Solomon in Rom 1–3 is unnecessary in the flow of the argument. However, I wonder whether his comparison between the two texts is necessary in interpreting Paul's expression and logic. It is unclear whether Paul actually has the Wisdom of Solomon in mind. Moreover, if Paul did have it in mind, then Campbell's view that Rom 2:1–5 is about a Jew is hard to maintain. Wisdom of Solomon mentions that God's grace is not only for the Jews, but also for the gentiles (Wis 11:23 [about Egyptians]; 12:10 [about Canaanites]).[73] Thus, Campbell's argument regarding intertextuality is not convincing.

Fifth, Campbell questions whether the role of the person in Rom 2:1–5, whose problem is judging other people, is appropriate in the flow of Paul's argument. He seems to take no heed of the voice of the text. The main issue in 2:1 is not about one's judgment of others but the lack of performing righteous deeds. The behavioral dimension appears as the main reason for God's judgment in 2:2.[74]

Sixth, Campbell says that the mention of repentance in 2:4–5b is unnecessary and makes the flow messy. This claim results from his misunderstanding of the rhetorical function of these verses. If 1:18–32 and 2:1 are about the same group, as I have mentioned above, the interlocutor in 2:4–5b shares the same fundamental sinful nature. They do not want to accept God as their God (1:28) and do not repent (1:32). Accordingly, there is no possibility for the interlocutor in 2:4–5b to repent. The aim of this expression is not to give hope to the interlocutor, but to demonstrate his or her sinfulness. Contrary to Campbell's thought, 2:4–5b is necessary to show the willful disobedience of sinful humans. Even though they know God's grace, they reject it and adhere to their sinfulness.

Seventh, for Campbell, two contrasting groups in Rom 2:6–10 are unrealistic, so this part does not align with JT's reading. It is true that in the real world after the fall, there is no purely good or evil person. However, he does not consider several aspects of these verses. One as-

---

73. Ibid., 132–33.
74. Ibid., 134; Wilckens, *Der Brief an die Römer*, 1:23–24; Schreiner, *Romans*, 107; contra Barrett, *Romans*, 44.

pect is the function of 2:6–11. Focusing on the human response, these verses introduce God's principle in dealing with his creation, which is the last phase of the interaction between God and humans. Accordingly, it is understandable to set up two contrasting groups in order to explain God's just response to humans. Even though Campbell knows the function of 2:6–11, he denies it in order to establish his alternative reading.

Another aspect is the nature of sin. The good and evil in this part do not simply refer to moral activities. Rather, it is about the human response to the revelation of God's attributes, his will, and humans' relationship with their Creator. In light of human morality, absolute and perfect goodness is impossible. However, with regard to sin in relation to God, the concept of a "half sin" does not exist. Every sin is sin, and it breaks people's relationship with God. In this sense, there are only two kinds of people with regard to sin, sinners and non-sinners.

The third aspect is the rhetorical intention. Setting up two contrasting groups is not to give the hope of human-initiative salvation to the readers. On the contrary, Paul's intention is to show that all humans are undeserving of God's salvation because of their sin. Thus, contrary to Campbell's understanding, the contrasting groups that explain God's dealings with humans in 2:6–10 are pertinent to the flow of the argument.

Eighth, Campbell argues that the image of Christ as a judge in JT does not align with Romans and Pauline theology. However, he does not consider what the nature of letter writing is. The letter is a contingent-sensitive genre. Even though the writer has information on various topics, if a certain topic is not relevant to the audience, there is no need for the author to write about it. In this sense, the fact that Paul does not write about Christ as the Judge does not indicate his ignorance of this knowledge. It is more probable that Paul and the Roman church already shared the knowledge of Christ's return as the Judge according to what Christ himself taught in the Gospels (e.g., Matt 16:27; 25:31–33; Mark 13:26–27; John 5:22, 26–27; cf. Acts 10:42). Moreover, contrary to Campbell's claim, the concept of Christ as the Judge appears in 2 Cor 5:10, which he regards as part of the so-called genuine Pauline corpus.[75] Here, Paul depicts Christ as the Judge who will perform his retributive justice with the principle that each person will be rewarded in accor-

---

75. "For we must all appear before *the judgment seat of Christ*, so that each one may receive what is due for what he has done in the body, whether good or evil" (ESV).

dance with his or her deeds. This principle is the same one mentioned in Rom 2:6–11. Thus, Campbell's argument is unconvincing.

Ninth, Campbell claims that the content of Rom 2:21–23 does not help in following JT's reading. He insists that Roman Christians would have understand what Paul says in this part because there was an actual historical person for the case of temple robbery mentioned in 2:21b–22.[76] However, he does not consider that the actual person is not the Jewish teacher, whom he establishes as the real opponent of Paul. That is, if the historical example in 19 CE makes the Roman church understand the sinfulness of the Jewish teacher, it is also possible that the same example makes the Roman church evaluate the sinfulness of the Jews. Thus, since JT and his alternative reading have the same problem, his critique of JT's reading of 2:21–22 is meaningless.

Tenth, Campbell contends that Rom 2:14–16 does not harmonize with JT because it deals with the possibility of the salvation of gentiles. This, too, results from his misinterpretation of the text. The text never mentions the salvation of gentiles. Romans 2:14 says that if the gentiles do what the law requires by nature, their actions are a law to themselves (οὗτοι . . . ἑαυτοῖς εἰσιν νόμος). We should take note of the expression; Paul never says that they will be saved, but that the gentiles come to be in the same state as the Jews, who already have the law. In other words, the gentiles who do the law by nature can stand at the same starting line as the Jews. Final salvation is another matter. Both Jews and gentiles should run their own race by keeping God's will through the law in order to receive God's positive response as in Rom 2:6–11.[77] However, Paul does not mention their salvation even in Rom 2:15–16. Thus, Campbell's reading cannot be supported by the text.

Lastly, according to Campbell, JT's reading of Rom 2:25–29 is wrong because it redefines the identity of both Jews and gentiles. However, the text itself does not support such an interpretation. What vv. 23–26 say is that if the uncircumcised gentiles obey the law by nature, they can be regarded as being in the same state as the Jews with respect to the law. Of course, this does not mean they are saved. Just as in the case of the law in 2:14–16, what Paul wants to convey is that without obeying the law the identity marker of the Jews is meaningless for salvation. Thus, JT

---

76. Campbell, *The Deliverance of God*, 561.
77. Lee, *Paul's Gospel in Romans*, 160–64.

does not misunderstand the text; rather, Campbell misunderstands the text and ascribes this misunderstanding to JT.

Response to Campbell's Alternative Reading

Based on his critique of JT, Campbell establishes an alternative reading of Rom 1:18—3:20. As far as I know, his reading is unique in the history of the interpretation of Romans. Many reviewers have evaluated his reading in various ways. Here I would like to add just two points of criticism.

First, I am doubtful of his ability to catch the echoes concerning the opponent in Romans. The fundamental assumption of his rereading of Romans is the existence of the Jewish Teacher. He believes that 1:18—3:20 is Paul's dialogue with the Teacher, and his reading seems to involve finding the echoes concerning this Teacher. He asserts that he can delineate the voices of Paul and the Teacher by examining features such as speech-in-character. However, his division of the text, especially in relation to the diatribes in Romans, plants a seed of doubt about his ability to hear the echoes. There are several examples. One is that he splits Rom 3:9 into two parts and puts each part into different units. Romans 3:9a is the first question of the diatribal interaction, and Rom 3:9b is its answer. In this case Campbell's method has led him to split a verse that cannot be split—or at least ought not to be split—casting doubt on the reliability of his method.

Similar things happen in his interpretation of Rom 5–8, where he believes he finds the true gospel of Paul. In his article "Christ and the Church in Paul: A 'Post-New Perspective' Account," Campbell explains Paul's main argument in Rom 5–8 with four main sections, 5:12–21; 6:1–23; 7:7–25; and 8:1–13. The problem is his subdivision of these sections. He divides 7:7–25 into vv. 7–13, 14–24, and 25.[78] Even though another diatribal question appears after v. 7, in v. 13, he neglects it altogether and regards v. 14 as the beginning of another unit. Likewise, with regard to 6:1–23, he seems to view vv. 1–12 as one unit and vv. 13–23 as another. Here, too, he does not consider the existence of the diatribal question and answer. In addition, he treats 7:1–4 as an isolated unit. However, these verses should be connected to 6:15–23 for two reasons. One is

---

78. Campbell, "Christ and the Church in Paul," 134–35.

that, unlike the other parts of 6:1—7:25, where the new unit begins with a diatribal question (6:1, 15; 7:7, 13), 7:1 begins with "or" (ἤ). This indicates that 7:1 is not the beginning of a new unit, but another sub-unit connected to 6:23. Another reason is that 7:1–4 has a topical connection with regard to one's state under the law. Consequently, 7:1–4 appears to be a follow-up of the argument in 6:15–23.[79] But Campbell does not seem interested in these relations. All the cases noted above are related to the diatribal interaction, which is the best resource for hearing the echoes of Paul's counterpart. Nevertheless, Campbell consistently fails to catch the significance of this textual voice, and it makes us doubt his capacity to hear the echoes of the Teacher in Romans.

The second criticism that I want to add concerns the participants in Rom 1:18–32 and 2:1–5. This is a matter of life and death for his rereading because his rereading is mainly built upon the idea that Rom 1:18–32 is about the sinfulness of gentiles and that Rom 2:1 is about that of the Jew. However, as I have pointed out, it is more persuasive to say that both Rom 1:18–32 and 2:1–5 deal with the same group. If my argument is correct, his whole argument cannot be maintained. He has confidence in his rereading on the basis of his ability to hear the echoes of the Teacher, but I still doubt whether what he hears is the real voice of Paul's Teacher.

CONCLUSION

So far I have investigated Campbell's innovative interpretation of Romans. I now summarize and give an overall evaluation of it through the metaphor of building a house. Through his lenses, he looks at the seemingly old house, that is, the traditional understanding of Rom 1:18—3:20, and thinks that the old house is very problematic and awkward. Then he analyzes and deconstructs the old house with his interpretation of the text. Lastly, he selects a totally brand new kind of house based on the voices in the dialogue between Paul and the Jewish Teacher.

However, there are fatal mistakes at every stage of this process. At the first stage, his premises are not solid. Especially problematic is the fact that the clear-cut dichotomy between contract and covenant is not supported in Scripture. Also, his belief that Rom 1:18—3:20 is about

---

79. Garlington, *Faith, Obedience and Perseverance*, 116; Porter, "A Newer Perspective on Paul," 384–85; Witherington, *Paul's Letter to the Romans*, 167–78; Lee, *Paul's Gospel in Romans*, 333.

human ethical incapacity is groundless. This part of Romans is about the relationship between God, who is the Creator and gracious initiator, and humans. Their relationship consists of their progressive interaction: God's initiative—negative human response to God—God's just response/reward to human beings. The main focus is on the human response and its result. Although it is true that the apocalyptic framework appears in Rom 5:12—8:39, the framework of the interactive relationship between God and humans stands on its own in explaining the problem of all humans.

At the second stage, his analysis of the old house and his deconstructing process are also problematic. His analyzed old house can be rejected, because his premises are inadequate. Additionally, in the deconstruction process, he confuses bystanders because the kind of house he is breaking apart is not clear. Some of what he tries to break really exists in the old house, as with the issue of perfect obedience in relation to God's positive response, but most of his criticisms seem to come from the imposition of his own erroneous reading onto his reconstructed target house, JT. For example, he aims to break a window in showing that Rom 1:18—3:20 deals with ethical issues, but there is no such window in the old house. Also, he is trying to destroy the picture that hangs on the wall by saying that Rom 2:14–16 is about the salvation of the gentiles, but such a picture does not exist in the old house.

At the third stage, his alternative house is not solid. He builds a new house with the echoes of the dialogue between Paul and his real opponent, a Jewish Teacher. However, in spite of his strong claim to hear the voice of the opponent, it is doubtful that he has the capacity to catch the echoes of the voice of the Teacher. This is because he does not concentrate on the diatribal interaction in Romans.

For these reasons, this essay concludes that Campbell's attack cannot shake the foundation of the traditional understanding of Paul's gospel. This means that using Rom 1:18—3:20 to answer the topical question "Is the gospel good news?" gives a helpful answer, because all humans are under God's wrath, as Rom 1:18—3:20 indicate, and there is no way aside from Christ for humans to escape from their present and future situation. This situation comes as a result of humans' sinfulness in not wanting to accept God, the Creator, as God and in rejecting a God-initiated relationship with him. The gospel analyzes the human predicament correctly and provides two options for all human beings.

One is to die with their sinfulness, and the other is to experience God's salvation through Jesus. The choice is theirs.

BIBLIOGRAPHY

Alexander, T. D. "Abraham Re-Assessed Theologically." In *He Swore an Oath: Biblical Themes from Genesis 12–50*, edited by R. Hess et al., 7–23. Cambridge: Tyndale, 1993.

Barrett, C. K. *A Commentary on the Epistle to the Romans*. London: Adam & Charles Black, 1957.

Brown, Alexandra. Review of *The Deliverance of God: An Apocalyptic Rereading of Justification in Paul*, by Douglas A. Campbell. *ThTo* 68 (2011) 85–88.

Buchanan, G. W. "The Covenant in Legal Context." In *The Concept of the Covenant in the Second Temple Period*, edited by S. E. Porter and J. C. R. de Roo, 27–52. Supplements to the Journal for the Study of Judaism 71. Leiden: Brill, 2003.

Campbell, Douglas A. "An Apocalyptic Rereading of 'Justification' in Paul: Or, an Overview of the Argument of Douglas Campbell's *The Deliverance of God*—by Douglas Campbell." *ExpTim* 123 (2012) 382–93.

———. "An Attempt to be Understood: A Response to the Concerns of Matlock and Macaskill with *The Deliverance of God*." *JSNT* 34 (2011) 162–208.

———. "Christ and the Church in Paul: A 'Post-New Perspective' Account." In *Four Views on the Apostle Paul*, edited by T. R. Schreiner et al., 113–43. Grand Rapids: Zondervan, 2012.

———. "The Current Crisis: The Capture of Paul's Gospel by Methodological Arianism." In *Beyond Old and New Perspectives on Paul*, edited by Chris Tilling, 37–48. Eugene, OR: Cascade, 2014.

———. *The Deliverance of God: An Apocalyptic Rereading of Justification in Paul*. Grand Rapids: Eerdmans, 2009.

———. "Douglas Campbell's Response to Brittany E. Wilson." In *Beyond Old and New Perspectives on Paul*, edited by Chris Tilling, 192–95. Eugene, OR: Cascade, 2014.

———. "Douglas Campbell's Response to Chris Tilling." In *Beyond Old and New Perspectives on Paul*, edited by Chris Tilling, 74–77. Eugene, OR: Cascade, 2014.

———. "Rereading Romans 1–3." In *Beyond Old and New Perspectives on Paul*, edited by Chris Tilling, 133–60. Eugene, OR: Cascade, 2014.

———. "What Is at Stake in the Reading of Romans 1–3? An Elliptical Response to the Concerns of Gorman and Tilling." *JSPL* 1 (2011) 113–37.

Carson, D. A., et al., eds. *Justification and Variegated Nomism*. 2 vols. WUNT 2.140; 2.181. Tübingen: Mohr Siebeck; Grand Rapids: Eerdmans, 2001–2004.

Cayzer, Jeffrey F. Review of *The Deliverance of God: An Apocalyptic Rereading of Justification in Paul*, by Douglas A. Campbell. *Review of Biblical Literature* (2013). https://www.bookreviews.org/bookdetail.asp?TitleId=7267&CodePage=7267

Cousar, Charles B. Review of *The Deliverance of God: An Apocalyptic Rereading of Justification in Paul*, by Douglas A. Campbell. *Int* 64 (2010) 414–16.

De Boer, Martinus C. Review of *The Deliverance of God: An Apocalyptic Rereading of Justification in Paul*, by Douglas A. Campbell. *CBQ* 73 (2011) 610–11.

Dumbrell, W. J. *Covenant and Creation*. Crownhill, UK: Paternoster, 2013.

Fiore, Benjamin. Review of *The Deliverance of God: An Apocalyptic Rereading of Justification in Paul*, by Douglas A. Campbell. *TS* 72 (2011) 191–93.

Bible

Freedman, D. L. and D. Miano. "People of the New Covenant." In *The Concept of the Covenant in the Second Temple Period*, edited by S. E. Porter and J. C. R. de Roo, 7–26. Supplements to the Journal for the Study of Judaism 71. Leiden: Brill, 2003.

Garlington, Don. *Faith, Obedience, and Perseverance: Aspects of Paul's Letter to the Romans*. WUNT 79. Tübingen: Mohr Siebeck, 1994.

Gaventa, B. R. "Rescue Mission: A Review of *Deliverance of God: An Apocalyptic Rereading of Justification in Paul* by Douglas A. Campbell." *ChrCent* 127 (2010) 36–37.

Gorman, Michael. "Douglas Campbell's *The Deliverance of God*: A Review by a Friendly Critic." *JSPL* 1 (2011) 99–107.

Hegermann, H. "διαθήκη." In *EDNT* 1:299–301.

Hilborn, D. "A Response to Campbell's 'Connecting the Dots.'" In *Beyond Old and New Perspectives on Paul*, edited by Chris Tilling, 114–23. Eugene, OR: Cascade, 2014.

Jewett, R. *Romans*. Hermeneia. Minneapolis: Fortress, 2007.

Jipp, J. W. "Douglas Campbell's Apocalyptic, Rhetorical Paul: Review Article." *HBT* 32 (2010) 183–97.

Kahn, Charles H. *Plato and the Socratic Dialogue: The Philosophical Use of a Literary Form*. Cambridge: Cambridge University Press, 1996.

Kim, Seyoon. *Paul and the New Perspective: Second Thought on the Origin of Paul's Gospel*. Grand Rapids: Eerdmans, 2002.

Kruse, C. G. *Paul's Letter to the Romans*. PNTC. Grand Rapids: Eerdmans, 2012.

Lee, Jae Hyun. *Paul's Gospel in Romans: A Discourse Analysis of Rom 1:16—8:39*. LBS 3. Leiden: Brill, 2010.

Macaskill, Grant. Review of *The Deliverance of God: An Apocalyptic Rereading of Justification in Paul*, by Douglas A. Campbell. *JSNT* 34 (2011) 150–61.

Matlock, R. B. "Zeal for Paul but Not According to Knowledge: Douglas Campbell's War on Justification Theory." *JSNT* 34 (2011) 115–49.

McConville, G. J. "בְּרִית." In *NIDOTTE* 1:747–55.

McDonald, Lee Martin, and Stanley E. Porter. *Early Christianity and Its Sacred Literature*. Peabody, MA: Hendrickson, 2000.

Mendenhall, G. E., and G. A. Herion. "Covenant." In *ABD* 1:1179–1202.

Moo, D. J. Review of *The Deliverance of God: An Apocalyptic Rereading of Justification in Paul*, by Douglas A. Campbell. *JETS* 53 (2010) 143–50.

———. *The Epistle to the Romans*. NICNT. Grand Rapids: Eerdmans, 1996.

Osborne, Grant R. *Romans*. IVPNTC. Downers Grove, IL: InterVarsity, 2004.

Perry, Peter S. Review of *The Deliverance of God: An Apocalyptic Rereading of Justification in Paul*, by Douglas A. Campbell. *CTM* 39 (2012) 166–67.

Porter, C. L. "Rom 1.18–32: Its Role in the Developing Argument." *NTS* 40 (1994) 210–28.

Porter, Stanley E. *Idioms of the Greek New Testament*. Sheffield: Sheffield Academic, 1992.

———. "A Newer Perspective on Paul: Romans 1–8 Through the Eyes of Literary Analysis." In *The Bible in Human Society: Essays in Honour of John Rogerson*, edited by M. Daniel Carroll R. et al., 366–92. Sheffield: Sheffield Academic, 1995.

———. "Paul of Tarsus and His Letters." In *Handbook of Classical Rhetoric in the Hellenistic Period (330 B.C–A.D. 400)*, edited by S. E. Porter, 533–85. Leiden: Brill, 1997.

Schreiner, T. R. Review of *The Deliverance of God: An Apocalyptic Rereading of Justification in Paul*, by Douglas A. Campbell. *BBR* 20 (2010) 289–90.

Schreiner, T. R., et al., eds. *Four Views on the Apostle Paul*. Grand Rapids: Zondervan, 2012.

Scott, J. M. "Covenant." In *The Eerdmans Dictionary of Early Judaism*, edited by J. J. Collins and D. C. Harlow, 491–94. Grand Rapids: Eerdmans, 2010.

Seifrid, M. Review of *Deliverance of God: An Apocalyptic Rereading of Justification in Paul*, by Douglas A. Campbell. *Them* 35 (2010) 307–9.

Smith, J. Warren. "'Arian' Foundationalism or 'Athanasian' Apocalypticism: A Patristic Assessment." In *Beyond Old and New Perspectives on Paul*, edited by Chris Tilling, 78–92. Eugene, OR: Cascade, 2014.

Tilling, Chris, ed. *Beyond Old and New Perspectives on Paul*. Eugene, OR: Cascade, 2014.

———. "Campbell's Apocalyptic Gospel and Pauline Athanasianism." In *Beyond Old and New Perspectives on Paul*, edited by Chris Tilling, 49–77. Eugene, OR: Cascade, 2014.

Torrance, J. B. "The Contribution of McLeod Campbell to Scottish Theology." *SJT* 26 (1973) 295–311.

———. "Covenant or Contract? A Study of the Theological Background of Worship in Seventeenth-Century Scotland." *SJT* 23 (1970) 51–76.

Weinfeld, M. "$b^e rit$." In *TDOT* 2:253–79.

Westerholm, Stephen. *Perspectives Old and New on Paul: The "Lutheran" Paul and His Critics*. Grand Rapids: Eerdmans, 2004.

Wilckens, Ulrich. *Der Brief an die Römer*. EKKNT. Neukirchen-Vluyn: Neukirchener, 2014.

Williamson, Paul R. "Covenant." In *Pentateuch*, Vol. 1 of *Dictionary of the Old Testament*, edited by T. D. Alexander and D. W. Baker, 139–55. Downers Grove, IL: IVP, 2003.

Witherington, Ben, III. *Paul's Letter to the Romans: A Socio-Rhetorical Commentary*. Grand Rapids: Eerdmans, 2004.

8

The Gospel as God's Gift
Good News from Ephesians 1:1—3:12

Lynn H. Cohick

INTRODUCTION

Is THE GOSPEL GOOD news for Paul? The question is a good one, to which a quick answer might hide the tremendous cost of following this good news (2 Cor 11:23–29) and, ironically, limit the scope of the good news' effect. In one of the earliest examples of shaping Paul's good news, the *Acts of Paul and Thecla* portrays Paul as an ascetic. His protégé, Thecla, embraces the virginal life amidst attacks by her family and local government officials and survives to preach the gospel. Her fame as a proto-martyr continues unabated for centuries in the early church. The church's focus on martyrdom rightly reminds us today of the importance of the body within Paul's theology. The martyrs, naturally, were focused on living faithfully now, so as to enjoy their raised body in the new heavens and new earth. I will argue that Paul's emphasis on Christ as God's gift of salvation encourages us to think about our sanctification as well, becoming like Christ in this present age. Yet the gospel as presented in the *Acts of Paul and Thecla* ignores Paul's own context of a church made up of Jews and gentiles; this could give a lopsided view of his message of good news.

I hope to demonstrate how the gospel is good news for Paul by examining Paul's message to the Ephesians from two different angles.[1] A partial answer to the question of whether the gospel is good news for Paul can be found in Paul's grappling with the ramifications of salvation in Christ for the Jew and for the Gentile. The New Perspective on Paul (NPP) is helpful here, alerting us to the contours of Second Temple Judaism with its claims of election by God and its subsequent obedience to God's law. Jews were not trying to earn salvation through the law or otherwise. Nevertheless, Paul pairs "not of yourselves" and "not by works" in Eph 2:8–9, raising the question of why his (mainly) gentile congregations would imagine their salvation to be of themselves. The NPP does not seem to offer much guidance, but a way forward is found in Paul's statement about salvation being a gift. Placing God's gracious gift within the system of benefaction or gift-giving in the ancient world provides a necessary vantage point from which to discuss the subtleties of Paul's claims. Therefore, I will examine Eph 2:8–10 through the analytical lenses of both the NPP, with its focus on Second Temple Judaism, and the Greco-Roman benefaction system, in which both gentiles and Jews participated.[2]

Having explored the context of ancient gift-giving and the various understandings of "gift" from which Paul might have drawn, we will circle back to the statement "by grace you have been saved, through faith (διὰ πίστεως)" and isolate the last phrase for analysis (Eph 2:8). The phrase διὰ πίστεως has been pulled into the wider debates surrounding the phrases that speak of our faith in Christ or Christ's own faithfulness, the πίστις Χριστοῦ phrases.[3] Typically, this discussion swirls around two poles. Most argue that the phrase signals the believer's response of faith to God's work in Christ. Some suggest it refers to Christ's faithfulness

---

1. The question of the authorship of Ephesians is a lively one, but space constraints prevent me from discussing the details. I include myself among the number of scholars who believe this epistle is in some fashion written directly by or under the direction of the apostle Paul. Gorman, *Apostle of the Crucified Lord*, 499–504; Wright, *Paul and the Faithfulness of God*, 60. See also Campbell, *Framing Paul*, 337, who argues that Ephesians should be understood as Paul's letter to the Laodiceans.

2. In *Were the Jews a Mediterranean Society?* Schwartz argues a contrasting view, claiming that Jews in the Roman period rejected institutionalized reciprocity in gift-giving; they instead focused on solidarity within the Jewish communities.

3. Διὰ πίστεως Ἰησοῦ Χριστοῦ (Rom 3:22; Gal 2:16); διὰ πίστεως Χριστοῦ (Phil 3:9); ἐκ πίστεως Χριστοῦ (Rom 3:26; Gal 2:16); ἐκ πίστεως Ἰησοῦ Χριστοῦ (Gal 3:22); ἐν πίστει (Gal 2:20).

as demonstrated by his death for sin on the cross. Yet considering the ancient benefaction system, another possibility surfaces that might link the two options. If one understands the phrase διὰ πίστεως in Eph 2:8 as implying a reference to Christ's faithfulness and interprets this phrase within the expectations of the gift-giving protocols, then the believer's faith may also be in view, for accepting a gift carries obligations.

SUMMARY OF PASSAGES

Our focus is on Eph 2:8–10, but to appreciate Paul's message in this passage, we must connect it with what precedes and follows. Therefore, I offer a brief summary of Eph 2:1–10 and 3:1–12 and highlight key passages within Ephesians that pertain to the ideas and terms used in our main verses.

Summary of Eph 2:1–10

Paul begins this passage with a description of the gentile believers' past as one of disobedience, sin, and submission to the ruler of the air. The world's misalignment is evident in Jews' lives as well, declares Paul, for they might succumb to the desires of their flesh. In 2:5, Paul notes that, indeed, "we"—that is, Jew and gentile—are dead in our trespasses with language quite similar to 2:1. Into this hopeless situation, God's great love and mercy makes a way; his riches are expressed as grace that saves. The Father makes alive in Christ the Son, according to the plan of salvation laid out in 1:7–10 (see below). Paul makes clear that redemption on the cross by Christ effects God's plan; it is proof of God's riches of grace. In ch. 2, Paul declares that God makes us alive, raises us, and seats us in the heavenlies, as we are in Christ Jesus. In this, God shows his "riches of his grace" (2:7).

Twice in this passage (2:5, 8), Paul declares, "By grace you have been saved," and in the second occurrence he adds "by/through faith." In 2:8, he continues with "this is not of yourselves," which is paralleled by the phrase "not by works." Sandwiched between these two negative clauses is the positive declaration, "It is the gift of God." Paul explains that God's gift precludes any boasting, and he concludes that believers are God's workmanship or creative work, designed and equipped to do good works that God establishes.

Most conclude the gift is salvation, and while I do not disagree, I hope to show that we can nuance Paul's thought here even more. I argue below that "gift" and "grace," conceptually, are located in the system of benefaction, which also includes assumptions about the worthiness of the gift's recipients. Additionally, a second social structure, represented by the NPP, plays within this text, namely, the stunning, counter-intuitive embrace of gentiles through Christ's blood shed on the cross. These two narratives support Paul's conclusions about God's gift as being not "of yourselves" and as making a new category of human experience, being "in Christ."

Summary of Eph 3:1–12

Ephesians 3:1–12 includes Paul's explanation of his calling as a servant to the gospel. He also explains the content of the gospel as a mystery now revealed (3:3–5) to both humans and to the rulers and authorities of the heavens (3:10), a mystery of inclusion of gentiles as co-heirs with Israel of God's promise in Christ (3:6). Paul further explains that the gospel contains the riches of Christ (πλοῦτος τοῦ Χριστοῦ; 3:8), who expresses the "manifold wisdom of God" (ἡ πολυποίκιλος σοφία τοῦ θεου; 3:10) now through (διά) the church. God through Christ accomplished his eternal purpose, namely, that in Christ we have bold access, with confidence, to God (3:12).

Paul speaks of the gift of the grace of God given to him (τὴν δωρεὰν τῆς χάριτος τοῦ θεοῦ τῆς δοθείσης μοι; 3:7) that enabled him to preach this mystery now revealed. He weaves the gospel at the cosmic level with his own gift as the preacher of that gospel to illustrate by the latter the ironic and counter-intuitive nature of this Christ-gift. Paul sees his own low status among the saints (3:8) as a perfect illustration of what the gift does. The gift reveals God's wisdom to the rulers of the heavens, the same forces that control the world and shape perceptions of good and evil, right and wrong, and worthy and unworthy.

A Brief Note on Eph 1:7–13

Paul explains that Christ's blood gains for us redemption and forgiveness of sins (1:7) and that this represents God's riches of grace lavished on us (1:8). Paul explains that "we" were chosen and "we" were the first to hope in Christ (1:11–12). Likely, he refers here to the Jews who embrace Jesus as God's Messiah. He continues that "you" also are included in Christ based on your hearing and believing (πιστεύσαντες) and are thus sealed with the Holy Spirit (1:13). This refers to the gentile believers in Ephesus, who make up the majority of the churches in Ephesus and the surrounding area.

ANSWERS FROM THE NEW PERSPECTIVE ON PAUL

The contrast between faith and works is centuries old and is deeply embedded in the Protestant psyche. Formed in the crucible of the Reformation debates, the basic argument contends that Jews (and more directly the [Catholic] Church) in Paul's day trusted in their own merit or works, that is, their own accomplishment of the law's demands, to stand justified before God. Said another way, they earned their salvation by their own works. E. P. Sanders' work on Second Temple Judaism challenged the assumption that Jews in the first century followed the law in order to be saved. Instead, Sanders suggested that Jews followed God's law as an expression of obedience and not as a way to be justified or to earn their salvation.[4] His theory of "covenantal nomism" stresses Israel's election by God and their subsequent obedience as maintaining the relationship afforded by God's election. Numerous scholars in the last few decades have explored this trajectory, with the result that the field of the NPP is wide-ranging and diverse. For our purposes, such studies have opened the door to further reflection on the meaning of "faith" and "works of the law" within Paul's epistles.[5] We turn now to focus on the insights gained by using the NPP's assessment of Second Temple Judaism and, by extension, Paul's discussion of the law.

The Use of "We" and "You" in Ephesians 1:11—2:22

The alert reader will notice that in 1:11 Paul shifts to speaking about "we" and "you" from his earlier general address about "us" in Christ. He notes that "we" were first chosen and "we" were the first to hope in Christ. In 1:13 he adds that "you" were added to the community through hearing and believing the gospel. It might be that at this point the reader is thinking about location. Paul is from Judea, so naturally, he would

---

4. Sanders, *Paul and Palestinian Judaism*.
5. Wright, *New Testament and the People of God*; Dunn, *New Perspective on Paul*; Yinger, *New Perspective on Paul*.

hear about the Lord's work before someone in Ephesus might. But suspicions that more is going on are confirmed in 2:1, when Paul identifies the Ephesian believers as having once lived under the ways of the (evil) ruler of this world; this is contrasted with "us" Jews who also lived in the midst of such a world but did not follow the spirit who worked in "sons of disobedience" (2:2). Nevertheless, Paul makes clear that both groups fall under God's wrath and are objects of God's great love. In 2:4 Paul describes believers as a group, "we" who are alive with Christ. He continues using "we" until 2:10, with two interesting exceptions, to which I will return. In 2:11 Paul explicitly speaks of gentiles, "you" who were uncircumcised, and in 2:14 makes clear that two groups, gentiles and "Israel," are brought together in Christ, who is our peace. Thus, by the time readers get halfway through ch. 2, they realize that Paul sees two groups making up the church—"we" Jews and "you" gentiles.

If that is the case and all come to Christ by God's grace, then why does Paul say twice that "by grace *you* have been saved" (2:5, 8)? Does this statement imply that Jews might gain salvation another way? Few would find room for this conclusion in Paul.[6] If we accept that Paul believes Jews as well as gentiles are saved by God's grace, then why is there a shift in his use of pronouns? Perhaps it is a pastoral move to reassure his listeners of their place in Christ alongside Jewish believers. Again, it may be that Paul's explanation of God's grace, which is God's gift, requires a pointed statement on the surety of their salvation by grace. Paul will carefully allay their fears in 2:11–22. The NPP encourages these questions, for it emphasizes the historical reality that Paul's churches wrestled with the inclusion of gentiles into the holy community of believers in Christ.

Why Not Speak of "Being Justified"?

Further questions emerge as we look closely at the clause "by grace you have been saved," coupled with "not of yourselves" and "not by works." Many have remarked that in Eph 2:5–10, we find neither language of δικαιοσύνη (righteousness) nor the verb δικαιόω (to justify) when we would expect it due to the language of "works." Clinton Arnold notes that many see this omission as evidence for a deutero-Pauline author, although Arnold himself suggests that Paul would only use justifica-

---

6. For an affirmative answer, see Gager, *Reinventing Paul*, 59–61.

tion language when speaking against Judaizers, an enemy not present in Ephesus.⁷ I would add that, while we may not have opponents urging gentile circumcision, Paul finds the unity in Christ of these two groups to be an excellent picture of the power and riches of the gospel. Indeed, gentiles as co-heirs with Israel is the mystery now revealed, astonishing the rulers and authorities and expressing God's surpassing wisdom (3:6, 10).

As another way to examine δικαιοσύνη in Paul, Paula Fredriksen puts forward the interesting proposal that some Jews at this time, including Josephus, understood the Ten Commandments as encouraging two distinct but mutually reinforcing virtues: εὐσέβεια and δικαιοσύνη.⁸ The first five commandments, or the First Tablet, emphasize piety towards God and were considered to focus on the virtue εὐσέβεια. The second five commandments, or the Second Tablet, focus on acting justly to one's neighbors and exhibiting right conduct (do not steal, covet, murder, commit adultery, bear false witness), and center on the virtue δικαιοσύνη. Interestingly, she notes that Paul never uses the term εὐσέβεια,⁹ and she speculates that perhaps this omission is due to Paul's conviction that, at this eschatological moment, gentiles are invited to leave their idolatry and have piety towards the one true God through Christ and not by becoming Jewish proselytes. Fredriksen argues that for Paul the grace of God made effective in the cross of Christ (Eph 1:7) is the "eschatological fiat" by which God incorporates gentiles into the fellowship of believers in the Messiah.

While an argument from silence is difficult to sustain, Fredriksen's insight on the use of the term δικαιοσύνη might help explain its absence here in Eph 2:8–10, for Paul speaks about salvation broadly as the shifting of gentiles from their idolatry to worshiping the one true God. Stronger support for her position is found in Eph 4:24, where Paul speaks about right behavior through a believer's life in Christ and the Spirit. The context in ch. 4 focuses on commands that pertain most directly to "love your neighbor." Applying Fredriksen's argument to Ephesians at the very

---

7. Arnold, *Ephesians*, 140. See also Bruce, *Colossians, Philemon, and Ephesians*, 289.

8. Fredriksen, "Paul's Letter to the Romans," 801–8.

9. Ibid., 805. The term is found in each of the Pastoral Epistles, which Fredriksen does not consider to be written by Paul.

least offers a rationale for Paul's decision to use "to save" (σῴζω) over against language of righteousness (δικαιοσύνη) and "to justify" (δικαιόω).

Why Speak of Being "Saved" without Using the Verb "Justified"?

Perhaps our relentless focus on "faith" over against "works" with its notion of justifying belief has dimmed our appreciation of the fact that Paul often uses the verb σῴζω ("to save" or "to deliver") in connection with faith. In Rom 10:10–11, Paul expresses the gospel truth that each person who confesses with their mouth and believes (πιστεύω) with their heart will be saved. Paul continues that this belief justifies (see also Rom 10:13). In 1 Cor 1:18, 21, Paul links "to save" with "those believing." Thus, while these terms each carry nuanced meaning, Paul seems comfortable using "to justify" and "to save" in related ways as he fills out the message of the gospel.

Arguably, much of today's discussion about "faith" and "works" flows from Luther's critique of the Church. In a penetrating essay, John Barclay engages with Luther's assessment of "works of the Law" over against "faith."[10] Contrary to the commonly held view that Luther preached against "works," Barclay contends that Luther does not sharply differentiate between law and grace, or works and faith, as if contrasting two soteriological plans; rather, Barclay argues that Luther juxtaposes "two conceptions of the role of practice in salvation."[11] That is, Luther does not contrast the historical practice of the Torah with Spirit-generated faith. Instead, Luther offers a theory about religious practice that sets in opposition those who promote self-effort or self-trust and those who resist any practice as relevant for salvation. But is this really what Paul conveyed? Barclay maintains that, for Luther, "what matters in this abstract theoretical distinction is not the content of the practices, or even their cultural-religious context (in Judaism, Islam, or even Christianity), but the location of practices itself (of any sort) in relation to soteriology."[12] He contends that Luther's reading of Paul fails to consider the conventions of benefaction and gift-giving/grace in the ancient world, and he invites readers to look afresh at Paul's complicated (at least

---

10. Barclay, "Paul, the Gift and the Battle," 36–56. See also Barclay, "Under Grace," 61.
11. Ibid., 40.
12. Ibid., 41.

from our standpoint) engagement with Torah and Christ through such a lens.

GIFT AND GRACE VIEWED FROM THE ANCIENT BENEFACTION SYSTEM

It is not enough to highlight the importance of historical Jews within Paul's letters and to seek to portray Second Temple Judaism accurately, for in Ephesians, Paul does not say "not by works of the law" but "not by works." The NPP might suggest that Paul uses the shorthand "by works" in speaking about the place of the law within the believers' community and that all would know he meant "works of the law." But a niggling question remains: why would a gentile imagine that salvation could be "of themselves"? We can better understand this phrase and its parallel phrase in 2:9, "not by works," by looking at "gift."[13]

What Is the Ancient Benefaction System?

Gift-giving in the ancient world was part of a pervasive, complex, non-legal institution of benefaction.[14] The term "grace" (χάρις) can also be translated as "gift." Paul uses the ordinary Greek terms expressing favor or benefaction as he shapes his understanding of the gospel. This being the case, readers today should become acquainted with the features of the ancient benefaction system. Several characteristics of gift-giving, or benefaction, play a key role in our argument.[15] First, the one who gives the gift should give wisely. Usually, that means the gift should be given to one who will benefit from it and further the gift giver's goals as well (see Philo, *De posteritate Caini* 142–147). To give a gift without considering the worthiness of the recipient was viewed as imprudent, and perhaps even arrogant, because it disregarded the needs of the community. With

---

13. Harrison, *Paul's Language of Grace*, 104, critiques the NPP in his assessment of Paul's language of grace, explaining that "two pieces of Pauline polemic (Rom 10:2–3; Phil 3:5–6) indicate that the apostle was as much critiquing the rise of a merit theology within first-century Judaism . . . as the exclusivism of certain Christian Jews in the early house-churches." I appreciate Harrison's thorough study of the primary material but do not agree with several of his negative assessments of the NPP.

14. Mott, "The Power of Giving and Receiving," 60, says that "the act of benefitting set up a chain of obligations."

15. Barclay speaks about the system of gift-giving in his lecture "Paul and the Gift," given to the Centre for Social Scientific Study of the Bible, St. Mary's University College, Twickenham.

everything but dirt and death in short supply, careless dispersal of gifts could ruin a community.

Second, as implied in the above comments, the recipient is worthy of the gift in some way. The gift might exceed all expectations, and the recipient may not fully take advantage of everything the gift offers, but the basic assumption is that, in some way, the recipient deserves the attention of the giver. Yet it must be stated clearly that the recipient did not "earn" or "deserve" the *gift*—that would make it payment or wages. Barclay notes, "Pay was based on calculable equivalence; it was contractual, legal and therefore necessary. By contrast, gifts were ill-defined in value, were personal and voluntary, and were therefore inherently noble."[16] Because the gift is given benevolently, the recipient cannot boast that their efforts won them the prize. It is simply that the gift-giver believed the recipient would be most deserving of the gift, as a reward for past deeds or on the promise of good things to come. Said another way, Seneca states that a gift becomes a non-gift if the recipient is not esteemed by the gift giver (*De beneficiis* 1.15.6).

Third, the recipient of the gift must be grateful (Seneca, *De beneficiis* 3.1.1; 4.18.1) and must show honor to the gift giver. If possible, he or she should repay the gift, but most often the gift's value far exceeds the recipient's capacity to repay. The gift giver ideally takes no notice of such honor or repayment, for the giving of the gift is in itself a joy; nevertheless, an ungrateful recipient would not likely receive another gift. The purpose of the gift is to create a relationship or bond between giver and receiver. The gift includes obligations for the recipient, but these further a mutually satisfactory network.[17]

The Perfect Gift

As a way to think about our perceptions of the perfect gift and thus speak more clearly about gift-giving in the ancient world, Barclay lists six ways one can think about how a gift is perfected, that is, he describes a gift based on an extreme endpoint presented for definitional clarity.[18] First, he cites superabundance or the gift's large scale or enduring per-

16. Barclay, "Believers," 200.

17. Harrison, *Paul's Language of Grace*, 80, notes the unease with which the ancient world viewed ingratitude as well as the emphasis placed on recipients acquiescing to their benefactor's requests.

18. Barclay, "Paul and the Gift." See also Barclay, "Grace/Gift in Paul."

manence. The ancients spoke about the gift of great scale. Both Philo and Seneca note that God/the gods give gifts on a superabundant scale, such as the gift of nature, which provides food and water and life itself (Seneca, *De beneficiis* 4.25.1–2; Philo, *Legum allegoriae* 3.161–165). This gift is a perfect gift due to its scale relative to any possible human effort or work to merit such munificence.

A second way to think about the perfect gift is to note the giver's single-minded focus of benefaction. This perfection is known as singularity. Philo, denying that God gives evil, connects God's singularity with giving only the good (*De Abrahamo* 268).

A third possible understanding of the perfect gift is that it is unconstrained; that is, it is not in response to a prior event. The gods/God give in such manner, for they are not beholden to humans. Often the ancients would speak of parents and children in this way, noting that it is practically impossible for children to show adequate gratitude to their parents for the latter's unconstrained giving to them (Seneca, *De beneficiis* 3.29.1–38.3). Philo can also speak of this aspect of a perfect gift when cautioning against pride, for all good deeds and thoughts have first been shaped in the mind of God (*De confusione linguarum* 123–27; *De ebrietate* 73, 75).

A fourth way to think about the perfect gift is to look at the categories of congruity and incongruity (unconditionality). For Seneca, in small gifts the giver can be indiscriminate in his/her giving, so the gift could be incongruous with the recipient. But in large gifts, the giver must be selective (*De beneficiis* 1.15.6). Said another way, the gift must be in congruity with the recipient's worthiness (*De beneficiis* 1.1.1–2). Interestingly, the Essenes sang of the incredible incongruity of God's grace, as their psalms depict humans as dreadful, immoral sinners (1QH[a]). They paired this idea with a strong conviction of God's election of his special people.

A fifth way to imagine how to give a perfect gift is to note the effect of that gift; is the gift efficacious? Philo, in speaking of human virtues, stresses that they ultimately come from God, who enables virtuous living (*Legate ad Gaium* 2.44–48). Seneca notes that one cannot rightly boast in one's talents, for they are gifts from the gods (*De beneficiis* 4.6.4–5).

Finally, Barclay speaks of reciprocity, the circularity of the gift, which establishes a pattern of exchange. Most ancient writers stressed this aspect of gift-giving, as it built relationships and cemented alliances

(Aristotle, *Ethica nicomachea* 1157b7–8). The return gift might not be of the same size or configuration; indeed, the gifts of the gods were above repayment except through ongoing expressions of honor and gratitude by the recipient. Seneca is most concerned about the rise of ingratitude as he examines his culture, and he emphasizes reciprocity in the circle of gift-giving (*De beneficiis* 3.6.1–2). Today, by contrast, we in the West tend to value non-circularity and the unilateral gift. In sum, Barclay urges that readers today should not "attempt to measure the *degrees* of emphasis given to the Pauline motif of divine gift/grace, but trace the different *kinds* of emphasis (or 'perfection') to which it has given rise."[19]

How Did Jews See God's Grace and See God as a Gift Giver?

Philo's opinions were noted above because they compare with the work of Seneca, a gentile philosopher who was a near contemporary of Philo; in many ways Jews and Greeks shared assumptions about proper gift-giving. Moreover, the evidence suggests that Jews in the Second Temple period held firmly to God's grace/gift. Debate centered on how such grace was related to God's mercy and justice and his wisdom revealed in the cosmos. As Barclay states succinctly, "If they [Jews] all believe in 'grace', they disagree about its meaning and operation."[20] We see that Philo links worthiness (ἄξιος) with χάρις but not in the sense that the former earned the latter (*De sacrificiis Abelis et Caini* 54–57; *De vita Mosis* 2.242). Instead, Philo shows that God is rational, just, and fair and so gives gifts to those who are worthy (*Legatio ad Gaium* 3.77, 79, 83, 95, 166). Abraham, for example, receives God's grace in the gift of covenant, yet Philo also states that Abraham was rewarded in his search for God (*De migratione Abrahami* 77). Abraham did not earn his gift, but he was a suitable recipient; thus, God gave grace in a wise and just manner.

Jonathan Linebaugh examines grace and righteousness in the Wisdom of Solomon and compares that with Paul's argument in Romans.[21] He notes that Wisdom of Solomon categorizes God's grace with his divine justice. The book promotes the exodus as God's grace shown to the Israelites, for they did not deserve such a gift. More specifically, Wisdom of Solomon says that the gift of God is Sophia, that

19. Barclay, "Grace/Gift in Paul," 8–9.
20. Ibid., 4.
21. Linebaugh, *God, Grace and Righteousness*.

is, Wisdom (8:21), who delivers or saves the Israelites and destroys its enemies. In this act, God showed grace to the righteous and thus demonstrated that he is just. Linebaugh argues that for the author of Wisdom of Solomon, God's grace is conditional in that it rightly relates the gift to the recipient, but not in terms of "a calculable equivalence between human worth and subsequent divine benefaction (it is a gift, not pay); it is about the stability of the cosmos and the goodness and justice of God."[22] One is not saved because one is worthy; those who are saved by Wisdom are worthy. As Linebaugh helpfully notes, Wisdom of Solomon is unequivocally clear: God saves. The question the book addresses is "*whom does he save? Answer: the worthy, because God is just and good.*"[23]

Therefore, the contrast is not between earning and not earning something, but between a gift given to someone worthy of it and someone unworthy of it. Linebaugh makes the point that "human worth is a *condition* of divine grace, but it is never its *cause*; that role belongs exclusively to Wisdom (8:5, see also 9:18)."[24] Thus, when Wisdom speaks of "reward" (μισθός) given to those brought out of Egypt, whose labors were rewarded in their deliverance, it is not the case that the ancient Israelites are said to earn their deliverance. "The fittingness of grace is not an indication of commercial exchange; it is a reflection of the rationality and goodness of the gift-giving God."[25]

Characteristics of God's Gift in Christ

When we examine Paul next to Barclay's six characteristics of the perfect gift, we see that Paul would seem to agree that the perfect gift of salvation in Christ is superabundant and is unconstrained or is given spontaneously. Paul includes God's focus on destroying sin and death by way of Christ's work; therefore, the gift of Christ is not singular in relation to our personal salvation. Paul imagines reciprocity, seen in his insistence that a believer walk in godliness. Of course, for Paul (and other Jews), these godly actions are in some way established and enabled

---

22. Ibid., 164. He notes, "This does not necessarily imply a cooperative soteriology . . . but it does indicate that the objects of salvation correspond to a preconditional standard of worth" (48).

23. Ibid., 52 (italics original). See also p. 164, which states, "for *Wisdom* . . . grace means . . . an unearned though explainable benefit given to a suitable recipient."

24. Ibid., 162 (italics original).

25. Ibid., 165.

by God.[26] Yet growing from his perception of God's work in Christ, Paul argues innovatively for the incongruity of God's gift.[27] God disregards one's ethnic or social worth when giving grace. The distinctive aspects of a person (wealthy or poor, male or female, Jew or gentile) need not disappear, but they have no social value when considering God's grace.

Interestingly, Paul typically uses the feminine term "gift" (e.g., Eph 3:7; 4:7).[28] It is only here that he uses the neuter term, and this could reflect a nuanced distinction between the terms, with the neuter noun suggesting a cultic offering and the feminine term stressing a free gift, as in the Latin *gratis*. Perhaps Paul chose the neuter noun "gift" in 2:8 to reflect on Christ's death on the cross as a sacrifice to God. It may also be that the neuter was chosen to connect "gift" with the neuter term "riches" (τὸ πλοῦτος) in 2:7, linking the two with the neuter demonstrative pronoun "this." In so doing, Paul underscores the gift of God as the riches of his grace known to us in Christ.

Not of Yourselves

While we were sinners, Paul declares to the Romans, Christ died for us (Rom 5:6). God extends the gift of salvation to those who have no apparent congruity with the gift, no actual condition that make the gift a good decision. Paul addresses the incongruity and unconditioned aspects of God's gift in Christ in Eph 2:8–9 when he qualifies God's gift as "this not of yourselves"[29] and "not by works." Thus, when Paul says "not of

---

26. This is not to ignore Jesus' insistence: "Store up for yourselves treasures in heaven ... For where your treasure is, there your heart will be also" (Matt 6:20–21 NIV2011). For a discussion of "reward," see Anderson, *Sin*, 146–47. Two insights are relevant to our paper. First, he emphasizes Col 2:14 with its promise that God in Christ erased the believers' χειρόγραφον ("legal indebtedness" NIV2011), noting that this idea comes from Second Temple Judaism and the LXX. Second, his perception that almsgiving is understood as "loaning to God," who then repays all out of proportion to the "loan," provides another avenue to explore notions of reward, work, and grace/gift (see Tob 4:11: δῶρον γὰρ ἀγαθόν ἐστιν ἐλεημοσύνη πᾶσι τοῖς ποιοῦσιν αὐτὴν ἐνώπιον τοῦ ὑψίστου, translated in the NRSV as "Indeed, almsgiving, for all who practice it, is an excellent offering [gift] in the presence of the Most High."

27. Barclay, "Under Grace," 64.

28. Paul links the feminine "gift" with God's specific calling in his life to be an apostle to the gentiles (3:7) and with Christ's gift to each believer, namely, "the grace" according to the measure or standard of Christ's gift (4:7).

29. "This" is the neuter demonstrative pronoun, τοῦτο, which is grammatically unconnected to the feminine nouns χάρις (grace) and πίστις (faith), but which may reflect the closest neuter antecedent πλοῦτος (riches).

yourselves," he means that there is no social worth connected with God's good choice to extend grace to individuals. For Paul, there is a deep wisdom here, as God amazes the powers and principalities (Eph 3:6–12), and as he scuttles the wisdom of the Greeks (1 Cor 1:26–28). In this Paul is an outlier among many of his Jewish compatriots for most Jews concluded that, "God's gifts were good precisely in being distributed to those who in some ethnic, intellectual, economic, or moral dimension were regarded as more worthy than other potential recipients."[30]

Not by Works, So No Boasting

Additionally, the gift is unconditioned, but not unconditional, according to Barclay. The conditions include agreeing to die and to be raised to new life. The gift is enjoyed, if you will, by the new person, for the old self dies. The new "masterpiece" (ποίημα; Eph 2:10) is now fit to do good works under God's empowerment and guidance. It is because we are God's ποίημα that boasting is excluded. In this sense, then, God wisely gives his gifts, for they pay eternal dividends for his people and grant immortality and everlasting relationship between the Giver, the gift, and the recipients.

God's Gift Kills, Makes Alive, Brings Forth a New Person

Does this act of gift-giving make God illogical, irrational, or unjust? Is God capricious, giving gifts to good folks and bad alike? These are not idle questions; the issue goes deep to the very character of God and the moral constancy of the cosmos. Paul himself raises the question in Rom 3:4 and 9:6. Paul can defend God's gift-giving as logical and rational if one recognizes certain features of this gift. God's gift brings death—the one who accepts God's gift dies. And the gift also makes alive, but now the person's life is hidden in Christ and will rise in the bodily resurrection to come, when Christ the Savior returns. God makes the person new, and thus actually and ultimately worthy, through Christ. In the end, Paul challenges and reshapes aspects of the benefaction system, but also assures believers that God's perfect gift of salvation reflects God's good and just wisdom.

---

30. Barclay, "Grace/Gift in Paul," 4.

Summary Statements on Benefaction and Ephesians

Paul's message in Eph 2:5–9 is often summarized, "You (and we) have been saved by grace through faith and not by your own works or good deeds that seek to self-justify before God." This abridgment of the verses, however, fails to consider Paul's central statement that "it is the gift (δῶρον) of God." The NPP and Sanders' covenantal nomism only go so far, for they fail to consider the ways "gift" and "grace" sounded to ancient ears. Paul works within the system of benefaction and must connect with and distinguish his understanding of God's gift of salvation in Christ from other ways of constructing gift-giving. The qualifying phrase "not by works" challenges the default assumption that most in the Greco-Roman world held about giving and receiving. Paul declares that unlike the benefaction system in which they operate, God gives the greatest gift of all, salvation in Christ, to those who have no apparent worthiness. Moreover, God does not give based on the knowledge that the recipients will become worthy in themselves.

The gift is achieved by Christ's effective death on the cross, which brings forgiveness of sins and new life and which sets in motion the ultimate unification of all things under Christ (1:10). Lest the believers imagine that they are suited for the gift, or, if unsuited, that God is capricious or unreasonable in his gift-giving, Paul reminds them that the gift does not affirm them in themselves in their current or any possible future state, but actually makes them new in a way that perfects what they were created to be—God's masterpiece.

By Faith

Having examined the key terms "gift" and "works," we have one important and hotly contested phrase yet to explore. Paul tells the Ephesians that they have been saved by grace through faith (πίστις). We will look at the basic definitions of πίστις and then consider the major interpretations of this phrase.

Definition of "Faith"

Matlock offers a useful summary of definitions in BDAG, L&N, and LSJ.[31] Overall, the lexicons speak of πίστις as (1) assurance, confidence, trust in others, proof; (2) trustworthiness, faithfulness; (3) pledge of loyalty,

---

31. Matlock, "Detheologizing the ΠΙΣΤΙΣ ΧΡΙΣΤΟΥ Debate," 1–23.

promise; and (4) true piety, body of belief. The verb πιστεύω carries the sense of believing that something or someone is true or trustworthy. Douglas Campbell notes that in Philo and Josephus, "one gives signs *of* faithfulness, but entrusts valuable things *to* the faithful."[32] He continues that πίστις can denote the actual proof, which creates knowledge, but much less often does it suggest act of belief. The term "truth" (ἀλήθεια) is used to speak about a reliable or trustworthy bit of evidence. Barclay suggests the nuance in Paul's usage: "'Faith' in Pauline discourse is not a general stance of trust towards God but orientation to a specific event, the death and resurrection of Christ, which altered the structures governing the whole of life, 'external' works included."[33]

Focus on Eph 3:12

In the center of Paul's letter to the Ephesians, he weaves a discussion of the mystery of salvation with his own situation as a prisoner of Christ Jesus who is tasked with the job of preaching the gospel to gentiles. God's grace (χάρις) in Paul's life establishes him as an apostle, granting insight into the mystery of God's redemptive plan. Paul declares this mystery of Christ (3:4) to be that gentiles are now included as fellow heirs, of one body together, and fellow sharers of "the promise in Christ Jesus through the gospel" (3:6). Paul continues to explain this gospel as the fathomless riches of Christ (3:8), which are now revealed to the rulers and authorities in the heavenlies (3:10).

The plan of God is accomplished in Christ Jesus our Lord (3:11), in whom (ἐν ᾧ) believers find bold access and confidence before God (3:12). The final phrase in this verse, διὰ τῆς πίστεως αὐτοῦ, may denote Christ's work in our salvation, in the fulfillment of the mystery, the inheritance in the Messiah for gentiles alongside Jews.[34] It may also highlight the believer's faith in Christ.[35] Several points bear on the interpretation of this phrase. First, the pronoun certainly refers to Christ, specifically Christ Jesus our Lord (3:11). Second, with the exception of Eph 3:12, the noun πίστις is anarthrous in key verses in Romans, Galatians, and Philippians, as well as in Eph 2:8.[36] Most exegetes, however, are unwill-

32. Campbell, *The Quest for Paul's Gospel*, 179.
33. Barclay, "Paul, the Gift and the Battle," 42.
34. Foster, "Πιστις Χριστου Terminology," 99–109.
35. Bell, "Faith in Christ," 111–25.
36. See p. 149 n. 3 above for references.

ing to put all the weight of their argument on this fact.[37] Those who argue that the article indicates the subjective genitive (faithfulness of Christ) are obliged to acknowledge that the other seven examples (plus Eph 2:8) must therefore be objective genitives (faith in Christ).[38] And those who argue for the objective genitive worry that even one example of a subjective genitive might open the door to the possibility of including "the faithfulness of Christ" among the exegetical choices in the other verses. Overall, it seems that the grammar and syntax within the New Testament itself does not offer a watertight argument for either position.

Ephesians 3:1–13 speaks of salvation using language found in the earlier two chapters, but with new connections or emphases. Paul notes the inscrutable riches of Christ (3:8), which calls to mind 1:7, where Paul speaks of the riches of God's grace, given to us in the Beloved, whose shed blood brings redemption and forgiveness of sins. Then, in 2:7, Paul announces again that these incomparable riches of God's grace are manifest in Christ Jesus. In 2:13 Paul mentions the blood of Christ that brings close to God those who were far away (gentiles); they are "in Christ." A few verses later, Paul adds that reconciliation before God of both Jew and gentile and the creation of one body have been accomplished through the cross (2:16). When we read 3:8, then, we are prepared to see Christ's work described as "riches" for the salvation of gentiles, who, together with "Israel," share in Christ the promise of redemption (3:6). Consistently in all three chapters, Paul insists that these riches are found in Christ, result in reconciliation with God, and create a new entity—Jew and gentile as one body. Paul links the gospel mystery—that gentiles are included in God's family in Christ—with God's redemption plan (οἰκονομία; 3:9), which is accomplished in the inscrutable riches of Christ. Moreover, the cosmos will be unified under Christ (1:10). The eschatological and cosmic vantage point allows Paul to draw into view the rulers and authorities of this age.

---

37. Foster, "First Contribution."

38. Barclay, "Paul, the Gift and the Battle," 55. See also Barclay, "Pure Grace," 15: "The concern with questions of agency which motivates the work of J. Louis Martyn, and lies behind many of the arguments for the 'subjective genitive' interpretation of *pistis Christou* (as 'the faithfulness of Christ'), seems fully comprehensible as a reaction against contemporary forms of Christian moralism and gospel-less activism. But it is liable to overload Paul's discourse and his theology of grace with additional dimensions and perfections beyond the horizon or the interests of Paul himself."

Focusing on Christ's riches noted in 3:8, I suggest that these riches, which include redemption, reconciliation of humans to God, and peace between Jew and gentile, are captured by the phrase in 3:12, διὰ τῆς πίστεως αὐτοῦ, specifically pointing to the work of Christ, his faithfulness unto death, that effects this salvation plan of God. Paul builds an argument that connects the faithfulness of Christ with the work of Christ in making gentiles co-heirs with Jews in God's family. Foster concludes, "In this context a subjective rendering of διὰ τῆς πίστεως αὐτοῦ most satisfactorily coheres with the overarching train of thought that the new administration ... is inaugurated and revealed through Christ."[39] Foster's conclusion, however, need not diminish a believer's faith or trust in God's salvation plan. It seems to me that Paul addresses this when he notes at the beginning of 3:12 that believers are "in Christ" (ἐν ᾧ). They participate in Christ's life, accepting God's call to live worthy of this calling (4:1, 4).

Focus on Eph 2:8

These observations inform the reading of Eph 2:8, with its phrase διὰ πίστεως. One might argue that Paul's focus here is on the believer's response to Christ's work. For example, Arnold points to Eph 1:13, with its participle πιστεύσαντες ("believing"), and argues that the wider context shared by these verses stresses the gentiles' faith in the gospel message. Such reasoning is sound,[40] and I find myself strongly influenced by the position's cumulative arguments. Nevertheless, Paul may be suggesting Christ's faithfulness if we link this verse with the similar phrase in 3:12 and draw connections between πίστις, δῶρον, and πλοῦτος in chs. 2 and 3. Paul depends on his listeners linking "riches" in 2:7 with "gift" in 2:9 through salvation by grace. Paul distinguishes "by faith" from "not of yourselves," perhaps intending to create a picture in his listeners' minds that puts Christ in the forefront. "By faith" is their cue to imagine Christ seated in the heavenlies, full of riches unto salvation. Paul consistently promotes Christ as God's "indescribable gift" (2 Cor 9:15 NIV2011, see also 8:9), as the Son who gave himself (Rom 8:32; Gal 1:4).

---

39. Foster, "First Contribution," 88. See also O'Brien, *Ephesians*, 249.

40. See also Campbell, *The Quest for Paul's Gospel*, 188, who states that Eph 1:15 "clearly denote[s] Christ as the object of *pistis*, and the sense as 'faithfulness,' because of its parallel function in context to that other great attribute of ongoing Christian existence, love, in Eph. 1:15."

CONCLUSION: THE GOOD NEWS OF THE GOSPEL

The gospel is good news for Paul because it declares God's gift to the cosmos, to humanity, and to each individual. We have explored Paul's argument that God's gift is shown in his grace, which brings salvation. Ephesians 2:8–10 expresses and holds together these essential elements of salvation by speaking of God's gift, which reflects the riches of Christ and which is given without consideration of the individual's worthiness.

Capturing Paul's meaning in Eph 2:5–10 requires operating within at least three narratives and two time zones, if you will. Paul lives within a worldview that separates humanity into Jews and non-Jews, the people of God and idolaters. He exists within the ubiquitous system of benefaction, a foundational structure of his world, structuring communities and political and economic exchanges.[41] And Paul preaches a new narrative, one with unbreakable links to the God revealed in the Hebrew Scriptures and to the people called in his name.[42] Paul's testimony speaks of a new covenant, promised by the prophets of old and now realized in the Messiah Jesus. This story requires two time zones, the present age, characterized by the light breaking forth in darkness, and the age to come, when believers with resurrected bodies enjoy the full realization of their hope—immortal, embodied life in the new heavens and new earth.[43] I suggest Paul takes these realities, together with an eschatological perspective, and presents an explanation of our salvation. He states to the Jewish and the gentile believers that God gifts them with salvation.

---

41. This language of structured structures and structuring structures is found in the French sociologist Pierre Bourdieu (1930–2002). For an accessible, brief introduction to his ideas, see Swartz, "The Sociology of Habit," 61–69. Barclay, "Under Grace," 73, calls upon Bourdieu's insights in discussing the importance of embodiment for Paul's theology: "the refashioning of the self cannot take effect without refashioning the practices of the body."

42. Watson, "Is There a Story in These Texts?" 232, offers summary remarks on the "ambivalence" of scholars towards discerning narrative in Paul. He suggests this ambivalence is based on Paul's reinterpretation of Israel's history in "the light of the singular divine saving action." Watson suggests that the "question is whether, for Paul, this life [of Christ] can be presented *both* as the singular divine saving action *and* as a narrative."

43. Hays, "Apocalyptic *Poiēsis* in Galatians," 216, speaks of Paul's "*poiēsis*—his imaginative renarration of a symbolic world in which the gospel story reshapes everything." He cites three major motifs of this renarration: (1) God the Father rescues his people in an unexpected way and forms a new community; (2) the cross is the decisive pivot point in history, which ends human slavery to sin and makes a new creation possible; and (3) humans gain all this through participation in Christ.

That gift is unconditioned and incongruous; it does not depend on their suitedness for the gift or any potential they might carry to use the gift. The gift must be this way because the gift is death and new life in Christ.[44]

BIBLIOGRAPHY

Anderson, Gary A. *Sin: A History*. New Haven: Yale University Press, 2009.

Arnold, Clinton E. *Ephesians*. Grand Rapids: Zondervan, 2010.

Barclay, John M. G. "Believers and the 'Last Judgment' in Paul: Rethinking Grace and Recompense." In *Eschatologie—Eschatology: The Sixth Durham-Tübingen Research Symposium: Eschatology in Old Testament, Ancient Judaism and Early Christianity*, edited by H.-J. Eckstein et al., 195–208. WUNT 272. Tübingen: Mohr Siebeck, 2011.

———. "Grace/Gift in Paul." In *The Oxford Handbook of Pauline Studies*. Oxford Handbooks Online. http://www.oxfordhandbooks.com/view/10.1093/oxfordhb/9780199600489.001.0001/oxfordhb-9780199600489-e-001

———. *Paul and the Gift*. Grand Rapids: Eerdmans, 2015.

———. "Paul and the Gift: Gift-Theory, Grace and Critical Issues in the Interpretation of Paul." Plenary to the Centre for Social Scientific Study of the Bible, St. Mary's University College, Twickenham. 3 May 2013. http://www.stmarys.ac.uk/news/news/school-of-theology-philosophy-and-history/2013/05/inauguration-of-st-marys-centre-for-the-social-scientific-study-of-the-bible/.

———. "Paul, the Gift and the Battle over Gentile Circumcision: Revisiting the Logic of Galatians." *ABR* 58 (2010) 36–56.

———. "Pure Grace? Paul's Distinctive Jewish Theology of Gift." *ST* 68 (2014) 4–20.

———. "Under Grace: The Christ-Gift and the Construction of a Christian *Habitus*." In *Apocalyptic Paul: Cosmos and Anthropos in Romans 5–8*, edited by Beverly Roberts Gaventa, 59–76. Waco, TX: Baylor University Press, 2013.

Bell, Richard H. "Faith in Christ: Some Exegetical and Theological Reflections on Philippians 3:9 and Ephesians 3:12." In *The Faith of Jesus Christ*, edited by Michael F. Bird and Preston M. Sprinkle, 111–25. Peabody, MA: Hendrickson, 2009.

Bruce, F. F. *The Epistles to the Colossians, to Philemon, and to the Ephesians*. Grand Rapids: Eerdmans, 1984.

Campbell, Douglas. *Framing Paul: An Epistolary Biography*. Grand Rapids: Eerdmans, 2014.

———. *The Quest for Paul's Gospel: A Suggested Strategy*. London: T. & T. Clark, 2005.

Dunn, James D. G. *The New Perspective on Paul: Collected Essays*. WUNT 185. Tübingen: Mohr Siebeck, 2005.

Foster, Paul. "The First Contribution to the *Pistis Christou* Debate: A Study of Ephesians 3.12." *JSNT* 85 (2002) 75–96.

---

44. I am grateful to Michael Thomson of Eerdmans Publishing for allowing me to see a pre-publication draft of John Barclay's *Paul and the Gift* when preparing this essay. Barclay treats Ephesians as deutero-Pauline and briefly comments that this epistle presents "work" as moral achievement, a position that Augustine would eventually promote. I found Barclay's essays and arguments very useful in interpreting Ephesians as part of Paul's corpus.

———. "Πιστις Χριστου Terminology in Philippians and Ephesians." In *The Faith of Jesus Christ*, edited by Michael F. Bird and Preston M. Sprinkle, 99–109. Peabody, MA: Hendrickson, 2009.
Fredriksen, Paula. "Paul's Letter to the Romans, the Ten Commandments, and Pagan 'Justification by Faith.'" *JBL* 133 (2014) 801–8.
Gager, John G. *Reinventing Paul*. Oxford: Oxford University Press, 2000.
Gorman, Michael J. *Apostle of the Crucified Lord: A Theological Introduction to Paul and His Letters*. Grand Rapids: Eerdmans, 2004.
Harrison, James R. *Paul's Language of Grace in Its Graeco-Roman Context*. WUNT 2.172. Tübingen: Mohr Siebeck, 2003.
Hays, Richard B. "Apocalyptic *Poiēsis* in Galatians: Paternity, Passion, and Participation." In *Galatians and Christian Theology: Justification, the Gospel, and Ethics in Paul's Letters*, edited by Mark W. Elliott et al., 200–219. Grand Rapids: Baker, 2013.
Linebaugh, Jonathan. *God, Grace and Righteousness in Wisdom of Solomon and Paul's Letter to the Romans*. NTSup 152. Leiden: Brill, 2013.
Matlock, R. Barry. "Detheologizing the ΠΙΣΤΙΣ ΧΡΙΣΤΟΥ Debate: Cautionary Remarks from a Lexical Semantic Perspective." *NovT* 42 (2000) 1–23.
Mott, Stephen Charles. "The Power of Giving and Receiving: Reciprocity in Hellenistic Benevolence." In *Current Issues in Biblical and Patristic Interpretation: Studies in Honor of Merrill C. Tenney*, edited by Gerald F. Hawthorne, 60–72. Grand Rapids: Eerdmans, 1975.
O'Brien, Peter. *The Letter to the Ephesians*. PNTC. Grand Rapids: Eerdmans, 1999.
Sanders, E. P. *Paul and Palestinian Judaism: A Comparison of Patterns of Religion*. Philadelphia: Fortress, 1977.
Schwartz, Seth. *Were the Jews a Mediterranean Society? Reciprocity and Solidarity in Ancient Judaism*. Princeton: Princeton University Press, 2010.
Swartz, David. L. "The Sociology of Habit: The Perspective of Pierre Bourdieu." *The Occupational Therapy Journal of Research* 22 Supplement (2002) 61–69.
Watson, Francis. "Is There a Story in These Texts?" In *Narrative Dynamics in Paul: A Critical Assessment*, edited by Bruce W. Longenecker, 231–39. Louisville: Westminster John Knox, 2002.
Wright, N. T. *The New Testament and the People of God*. Minneapolis: Fortress, 1992.
———. *Paul and the Faithfulness of God*. Minneapolis: Fortress, 2013.
Yinger, Kent L. *The New Perspective on Paul: An Introduction*. Eugene, OR: Cascade, 2011.

Theology

9

"The Word Became Flesh"
Christian Theology and Science as Coinherent, Not Conflicted . . . A Post-Intellectual Approach

W. Ross Hastings

INTRODUCTION

I HAVE FOUND OVER the years of playing the occasional golf game (with people I do not know) that it is best to try to keep my vocation as a pastor or professor of theology a secret. On one occasion on Burnaby Mountain, one chap I was joined with swore like a trooper all the way through the first nine holes, which he played abominably. A blue hue followed him everywhere he played a shot. At the tenth, he found himself under a tree, swung with full abandon, and wrapped his shaft around a branch. After taking swears and cusses to a new level, he turned to me, and I kid you not, in his next breath asked me, "So what do you do for a living?" I told him that I played a lot of rugby and was used to this kind of language and that it was really a matter between him and God anyway; he was not much put at ease. When I told him that I have a Ph.D. in chemistry and that my first career was in science teaching before becoming a pastor and theologian, he looked utterly bewildered. He then said what is almost always said to me in this situation, "How do you put those two things together?" That is the question I want to try to answer in this paper.

Theology

When it comes to the relationship between science and the Christian faith, Denis Lamoureux, in his book *Evolutionary Creation*, has reflected what I am afraid is the sad truth: Bad theology and bad science have characterized the Christian tradition, and we have not learned from it! Lazar Puhalo, Orthodox theologian and scientist, believes that a primary reason for the conflict model has not so much been modern science, as if it were some kind of "international plot" to overthrow Christianity; it is rather the "bad" scholastic theology of the West in both the Catholic and Protestant traditions and a fundamentalism that is present especially within the latter. These Western traditions, he asserts, were shaped more by the influence of Greek philosophy, specifically that of Aristotle through Islamic philosophy and of Neoplatonism through Augustine and his "analogy of being." Puhalo states that "Aristotle had written on the essence of natural mechanisms, but he favoured the search for truth in philosophical processes rather than experimental ones. It was Aristotelianism that formed the dogmatized canon of 'scientific fact,' or at least the canon of acceptable thought."[1] He insists that under scholasticism, philosophy sat over both science and theology, the former being determined by presuppositions about the unchangeable and static nature of the cosmos and by misreadings of Scripture and the latter being determined by philosophy's idolatrous reductionisms concerning God, robbing humanity of its relationship with creation and its formation through the empirical discoveries about creation through science. Puhalo does acknowledge that the systematic reasoning process of the scholastic West was ultimately crucial in the development of scientific process, but he says that it was the empiricism and apophaticism of the East, along with the nominalism and particularism of Ockham and Scotus, which together gave birth to science.[2]

The lack of dynamic interplay between science and theology is certainly missing in the fundamentalist quarter of the church today (with its literal six-day scientific creationism, which ignores science, for example), and it has failed to learn from the sad chapter concerning the relationship between the church and the findings of Copernicus, Giordano Bruno, and Galileo. During the medieval period, when scholastic theology emerged, both theology and science were essentially departments of Aristotelian (and, eventually, also Platonic) philosophy.

1. Puhalo, *Evidence of Things*, 36 n. 39.
2. Ibid., *passim*.

It was in this context that scientists became the victim of "the breach of this harmony."[3] Puhalo gives a graphic illustration of this:

> Thus, when Bruno, the brilliant, if erratic disciple of William of Ockham and Erasmus, dared to venture toward authentic science, and strive for a more accurate knowledge of the solar system, he paid the supreme price. When Galileo made irrefutable discoveries about the solar system that conflicted with the Biblical interpretations of scholastic fundamentalism and upset the artificial tandem of a much repressed and suppressed science, he was quickly reminded of Bruno's fate and forced to renounce truth in deference to dogmatized ignorance. The question of truth was of no consequence; what mattered was the maintenance of the pseudo-harmony.[4]

Puhalo goes on to make the case, convincingly, in my opinion, that new or quantum physics is more compatible with the apophatic theology of the Trinity in the Orthodox tradition, although I fear he slightly overstates the case in terms of both the science and the theology. On the science side, the cautions of John Polkinghorne need to be heard. He refers to what "one might call quantum hype—the invocation of the peculiar character of quantum thinking as if it were sufficient license for lazy indulgence in playing with paradox in other disciplines."[5] On the theological front, I am in agreement with the Orthodox tradition concerning the ineffable and mysterious nature of the Trinity and am cognizant of the dangers of scholastic probing beyond mystery. I *do* think that the nature of matter at the quantum level *does* provide an analogy of the mystery of the Godhead, that there *is* an apophatic dimension to the knowledge of God, and that there *is* a glory that we may not approach (see John 1:18: "no one has ever seen God"; 1 Tim 6:15–16: "God, the blessed and only Ruler, the King of kings and Lord of lords, who alone is immortal and who lives in unapproachable light, whom no one has seen or can see"). The challenge is to know what the borders of that mystery are, for there are realities that *have been revealed* to us in the Christ event and in the Scriptures that describe them, and these must not be neglected. I only want to be as cataphatic as Scripture allows and to be as apophatic as the silence of Scripture. The Gospels, and particularly

---

3. Ibid., 33–34.
4. Ibid., 34.
5. Polkinghorne, *Quantum Physics and Theology*, ix.

John's, are fraught with statements and insinuations about the revelation of who God is as revealed in the historical coming of the Son:

> The Word became flesh and made his dwelling among us. We have seen his glory, the glory of the one and only Son, who came from the Father, full of grace and truth. (John 1:14)

> No one has ever seen God, but the one and only Son, who is himself God and is in closest relationship with the Father, has made him known. (John 1:18)

> "You do not know me or my Father," Jesus replied. "If you knew me, you would know my Father also." (John 8:19)

> "But if I do them, even though you do not believe me, believe the works, that you may know and understand that the Father is in me, and I in the Father." (John 10:38)

> "Don't you believe that I am in the Father, and that the Father is in me? The words I say to you I do not speak on my own authority. Rather, it is the Father, living in me, who is doing his work." (John 14:10)

> "On that day you will realize that I am in my Father, and you are in me, and I am in you." (John 14:20)

> "My Father will love them, and we will come to them and make our home with them." (John 14:23)

These expressions regarding the revelatory economic being and life of the Trinity in Christ by the Spirit were no doubt crucial in the formulation of the doctrine of the Trinity via Polycarp, Irenaeus, and the Cappadocians. The Niceno-Constantinopolitan affirmations are not too far a distance from the Johannine texts. The apophaticism arises when speculation begins regarding how the immanent Trinity relates to the economic Trinity.[6] It seems crucial, and here I align with Karl Barth, that the immanent Trinity, though distinct and containing elements of mystery, must *correspond* with what the economic Trinity is, or else we are back on our quest looking for God.[7] God *in se* must at minimum be

---

6. The relationship between the economic and the immanent Trinities has been closely studied by Chung-Hyun Baik. He references seven different proposals for the relationship within the tradition. See Baik, *Holy Trinity*.

7. If there is not a correspondence between what we know of God as he has revealed himself in the economy of redemption and what he really is, we are in difficulty, and revelation will have proved to be unreliable. Moreover, the Christian gospel will

Father, Son, and Holy Spirit, that is, God in three persons, who are one in essence and mutually internal to each other in perfect communion. This is legitimate biblically cataphatic theology. Much beyond that is difficult to know, and this is where apophatic wonder and silence is more appropriate than cataphatic speculation.

So, for example, who is the *font* of the eternal Trinity? The Cappadocian and Orthodox traditions have suggested that the Father is the *font* and that icons of the Father are illegitimate because the mystery of the very Godhead is being thereby revealed. The strength of conviction with which this is expressed actually betrays a cataphatism despite protest. The Athanasian tradition, championed by T. F. Torrance, for example, prefers to think of the *font* of the Trinity as the perichoretic communion of all three Persons. This issue of *font*, therefore, even though there are hints of its nature in Scripture, would seem to me to be a matter for the apophatic, and yet, as noted, it is viewed with dogmatism in these traditions. This is what makes the boundary difficult to ascertain with precision within theology. The dangers of a similarly apophatic approach in science is, of course, that "mystery" can lead to a failure to probe or to an invoking of a "God of the gaps" approach, in which God is invoked whenever there is a lack of understanding.

In light of even these boundary challenges in both disciplines, I am boldly suggesting in my title a way of bringing the two disciplines together in a way that suggests profound overlap while giving freedom for each to conduct its business in ways that are distinctive and particular to each discipline. While preserving the supremacy of theology, the queen of sciences, as first-order creedal theology (God as Creator), science contributes by enriching our understanding of that first-order theology. For me, the final authority in theology is always that of the Word of God as properly interpreted. The tradition of the church, reason, and experience also play a role in the discovery of truth, and it is in the latter two that science and the philosophy of science play a role. Another way to see this, beyond this Wesleyan quadrilateral, is to say that science contributes to the development of a second-order theology (e.g., the issue

---

be no more than a groping in the dark. As Barth famously said, if the revealed God does not reflect the real God, "the real God would remain behind revelation and we would be back on our quest" (Barth, *CD* 1/1, 350–51). Barth again states, "If the *tropos apokalupseos* is really a different one from the *tropos huparxeos* and if the *huparxis* is the real being of God, then this means that God in his revelation is not really God" (Barth, *CD* 1/1, 353).

of *how* God creates), thus making theology encyclopedic in the sense that theology overall must consider and respond to all reality, as it may be found in every realm of human scholarship. This posture towards science rests in the providence of God—his revelation in Scripture and the discovery through interaction with creation (science) cannot contradict. The coinherence of science and theology lies in the one God who is author of both, in Christ, by the Spirit.

Julian Huxley's view that with the discovery of evolution "there is neither need or room for the supernatural"[8] is unacceptable today even to postmodern philosophers without any religious faith. His proposal of a secular religion, one without revelation, does not appeal to me as a Christian, because in the history of Jesus Christ, there simply is revelation. Of course, it will be obvious that my title also stands in contradiction to the more respectful biologist Stephen Jay Gould, who advocated that science and faith should occupy separate "non-overlapping magisteria." There is at least an acknowledgement of theology as a magisterium. He also rightly gives freedom to each discipline in its *modus operandi*. He is worth quoting at some length here:

> To say it for all my colleagues and for the umpteenth million time (from college bull sessions to learned treatises): science simply cannot (by its legitimate methods) adjudicate the issue of God's possible superintendence of nature. We neither affirm nor deny it; we simply can't comment on it as scientists. If some of our crowd have made untoward statements claiming that Darwinism disproves God, then I will find Mrs. McInerney and have their knuckles rapped for it (as long as she can equally treat those members of our crowd who have argued that Darwinism must be God's method of action). Science can work only with naturalistic explanations; it can neither affirm nor deny other types of actors (like God) in other spheres (the moral realm, for example). Forget philosophy for a moment; the simple empirics of the past hundred years should suffice. Darwin himself was agnostic (having lost his religious beliefs upon the tragic death of his favorite daughter), but the great American botanist Asa Gray, who favored natural selection and wrote a book entitled Darwiniana, was a devout Christian. Move forward 50 years: Charles D. Walcott, discoverer of the Burgess Shale fossils, was a convinced Darwinian and an equally firm Christian, who believed that God had ordained natural selection to construct a history of life ac-

---

8. Huxley, "Evolutionary Vision," 252–53.

cording to His plans and purposes. Move on another 50 years to the two greatest evolutionists of our generation: G. G. Simpson was a humanist agnostic. Theodosius Dobzhansky a believing Russian Orthodox. Either half my colleagues are enormously stupid, or else the science of Darwinism is fully compatible with conventional religious beliefs—and equally compatible with atheism, thus proving that the two great realms of nature's factuality and the source of human morality do not strongly overlap.[9]

Nevertheless, I am not quite as content as Huxley to avoid the overlapping. I am hoping to show that there are overlapping realities and methodologies and limits to knowledge within good theology and good science. This essay is addressed primarily with the Christian audience in mind, with a view to inspiring a fresh and fearless engagement of Christians in science, given that we have, in large part, abandoned the field. It will perhaps serve also as integrative for scientists to see their work as priestly and as a valuable living out of what it means to be human. There was a day in Western Christianity in which this vast chasm was not present. Even as recently as in the nineteenth century, Charles Hodge spoke of theology and science as the "twin daughters of heaven,"[10] albeit he shortly thereafter went to battle against Darwinism. Under Hodge, 20 percent of the content of the *Princeton Review* was of a scientific nature. In recent times, Francis Collins coined the term "Bio-Logos," which reflects a move towards a relationship between the magisteria that Douglas E. Coe (in a cover blurb) describes as "not merely compatible but complementary." I am being a little bolder, taking liberty as a practicing theologian-scientist and as a once-practicing and still-engaged scientist-theologian. I wish to affirm that the disciplines of Christian theology and science are more than complementary. The two are coinherent. For clarity's sake, when I say science, I mean science and not secular naturalism or scientism; I mean science including the theory of evolution as teleological, not dysteleological. Science and theology are coinherent, not non-overlapping; they are compatible and complementary because they are coinherent, and they are coinherent because they cohere in the same person, who in turn is a coinherent person within the triune Godhead. I even suggest that, although divine and created reality are metaphysically distinct, by virtue of the mediacy of the Son

---

9. Gould, "Self-Appointed Judge," 118.
10. Hodge, "Princeton College," 137–38.

of God, who has entered eternally into a human body by means of the hypostatic union, there is some coinherence between divine and created reality, the latter being the stuff of scientific inquiry.

This coinherence model I am proposing has many similarities with the "mutuality model" of theology and science in the work of Alan Padgett, though, as will become apparent, I take issue with his departure from the tradition of seeing theology as a science.[11] He classifies his own view as between the "dialogue" and "full integration" models outlined by Ian Barbour (independence, conflict, dialogue, and integration).[12] His "collegial metaphor" between the disciplines is agreeable, but his "mutuality model" of the relationship between the disciplines falls short of what I am proposing, namely, a model of coinherence, which may be considered a sixth model. This moves beyond the mutuality model in that I am suggesting that theology and science are not merely interdependent, but mutually internal to each other. Admittedly, this is a model grounded in faith, coming from the theological side and particularly from the reality of the Trinity. But I believe it to be inherently integrative, and with Padgett, I believe in the importance of the mutuality of theology and science practiced within the rubric of image-bearing and affirm that stewardship is crucial for the saving of our planet and its new creation and restoration to a flourishing state of shalom.

I recognize that both the mutuality and the coinherence models are far from the lived reality of the contemporary church. I recognize that many Christians struggle to bring science and theology together. Too often Christians who are scientists struggle with dissonance, as they attend church on Sunday and experience practical atheism from Monday to Friday. Often Western Christians hold to a dualism of things material and things spiritual that goes back beyond the Enlightenment to Greek Platonic thought. The God of creation and the God of redemption are far apart. The Christ of creation and the Christ of reconciliation are distant for them. They assume that in salvation God will take us out of creation, but the biblical truth is that we are saved as whole beings for creation and that at the consummation we will be new creations, not disembodied spirits. The point of the resurrection of Jesus in a body seems to escape them!

---

11. Padgett, *Science*. Padgett does not consider theology to be empirical, an assumption I do make and explain here.

12. Barbour, *Religion*.

So, in light of this need, I will embark upon a defense of this coinherent position. To do so, I will reference John's great summation of the gospel in his prologue, John 1:1–14, and I will offer three main propositions that make coinherence a valid way to view the gospel and scholarship in science and indeed in any scholarly discipline.

> In the beginning was the Word, and the Word was with God, and the Word was God. He was with God in the beginning. Through him all things were made; without him nothing was made that has been made. In him was life, and that life was the light of all mankind. The light shines in the darkness, and the darkness has not overcome it . . . The true light that gives light to everyone was coming into the world. He was in the world, and though the world was made through him, the world did not recognize him. He came to that which was his own, but his own did not receive him. Yet to all who did receive him, to those who believed in his name, he gave the right to become children of God—children born not of natural descent, nor of human decision or a husband's will, but born of God. The Word became flesh and made his dwelling among us. We have seen his glory, the glory of the one and only Son, who came from the Father, full of grace and truth.

The opening phrase, "In the beginning," is an echo of Gen 1:1, and the creation statement in John 1:3, which provides the first major verb of the Logos's action—"through him all things were made"—confirms this. John 1 is the fullness of revelation about creation, indicating the specific role of the Son in creation. We learn here of a being who existed *as* God with respect to identity and essence and *with* God with respect to personhood and communion, before creation took place. So our passage starts before the beginning, before the Big Bang 14 million years ago, outside of time and space, in eternity. To understand truly who Jesus is, John says, we must begin with the relationship he shared with the Father "before the world began" (John 17:5, 24). This relationship is the central revelation of the gospel and the key to understanding all that Jesus says and does. But it also provides insight into the councils of the triune God prior to creation, which in turn provide insight into the nature of creation and the nature of the creatures chosen by God to care for it and manage it lovingly. This leads to the first principle.

Theology

ONTOLOGICAL CONSIDERATIONS

The Freedom of God as This Relates to the Contingent Nature of Creation and Revelation

I recently lost a good friend, my squash partner, who grew up where I did, that is, in Zimbabwe. As I was reflecting on his life at the memorial service, I quoted C. S. Lewis, who wrote a fair bit about friendship. One of the things Lewis realized about friendship is that it is a sheer *gift*. It is not required in the evolutionary process: "Friendship is unnecessary, like philosophy, like art, like the universe itself (for God does not need to create). It has no survival value; rather it is one of those things that give value to survival."[13] For my purposes in this essay, I note the fact that the ground on which Lewis places the unnecessary and contingent nature of friendship is the unnecessary and contingent nature of the universe. It is the freedom of God in creating and the resultant contingent nature of the creation that makes for an overlapping of the disciplines of science and theology. How so? One cannot decide beforehand on the nature of substances or the behavior of the orbits of the earth and the sun on some kind of *a priori* basis. One can try to predict based on previous results and known patterns, but these will have been discovered empirically. Of course, there have been times when the church has sought to preempt empirical findings based on spurious readings of Scripture, as in the cases of Copernicus and Brahe and Galileo. But when Scripture is read in the kind of manner that its texts should be read, that is, based on proper rhetorical and literary hermeneutics, it seems to me that we need not fear contradictions with science. In a similar manner, the core of Christian theology could not have been predicted on *a priori* grounds. This is true of the two great foundation stones of the faith—that God would become man (the incarnation) and that the one God, Yahweh, is three persons in one eternal communion, the Trinity.

With respect to the incarnation, this was a bombshell for the *a priori* assumptions of the Greek philosophy of the day. "God, spirit" could never be in contact with "man, flesh." But John the eyewitness apostle gives witness that this is precisely what happened. In 1 John 1 he writes:

> That which was from the beginning [the eternally divine Son], which we have *heard*, which we have *seen with our eyes*, which we have *looked at* and our *hands have touched*—this we proclaim

---

13. Lewis, *Four Loves*, 71.

> concerning the Word of life. The life appeared; we have seen it and testify to it, and we proclaim to you the eternal life, which was with the Father and has appeared to us. We proclaim to you what we have seen and heard, so that you also may have fellowship with us. And our fellowship is with the Father and with his Son, Jesus Christ [the Trinity is hinted at here].

The utterly unlikely reality that God could become human was arrived at by empirical study and reflection. *A posteriori* not *a priori*. What a surprise. And of course, the articulation of the doctrine of the Trinity was next, and again, it was not dreamed up in *a priori* fashion by Greek philosophy, even though terms with Greek philosophical background were used in describing the doctrine, terms such as *ousia*, *hypostasis*, and *homoousios*. I would argue that these terms were not merely used to reflect standard meanings, but were in fact commandeered by the church to describe realities they had come to know personally and historically.

As Paul Fiddes aptly states, "When the early church fathers developed the doctrine of the Trinity, they were not painting by numbers, they were finding concepts to express an *experience*. That is, they were attempting to articulate the richness of the personality of God that they had found in the story of salvation and their experience of it."[14]

There is thus a profound coinherence between science and theology that is grounded in God's free decision to create and to reveal himself in Christ.

The Freedom of God as This Relates to the Nature of Humanity as Graced Image Bearers

> In the beginning was the Word, and the Word was with God, and the Word was God. He was with God in the beginning. Through him all things were made; without him nothing was made that has been made. In him was life, and that life was the light of all mankind. (John 1:1–4)

I wish to borrow here from the anthropology of Karl Barth. The best news of the gospel is the election of the triune God to create and to be *for* humanity, to become one with humanity in Christ. The nature of humanity as defined first by this election, and not merely by evolutionary theory, is what gives humanity the capacity to engage in scholarship as image bearers of the God of wisdom, knowledge, creativity, and beauty.

14. Fiddes, *Participating in God*, 5.

What enables the human quest in science is the prior election of God to create and be for humanity in redemption, as revealed in the incarnation, death, and resurrection of Christ—the elect Man for all humanity. Anthropology, as it is determined first by the election of God, and not by evolution, accounts for the human capacity to do science and scholarship in general. This is an argument about the coinherence of theology and science from *ontology*, that is, the coinherence of theologians and scientists as graced image bearers.

The patristic-medieval tradition speaks of the image of God in three different ways: (1) as *relational* in the sense that it is established by the initiative of God and in covenantal relationship with him and also in the sense that relationality is embedded in the first humans ("male and female created he them" [Gen 1:27 KJV]), (2) as *structural* or ontological in the sense of cerebral and self-reflexive capacity and creativity, and (3) as *functional* in that the immediate command of God upon the first humans is to tend the garden and care for the earth. Jeremy Kidwell, in reviewing this tradition, has wisely commented that "appreciation for the polyvalence of the doctrine allows for a composite meaning."[15] Even so, most theologians have opted for the elevation of one of these viewpoints as primary, even if polyvalence is evident. To draw on Irenaeus, the image is recapitulated in Jesus, who, by his representative actions from incarnation to resurrection and ascension, makes possible the restoration of the *imago*. The resurrection was the first day of the new creation, and as Oliver O'Donovan states, the resurrection of Christ is the reaffirmation of creation;[16] and, I would add, with this comes the anthropological possibilities of science and theology in ways that are constructive intellectually and for the care of the environment.

The crucial piece for considering who both scientists and theologians *are*, then, is that they are human persons and image bearers, with, yes, remarkable cranial capacity, with, yes, ability to assess their own ideas, and with, yes, profound creativity. However, the design of God for image bearers was to be and do these things in participational relationship with him. When these capacities are exercised outside the core concept of relationality with God and other humans, the efforts of both theologians and scientists begin to be distorted and possibly destructive

---

15. Kidwell, "Elucidating the Image of God."
16. O'Donovan, *Resurrection*, 14.

for creation rather than a constructive continuation of God's work in the world.

Both disciplines are possible only because of the graced nature of human beings, who are made in the image of God and who are such only in the One true image of the invisible God, the last or *eschatos* Adam. There is a coinherence related to capacity, that is, by way of what human persons made in the image of God and made recipients of the cultural mandate can do and are to do. We have been made to be god-like creatures, and as such, we are characterized by curiosity and wonder and creativity and responsibility.

In my opinion, Barth's view of election as the "best news of the gospel" is therefore the "best news for scholarship." For Barth, the union of creation and covenant is the primary purpose of Gen 1 and 2. It is more about anticipation of the last Adam than it is about the first Adam. Barth viewed God's pre-historical purpose for humanity in Christ (all of humanity) as all-important, and like Irenaeus, he saw Christ's humanity as the recapitulation, indeed, the first-intended nature of God's purposes for the first Adam. It is really in the last Adam that the cultural mandate is fulfilled, and all that this means for the human pursuits of the sciences, the arts, and theological scholarship.

The crucial piece in all this is human participation. Even in the prelapsarian state, humans were only capable of being humans in relationship with God. Image-bearing may involve cerebral capacity, and it does involve the functions of earth-keeping, creation care, and work, which, according to Gen 4, includes things that smack of the arts ("Jubal; he was the father of all who play stringed instruments and pipes" [v. 21]) and the sciences ("Zillah also had a son, Tubal-Cain, who forged all kinds of tools out of bronze and iron"—metallurgists, i.e., chemists [v. 22]), but all of this is contingent upon being in communion with and being guided by God. Calvin sees this. He insists that even in prelapsarian days Adam participated in the life of the last Adam in the garden, for he was unfit for the divine presence on his own, not because of sin, but because of the metaphysical disconnect between God and humanity. Christ was the mediator even then.[17] The fall regrettably distances the

---

17. Calvin recognized that "even if man had remained free from all stain, his condition would have been too lowly for him to reach God without a Mediator" (*Institutes* 2.12.1 [1:465]). He insisted that it was Christ who was our Mediator even before the fall, by virtue of the fact that even from the beginning, "Christ was set over angels and

cerebral and creative capacities of humanity from the relational participation. In Christ, in whom all the treasures of wisdom and knowledge inhere, and who is in perfect relationship with the Father as a Man, the *imago* is recapitulated, and all in union with him are able to hold together their intellectual capacity with profound humility and responsible administration of their theological or scientific knowledge. That is, the ideal posture of the scientist must be as a theologian-scientist.

What about those who are not Christian? All are image bearers by creation and as reasserted by the incarnation and resurrection of Christ. If Barth is right, all humanity has, ontologically speaking, been justified in Christ. All are *designated* Christians. The incarnation has made a difference for all humanity, even if all humanity is not saved. Brilliant scientists, whether Christian or not, reflect the divine image in their IQ, craft, and creativity. Regrettably, as fallen humanity, we do not give thanks for the capacities we have, and we often do not show wider concern for the effects of our scientific advancements. The image is effaced but not erased in humanity. Humanity remains in relatedness to God even if not in relationship with God, and their intellectual, creative capacities remain. The advent of modernity ushered in mainly by science is not all bad. I for one do not want to be premodern again. I am glad about scientific advancement and medications and PowerPoint and Google; in every culture, including those that have embraced modernity, there is the good, the true, and the beautiful. There is also that which is sinister, and the advent of global warming is but one evidence of the imbalances of modern scientific humanity that is capable not only of great science but of destroying the whole earth (climate scientist Katherine Hayhoe recently made the comment that if the graphs continue as they are, by 2034, we will be in serious trouble). Christians in science have great potential for being redemptive in this age and for modeling the shalom of a priestly, humble approach to science.

---

men as their Head," as he was "'the first-born of all creation' [Col. 1:15]" (2.12.4 [1:467, bracketed biblical citation in source]). "Hence, whatever excellence was engraved upon Adam ... [was] derived from the fact that he approached the glory of his Creator through the only-begotten Son" (2.12.6 [1:471]). Thus, only by way of participation in Christ was Adam a "mirror" of God's glory (2.12.6 [1:471]). Only by way of Adam's dynamic "union with Christ" did God behold himself (which is to say: did God "image" himself) in Adam. Adam and Eve were continually reminded that their very lives, their very ability to "image" God, were utterly dependent upon communion (κοινωνία) with God.

In sum, I have chosen a somewhat controversial way of answering the question "What has the gospel got to do with scholarship?" I am suggesting with Karl Barth that the *best news of the gospel* is the election of the One Man Jesus Christ in eternity past. What does the best news of the gospel mean for scholarship?

Much has been made in recent biblical/theological scholarship of the importance of *history* in the outworking of the gospel. Thus, the gospel narrative according to a Kuyperian way of speaking is that of creation, the fall, redemption or reconciliation of creation, and consummation of creation. Along with this has been the stress on valuing *creation* and keeping creation, redemption of humanity, and the cosmos together. The gospel is not a gospel of evacuation, we have rightly stressed. The gospel entails a doctrine of creation in which creation matters, because creation is the product of God's creating action, because it has been pronounced good by the Divine Creator, because it has been entered into in the incarnation of the Son, and because by his resurrection Christ has reaffirmed the creation. The *creatio ex nihilo* and the *creatio continua* (continuing creative activity) have led, through the advent of the Christ of creation, to the *creatio ex vetere* (transformation of the old creation) in which humanity, in Christ, the last Adam, can participate. The Christian faith should, in light of God's estimation of and purpose for creation, foster the pursuit of science with the care of creation as its ultimate goal. Furthermore, the cultural mandate by which God passed on the baton of creating to his image bearers—for it was good but not perfect—positively urges the Christian becoming human, according to particular vocations, to be the scientists committed to understanding creation; to be priests of creation, giving creation a voice; to be the artists who in their painting and sculpting take their cue from the God of triune beauty who has created a beautiful world; and to be the musicians emanating sound that reflects the supreme harmony of all.

However, I want first to focus not so much on these important *historical* and *creational* commitments of the Christian faith, but on what happens in pre-history and pre-creation. For this is where the gospel begins. It begins in the eternal love of the triune Godhead, and it begins in the electing of God to create, to create humanity, and to be *for* humanity, in fact, to be for *sinful* humanity. I am not referring to a secret decretive act of God by means of which some individuals are chosen for salvation and some for perdition. I am choosing rather to opt for God's electing in eternity past, within his covenanting purpose, to choose the Son to become human, to become one with humanity, and to act vicariously for that humanity. I am electing to believe in the premundane election *by* God, including God the Son, and *of* God the Son to enter into sinful humanity, into the forsakenness of the divine "no" on humanity's sinfulness by way of the cross, and then into the divine "yes" of the resurrection, in which humanity finds its reality and function as image-bearing persons, scientists, artists, and economists. I am electing to believe the good news that, because of the incarnation and resurrection, God has elected to be for humanity. Because the One really real Human, Jesus Christ, is in fact the last Adam, and because his covenant people with him are that communal last Adam, humanity in Christ has not only been redeemed and reconciled, but humans have participated together in the pursuit given to image bearers of Yahweh in the now to care for creation, to probe its secrets, to be creative as God is creative, and to participate in the *creatio ex vetere*, perceiving the prods of the Spirit towards the consummation.

But people are to do all of this as graced humans, humans elected in Christ and in participation with Christ, who can only study any of these disciplines as humans engraced and with the ideal that each pursues their vocation in gratitude. The two acts of God, revelation and election, work to establish humanity in the reality of grace, which creates the possibility of human reciprocity in gratitude. Humanity is thus ontologically grounded in the realities of divine grace and the truly human response of gratitude. This act of gratitude is a uniquely human reality that can only be uniquely directed to God in both disciplines. In this way, the encounter of grace opens the door for human freedom and human responsibility. These two realities lived in obedience to the Word of God—as a result of God's invocation—form the very basis of an ontological description of humanity that is true to our reality as created by the Creator God. This ontological description is not the sum of human self-understanding but the beginning of it. This is what humanity is without separating humanity from creation or the Creator.

Karl Barth freely admits that many forms of anthropological understanding derived from sociology, psychology, biology, existential philosophy, naturalism, and evolutionary science hold some significance, for "in their limits they may well be accurate and important."[18] They all describe humanity in its uniqueness based on the unique methodologi-

---

18. Barth, *CD* 3/2, 122.

cal features of each field of study. These descriptions can be helpful, useful, and accurate, but they cannot fully describe humanity, he insisted. For they are "all bracketed, and no decisive enlightenment about man is to be expected from within these brackets, but only from a source outside. This source is God."[19] True humanity cannot be understood apart from God. To remove the Creator from the definition of humanity is to remove the foundation of what humanity is. Barth suggests that "if we think of man in isolation from and independence of God, we are no longer thinking about real man."[20] For him humanity exists because of the election of God and only in relationship with God. Outside of this relationship humanity ceases to be human. The significance of this relationship means that it "is not peripheral but central, not incidental but essential to that which makes him a real man, himself."[21] Evolutionary understandings of humanity that pay particular attention to humanity's environment are no doubt helpful in understanding humanity. But as Barth states, "If man does not know himself already, long before his attention is directed to these phenomena, he will be blind even though he sees. In face and in spite of these phenomena he will always look on the wrong side. He will always think with the animal and the rest of creation generally."[22] The created and reaffirmed nature of the human person as made in the divine image answers the "who" question, and it is crucial to all humble scholarship, be it scientific or theological. The subject in the disciplines is the same, image-bearing humanity with divinely endowed capacities and, hopefully, relationship with the Creator that forms the character that bears the capacities and guides their use. Scientists themselves, with all their brilliance and creativity, strike me as anthropological evidence of the God they sometimes deny.

The Goodness of God as This Relates to the Distinctness and Goodness of Creation

"In the beginning was the Word, and the Word was with God, and the Word was God. He was with God in the beginning. Through him all things were made; without him nothing was made that has been made"

19. Ibid.
20. Ibid., 123.
21. Ibid.
22. Ibid., 90.

(John 1:1–3). This verse reflects a movement from eternity into time. Here is the specific statement of the Son's specific role in creation. Paul echoes this in Col 1:15–17: "The Son is the image of the invisible God, the firstborn over all creation. For in him all things were created: things in heaven and on earth, visible and invisible, whether thrones or powers or rulers or authorities; all things have been created through him and for him. He is before all things, and in him all things hold together." In John 1:1–3 John stresses by stating both positively and negatively—that the Word is the agent of all creation (1:3)[23]—and that there were no exceptions (the existence of absolutely all things came by this Word).

Two further ontological realities serve to demonstrate the overlap between theology or the Christian faith and science. The first is the clear distinction good theology provides between God and the creation, the metaphysical remove, as it were, between these two realities. Creation is not God. This distinction is implicit in our text. Clearly the Word, who is God, is distinct from "all things that are made," that is, the creation. But here, the fact that the triune God works through the agency of the Son (and the Spirit elsewhere) is suggestive of some metaphysical distance, especially when it is most likely that, in the eternal covenant of God, the Son, to borrow another Barthian concept, is *incarnandus*, that is, he has an orientation towards the incarnation in eternity past and therefore towards agency in the creation.

But this theological reality must not be emphasized to the expense of another one. What God creates through the Word is good. It may not be God, but it is good. It is not, as in the Greek world, inferior to spirit. This was emphasized in the Genesis account, and it is recapitulated here and also in John 1:3 and 14: "Through him all things were made; without him nothing was made that has been made"; "The Word became flesh and made his dwelling among us. We have seen his glory, the glory of the one and only Son, who came from the Father, full of grace and truth." The Son in creation, in a created body, is no less glorious than in pre-incarnate days, albeit that glory may be veiled. This vindicates the goodness of matter.

---

23. The first chapter of Genesis hints that the Spirit was also active in creation, brooding over the primeval waters. A biblical understanding of creation is Trinitarian in nature. Irenaeus spoke of the Son and the Spirit as the two hands of the Father in creation.

These two theological realities are actually the cornerstone for the proposal that Christianity was the seedbed for the development of modern science in the first place. That creation was *good* made it worth studying and engaging with in an empirical manner. That it was *not God* and *not sacred* rendered it accessible. Some cultures of a pantheist variety could never develop science, for they were simply too fearful of the matter they sacralized and too fearful of tampering with the gods. Other cultures, like the Greek one, did not develop science, for they downplayed the importance of the material realm and thought experimentation within it to be unnecessary. It is possible to argue historically that science actually is the offspring of a Western Christian culture, even if in modernity the child has become a rebellious teenager.

Thus, science is coinherent within Christian theology, with a compatibility stemming from a high, but not too high, view of created matter. Matter matters and is worthy of study. It has its own identity, its own particularity. It is not inferior to things mental or spiritual, as in Platonism. Yet it is not sacralized, as in paganism or animism. That is, it is not to be considered equal with God. It is God's creation, and he is distinct from it. It is not too sacred to study. One can also argue that the freedom to study creation in its own right, which the Enlightenment prospered, in fact had its roots in a Christian doctrine of creation with roots as far back as the medieval church, as Michael Foster has indicated. Loren Wilkinson writes:

> In the 1930's M.B. Foster, an Oxford philosopher, published three articles (in the prestigious philosophical journal *Mind*) on "the Christian Doctrine of Creation and the Rise of Modern Science." In those days the scholarly and popular consensus on that subject was largely unanimous: if there was any influence of Christianity on the development of science it had been negative. Bertrand Russell's words at the beginning of his *History of Western Philosophy* are typical of the mood. Whereas science gives us genuine knowledge, says Russell, theology "induces a dogmatic belief that we have knowledge where in fact we have ignorance, and by doing so generates a kind of impertinent insolence towards the universe." The supposed effect of this conjectured "insolence towards the universe" had been catalogued a few decades earlier in an influential (and typical) book by John Wilson Draper provocatively titled *History of the Conflict Between Science and Religion*. Draper's conclusion was that through its disparagement of science Christianity had become

"a stumbling block in the intellectual advancement of Europe for more than a thousand years." Foster's meticulously reasoned articles—written not as Christian theology or apologetics, but simply as a careful exercise in the history of thought—were the beginning of a slow but thorough change in this image of "warfare." Though many people (including many Christians who should know better) still use such language of conflict, it is now widely acknowledged that some aspects of medieval Christianity were not only a fertile seedbed for modern science but also quite possibly a necessary condition for its eventual development. The main point of Foster's exhaustive (and largely irrefutable) argument was that Greek science had never moved beyond its embryonic stage, because it assumed that genuine knowledge was (as in a mathematical proof) always a matter of abstract reasoning from certain first principles. Though the physical world could provide examples and illustration of these ideal truths, it was never their starting point. In contrasting modern empirical science with ancient Greek attempts at science, concludes Foster, "In each case the modern procedure will be found to differ from its ancient counterpart by the part which sensuous experience plays in it." "Sensuous experience," of course, is nothing new; it was certainly not new to the Greeks. But the Christian experience of the Creator-God of love who invented physical reality, and who, in Jesus, became a part of it, changed forever how we value that knowledge. We cannot know the world God has made simply by thinking about it. What God does, like who God is, is inexhaustible, surprising and gracious. Knowledge comes through engaged experience, not detached contemplation. The Psalmist said it well: "Taste and see that the Lord is good." This recognition that sensuous experience is the source of knowledge is basic to Hebrew understanding. And it is here, rather than in Greek ideas of the superiority of the knowledge abstracted from the senses, that the tradition of empirical science took root.[24]

The Goodness Yet Incompleteness of Creation Assumes a Place for Human Endeavor

The fact that the creation described in Gen 1 was good and very good leaves room for the notion that it was not perfect, thus creating a role for humanity's participation with God in his management and perfection of this creation. That is, image-bearing humans have a required role of

---

24. Wilkinson, "New Story of Creation," 26–36.

being receivers of the baton, and the role of science comes within this, as we have already indicated. The eschatological fulfillment of creation is, of course, in a primary sense found in Christ, but as humans in Christ, the image is recapitulated. It is thus entirely fitting that Christians, those in Christ, might take their place as priests of creation, pursuing its understanding, utilizing its resources, and managing it within the wider creation. This is an enterprise most fitting for human persons fully alive! There is a Christian theology of vocation, which I believe is crucial for the healthy functioning of scientists. In their endeavors they are participating in God's work in the world. Scientific research can be brutally difficult, lonely, and fraught with doubting with respect to its significance. Scientists need a sense of vocation, a sense that they are doing what it is humans are intended to do—to participate in creation and to do so by seeking to understand it. They are being mission-al in their work. There is still a need for the overcoming of dualism in the church with respect to the clergy-laity distinction. Theology gives a sense of vocation to the scientist, and it is a lofty one—to be priests of Christ's creation.

The Contingency and Goodness of Creation is Defined by Its Being Granted Its Own Particularity and "Thisness" (HAECCITAS) and Certain Degrees of Freedom

"Through him all things were made; without him nothing was made that has been made" (John 1:3). This verse stresses, in light of who the Word is in context, the closeness yet metaphysical distance of Christ to creation and his crucial centrality to God's ultimate purpose for creation. Creation was, as Athanasius insisted, a free act of the will of God. It is to be distinguished from the generation of the Son by the Father and from the procession of the Spirit, which come from within the being of the Father. The triune God did not need to create, as if to overcome some deficit, but created in an overflow of divine love expressed in divine volition. Thus, what he created was distinct from himself, having its own particularity and degree of freedom. The *contingency of creation gave to a good creation degrees of freedom*. This must be held in tension with the reality that all of creation is under the sustaining and sovereign rule of God the Creator, in the Son and by the Spirit.

At this point there are tensions in the Christian tradition, and much thought still needs to be applied to the ways in which the sovereignty of God interacts with the particularity and freedom of molecules, subatomic particles, and all matter in the cosmos. Some degrees of freedom seem to have been granted to even the first particle or particles created *ex nihilo* by God, such that the big bang occurred and then, over the next 14 billion years, the development of a habitable earth and the evolution of plants, animals, and humans transpired. One side of the tradition has tended to emphasize the participation of all matter in the life of God, thus explaining the directed or teleological nature of evolution.

It would be naive to assume this is a new issue. There is a dialogue that goes back centuries. On the one hand, there is a stream of thought from Augustine on that may be called a participatory view of creation. This is grounded in the belief that correspondence between the Creator and the creation is analogical, not univocal. The doctrine of the *analogia entis* is at the heart of Catholic thought, and a modification of it has been proposed within the Protestant tradition by Bonhoeffer and Barth, termed the *analogia relationis*. Both positions agree that creation is not stridently autonomous.

Thomas Aquinas, for example, did not believe in a graceless nature. Even nature was "engraced," because creation is a gift. He also did not, in his desire to maintain the integrity of creation, think of it as having a "brute autonomy" or a "seized autonomy," but rather thought of it as having a graced or gifted autonomy. A participatory ontology "understands transcendence as an essential feature of material reality."[25] There is always a danger in this kind of *methexis* participation theology, which is the loss of the particularity of the creation and its parts.

As Wilkinson points out, the Franciscan tradition, originating with Francis of Assisi himself and the thirteenth-century Franciscan philosopher Bonaventure, offered a new kind of attention to the particulars of creation as a seedbed for science. Their prodigy, Franciscan philosopher Duns Scotus, a careful thinker dubbed the "subtle doctor," offered a defense of the centrality of the will (voluntarism) in God's creation and challenged Thomas by suggesting that both creation and the incarnation transcend reason and are evidence of "irrational love" or love's extravagance. Scotus, in affirming the univocity of being (*Opus oxoniense* 1.3.1–2),[26] that is, that we can indeed speak univocally of God with respect to our being (God exists, and we exist), recognized the risk in the assertion that we do not exist by material participation and that our

25. Smith, *Radical Orthodoxy*, 185.
26. Quoted in Grenz, *Named God*, 55.

being is our own. The risk is that humans will take up their autonomy as independent of God rather than in relational participation with God. Scotus avers that, from the beginning, God had willed to assume the consequences of human autonomy by way of the cross. Thus, creation was itself a kenotic act of God.

Whatever we think of Scotus, whether a hero or a villain, he is to be credited with an awareness of the irreducible uniqueness and particularity of things, that is, the "thisness" (*haeccitas*)[27] of things that encouraged the pursuit of science. His view also of the "the primacy of Christ," that is, creation for incarnation, not vice versa, has much to contribute towards a theodicy. How is all this relevant to the science of origins?

1. No Christian theologian-scientist can avoid the notion of an *ex nihilo* creation of at least something, for it is this that upholds a distinction between God and his creation. Whether it is the first subatomic particles or atom, the first cluster of atoms or molecules that formed the Big Bang, or all of creation in a fiat moment (so Augustine, based on Sir 18:1, which he considered to be canonical), none can avoid the *ex nihilo* piece of creation.

2. However, it seems that after the creation of the first piece of matter, creation is given some degree of freedom and some degree of participation in God. Or perhaps, in the spirit of Karl Barth, the God who loves in freedom has granted freedom to his creation, but this freedom is found in God's freedom. Creation acts in freedom as God acts in freedom, and in his acting in freedom, creation acts in freedom. This seems to preserve both the ideas of freedom and participation.

Thus, although there was an *ex nihilo* creation by Christ of whatever the initial creation substances were, this gave way to a creation that God permitted to evolve in its own way over 14 billion years, or so it seems. If Christ made all things, he must have been involved in this process, watching over its development. Creatures were also granted freedom (contingency but dependence). This is an important piece for a theodicy, that is, in the reconciling of the presence of evil and suffering with the notion that creation was brought into existence by a good God. Creation was in itself a kenotic act on behalf of God before the incarnation took place (perhaps both went together in the eternal purposes

---

27. Scotus, *Ordinatio* II, d. 3, p. 1. q. 2, n. 48.

of God, given the seminal place of the incarnation and resurrection in the formation of the new creation from the old). As Polkinghorne has stated, "the existence of free creatures is a greater good than a world populated by perfectly behaving automata." However, with realism, Polkinghorne notes "that good has the cost of mortality and suffering."[28] This then leads him to speak of the transformation of the old creation into the new, the second stage of God's creation, that is, its redemption and reconciliation by Christ, one that happens not by creation *ex nihilo*, but *ex vetere*. Why does this happen in this way? What is the purpose of this old creation? The answer lies in part in the freedom spoken of and in the consequences that such freedom incurs. Another answer lies in the fact that somehow, in the providence of God, more glory is revealed of the God who redeems a contingent universe than one who creates perfect automata. This has overlap with, surprisingly, Stephen Jay Gould's views on biological determinism. In an article defending Gould's view, John Horgan states,

> I used to be tough on Stephen Jay Gould, the great evolutionary biologist, who died in 2002. I found him self-righteous and pompous, in person and on the page. In an August 1995 profile of him for *Scientific American* I summed up his worldview, which emphasizes the role of randomness, or "contingency," in shaping life, as "shit happens." But I admired Gould's ferocious opposition to biological determinism, which he defined as the view that "the social and economic differences between different groups—primarily races, classes and sexes—arise from inherited, inborn distinctions and that society, in this sense, is an accurate reflection of biology." I loathe biological determinism, too, and so I must defend Gould against charges that he was a fact-fudging "charlatan," as the anthropologist Ralph Holloway of Columbia University put it.[29]

The Relational and Personal Nature of the Triune God is Mirrored in the Relationality of Creation

"In the beginning was the Word, and the Word was with God [as a person in relation, *perichoresis* of essence, *circumincessio*], and the Word was God. He was with God in the beginning (*perichoresis* of act, *circum*-

---

28. Polkinghorne, *Science and the Trinity*, 165.
29. Horgan, "Defending Stephen Jay Gould's Crusade."

incessio). Through him all things were made; without him nothing was made that has been made" (John 1:1–3). "And the Word was with God . . . " This phrase indicates both the equality and the distinctness of the Person of the Word. That the Word is with God implies that the Word is distinct from God, and yet the phrase that follows indicates that he was, at the same time, fully God. The preposition "with" (Gk. *pros*) in a context like this is used to indicate personal relationship, not mere proximity (cf. Mark 6:3). Here we have conveyed the mystery of the Trinity, in which the Son is both "with" as to his person and "God" as to his essence. The Persons have irreducible identity and are distinct, and yet they are one by communion or coinherence, each in the other, one in essence and one in complete mutuality.

I do not wish to point to things in nature that have some resemblance to threeness in oneness. All analogies for the Trinity are heretical, save the one sanctioned in Scripture—humanity in the image of God. But I do wish to suggest that there is something about creation that reflects some of the *concepts* of the Trinity, which will not be surprising to find, given he is the Creator. Take, for example, the nature of electrons that is fundamental to all matter. When we first learn chemistry, our teachers draw electrons as if they were particles that fill shells around the atom. As we advance, however, we learn that electrons have both particulate nature and wave nature (as per the Schrödinger Wave Equation). They show particulate nature and wave nature all at the same time, and their location is described more by a cloud than a particle. Something called the Heisenberg Uncertainty Principle reflects the non-locatedness of electrons, which are described as present in orbitals, not as particles in circular orbits.

Polkinghorne (an Anglican minister and theoretical physicist), in his book *Science and the Trinity*, expresses the belief that both science and theology are best done from the bottom up, from a faith-seeking-understanding perspective. He develops the analogy between relationality in God the Trinity and in matter. Thus, he states, "I shall make what some of my scientific colleagues might think was an over-audacious claim, that a deeply satisfying intellectual candidate for the title of a true 'Theory of Everything' is in fact provided by Trinitarian theology." He clarifies that it is not that we can infer the Trinity from nature, but "that there are aspects of our scientific understanding of the universe that become more deeply intelligible to us if they are viewed in a Trinitarian perspective."[30] Later, he illustrates this in a number of ways. These include Einstein's Theory of General Relativity, which showed that "space, time and matter are closely connected in a kind of integrated package, in which matter curves spacetime and spacetime curves the paths of matter."[31] He refers also to the phenomenon of relationality within quantum mechanics. Einstein's EPR (Einstein-Podolsky-Rosen) effect "showed that quantum theory implied that once two quantum entities have interacted with each other, they remain mutually entangled however far they may eventually separate."[32] He notes the fact that Einstein thought there was something "spooky" about this and wondered whether the quantum account was incomplete. However, as Polkinghorne points out, "the beautiful experiments of Alain Aspect and his collaborators have shown us that non-locality is indeed a property of nature." He generalizes to say that "twentieth-century science has revealed a deep-seated interconnectivity present in the fabric of the physical world."[33] Thus, he is convinced that the Trinitarian perspective, such as is expressed in John Zizioulas's *Being in Communion*, which Polkinghorne suggests could equally well have the title "Reality is relational," does indeed reveal deeply intelligible but otherwise hidden features of nature, such as non-locality. This theme is developed further by a number of authors in the 2010 volume *The Trinity and an Entangled World: Relationality in Physical Science and Theology*, edited by Polkinghorne, probing relationality in both matter, including the property of quantum entanglement,[34] and God.

Creation is both substantial and relational. The classical Trinitarian theological assertion of God as both being and being-in-relation, or, in fact, persons in relation, may have some parallels in the scientific shift from classical physics to relativity and quantum theory. The concept of complementarity in microphysics presents an analogous problem to the

---

30. Polkinghorne, *Science and the Trinity*, 61.
31. Ibid., 73.
32. Ibid., 73–74.
33. Ibid.
34. See Polkinghorne, ed., *Trinity and an Entangled World*. Chapters 2 (Jeffrey Bub) and 3 (Anton Zeilinger) deal with this theme of quantum entanglement, a phenomenon hinted at above. This is a phenomenon in the subatomic world, where interaction "can bring about states that have to be considered as a single unified system, even though composed of constituents that may spatially be widely separated" (vii).

question about being and becoming; how can a physical phenomenon like light have qualities of both a wave and a particle?

The paradigm shift in Barth's thought with respect to relations in the Godhead is perhaps analogous to the shift in the new physics. Once the shift is made, the possibility that there could be a being that is apart from relations is nonsense, as is the notion that light must be either wave or particle, and cannot be both. Being and relations are simultaneous to one another. Being is inseparable from the relations that constitute any human person's existence, all of which are simultaneous, multi-leveled, and complex.

I stress, though, that the doctrine of the Trinity is not an exercise in mathematics. For example, in response to the charge that 1+1+1=3, not one Christian apologist has countered that 1x1x1=1. God is not and cannot be the result of multiplication! Barth has correctly emphasized that the oneness of God is not to be confused with the "singularity" that is connected with numerical unity. As he states, unlike numerical oneness, the "revealed unity does not exclude but includes a distinction."[35] In other words, God is Father, Son, and Holy Spirit, three persons sharing the same divine nature (preferred to substance) in a oneness of communion. The doctrine of the Trinity was formulated in response to the historical event of the incarnation, the presence in history of a man who was God the Son. The immanent Trinity, who God is *in se*, is understood from who he is *pro nobis*, or for us, in the economy of redemption.

These are ontological indications of an overlap between theology and science. But now we come to things epistemological.

> In him was life, and that life was the light of all mankind. The light shines in the darkness, and the darkness has not overcome it . . . The true light that gives light to everyone was coming into the world. He was in the world, and though the world was made through him, the world did not recognize him. He came to that which was his own, but his own did not receive him. Yet to all who did receive him, to those who believed in his name, he gave the right to become children of God—children born not of natural descent, nor of human decision or a husband's will, but born of God. (John 1:4–13)

---

35. Barth, *CD* 1/1, 354–55.

EPISTEMOLOGICAL CONSIDERATIONS

The best news of the gospel, that God has elected to create and redeem humanity in Christ, has been revealed in a historically empirical way that requires faith as the grounding of understanding. The receiving of the revelation of the gospel is consonant with the way in which all knowledge is gained. I will argue that, likewise, in science there is no such thing as unprejudiced knowledge. There is no pure reason and no pure objectivity. All knowledge is based on faith, and it is "engraced." This is in the nature of our human constitution as related to God. This is an argument about the coinherence of theology and science from *epistemology*.

Jim Houston once ended a lengthy discussion on how we know God with the statement "Some people think I am anti-intellectual. I am not. I am post-intellectual." Reason, the life of the mind, and its pursuits come after faith. Reason is always post-faith. That this is true in the realm of Christian theology is well known and has been acknowledged since Augustine through to Anselm and on to Karl Barth. Knowledge in theology is always faith seeking understanding. It is always *a posteriori* and not *a priori*. What may come as a surprise to many of us is that science, indeed all knowledge, is arrived at in the same way.

Contrary to the scientism of logical positivism, the belief in the privileging of scientific knowledge, the primacy of science over religion, there is no science until we have criticized the critical and deconstructed the notion of pure reason. As Alan Padgett explains so well, in science, despite the aversion of scientism to metaphysics, "explanations are always attached to some metaphysical commitments."[36] I do not practice science until I have first understood faith or prejudices or tacit understanding or knowledge as personal knowledge. I am a post-scientist in that respect, not just because I am no longer practicing science, though I am trying to practice theological science, as T. F. Torrance called it.

The compatibility of Christian theology with science lies in how we know what we know. It is compatibility by way of *empiricism*. I have shown above how, in some surprising and very significant ways, the gospel was and is compatible with science and was indeed instrumental in the development of science in the Western world. This is in contrast to the world of the ancient Greek philosophers, who did not and could

---

36. Padgett, *Science*, 13.

not develop empirical science. I am contending that there is a profound consonance between scholarship in theology (what Torrance called "Scientific Theology") and scholarship in science. I do not really favor the term integration. I see no need to integrate science and theology, because in my mind they are already one. God is the author of both, and even though these disciplines have their own particularities and methodologies, they are one in their epistemologies and one in their conclusions regarding the universe and God. They do not need to be integrated except in our own dualistic Western minds.

Now, this is perhaps counterintuitive for moderns. Edwin Judge, one of the leading experts in first- and second-century history, who founded Macquarie University's ancient history department, challenges fundamental aspects of modern worldviews or dominant thought structures.[37] In today's world the popular understanding is that there is a massive contrast between the world of science or rationality and the world of the religious, which is considered to be a realm of belief that has no ground in evidence. Religious people are considered to have a reliance on myths and live within a cocoon of faith in which beliefs are held within some kind of reinforced circle based on desire, for any number of reasons, to believe in those things. These are to be contrasted with "evidenced" persons—those under the rule of science, who do not go into a question with preconceived answers. Science is considered to be unprejudiced, to be reason without faith, and to be inquiry from outside of one's own mind. And where did this rule of rationality begin? The common answer is: with the Greeks. It was the pre-Socratic, Socratic, Platonic, and Aristotelian minds that introduced philosophy and reason. This was supposed to have smashed the world of religion. It gave the world the gift of logic and reason. The saga continues along the lines that Christianity then snuffed that out, giving rise to the dark ages, the world of dogma, faith, and mysticism—a return to instinctual religion. Then, at the Renaissance, thankfully, science and rationality were recovered for the human race, and people were freed from the shackles of mystical religion. This worldview, a commonly held narrative, has been shown by Judge and philosopher Karl Popper, convincingly, to my mind at least, to be absolutely untenable. It is simply wrong.

---

37. "Edwin Judge." The account following here of Greek philosophy is a summation from a conversation with Judge.

THEOLOGY

Recall the question of the cussing golfer, "How do you put those two things together?" His reaction epitomizes the Enlightenment dichotomization of fact (known by reason, the realm of science) and values or faith (known by faith, the realm of religion). The dictum of Augustine and Anselm that the pursuit of truth is always a "faith seeking understanding" prospect (*credo ut intelligam*) has for me been the basis on which I have sought, on the one hand, to debunk the scientific naturalism of the secularist and, on the other hand, to encourage overly confident Christians to realize that their pursuit of knowledge is also *credo ut intelligam*. The kind of certainty that some Christians seek about the tenets of their faith (and that some rationalistic apologists proclaim to be possible) is more a product of the Enlightenment than it is of the truly Christian way of knowing.

One important thinker in this area, as Judge indicates, was Karl Popper. Speaking against the school of Vienna, he denied that at the heart of the scientific endeavour is accumulated evidence that proves truth, saying instead that the scientific endeavour involves attacks against the hypothesis and then successive disproofs, giving rise to the next hypothesis. Science does not work by what is in the mind already, although there may be a tentative hypothesis in the mind. It works by the experimental method, not through its concepts. Popper attacked Plato and the Platonic mirage of Idealism, with its idea that truth lies in the perfect form. For Plato, particular things were faulty, and truth lay beyond sensory data. In Greek philosophy, the world was utterly predictable on the basis of logic, and it was not subject to change. In the pre-Socratic philosophers, and then Plato and Aristotle, a manner of understanding the world was being developed using the mind alone, using reason to explain everything; and behind this was the assumption, the magnificent hypothesis, that the universe is logical and unsurprising. This was simply wrong, not that there is not a certain order and logic behind it that permits scientific discovery—an orderly Periodic Table, for example. But this axiom of Classical Greek philosophy is simply wrong. The idea was that logic ruled everything, that the mind could deduce necessary truths, as in mathematics, music, or the music of the spheres. Thus, Aristotelian logic was absolute. Logic came from Logos and from calculation. Mathematics was considered to be a form of knowledge. The universe was simply all musical spheres with balancing parts expressed mathematically. Therefore, Empedicles accepted Parmenides' statement

"Change is impossible." So what did you do with the appearance of change? You suggested it was delusion. Empedicles not only explained the appearance of change as a delusion, but suggested that the senses were recording a process of circular rotation. The cosmos was a beautiful prison. The universe could not be changed, as such an occurrence would mean that it had not been complete.

Of course, the Christian doctrines of creation, the incarnation, and the resurrection stand in contrast to this, and they are much more consonant with what we know of the universe from modern science. This gospel also comes to be known in the same way as science; both are post-intellectual.

Two important contributors to helping us understand how we actually attain scientific knowledge have been Michael Polanyi, who speaks of all knowledge as tacit and as personal, and John MacMurray, who argued that the nature of human beings is personal rather than mechanical or organic. Epistemologically, how we "know" what we know is the same in all spheres of knowledge. It is personal knowledge. It is tacit. It is arrived at empirically. When God revealed himself to Moses in the burning bush as "I am who I am" (Exod 3:14), he was really saying, "Do not try to guess who I am intellectually in some kind of disembodied way." There is mystery, but it is revealed ultimately in the embodied person of the Son, whom we could see, hear, and touch. In the same way, in science, we do not discover things by guessing or by mathematics, but by experimentation and by trial and error, and what we discover is often surprising.

The profound words about truth-seeking written by Thomas Merton are greatly helpful here: "We make ourselves real by telling the truth . . . To destroy truth with truth under the pretext of being sincere is a very insincere way of telling a lie . . . A man of sincerity is less interested in defending the truth than in stating it clearly, for he thinks that, if the truth can be clearly seen, it can very well take care of itself. Fear is perhaps the greatest enemy of candor."[38]

My own interest in theology and science arises out of a curiosity to know the truth that takes care of itself in every realm of reality and that sets us free. It is motivated by the presupposition that all truth is God's and that all truth concerning the creation of the universe and its reconciliation is centered in the God-Man Jesus, who said, "I am the

38. Merton, *No Man Is an Island*, 198–99, 205–6.

truth" (John 14:6). Merton's assumption about truth is that it *can* be known. He is thus distinct from the endless deconstruction characteristic of extreme forms of postmodernity or Nietzchean nihilism. Merton does not in this statement assert *how* one knows the truth. He is saying something about a tendency within the church, historically and to this day, to deny truth discovered scientifically if it seems to be in contradiction with cherished ways of interpreting certain Scriptures. My interest is in the ways of knowing what we think we know both in theology and in science. I wish to show that there is coherence in the way we know, irrespective of the discipline. In probing this, I am suggesting a coinherence between the disciplines that moves well beyond non-overlapping magisteria. The epistemology is a prime case in point. We come to knowledge of the surprising nature of the incarnation and the triune God in theology through historical experience and continued experiences and encounters as the apostolic community. In science, we come to knowledge with presuppositions and reasonable hypotheses, and we seek by experimentation to test our hypotheses, and we are open to surprises. The more deeply we probe nature, the less certain we are and the more surprised we are.

The advent of postmodernity in its more moderate forms has actually served to narrow the gap between science and theology with regards to this issue of epistemology. As I have written elsewhere,

> True postmodernity has demonstrated that reason is never unprejudiced and Radical Orthodoxy has shown convincingly that there is specifically no neutral secular sphere, including that of science. As Jamie Smith suggests, "RO's project is aimed at unveiling the religious status of this modern vision, thus alerting us to the ways in which these core values or doctrines of modern life are, in the end, competitors of the Gospel of Christ." Secularism is an alternative confession. It does not merely form values by borrowing capital from its original Christian roots, but it is "actually *constituted* in its secularity by 'heresy' in relation to orthodox Christianity, or else a rejection of Christianity that is more 'neo-pagan' than simply anti-religious. Secular theory, then, is supported not by a neutral universal rationality (as it claims) but by simply another *mythos*, an alternative confession." Smith comments that these RO conclusions in fact mirror the postmodern critique of metanarratives made by Lyotard, for example. Smith's exhortation that Christians can engage in the public square of ideas on the basis that all engagement by everyone is faith-based,

given the fideistic nature of reason, the myth of neutral secularity, is timely.[39]

Of course, this has not yet pervaded modernity and secularism, and scientism is still very much publicly viable, its core being the conclusions of the Enlightenment. The Enlightenment has at its heart the notion of "prejudice against prejudice"[40]—where the most dangerous prejudice is the religious. Therefore, as Smith concludes, "political (and academic) rhetoric indicates that modernity is a thriving project."[41] Evidence that this has pervaded the church abounds also, most notably in theologies of both liberal and conservative kinds that are apologetic projects that employ supposedly autonomous reason.[42] Fundamentalism in particular is "but a mirror of modernism"[43] in its engagement also on the assumption of neutral, objective reason.

Thus, postmodernity still has its work to do in secularistic science. Michael Polanyi (*Personal Knowledge*) and Alasdair McIntyre (*After Virtue*) have exposed the fallacies of a rationalistic world view, scientism, and the reliability of pure reason, suggesting that total objectivity is a myth, even for scientists. The idea of the infallibility and supremacy of the reason of the autonomous human mind, and of a pristine secular space untarnished by religious faith, which dominated many Western countries, has in fact, by means of postmodernity (so Lyotard), been shown to be a myth. Postmodernity's contribution to the contemporary postfoundationalist milieu does at minimum create some windows for the gospel and an "unapologetically confessional theory and practice" of the Christian church. The realistic revelationism expressed in Karl Barth's commitment to Anselm's epistemological conviction that theology is faith seeking understanding provides a window arising from a consonance between postmodernity and Christian theology done in this way.

39. Hastings, *Missional God*, 52.
40. A phrase coined by Gadamer, *Truth and Method*, 276.
41. Smith, *Radical Orthodoxy*, 32.
42. Smith cites Herman Dooyeweerd in relation to this point: "Theology is itself in need of a transcendental critique of theoretical thought" (*In the Twilight of Western Thought*, 6). He cites the influence of Tübingen on much twentieth-century theology, including fundamentalist and early evangelical theology which presumes upon a neutral, 'objective' reason to warrant their theological project and by so doing ends up being correlationist and accommodationist.
43. Smith, *Radical Orthodoxy*, 37.

Theology

The quest for indubitable certainty in modernity (Descartes), now counteracted by postmodern deconstructionism, saw science as that realm of certainty. It was the method of Descartes that specifically led us down the blind alley of seeking absolute certainty in science. As Lesslie Newbigin has pointed out, the crucial issue is the "starting point" of knowledge. That of Descartes was anthropological: "his own existence as a thinking mind" ("I think, therefore I am").[44] This was for Descartes a self-evident and irrefutable truth. The thinking self, as opposed to the feeling self or the acting self, once made the starting point, opened up three dualisms which became part of modernity:

1. The first dualism is the dualism between the thinking mind and the world of things outside of the mind, extended in space (*res cogitans* and *res extsensa*). As Newbigin states, for Descartes, "The thinking mind was not extended in space" but was, "so to speak, a single point, an eye looking from outside into the cosmos extended in space. The mental world and the world of material things belong, as it were, to two quite different and separate realms of being." But, as Newbigin concludes, this has led to the popular idea that God, who belongs to the mental or spiritual world, cannot influence or interfere with the material world. The world of pure thought, as, for example, in mathematics, hovers above the "real"—that is, the material world—but is not part of it. This dualism is very similar to that which dominated classical thought, namely, the sharp distinction between a world of pure forms or ideas and the sensible world with which we are in contact through our five senses.[45]

The difference is, of course, that the modern mindset involved the empirical approach, which tested the theory of the mind with experiment. Mathematics goes with science as the means of the expression of empirical findings. Yet, still within modernity, there is this dualism. In fact, the moment a mathematical formula is expressed, it becomes distant from reality. Into this dualism comes the word of the Lord:

And the Word became flesh and dwelt among us (John 1:14).

---

44. Newbigin, *Proper Confidence*, 36.
45. Ibid., 36–37.

Newbigin explains how the "early church had to overcome this dualism in order to affirm as public truth the gospel's central statement that the *logos* was identical with the Man, Jesus of Nazareth. It could do so because the starting point of its thinking was in the Bible, where this dualism is absent."[46] Paul affirmed that the one God in Christ was the creator of things visible and invisible. Newbigin also states that as long as this dualism persists, the gospel can never be accepted as "public truth," but only as "private opinion." He believes that developments in physics and mathematics in the past 100 years have sought to overcome this dualism, this being especially the case with quantum physics, in which "the observer and the object of observation do not belong in separate worlds" but "interact."[47]

2. The second dualism is closely related to the first. It is that expressed in the words "objective" and "subjective." This dichotomized language is so much a part of our vocabulary today that it is "hard to think in a way that is not controlled by them." Of course, there is always a subject and the object of the subject's inquiry, but it is the wide separation between the two that Descartes' method encouraged, resulting in two types of truth claims: those that communicate objective knowledge and those that express subjective experience. In the nineteenth century, science came to be known as the source of objective knowledge and "the locus of public truth," and it replaced religion, which was deemed to be subjective experience. Only science could offer objective facts that were universally true irrespective of culture and other contingent elements of a human person.

What the Christian gospel proclaims is that there is only personal encounter and that the objectivity is imperfect and uncertain, always mixed with some subjectivity. There has been historical encounter, real objectivity but not of a disembodied and disconnected kind.

And the Word became flesh and dwelt among us. *And we beheld His glory* (John 1:14) ... That which was from the beginning, which we have heard, which we have seen with our eyes, which

---

46. Ibid., 37.
47. Ibid.

we have looked at and our hands have touched—this we proclaim concerning the Word of Life (1 John 1:1).

3. The third dualism was that between *theoria* (theory) and *praxis* (practice). Newbigin comments on the fact that these two words are absent from the Bible "because they express a way of understanding which is foreign to the Bible," but is deeply entrenched in our culture. We picture a thing in our minds as it ought to be, and then, as second step, we check out what's "real." In the Bible, the vision of something is present but is second to hearing. Above all, in the Bible, the "ultimate reality" "is personal," and we are "brought into conformity with this reality not by the two-step process of theory and practice, vision and action, but by a single action compromised of hearing, believing and obeying."[48] "The operative contrast," says Newbigin, "is not between theory and practice; it is between believing and obeying on the one hand and the refusal of belief and obedience on the other." These two actions of believing and obeying are one in Hebrew thought, where "to know" is not a reality until "to do" takes place. Similarly, in the New Testament, when Jesus calls Simon Peter, it is not to a world of disembodied belief that he calls him. It is expressed as "Follow me." It is a holistic response. As Newbigin affirms, the theory-practice dualism is a denial of good anthropology: "the human person is not a mind attached to a body but a single psychosomatic being. This again poses a challenge for Christianity in the public square," for it cannot be "propagated as a theory or a worldview and certainly not as a religion."[49]

In addition to the work of quantum physics, that of scientist-turned-philosopher Michael Polanyi has, of course, placed a significant dent in this dichotomy or dualism. It was he who coined the term "personal knowledge." He specifically exposed that the objective-subjective dualism is fallacious and that in fact "all knowing of reality involves the personal commitment of the knower as a whole person."[50]

In sum, it would seem impossible to find any coinherence between theology and science without sharing a common epistemological com-

---

48. Ibid., 38–39.
49. Newbigin, *Proper Confidence*, 39.
50. Ibid., 39.

mitment to the fearless pursuit of truth no matter its source—all truth is God's truth. But we must also all acknowledge that faith commitments affect how we see truth in theology, and we must plead with others to see that this is always true in the pursuit of truth, including scientific truth, as people like Polanyi have shown. All knowledge is humble knowledge. One has to admit that, while prejudices do influence science, the levels of certainty achieved by some of the harder sciences, in which conclusions are tested by instrumentation and reproducibility, are of a higher level than some of the softer sciences. It is, however, at the higher level of the philosophy of science that theology and science share the common limits of reason.

The commonality of the ways of knowing in science and theology in fact prompted T. F. Torrance to suggest that *critical realism* is common to both.[51] This led him to speak of a scientific theology. "Scientific theology," according to Torrance, "is active engagement in that cognitive relation to God in obedience to the demands of His reality and self-giving."[52] As Martin Davis expresses it, "a scientific theology seeks to bring knowledge of God into clear focus, so that the truth of God may shine through unhindered and unobscured by the "opacity" of the human mind."[53] Torrance states, "That is to say, we seek to allow God's own eloquent self-evidence to sound through to us in His Logos so that we may know and understand Him out of His own rationality and under the determination of His divine being."[54]

As Davis notes, "against the Kantian disjunction between the knower and the known, God's own 'eloquent self-evidence' has sounded through to us both in the mediation of revelation in ancient Israel . . . and particularly and most clearly in the incarnation of the Word (Logos) of God in Jesus Christ, who is 'of one being with the Father' (*homoousios to Patri*)."[55]

Torrance's scientific theology is a *via positiva* (rather than *via negativa*) approach to knowledge of God developed in accordance with God's

---

51. Similarly, John Polkinghorne (*Quantum Physics and Theology*, xi) expresses the opinion that, in the comparison of science and theology, "both are best understood as leading to a critical realist account of what is the case."

52. Torrance, *Theological Science*, ix.

53. Davis, "T. F. Torrance."

54. See Torrance, *Space, Time, and Incarnation*, v–viii.

55. Davis, "T. F. Torrance."

THEOLOGY

historical self-revelation in the history of Israel and the incarnation of Jesus Christ. This is one further notable example of coinherence.

DOXOLOGICAL CONSIDERATIONS

The best news of the gospel is that in his electing to be for his creation and especially humanity, God will himself be glorified, and the essential posture of both theologians and scientists must be one of worship. This has the overarching telos of *doxology*. Doxology relates to the perception of goodness and beauty. This takes its cue from the Son made flesh, who is glorious: "The Word became flesh and made his dwelling among us. We have seen his glory, the glory of the one and only Son, who came from the Father, full of grace and truth" (John 1:14).

The full regal glory of the incarnate Son may be veiled, but the disciples saw its unveiling. His moral glory was unchanged. The enfleshed Word is glorious. He will one day be seen in human flesh as still the One who is all the glory in Immanuel's land. In fact his glory and that of his church together with him will bring an unveiling of the glory of creation.

This involves contemplative appreciation of beauty in both theology (such Jonathan Edwards, Hans Urs von Balthasar) and science, a sense of curiosity and wonder that is transformative. Part of this is the acknowledging of mystery and the limitations of human knowledge in both disciplines.

The tragedy referred to above, of the distancing of theology and science through scholasticism, from Orthodox scientist-theologian Puhalo's perspective was the depriving of the "Christian community of its primary vocation to love God's creation as God loves it. It deprives us of the world itself." Historical and scientific "facts," artificially grounded "in ideology and philosophical theories" displace an "empirical regard for nature, which science may deepen our appreciation of."[56] Scholasticism, which all traditions have been influenced by, has also reduced spirituality to a cognitive dimension. Puhalo makes the point that theology for the Orthodox was always the journey of purification through *theoria* (theology), that is, experiential knowledge of God, and on to *theosis*. The wonder of creation as discovered in science is therefore part of this *theoria*, or theology, by its very definition. Innate to this was a posture of wonder and silence rather than mastery of the reality we encounter

---

56. Puhalo, *Evidence of Things*, 42.

by our words and concepts. In science this is to acknowledge the difference between *models of creation* and *creation itself*, which parallel the difference between what we call "theology" and who God really is in himself. So many conflicts between science and theology have been between "models of creation" that were mistaken for creation itself. The language we use for science and for theology is limited. Puhalo states that "linguistically based assumptions are derived from the presumption of visualizability." Thus, he suggests that when we use language for the unseen that has been developed from the matrix of what is visible and is "a developed system of imitation of, and metaphor for, things heard and seen," idolatry is the inevitable result, and "this is just what St. Gregory the Theologian warns us against when he says, 'Every concept of God is merely a simulacrum, a false likeness, an idol: it cannot reveal God Himself' (*Against Eunomius*, Discourse 3).[57]

This is the point at which Puhalo venerates his own tradition, which has been protected from this idolatry arising in scholasticism, by the concept of *apophatic*, or negative, theology, that is, theology based on the belief that we cannot really describe or define anything that God is, but can "only circumscribe our understanding of Him by saying what He is not."[58] Even though God has been revealed in Christ, and even though we can know him by his energies, when it comes to his divine *essence*, we still can neither describe nor visualize it. In fact, as Abba Isaak has said, "Speech is the language of this world, but silence is the mystery of the age to come." This precludes the visualization of "things yonder," says Puhalo.

> The goal to which apophatic theology leads—if, indeed, we may speak of a goal or ending when it is a question of an ascent toward the infinite—is not a nature, an essence, or a person; it is something that transcends all notions both of nature and of person: it is the Trinity.[59]

Mathematics is to science what theology is to the reality of God. It is an attempt at description. But fascinatingly, Puhalo says that mathematical formalisms in quantum mechanics are "an expression of

---

57. Ibid., 72.
58. Ibid.
59. Lossky, *Mystical Theology*, 44.

speechlessness."[60] There is a real coinherence between theology and science here.

One of the things that brings about the speechlessness in the science world is beauty. I am often stunned into silence by the beauty and symmetry of molecules I have studied. I also have often been in awe of organic synthetic chemistry for the artistry beyond science in their synthetic pathways and molecular creations. But the beauty of both the micro and the macro effect wonder. Gerard Manley Hopkins expressed this inimitably.

> "God's Grandeur":
>
> THE WORLD is charged with the grandeur of God.
> It will flame out, like shining from shook foil;
> It gathers to a greatness, like the ooze of oil
> Crushed. Why do men then now not reck his rod?
> Generations have trod, have trod, have trod;
> And all is seared with trade; bleared, smeared with toil;
> And wears man's smudge and shares man's smell: the soil
> Is bare now, nor can foot feel, being shod.
> And for all this, nature is never spent;
> There lives the dearest freshness deep down things;
> And though the last lights off the black West went
> Oh, morning, at the brown brink eastward, springs—
> Because the Holy Ghost over the bent
> World broods with warm breast and with ah! bright wings.[61]

Doxology also relates to *telos*. The eschatology of John Polkinghorne is useful to us here in understanding the coinherence of theology and science in a doxological way. I will here summarize it and add some of my own reflections.

It seems to me that creation must be viewed in four stages. There was an initial creation of seminal materials *ex nihilo*. Then, secondly, there was the gradual development of that creation under the providence of God, but with a real measure of freedom or contingency for the substance of creation and particularly its human creatures, who were made in the divine image. These humans represent a third stage of creation, when humans were breathed into with the breath of God and made in the divine image (a coronation of *homo sapiens* in the *imago*

---

60. Puhalo, *Evidence of Things*, 76.
61. Hopkins, "God's Grandeur."

Dei). Then comes the fall, and with it the presence of evil and suffering in the world. Fourthly, the last revealed chronologically, but, I would argue, the first intended by God, is the creation redeemed by means of Christ who enters creation to redeem and reconcile it by his incarnation, death, and resurrection. There are two stages within this redemption, one of which occurs in this present age, at which point there are signs of that redemption in the church and humanity that takes place under the influence of the kingdom of God. Wherever people in Christ live the lives of persons alive in Christ and in the fullness of their humanity work for the glory of God and steward his creation wisely, there the new creation is visible. The church especially, as it feeds on the physical, created elements of bread and wine, is a sacrament of a reconciled cosmos. The fullness of the eschaton will, however, reveal a new creation in its more fully developed stage. While in this old creation the creation reveals something of the nature and glory of God, the relationship between the Creator and his creation is at a metaphysical and relational distance. This is what leads Polkinghorne to reject the notion of panentheism in this creation. He does interestingly, however, posit an eschatological panentheism in which there are not just *some* evidences of the sacramental, as in the now. Rather, when creation is fully reconciled, all of creation will be sacramental. Thus, whereas the old creation has functioned with a veil over God's presence, the new creation will function with this veil removed. The revelation of the glory of Christ, and with it the revelation of the reflected glory of the church, will usher in the freedom of creation, and its every aspect will be fully and obviously iridescent with the glory of God. This eschatological view of creation is possible only by closely linking Christ and creation.

This doxological aim is what makes both theological and scientific vocations one. And this is what makes the sheer hard work in both worthwhile. But as we well know, the kingdom of God has already broken into history in Christ, and therefore a doxological orientation both in theology and in science is highly appropriate. Christ comes to recapitulate the old Adam's orientation.

Doxology also relates to going back to the future. The vocation of the first human persons depicted in the garden of Eden was a doxological orientation to creation. These persons were called to see, to know, to name, and to delight in creation. They were also called to offer/oblate. For Alexander Schmemann, to name it was to bless it, for it revealed the very essence of the thing as a gift given by the Creator. So everything that exists does so as a gift of God, and it exists to make God known to man, to enable his life to be one of communion with God. "O taste and see that the Lord is good" (Ps 38:4) is the summation of the gospel. God blesses all that he creates. It is in love that God made food for humanity, for example. As Schmemann says, "Behind all the hunger of our life is God. All desire is finally a desire for him."[62]

This removes all dualism from life with God. The task of naming and blessing the creation was not a religious or cultic act, but a way of life, an earthy spirituality. The idea of eating and drinking in communion with God is not an encouragement to escape the earthly, physical realm for a spiritual mysticism or evacuation theology, nor is being for the life of the world a crass activism distanced from contemplation and communion. *Homo sapiens* we may be, but we are not first that or just that in Yahweh's eyes. Rather, we are *homo adorans*. The human is first defined as a priest. The *imago* in its very essence is humanity in relationship to God and, as such, a mediator of God's love to creation and a thankful consumer and blesser of God on behalf of creation. He receives the world from God for his hunger, and he offers it back to God as a blesser, as an offerer of eucharist. As Schmemann says, "The first, the basic defintion of man is that he is *the priest*. He stands in the center of the world and unifies it in his act of blessing God, of both receiving the world from God and offering it to God—and by filling the world with this eucharist, he transforms his life, the one that he receives from the world, into life in God, into communion with him. The world was created as the 'matter,' the material of one all-embracing eucharist, and man was created as the priest of this cosmic sacrament."[63]

This is the posture of the scientist and of the theologian.

BIBLIOGRAPHY

Baik, Chung-Hyun. *The Holy Trinity: God for God and God for Us: 7 Positions in the Immanent-Economic Trinity Relation in Contemporary Trinitarian Theology*. Eugene, OR: Pickwick, 2010.

Barbour, Ian. *Religion in an Age of Science*. San Francisco: Harper & Row, 1990.

Barth, Karl. *Church Dogmatics* 1/1: *The Doctrine of the Word of God*. Edited by G. W. Bromiley and T. F. Torrance. Translated by G. T. Thomson. Edinburgh: T. & T. Clark, 1936.

62. Schmemann, *For the Life of the World*, 14.
63. Ibid., 15.

———. *Church Dogmatics 3/2: The Doctrine of Creation*. Edited by G. W. Bromiley and T. F. Torrance. Translated by H. Knight et al. Edinburgh: T. & T. Clark, 1960.

Calvin, John. *Calvin: Institutes of the Christian Religion*. Edited by John T. McNeill. Translated by Ford Lewis Battles. LCC 20. 1960. Reprint, Philadelphia: Westminster, 1967.

Davis, Martin M. "T. F. Torrance: Scientific Theology and Critical Realism." *God for Us!* 2 January 2010. http://martinmdavis.blogspot.ca/2010/01/t-f-torrance-scientific-theology-and.html.

Dooyeweerd, Herman. *In the Twilight of Western Thought: Studies in the Pretended Autonomy of Philosophical Thought*. Nutley, NJ: Craig, 1965.

"Edwin Judge." Gospel Conversations. http://www.gospelconversations.com/who-are-we/edwin-judge/.

Fiddes, Paul S. *Participating in God: A Pastoral Doctrine of the Trinity*. Louisville: Westminster John Knox, 2000.

Gadamer, Hans-Georg. *Truth and Method*. Translated by Joel Weinsheimer and Donald G. Marshall. Rev. ed. New York: Continuum, 1989.

Gould, Stephen Jay. "Impeaching a Self-Appointed Judge." *Scientific American* 267 (1992) 118–21.

Grenz, Stanley. *The Named God and the Question of Being: A Trinitarian Theo-Ontology*. Louisville: Westminster John Knox, 2005.

Hastings, W. Ross. *Missional God, Missional Church: Hope for Re-evangelizing the West*. Downers Grove, IL: IVP Academic, 2012.

Hodge, Charles. "Princeton College and the General Assembly." *Nassau Literary Magazine* (1893) 137–38.

Hopkins, Gerard Manley. "God's Grandeur." Sparknotes. http://www.sparknotes.com/poetry/hopkins/section1/.

Horgan, John. "Defending Stephen Jay Gould's Crusade Against Biological Determinism." *Cross-Check*, 23 June 2011. Scientific American. http://blogs.scientificamerican.com/cross-check/2011/06/24/defending-stephen-jay-goulds-crusade-against-biological-determinism/.

Huxley, Julian. "The Evolutionary Vision: The Convocation Address." In *Evolution After Darwin*, edited by Sol Tax and Charles Callender, 242–62. Chicago: University of Chicago Press, 1960.

Kidwell, Jeremy. "Elucidating the Image of God: An Analysis of the *Imago Dei* in the Work of Colin E. Gunton and John Zizioulas." MCS thesis, Regent College, 2009.

Lewis, C. S. *The Four Loves: An Exploration of the Nature of Love*. New York: Harcourt Brace, 1960.

Lossky, Vladimir. *The Mystical Theology of the Eastern Church*. Cambridge: James Clark, 1957.

Merton, Thomas. *No Man Is an Island*. Boston: Shambhala, 1955.

Newbigin, Lesslie. *Proper Confidence: Faith, Doubt and Certainty in Christian Discipleship*. Grand Rapids: Eerdmans, 1995.

O'Donovan, O. *Resurrection and the Moral Order: An Outline for Evangelical Ethics*. Grand Rapids: Eerdmans, 1986.

Padgett, Alan G. *Science and the Study of God: A Mutuality Model for Theology and Science*. Grand Rapids: Eerdmans, 2003.

Polkinghorne, John. *Quantum Physics and Theology: An Unexpected Kinship*. New Haven: Yale University Press, 2007.

———. *Science and the Trinity: The Christian Encounter with Reality*. New Haven: Yale University Press, 2004.

Polkinghorne, John, ed. *The Trinity and an Entangled World*. Grand Rapids: Eerdmans, 2010.

Puhalo, Lazar. *The Evidence of Things Not Seen: Orthodox Christianity and Modern Physics*. 2nd ed. Dewdney, BC: Synaxis, 2005.

Schmemann, Alexander. *For the Life of the World: Sacraments and Orthodoxy*. New York: St. Vladimir's Seminary Press, 2004.

Smith, James K. A. *Introducing Radical Orthodoxy: Mapping a Post-Secular Theology*. Grand Rapids: Baker, 2004.

Torrance, Thomas F. *Space, Science, and Incarnation*. Oxford: Oxford University Press, 1969.

———. *Theological Science*. Oxford: Oxford University Press, 1978.

Wilkinson, Loren. "The New Story of Creation: A Trinitarian Perspective." *Crux* 3 (1994) 26–36.

10

The Spirit of the Gospel

STEVEN M. STUDEBAKER

THE PASTOR DECLARED THAT the essence of salvation is the forgiveness of sins and going to heaven because Jesus died on the cross. Most Christians, like the congregation that morning, say, "Amen." But is that what makes the gospel the good news? Absolution from moral guilt and participation in the everlasting kingdom are important aspects of the gospel. But the gospel is more than forgiveness of sins and heaven. What then makes the gospel good news? The Holy Spirit, as the Spirit of Pentecost, makes the life realized in Jesus Christ available to all people. The Holy Spirit, however, is too often overshadowed by Christocentric and crucicentric views of the gospel.[1] Although Christocentric expressions of the gospel are familiar and comfortable, bringing visibility to the Holy Spirit's role in the biblical drama of redemption is the goal of this essay. Emphasizing the Spirit does not displace Christ. Replacing one subordination with another one is not the way forward.

From the perspective of pneumatology, the key moments on a continuum of redemptive history are creation, incarnation, and Pentecost. They are not discrete and disparate economies of God's work in the world. In the incarnation, the Spirit's work in creation finds its fullest realization in the union of the Son with the humanity of Jesus Christ. Jesus Christ's subsequent ministry, crucifixion, and resurrection are made

---

1. E.g., endorsing Christocentrism, Gordon Fee asserts the principle that "Christ gives definition to the Spirit." Fee, *God's Empowering Presence*, 837.

possible by this fundamental pneumatological condition. At Pentecost, the Spirit makes the grace of union with the Son and participation in the fellowship of the triune God universally available to all people. The first section of this essay sets out the narrative of the Spirit within the Old Testament. Although this narrative takes greater clarity in the New Testament, especially around the themes of incarnation and Pentecost, the Old Testament material is important because it establishes the basic plot features of the Spirit's work. The second and third sections show that the Spirit's work in the incarnation of Christ and as the gift of Pentecost continues and clarifies the narrative of the Spirit that begins with creation. The fourth section shows the parallel between the Spirit's work in the incarnation and the grace of the good news. The final section shows that the Spirit of the gospel brings more transformational and relational emphases than traditional Christocentric approaches.

THE SPIRIT AND CREATION AND REDEMPTION

The gospel begins in Gen 1:2 from the perspective of pneumatology. Creation is a work of God's Spirit, and creation is redemption. The biblical story of salvation cannot be appreciated without grasping those two fundamental points. First, Gen 1 is simply neither a creation story nor a scientific report. Before the days of creation, "the earth was formless and empty, darkness was over the surface of the deep, and the Spirit of God was hovering over the waters" (Gen 1:2).[2] Before the light and life of creation, an evil thrall binds the earth in a void of blackness.

Genesis 1 reflects a cosmology common throughout the ancient Near East (ANE). Primal pandemonium preceded the present world of order and life. Genesis 1 does demythologize the Babylonian and Canaanite creation myths. Gone is the primordial battle between dragon-like chaos gods (e.g., Rahab and the multi-headed Leviathan) out of which the victor brings order to the world. Nevertheless, it retains the basic narrative of ancient Near Eastern cosmology—a transition from dark abyss to fecund creation.[3] Where before all lies in darkness, God brings light. From the formless void, God crafts fields and mountains

---

2. For more on the meaning of "Spirit" in Gen 1 and especially the ANE context of wind-gods, see my *From Pentecost to the Triune God*, 54–60.

3. Note, however, that Ps 74:12–17 and Job 26:12–13 retain the *Chaoskampf* characteristic of the ancient Near East. Habel, *The Book of Job*, 192. For a comparison of biblical creation stories with ANE alternatives, see Tsumura, *The Earth and the Waters*.

and fills them with living creatures. Creation is not a natural and neutral process. It is a transition from a place of doom to hope, life, and goodness. This transition may create questions for Christian theodicy—for example, how could the original state be evil, if God creates everything? That is a good question for philosophical theology. It is, however, neither the problem of the biblical narrative in general nor the creation story in particular. The creation story in Gen 1 starts with the problem common to ANE cosmology. Waters of the deep covered the earth. The earth was without order and life. Out of this darkness and void God brings forth the spaces—sky, land, and sea in days one through three of creation—and fills them with the stars, planetary bodies, the living creatures, and human beings in days four through six of creation.

Second, creation is a story of the Spirit. The Spirit of God hovering over the primal elements is the threshold of creation. The Spirit of God contrasts with the earth that stands shapeless, empty, and dark.[4] The Spirit is the catalyst of creation. The Spirit of God hovering over the waters, who initiates the transition of the primal chaos to the verdant creation, is the pneumatological threshold of creation.[5] The habit, conditioned by traditions of Christocentrism, is to begin the creation account with the Word in Gen 1:3: "And God said . . . "[6] The Spirit hovering over the abyss, however, is the beginning of creation.[7] Connecting creation to the agency of not only divine *logos*, but also *pneuma* in Gen 1, is consistent with Ps 33:6–7: "By the word of the LORD were the heavens made, their starry host by the breath of his mouth." The Spirit of God in Gen 1:2 is a pneumatological transition from cosmic chaos to God's creation. At the initiative of God's Spirit, the days of creation emerge from the primal pandemonium. The biblical story portrays the Spirit of God as

---

4. Hildebrandt, *An Old Testament Theology*, 32–35. For similar interpretations, also see Freedman, "רוח אלהים—and a Wind from God," 9–13; Sailhamer, *The Pentateuch as Narrative*, 32, 87.

5. Psalm 33:6–7 also portrays creation as the product of God's word and Spirit. For reading *ruach* as Spirit of God in Gen 1, see Studebaker, *From Pentecost to the Triune God*, 54–67.

6. Karl Barth, for example, maintains that the Spirit hovering over the primal elements is impotent, and that the power of creation lies in the Word of God. Barth, *CD* 3/1, 108. Biblical scholars are sometimes no less prone to downplay pneumatology in the creation story (e.g., Waltke, *Genesis*, 69).

7. Brodie, *Genesis as Dialogue*, 133.

the key agent that redeems the elements from that dark abyss and ushers in a world ordered for the flourishing of life.

The relationship between creation and redemption and the Spirit's role in them is seamless. The psalmist describes creation as an act of salvation, declaring that "you, O God . . . bring salvation upon the earth. It was you who split open the sea by your power and broke the heads of the monster in the waters . . . you established the sun and moon . . . set all the boundaries of the earth" (Ps 74:12–17).[8] Isaiah portrays the Spirit's redeeming work as a work that parallels creation. The coming of the Spirit transforms the *desert* into a *fertile field* and enables the people of God to live in justice and righteousness. Just as the Spirit brought life to the formlessness and emptiness of the primeval abyss, so the Spirit redeems the barren land and makes it a land of abundance (Isa 32:15).

The creation of human life in Gen 2 continues the portrayal of creation as an act of redemption and of the Spirit. In Gen 2:7, human life emerges when God breathes life into lifeless dust. The text presents a picture not of a body that gets a soul or spirit, but rather of dirt animated by God's breath. The entirety of human life is a gift of the Spirit of God and not only its inner spiritual element. The dirt is dead until the Spirit vivifies it.[9] The breath of God brings life to the dust. By the life-giving presence of the Spirit of God, the dust becomes a human being that can live in fellowship with its Creator, other human beings, and the rest of creation. Genesis 2:7 presents a pneumatological anthropology. To be human is to be a creature uniquely vitalized by God's Spirit for a unique relationship with God and creation.

The human creation story does not permit a division of life into *natural* and *spiritual*. Human beings do not have a *natural* or secular existence. The Spirit gives life to them for no other reason than for them to live in fellowship with their God and each other. The use of the term "creation" is unfortunate because it implies its counterpart, "redemption." The inevitable result is that creation and redemption become not only binary but ranked categories. God creates the world and then later does the more important and spiritual work of redemption. It is better to deny neither creation nor redemption, but to recognize their con-

---

8. Note that this creation account retains elements of the *Chaoskampf* characteristic of comparative ANE origin stories.

9. Levison, *Filled with the Spirit*, 14–15; Montague, *The Holy Spirit*, 5; Walton, *Genesis*, 166.

nection/unity. Creation, in the biblical narrative, is not a natural activity of "creation" as the traditional categories imply. Creation is an act of redemption. God redeems the primal elements from darkness and formlessness by creating an ordered world in which life thrives. Creation is the realm of God's redeeming work, but creation and redemption are not perceived in terms of natural and supernatural. Redemption is not a spiritual act that comes to a natural world; rather, it gives creation its divinely ordered shape.

In the creation of human life in Gen 2:7, God redeems dirt by breathing life into it. The life given to Adam is not a *natural* life to which a *spiritual* life is later added. Relationship with God is not a *superadditum* of grace added to human beings otherwise living natural, secular, or non-spiritual lives. The biblical creation story does not support a *supernatural anthropology*.[10] Giving Adam the breath of life created his life, but created it for no other reason than for Adam to live in this world in loving relationship with God and the rest of creation, eventually including Eve. Adam never had a *natural* existence. He was from the beginning created for nothing other than relationship and life with God in and for this world. Redemption does not paste a spiritual life onto a lesser natural life. Moreover, the life given by the Spirit is not for heaven, but for this world. Eden is a picture of abundant and joyful life in this world. For this reason, the Old Testament prophets portray God's redemption as first bringing (exodus) and restoring (from exile) the people to prosperous and peaceful life in the land of promise. Redemption is the work of God's Spirit that enables human beings to realize God's dream for them—it breathes life into lifeless dirt; just as Paul said, you were dead in your sins, now alive in Christ, etc.

The book of Exodus has two back-to-back accounts of the deliverance of the people of Israel from Pharaoh. Both use pneumatological imagery to describe the divine agency of their salvation. In the prose account, "the Lord drove the sea back with a strong east wind and turned it into dry land" (Exod 14:21). The poem or Song of Moses intensifies the personal aspect of the wind that drives back the water of the sea. Exodus 15:8 and 10 declare, "By the blast of your nostrils the waters

---

10. For this term, see Martin, *Capitalizing Religion*, 56. Martin argues that the separation of the spiritual and physical derives not so much from lingering vestiges of Platonism, but from the late-medieval and early-Reformation currents in theology (54–56).

piled ... [Y]ou blew with your breath and the sea covered them." The song attributes both the act of restraining the waters for the Israelites (deliverance) and of swamping Pharaoh's army (judgment) to the *ruach/* Spirit of God.[11] Both texts interpret the physical phenomenon that caused the sea to recede for the Israelites and cascade over the Egyptians as the direct intervention of Israel's God and describe that activity in pneumatological terms.

Isaiah makes the connection between the Spirit of God and divine agency in redemption through the sea even more telling: "Then his people recalled the days of old, the days of Moses and his people—'where is he who brought them through the sea, with the shepherd of his flock? Where is he who set his Holy Spirit among them, who sent his glorious power to be at Moses' right hand, who divided the waters before them ... who led them through the depths? [T]hey were given rest by the Spirit of the Lord'" (Isa 63:11–14).[12] Deuteronomy 32:10 connects the theophanic glory of the exodus with the hovering Spirit of God in Gen 1:2. The creation and exodus stories also possess parallel images. The light that shines in the primordial darkness, the division of the waters, and the appearance of the dry land compares with the glory of the Lord that guides the Israelites through the darkness and the receding waters that open up the dry seabed for the Israelites.[13] In other words, pneumatology developed and became an important category for understanding God's presence and redemptive work in the history of the people of Israel. Moreover, the redemptive work of the Spirit has strong associations with the Spirit's work in creation.

Isaiah links Yahweh's creative and redemptive activity with the restoration of Israel from exile.[14] In Isa 32 the Spirit renews (recreates) the land of promise: "Citadel and watchtower will become a wasteland forever, the delight of donkeys, a pasture for flocks, till the Spirit is poured upon us from on high, and the desert becomes a fertile field, and the

---

11. Al Wolters argues that Exod 15:8 does not refer to the deliverance of the Israelites and that Exod 15:8 and 15:10 both refer to the flood of water that destroyed the Egyptian forces. Although I agree with Wolters that the Song primarily showcases the destruction of Pharaoh and his army, Exod 15:8 and 10 appear to connect the two aspects—deliverance and judgment—of the one event. See Wolters, "Not Rescue but Destruction," 223–40.

12. Eichrodt, *Theology of the Old Testament*, 2:60–61.

13. Kline, *Images of the Spirit*, 14–15.

14. Anderson, *Understanding the Old Testament*, 449–50.

fertile field seems a forest. Justice will dwell in the desert and righteousness live in the fertile field . . . peaceful dwelling places, in secure homes" (vv. 14–18). The *wasteland* echoes the desolation of the earth before creation. The arrival of the Spirit transforms the desolate desert into a place of abundance. Thus, Isaiah ties together the creative and redemptive activity of God and associates that activity with the Spirit of God.

Ezekiel's prophecies of restoration from exile also integrate pneumatology, creation, and redemption. Ezekiel promises that Yahweh will put the Spirit of God in the exiled people of Israel and that the Spirit will return them to their homeland.[15] Ezekiel uses the metaphor of the Spirit of God resurrecting a valley of dry bones to portray Israel's repatriation (Ezek 36–37, esp. 37:1–14). Yahweh charges Ezekiel to "prophesy to the breath; prophesy, son of man, and say to it, 'this is what the Sovereign Lord says: Come from the four winds, O breath, and breathe into these slain, that they may live'" (Ezek 37:9). The "breath," the "four winds," and the divine power that will bring new life to the people of Israel is the Spirit of Yahweh (Ezek 37:14).[16]

Ezekiel's use of pneumatological images to describe Yahweh's fulfillment of the promise to restore the people of Israel coheres with the Genesis creation stories.[17] The Spirit of God, the divine power that emancipates the people of Israel from their desolation in captivity and returns them to Jerusalem as the faithful covenant people of God, is the same Spirit who moved over the mayhem of Gen 1:2 and brought forth a world teeming with life.[18] The Spirit of God breathing new life into the dead bones of exiled Israel parallels God breathing life into the dirt in Gen 2:7.[19] In short, redemption is creation. The creation narrative of

15. See Block, "The Prophet of the Spirit," 38; Joyce, *Ezekiel*, 204; Robson, *Word and Spirit*, 269; and Wright, "The Concept of *RUACH*," 146.

16. For the ANE context of associating divine presence and agency with the four winds and other meteorological phenomena, see Woodhouse, "The Sun God," 136–37; Hasenfratz, "Patterns of Creation in Ancient Egypt," 175; Kákosy, "The Ptah-Shu-Tefnut Triad," 219–29. Furthermore, the Egyptian high god Shu, who was associated with the air and was the ultimate source of the winds and reigned with his sister-goddess Tefnut, ultimately controlled the four winds and was a chief actor in ancient Egyptian cosmology (see Fabry, "רוח *rûah*"). The Assyrian king Adad-Nerari II arrogated to himself the sun god and likened his royal power with the "onslaught of the wind" and "the gale" (see Grayson, *Assyrian Royal Inscriptions*, 2:85–86.)

17. Robson, *Word and Spirit*, 269.

18. Vawter and Hoppe, *A New Heart*, 166–67.

19. Boone, "The Role of the Holy Spirit," 52–53; Joyce, *Ezekiel*, 209; and Yates,

Gen 1 and Isaiah and Ezekiel's promise of restoration to and revitalization in the land of Israel portray the Spirit as the agency of God that facilitates the transition from disrepair and despair to life and flourishing.[20] Ezekiel and Isaiah draw on the creation narratives and images to buttress faith in God's power to redeem the people of Israel. In other words, creation and soteriology are reciprocal categories.[21] The redemption from primeval chaos is a creative action. Exodus as redemption by the Spirit God, the same Spirit who tamed the primeval waters, from the threat of military annihilation leads to the creation of the people of Israel. Return from exile in Babylon and restoration to the land is a new exodus or re-creation of the people of Israel

THE SPIRIT AND THE INCARNATION

The New Testament has two pivotal events: incarnation and Pentecost. Yet because of Christocentrism, the work of Christ receives most of the attention. Even Pentecostals, though accentuating the Holy Spirit in their experience, subordinate pneumatology to Christology in their theology.[22] The solution is not to trade Christocentrism for pneumacentrism, but to recognize that Christology and pneumatology condition one another. Neither one can be understood in isolation from the other. Christ is the product of the Spirit's work. Yet at the same time, and consequently, the fullest and clearest window to the nature of the Spirit's redemptive work is the life and ministry of Jesus Christ.

The Holy Spirit's work in Christ is fundamental for understanding the Spirit's identity. Moreover, the Spirit's work in the incarnation

---

Spirit and Creation, 32–33.

20. George Montague does not think the pneumatological themes in the Exodus and Gen 1 stories are related and rather sees Gen 1 connected with the exilic and post-exilic pneumatology of Second Isaiah and Ezekiel (see Montague, "The Fire in the Word," 39). Without disagreeing with the historical-critical connection of Gen 1 with exilic and post-exilic pneumatology, reading the texts canonically also is appropriate. When read canonically, a theological consistency with respect to the images and activity of the *ruach*/Spirit of God emerges. Hebrew Scriptures describe God's redemptive presence in pneumatological categories.

21. Von Rad, *Genesis*, 45–46; Yates, *Spirit and Creation in Paul*, 151–54.

22. Recent exceptions to this tendency are Yong, *Spirit of Love*; Macchia, *Baptized in the Spirit*. For a critique of this tendency, see Dabney, "Saul's Armor," 115–17; Studebaker, "Globalization and Spirit Baptism," 87–108; Studebaker, "Pentecostal Soteriology and Pneumatology," 248–70.

shares continuity with the Spirit's creative-redemptive work in the Old Testament. First, the work of the Spirit in the creation-redemption episodes discussed in the Old Testament is paradigmatic for the Spirit's work in the incarnation. Put more forcefully, the Spirit's work that begins in Gen 1:2 with the redemption of creation from chaos, that is carried on further in breathing life into the dirt in Gen 2:7, and that revivifies the valley of dry bones in Ezek 37:1–14 finds its historical zenith in Christ and especially his resurrection by the Spirit (Rom 8:11). Thus, the angel Gabriel comforts Mary, "Do not be afraid . . . the Holy Spirit will come upon you . . . [s]o the holy one to be born will be called the Son of God" (Luke 1:35). The angel appearing before Joseph was more direct, declaring, "What is conceived in her is from the Holy Spirit" (Matt 1:20). The Spirit hovering over the waters gave structure to the formless primordial elements. The same Spirit established the hypostatic union of the Son and the humanity of Jesus, which formed the life and ministry of Jesus Christ. The Spirit's union of creation with Creator attains its highest possible concrete manifestation in Jesus Christ.[23]

Considering Christology from a pneumatological perspective means that Jesus is the Messiah in and through the agency of the Holy Spirit. Isaiah defines the messianic figure in terms of pneumatology. The source of the messiah's ministry is the investiture of the Spirit. Because the "Spirit of the LORD rests on him" he will govern with "wisdom" and "justice" (Isa 11:1–9). Isaiah 42:1 declares, "I will put my Spirit on him and he will bring justice to the nations . . . [A] bruised reed he will not break, and a smoldering wick he will not snuff out." These passages are not only significant for pneumatology, but also describe the nature of God's redemption. God desires justice, but not primarily retributive justice. God's justice aligns with what today is called social or restorative justice. Rather than the hammer blow of penal judgment, the prophetic vision focuses on the justice that heals the bruised reed and kindles the ember into a flame. The Spirit-anointed redeemer acts on behalf of the "poor" and "needy" (Isa 11:4), frees the captives, comforts the brokenhearted, and brings joy and abundance to those trapped in misery and austerity. Isaiah's vision is not heavenly, but earthy. The freedom,

---

23. Above and what follows contributes to the field of Spirit Christology. For background on and approaches to contemporary Spirit Christology, see Del Colle, *Christ and the Spirit*; Habets, *The Anointed Son*, 188–227. Also, see Studebaker, "Integrating Pneumatology and Christology," 5–20; Studebaker, *From Pentecost to the Triune God*.

comfort, and prosperity is not *spiritual* but earth bound. The people will rebuild their cities, restore their commerce, and live in righteousness with each other and their God (Isa 61:1–9). The justice of retribution is not absent. Isaiah 11:4 warns, "He will strike the earth with the rod of his mouth; with the breath of his lips he will slay the wicked." The focus remains, however, on social justice. The judgment visited upon the *wicked* comes because they have oppressed and exploited the poor. Rather than saving the bruised reed, they trampled it.

The Spirit constitutes Jesus the Christ. The Spirit is not the handmaiden of Christ. Traditional Christology emphasizes the Logos Christology of the Gospel of John. "In the beginning was the Word . . . [a]nd the Word became flesh" (John 1:1 and 14). Yet what transpired between John 1:1 and John 1:14? The synoptic Gospels of Matthew and Luke answer that question. What effected the transition from "the Word was with God" to "the Word became flesh" was an act of the Holy Spirit (Matt 1:20 and Luke 1:35). The incarnation of the Son in Jesus Christ was a result of the presence and activity of the Holy Spirit.

Jesus recognizes that the presence and power of the Spirit constitutes him the Christ. "Returning to Galilee in the power of the Spirit," Jesus enters the synagogue in Nazareth on the Sabbath. There he reads from the scroll of Isaiah: "The Spirit of the Lord is on me, because he has anointed me to preach good news to the poor. He has sent me to proclaim freedom for the prisoners and recovery of sight for the blind, to release the oppressed, to proclaim the year of the Lord's favor" (Luke 4:14–19). His subsequent ministry demonstrates that the Spirit is upon him. After self-identifying as the Spirit-anointed messiah of Isaiah, Jesus goes forth and frees a person tormented by an "evil spirit" and heals people suffering from various physical illnesses and infirmities (Luke 4:31—5:26). Jesus' anointing is from the Spirit. Jesus' messianic identity and ministry derive from the presence of the Spirit. "The Spirit of the Lord is on" him because the Spirit has anointed him "to preach good news to the poor."

Jesus' messianic ministry, moreover, remains rooted in the Spirit. Sandwiched between the healing of the man with a deformed hand and a man possessed by a demon that rendered him blind and mute, Matthew identifies Jesus as the Spirit-anointed messiah of Isa 42: "'Here is my servant whom I have chosen, the one I love . . . I will put my Spirit on him, and he will proclaim justice to the nations . . . A bruised reed he will not break, and a smoldering wick he will not snuff out, till he leads justice to victory'" (Matt 12:18, 20, quoting Isa 42:1, 3–4). Jesus, therefore, declares to the Pharisees, "If I drive out demons by the Spirit of God, then the kingdom of God has come upon you" (Matt 12:28). The people healed by Jesus are concrete examples of the "bruised reed" and the "smoldering wick." Jesus' healing demonstrates that he is the Spirit-anointed messiah. Moreover, the agency of the Spirit constitutes his messianic identity and ministry—what he does he does "by the Spirit of God."

Jesus' ministry derives from the presence and power of the Spirit in his life.[24] The Spirit enables Jesus' life from the inception of the incarnation to his baptism, his standing down Satan in the desert (Luke 4:1–13), and finally his resurrection (Rom 1:4; 8:11).[25] In Christ, the good news had come because he was the *chosen servant*, the Spirit-anointed messiah.

THE SPIRIT AND PENTECOST

The outpouring of the Holy Spirit on the day of Pentecost is a key event not only in the New Testament but in the entire history of redemption. Joel 2 identifies the outpouring of God's Spirit as the eschatological work of redemption. The life and ministry of Jesus Christ reflects this anticipation. Jesus' saving work does not reach its climax on the cross or even in the resurrection, but on the day of Pentecost with the outpouring of the Holy Spirit. This event is a decisive scene in the drama of redemption. It culminates the great movement of redemption that began with the Spirit hovering over the waters and continued with breathing life into the dirt and bringing about the incarnate life of Jesus Christ. Peter's Pentecost sermon identifies the outpouring of God's Spirit as the eschatological work of redemption (Joel 2:28–32).

The baptismal narratives in the Gospels define the nature of Christ's redemptive work in terms of pneumatology—Spirit baptism. Heralding the coming of the Messiah, John the Baptist also declares the nature of his salvation: "I baptize with water, he will baptize you with the Holy Spirit" (see Matt 3:11; Mark 1:8; Luke 3:16; John 1:33). In the Gospel of Luke, Jesus indicates that the goal of his work is the gift of the Holy

---

24. Dunn, *Romans 1–8*, 446.

25. Jewett, *Romans*, 106–7, 492; Osborne, *Romans*, 32, 201; Stuhlmacher, *Paul's Letter to the Romans*, 19, 122.

Spirit. In Luke 11:13, he promises that the "Father in heaven" will "give the Holy Spirit to those who ask him." Not just one among other gifts, the promise of the Holy Spirit is the gift *par excellence*. The Gospel of Luke closes with Jesus assuring the disciples that they will receive the promise of the Father and be "clothed with power from on high" (Luke 24:49).

Acts 1 continues that narrative. Jesus urges the disciples not to leave Jerusalem, but to "wait for the gift my Father promised ... For John baptized with water, but in a few days you will be baptized with the Holy Spirit" (Acts 1:4–5). The Acts narrative (esp. chs. 1 and 2) connects the inaugural promise of Jesus' ministry—John the Baptist's "I baptize with water, he will baptize you with the Holy Spirit"—with its fulfillment on the day of Pentecost. The outpouring of the Spirit of Pentecost therefore is eschatological. The day of Pentecost is the goal of the Christ's ministry. Jesus comes as the Spirit-anointed Messiah (Luke 1:35; 4:17–19; Acts 2:33) so that the life the Spirit made possible in him can be shared with "'all people'" (Acts 2:17).

That all four Gospels and Acts define the goal of Jesus' ministry as baptism in the Holy Spirit is significant. It indicates that the fundamental nature of his ministry and Christian salvation is pneumatological—it is the reception of and participation in the Holy Spirit. The threshold from the Spirit's work in the life of Christ to the outpouring of that possibility on all people is the day of Pentecost. The Spirit of Pentecost makes available to all people the historical realization of the life of God with humanity that took place in Christ. But what is the consequence for traditional Christocentric understandings of the gospel/grace?

THE SPIRIT AND GRACE

The gospel is good news because the Spirit makes the life of Christ available to all people, though not all participate in it. The Spirit's work in Jesus Christ is the paradigm of the Spirit's work as the Spirit of Pentecost. This section showcases two ways that the incarnate life of the Christ parallels the Spirit's work of grace—*Sonship* and sharing in the death and life of Christ.

The Spirit of Sonship

In Rom 8:14–16, Paul connects the Sonship of Christ with Christian identity as children of God the Father: "because those who are led by the Spirit of God are sons of God . . . For . . . you received the Spirit of sonship. And by him we cry, '*Abba*, Father.' The Spirit himself testifies with our spirit that we are God's children." Christians are children of God—that is, they have "sonship."[26] Their "sonship," moreover, parallels the Sonship of Christ. For that reason, they can call their Father "*Abba*." That the Spirit, not Christ, is the source of their "sonship" is notable. The Spirit makes Christians children of God. Connecting Christian identity with being children of God is not limited to Pauline theology. In the prologue to the Gospel of John, John defines the gospel as receiving new birth as God's children: "Yet to all who received him, to those who believed in his name, he gave the right to become children of God—children born not of natural descent, nor of human decision or a husband's will, but born of God" (John 1:12–13). John 3:1–8 clarifies that the Spirit of God is the source of this new birth that constitutes believers children of God.

Why is the Spirit the source of *sonship*? The Spirit's role in constituting Jesus the incarnate Son of God provides the answer. The indwelling Holy Spirit is the source of *sonship* because the Spirit constituted the sonship of Jesus Christ—the Holy Spirit was the agent of the incarnation of the Son of God. The Spirit's work in the incarnation is the paradigm of the Spirit's work as the Spirit of Pentecost. In other words, symmetry marks the Spirit's work in the incarnation and grace. What the Spirit achieved in the life of Christ is the mission of the Spirit of Pentecost. Jesus Christ was the incarnate Son of God through the activity of the Holy Spirit. The Spirit led and enabled the life and ministry of Jesus Christ (Luke 4:1 and 14). So also the Spirit constitutes believers children

---

26. I place "sonship" in quotation marks because that is the term Paul uses. "Sonship" sounds exclusive, but the wider context of Paul's theology makes it clear that the term is inclusive and means children of God. In Romans Paul emphasizes the inclusion of Gentiles in God's grace. In Gal 3:26–28, using the same image of Christians as "sons of God," Paul clarifies the gender inclusiveness of Christian identity as children of God: "There is neither Jew nor Greek, slave nor free, male nor female, for you are all one in Christ Jesus." I believe Paul uses the term "sonship" to accentuate the connection between Christ as the Son of God and the identity of Christians as children of the Father. My use of the term is inclusive and therefore denotes children of God.

of God and frees their lives from sin and enables them to live in righteousness (Rom 8:1–11).

The Spirit of Death and Life

In Rom 6:1–14, Paul parallels the Christian life with the death and resurrection of Christ.

Christ
- died to sin
- was raised to new life

Christians
- die to sin
- are raised to new life

Paul shows that Christ's life, death, and resurrection are a paradigm for redemption. He uses Christian baptism to illustrate the death-to-sin to new-life-in-Christ pattern of salvation. Paul points out that Jesus died *to*, not only *for*, sin (Rom 8:10). Christ died to sin because he never succumbed to temptation. But dying to sin is only half of the good news. Paul says of Christ, "The life he lives, he lives to God" (Rom 8:10). The crucifixion was the final and absolute manifestation of Christ's ongoing life of dying to sin and living *to God*. Death and new life are the negative and positive images of his comprehensive righteousness. Christ's righteousness consists not only in the absence of evil, but also in the active pursuit of God throughout his life.

Christ's death on the cross is the highest expression of his *death to sin* because death to sin becomes literal and absolute. Going down into the waters of Christian baptism symbolizes the Christians' participation in Jesus' ongoing life of death to sin and the absolute expression that takes on the cross. Rising from the waters of baptism represents the Christians' participation in Jesus' life of fellowship with God. Taken together, they are the way Christians participate in the righteousness of Christ. That is why Paul says, "In the same way, count yourselves dead to sin but alive to God in Jesus Christ" (Rom 8:11). What is the *same way* that Paul calls Christians to share with Christ? The previous verse answers this question: "The death he died, he died to sin once and for all; but the life he lives, he lives to God" (Rom 8:10). Facing abandonment by his friends and agonizing death, Jesus remained faithful to the Father, neither shirking his mission to embody the righteousness of God in the world nor lashing out in vengeance toward his tormentors. The Christian life parallels the death and resurrection of Christ.[27] Water baptism is a central rite for Christians because it symbolically and publicly enacts their participation in the death and life of Christ.

The death-to-life imagery of baptism and the historical experience of Christ's crucifixion and resurrection fit the broader canonical frame of God's redemptive work. Genesis 1 begins with "darkness over the surface of the deep." It is a place of menace and lifelessness. The hovering Spirit initiates the transition from darkness and doom to the light and life of the days of creation. The breath of God makes dust a living human being in Gen 2. In the story of the flood, water returns the world to a murky state, and God's Spirit then makes the floodwaters flee from the face of the earth and restores life to its surface and spaces. When the people of Israel face annihilation from Pharaoh's army, the Spirit of God makes a way for them. The bleached bones lying in a valley come alive again when God's Spirit blows on them. The same Spirit of life brings forth the incarnation of the Son of God and Jesus from the tomb.

The Spirit brings life where there is death, light to dark places, hope where despair reigns, and prosperity in place of scarcity. The Spirit of God takes the world, which is an empty, black void, and shapes it into a world full of life and vitality. The Spirit comes to human lives broken with and from sin and heals and transforms them in righteousness. The Spirit cultivates the life of Christ in "everyone who calls on the name of the Lord" (Rom 10:13). Being like Jesus is not a thin Christian moralism. It is more than tacking on spiritual disciplines. The essence of the Christian life is not religious calisthenics and moral asceticism. Being like Jesus is being the place where the Spirit of God brings human life into union with the eternal Son and fellowship with the Father. The gospel is the promise that through participation in Jesus Christ we may know the fellowship he shares with the Father ("that the love you have for me may be in them ... " [John 17:26]). The gospel is good news because the Spirit makes available the life realized in Christ and thereby fulfills the mission that began with the Spirit's first stirring over the primeval waters.

---

27. Fatehi, *The Spirit's Relation*, 206–15; Jewett, *Romans*, 490–91; and Yates, *Spirit and Creation*, 143–51.

THE SPIRIT AND THE GOOD NEWS

The good news is that the gospel is more than it is often portrayed in popular Christianity. Too often popular Christianity distills the gospel to the forgiveness of sins and the hope of heaven. Adopting a list of church activities and personal spiritual disciplines provides the proof that one is on their way to heaven. The forgiveness of sins, freedom from the burden, and the promise of participation in the everlasting kingdom of God are important elements of the gospel. But the Spirit of the gospel shows that the good news entails much more.

More Than Forgiveness

The heart of the gospel is a personal and life-changing relationship with Jesus Christ. The gospel promises that the Holy Spirit brings Christians into union with Christ, and in him they become children of God. Popular versions of the gospel, however, cast the fundamental relationship between God and human beings in legal and moral terms. God is a cosmic judge sitting enthroned in a heavenly courtroom, before which human beings stand guilty of sin. Because God is holy, God must punish sin. Human beings, bereft of means to meet the demands of divine justice, face everlasting suffering in hell. Reprieve from punishment depends on paying the price for sin. Jesus secures salvation by becoming the penal substitute. His death on the cross assuages God's wrath toward human sinners. Jesus' death on the cross is the only way to gain freedom from divine punishment and the forgiveness of sins.[28] Wayne Grudem puts it bluntly: Christ's death on the cross for sin was a "judicial execution . . . inflicted by the God the Father."[29]

Given this judicial emphasis, the gospel becomes almost entirely Christocentric and crucicentric. Even the resurrection loses importance, serving only to show the Father's approval of Jesus' death as the penal substitute. This view also affirms that God loves human beings. God's love led Jesus to die on the cross for them.[30] The essence of salvation is,

---

28. Calvin portrays the sinner's situation as "God's righteous curse bars our access to him, and God in his capacity as judge is angry toward us . . . for God's wrath and curse always lie upon sinners until they are absolved of guilt. Since he is a righteous Judge, he does not allow his law to be broken without punishment, but is equipped to avenge it" (Calvin, *Institutes*, 2.15.6 [1:501] and 2.16.1 [1:504]).

29. Grudem, *Systematic Theology*, 577, 579.

30. Calvin, *Institutes*, 2.16.2–3 (1:504–6).

nevertheless, a judicial exchange.[31] Sinners receive pardon of sin and the conferral of Christ's righteousness before the divine tribunal. The result is that, in popular preaching, the gospel becomes almost entirely about escaping everlasting punishment and having sins forgiven.

The eminent place of the outpouring of the Spirit of Pentecost calls for a revision of the Christocentric and crucicentric tendencies of traditional soteriology. The promise of salvation is the reception of the Spirit of Pentecost that transforms human beings into the image of Christ. The risen Christ does not send the Spirit of Pentecost simply for people to have their sins forgiven, but so that they have the opportunity to participate in his life as the incarnate Son of God. The Spirit is indispensable for receiving the gospel of Jesus Christ because the Spirit was central to making Jesus who he was. The Spirit's work of redeeming the earth from the floodwaters, saving the Israelites from annihilation by Pharaoh's army, and restoring the exiles and renewing their land reaches its fullest manifestation in Christ.[32] The Spirit of Pentecost is the historical threshold that reveals and makes universally available the perennial work of the Spirit.[33] The outpouring of the Spirit of Pentecost makes the life of the Spirit realized in Jesus Christ available to all people. The grace of Christ, therefore, can be no other than the gift of the Spirit.

Highlighting the Spirit's place in redemption does not displace Christology. Peter concludes the Pentecost address, "'Repent and be baptized . . . in the name of Jesus Christ so that your sins may be forgiven. And you will receive the gift of the Holy Spirit. The promise is for

---

31. Hans Boersma calls it an "economy of exchange." Boersma, *Violence, Hospitality, and the Cross*, 170–79. Boersma offers a compelling reformation of penal concepts and their integration with Irenaeus's theory of recapitulation in a Reformed theology of the atonement that overcomes what he calls the "Calvinist tradition's understanding of penal substitution [that] fell prey to juridicizing, individualizing, and de-historicizing tendencies that led to a view of the cross dominated by a strict economy of exchange that obscured the hospitality of the cross" (*Violence, Hospitality, and the Cross*, 19, 177–79). As the representative of the people of God (inclusive of Jew and Gentile), Christ, through the cross and resurrection, recapitulates Israel's exile and return from exile, and thus provides the way for the reconstitution of the people of God and their fulfillment in the eschatological hospitality of God.

32. See my discussion of the Spirit of Christ in *From Pentecost to the Triune God*, 78–87.

33. Note the term "universally" reflects the Joel 2 passage cited by Peter in the Pentecost sermon, which states that the Spirit will be poured out on "all people" (v. 28). Its use here should not be understood to connote soteriological universalism.

you and your children and for all who are far off'" (Acts 2:38–39). The promise is not compartmental, but comprehensive. Peter's summary of the gospel expresses its Christological and pneumatological nature.

Jesus Christ, the union of the eternal Son with human nature, fully manifests the Spirit's redemptive mission. Jesus is, nevertheless, *sui generis*. He is the incarnation of the Son of God in the particular human nature of Jesus. In Jesus Christ, the fellowship of the triune God comes to its most sublime historical expression. Christ is the definitive historical instance of the Spirit's work to bring creation into union with its Creator; he is the incarnation of the eternal Son of God. Core to the Christian faith is the belief that in Jesus we encounter not merely an inspired religious figure, but the incarnation of the Son of God. The Christian belief that Jesus saves depends on this fundamental conviction. Christians are not incarnations of the Son. Jesus, as the incarnate Son, is unique. He does, however, embody what the Spirit desires for all people. The promise of salvation is the reception of the Spirit of Pentecost that transforms human beings into the image of Christ. The point is that, on the one hand, Jesus Christ was a unique development in the history of redemption because he was the incarnation of the eternal Son of God. But on the other hand, the redemptive work brought about through the life of Jesus stands in continuity with the redemptive work that began with the Spirit of God hovering over the darkness of the deep.

More Than Heaven

"What on earth am I here for?" asks Rick Warren in the *The Purpose Driven Life*, telling people that Jesus saves and they are waiting to go to heaven. Why? Because for Christians, life on earth is temporary and their true "identity is in eternity, and [their] homeland is heaven."[34] Inspiring and encouraging millions in the pursuit of the Christian life, *The Purpose Driven Life* is, nonetheless, profoundly misguided. How is a message that flatly declares that most of life is insignificant, save for those precious moments of sharing the gospel, good news? Is the gospel really just about going to heaven?

The good news is that the life brought by the Spirit of Pentecost has little to do with the otherworldly and disembodied view of spirituality and salvation represented in Warren's popular view of the Christian life.

---

34. Warren, *The Purpose Driven Life*, 47–51, 282–83.

Redemption is this-world oriented. The Spirit's work begins with bringing forth a world in which life thrives, and it concludes with its renewal in the new heaven and the new earth and the liberation of creation from its bondage to decay (Rev 21:1–4; Rom 8:21). The incarnation of the Son of God indicates the this-world orientation of the Spirit's work. Christ becomes the means of salvation, not as a spiritualized savior, but as one of flesh and blood. The capstone of the Spirit's work in the life of Jesus is raising him from the dead, which becomes paradigmatic for Christian salvation ("if the Spirit of him who raised Jesus from the dead is living in you, he who raised Christ from the dead will also give life to your mortal bodies through his Spirit, who lives in you" [Rom 8:11]).

This-world orientation does not detract from the Christian hope in the everlasting kingdom. It does, however, indicate that the Spirit's redemptive work encompasses the totality of life and not the narrower notion of *spiritual* life. The Spirit's redemptive work is holistic. It redeems every corner of human life in this world—the fertile field of the prophets. This world is the arena of the Spirit's redemptive work. That is why Jesus heals people of their infirmities. The Spirit that realized the dream of God's desire for human beings in Jesus Christ enables him to restore the lives of people in this world. Jesus, therefore, declares to the Pharisees, "'If I drive out demons by the Spirit of God, then the kingdom of God has come upon you'" (Matt 12:27). Not will come, but has come.

Christian soteriology includes the hope of the everlasting kingdom of God. The Christian hope is not an ethereal, disembodied *heaven*, but *the city that is to come* (Heb 13:14). The Christian hope is earthy. It includes the "liberation of creation from its bondage to decay" and "the new heaven and the new earth" with the restoration of the "River of Life" (Rom 8:21; Rev 21–22). In 2 Cor 4:18, Paul says, "We fix our eyes not on what is seen, but on what is unseen. For what it seen is temporary, but what is unseen is eternal." Paul is not, however, promoting a spirituality of quasi-Christian Platonism. The *unseen* world Paul has in mind is a new creation with resurrected human beings. It is not an incorporeal and spectral *heaven* (2 Cor 4:10–14). The *unseen* of Paul's vision is the resurrected body and, along with his theology in Rom 8:11, the renewal of creation. The good news is that the Spirit that brooded over the primeval waters will one day complete the work of redemption in the resurrection of life in the everlasting kingdom of God. The Spirit that breathed life into the dirt of Gen 2:7 will one day fulfill God's dream for human beings.

CONCLUSION

The gospel is a story of the Spirit. It begins with creation and culminates in incarnation. The Spirit creates the humanity of Jesus Christ and brings about the union of incarnation for the same reason the Spirit delivered the primal elements from darkness and breathed life into the dirt of Gen 2:7. Redemption is the work of God's Spirit that fulfills God's dream for humanity and creation. The gospel is not primarily about the forgiveness of sins and going to heaven. The Spirit of God creates human beings for life in this world. The Spirit's work of redemption does the same. The everlasting kingdom has little resemblance to the disembodied, platonic afterlife of popular Christianity. The gospel is good news because it provides the opportunity to participate in the Spirit's work of redemption, a narrative of redemption that begins with the Spirit hovering over the waters of the deep and concludes with the "new heaven and new earth."

BIBLIOGRAPHY

Anderson, Bernhard W. *Understanding the Old Testament*. 3rd ed. Englewood Cliffs, NJ: Prentice-Hall, 1975.

Barth, Karl. *Church Dogmatics*, 3/1: *The Doctrine of Creation*. Edited by G. W. Bromiley and T. F. Torrance. Translated by J. W. Edwards et al. Edinburgh: T. & T. Clark, 1958.

Block, Daniel I. "The Prophet of the Spirit: The Use of *RWH* in the Book Ezekiel." *JETS* 32 (1989) 27–49.

Boersma, Hans. *Violence, Hospitality, and the Cross: Reappropriating the Atonement Tradition*. Grand Rapids: Baker, 2004.

Boone, R. Jerome. "The Role of the Holy Spirit in the Construction of the Second Temple." In *The Spirit and the Mind: Essays in Informed Pentecostalism*, edited by Terry L. Cross and Emerson B. Powery, 49–63. Lanham, NY: University Press of America, 2000.

Brodie, Thomas L. *Genesis as Dialogue: A Literary, Historical, and Theological Commentary*. New York: Oxford University Press, 2001.

Calvin, John. *Calvin: Institutes of the Christian Religion*. Edited by John T. McNeill. Translated by Ford Lewis Battles. 2 vols. Philadelphia: Westminster, 1960.

Dabney, D. Lyle. "Saul's Armor: The Problem and the Promise of Pentecostal Theology Today." *Pneuma* 23 (2001) 115–17.

Del Colle, Ralph. *Christ and the Spirit: Spirit-Christology in Trinitarian Perspective*. New York: Oxford University Press, 1994.

Dunn, James D. G. *Romans 1–8*. WBC 38A. Waco, TX: Word, 1988.

Eichrodt, Walter. *Theology of the Old Testament.* Translated by J. A. Baker. 2 vols. Philadelphia: Westminster, 1967.
Fabry, H.-J. "רוח *rûah*." In *Theologisches Wörterbuch zum Alten Testament*, edited by G. Johannes Botterweck and Helmer Ringgren, 7:385–425. 10 vols. Stuttgart: W. Kohlhammer, 1973–2000.
Fatehi, Mehrdad. *The Spirit's Relation to the Risen Lord in Paul: An Examination of Its Christological Implications.* WUNT 128. Tübingen: Mohr Siebeck, 2000.
Fee, Gordon D. *God's Empowering Presence: The Holy Spirit in the Letters of Paul.* Peabody, MA: Hendrickson, 1994.
Freedman, Tuvia. "רוח אלהים—and a Wind from God, Genesis 1:2." *Jewish Bible Quarterly* 24 (1996) 9–13.
Grayson, Albert Kirk. *Assyrian Royal Inscriptions: From Tiglath-pileser I to Ashur-nasir-apli II.* 2 vols. Wiesbaden: Otto Harrassowitz, 1976.
Grudem, Wayne. *Systematic Theology: An Introduction to Biblical Doctrine.* Grand Rapids: Zondervan, 1994.
Habel, Norman C. *The Book of Job: A Commentary.* OTL. Philadelphia: Westminster, 1985.
Habets, Myk. *The Anointed Son: A Trinitarian Spirit Christology.* Princeton Theological Monographs Series 129. Eugene, OR: Pickwick, 2010.
Hasenfratz, Hans-Peter. "Patterns of Creation in Ancient Egypt." In *Creation in Jewish and Christian Tradition*, edited by Henning Graf Reventlow and Yair Hoffman, 174–78. JSOTSup 319. London: Sheffield Academic, 2002.
Hildebrandt, Wilf. *An Old Testament Theology of the Spirit of God.* Peabody, MA: Hendrickson, 1994.
Jewett, Robert. *Romans: A Commentary.* Hermeneia. Minneapolis: Fortress, 2007.
Joyce, Paul M. *Ezekiel: A Commentary.* LOTS 482. New York: T. & T. Clark, 2007.
Kákosy, László. "The Ptah-Shu-Tefnut Triad and the Gods of the Winds on a Ptolemaic Sarcophagus." In *Essays on Ancient Egypt in Honour of Herman te Velde*, edited by Jacobus van Dijk, 219–29. Egyptological Memoirs 1. Groningen: Styx, 1997.
Kline, Meredith G. *Images of the Spirit.* Grand Rapids: Baker, 1980.
Levison, John R. *Filled with the Spirit.* Grand Rapids: Eerdmans, 2009.
Macchia, Frank D. *Baptized in the Spirit: A Global Pentecostal Theology.* Grand Rapids: Zondervan, 2006.
Martin, Craig. *Capitalizing Religion: Ideology and the Opiate of the Bourgeoisie.* New York: Bloomsbury, 2014.
Montague, George T. "The Fire in the Word: The Holy Spirit in Scripture." In *Advents of the Spirit: An Introduction to the Current Study of Pneumatology*, edited by Bradford E. Hinze and D. Lyle Dabney, 35–65. Milwaukee: Marquette University Press, 2001.
———. *The Holy Spirit: Growth of a Biblical Tradition.* New York: Paulist, 1976.
Osborne, Grant R. *Romans.* IVPNTC. Downers Grove, IL: IVP, 2004.
Rad, Gerhard von. *Genesis: A Commentary.* OTL. Philadelphia: Westminster, 1961.
Robson, James. *Word and Spirit in Ezekiel.* LOTS 447. New York: T. & T. Clark, 2006.
Sailhamer, John H. *The Pentateuch as Narrative: A Biblical-Theological Commentary.* Grand Rapids: Zondervan, 1992.
Studebaker, Steven M. "Globalization and Spirit Baptism." In *Pentecostalism and Globalization: The Impact of Globalization on Pentecostal Theology and Ministry*, edited by Steven M. Studebaker, 87–108. Eugene, OR: Pickwick, 2010.

———. "Integrating Pneumatology and Christology: A Trinitarian Modification of Clark H. Pinnock's Spirit Christology." *Pneuma* 28 (2006) 5–20.

———. *From Pentecost to the Triune God: A Pentecostal Trinitarian Theology*. Grand Rapids: Eerdmans, 2012.

———. "Pentecostal Soteriology and Pneumatology." *Journal of Pentecostal Theology* 11 (2003) 248–70.

Stuhlmacher, Peter. *Paul's Letter to the Romans: A Commentary*. Translated by Scott J. Hafemann. Louisville: Westminster/John Knox, 1994.

Tsumura, David Toshio. *The Earth and the Waters in Genesis 1 and 2: A Linguistic Investigation*. JSOTSup 83. Sheffield: Sheffield Academic, 1989.

Vawter, Bruce, and Leslie J. Hoppe. *A New Heart: A Commentary on the Book of Ezekiel*. Grand Rapids: Eerdmans, 1991.

Waltke, Bruce. *Genesis: A Commentary*. Grand Rapids: Zondervan, 2001.

Walton, John H. *The Lost World of Genesis One: Ancient Cosmology and the Origins Debate*. Downers Grove, IL: IVP, 2009.

Warren, Rick. *The Purpose Driven Life: What on Earth Am I Here For?* Grand Rapids: Zondervan, 2002.

Wolters, Al. "Not Rescue but Destruction: Rereading Exodus 15:8." *CBQ* 52 (1990) 223–40.

Woodhouse, Susanne. "The Sun God, His Four Bas and the Four Winds in the Sacred District at Saïs: The Fragment of an Obelisk (BM EA 1512)." In *The Temple in Ancient Egypt: New Discoveries and Recent Research*, edited by Stephen Quirke, 132–51. London: British Museum Press, 1997.

Wright, John T. "The Concept of *RUACH* in Ezekiel 37." In *Seeing Signals, Reading Signs: The Art of Exegesis: Studies in Honour of Antony F. Campbell, SJ for his Seventieth Birthday*, edited by Mark A. O'Brien and Howard N. Wallace, 142–58. New York: T. & T. Clark, 2004.

Yates, John W. *The Spirit and Creation in Paul*. WUNT 251. Tübingen: Mohr Siebeck, 2008.

Yong, Amos. *Spirit of Love: A Trinitarian Theology of Grace*. Waco, TX: Baylor University Press, 2012.

11

Can I Get a Witness?
Proclaiming the Gospel in a Post-Everything World

Lee Beach and Nicole Reid

INTRODUCTION: IS EVANGELISM STILL RELEVANT?

THE QUESTION "Is THE gospel good news?" has an implicit answer for many who are reading a book like this one. The question may seem rhetorical; "Of course the gospel is good news!" That is not to say that embracing the gospel does not have its challenges. For everyone who assents to it, there will be certain ways in which it causes us to live and think in patterns that are not in complete sync with the mainstream of our culture. For some it will come with drastic changes; believing in the gospel of Jesus Christ will mean extreme sacrifices and profound consequences. For those early Christians who were the first to embrace the gospel as well as those who came directly after them, the gospel may have seemed like good news on one hand, but it brought with it persecution and even martyrdom on the other. While these are indeed genuine realities that sometimes come with belief in the good news, the cost of belief does not take away from the fundamental reality that the gospel is the good news of God's grace, love, forgiveness, and salvation as it is found in the life and work of Jesus Christ. For those of us who have embraced this good news, it is indeed "good" news, even if it comes with certain costs. Even the early Christians who faced persecution called it "good news." That is why they were willing to suffer as they did.

However, for many (perhaps even most) people in contemporary Western culture, the answer to the same question, "Is the gospel good news?" is categorically "No!" For them the gospel is narrow, exclusive, preferential to some more than others, and irrelevant to modern life. Further, when we ask the question "Is the gospel good news?" we are implicitly asking a further question, "Is evangelism still relevant?" As other essays in this volume have made clear, the word "gospel" (*euangelion* in the original Greek) has etymological implications of proclamation. Thus, you cannot question the goodness of the gospel message without also considering whether proclaiming the message is also a good thing. Those of us who live in a Western cultural context understand that "evangelism" is not a positive word.[1] No matter how much those of us who are convinced Christians might understand evangelism to be a necessary aspect of our faith, for most people who stand outside of established Christianity, the question "Is evangelism relevant?" can be answered definitively: "No!" It is intrusive, presumptive, and just plain "not nice" for someone to try to thrust their religious beliefs on others.

One of the reasons that this is true is that we live in a post-everything society. We are post-Christian, post-institutional, post-denominational, and postmodern. There are several realities that accompany a post-everything culture that must be considered in order to understand the effect that this new culture has on the practice of evangelism. These realities include religious pluralism, diversity, relativity, alienation, division, and the lingering effects of colonial expansion. All of these factors contribute to the fact that Christianity is now just one voice among many; it no longer enjoys the place of singular privilege or elicits an automatic respect from the listener.[2] All of these cultural realities affect how evangelism is practiced in a post-Christian culture, because they challenge the certainty of one's faith. It is difficult for someone to believe in something that is not considered a universal certainty.[3]

However, post-everything does not necessarily mean post-religious. Another reason that evangelism is not necessarily seen as a positive initiative in contemporary Western culture is because of the religious realities that prevail in our current context. The religion of our post-

---

1. Stone, *Evangelism after Christendom*, 9–10.

2. Adeney, *Graceful Evangelism*, 57–58, 61, 139, 144. See also Ross, "Old Church and New Evangelism," 515.

3. Adeney, *Graceful Evangelism*, 58.

everything culture is a distinct one and perhaps has been best captured by Christian Smith and Patricia Snell in their book *Souls in Transition*. Smith offers that the prevailing religion of contemporary Western society is what he calls moralistic therapeutic deism. The primary doctrines of this brand of religious faith can be described by the following articles of faith:

- "A God exists who created and orders the world and watches over human life on earth."
- "God wants people to be good, nice, and fair to each other, as taught in the Bible and by most world religions."
- "The central goal of life is to be happy and to feel good about oneself."
- "God does not need to be particularly involved in one's life except when God is needed to resolve a problem."
- "Good people go to heaven when they die."[4]

While we may debate and quibble over the specific meaning of each of these ideas and reorganize them under different headings that we think more accurately render their meaning, the spirit of Smith and Snell's analysis accurately captures the prevailing religious commitments of our day. This broad but fair expression of Western religious ideals must be understood if we are truly to understand the meaning of the "good news" in a post-everything world. We are mistaken if we think that we live in a religiously neutral culture. The reality is that moralistic therapeutic deism is now *the* state religion, and we err if we do not understand that people are committed to it. If you are not sure about this, just try to tell someone who subscribes to this version of religious faith that they are wrong. Try to persuade them that their rather vague and nebulous understanding of God and his will for humanity is incorrect and that what they really need to believe is that Jesus is the true way to God and that they need to dedicate their lives to following him and his teachings. At best, you will receive an answer that respects Jesus and

---

4. Smith and Snell, *Souls in Transition*, 154–55. It needs to be acknowledged that for the purposes of this essay the concept of moralistic therapeutic deism encompasses the stream of "new age" type spirituality that exists in Western culture as well. This expression of spirituality is not necessarily "deistic," as it is highly personal in nature. However, in many of its expressions, it still encompasses the doctrinal contours that Smith identifies in his thesis.

your particular understanding of what it means to have faith in him. At worst, and more probably, you will receive an answer that reflects a belief that you would be better off keeping your own religious views to yourself. Your conversation partner will make clear to you that your views are decidedly narrow. It is fine if that is what you believe, but you should not expect that others should share your (rather antiquated) beliefs.

The challenge for proclaiming the "good news" (evangelism) in a context like the one, only briefly described here, is immense. The question, "How do we then proclaim the good news?" becomes a valid one for us to reflect on as we consider the various dimensions of the question "Is the gospel good news?"

WHAT IS EVANGELISM?

Prior to determining how best to undertake evangelism in the current North American milieu, it is important for us to come to some conclusions about what evangelism essentially is in its basic function. Much of the negativity surrounding the concept of evangelism stems from the particular experiences of evangelism that people have encountered. These experiences are usually, but not always, related to "proclamation evangelism."[5] In reflecting upon these experiences, one must ask the question "Is that really evangelism?" And if it is not evangelism, then what is it? According to Frances Adeney, there are three types of definitions that can be used when it comes to creating a conceptual framework of evangelism: inclusive, ideological, and lifestyle.[6] Inclusive definitions of evangelism are broad in nature, as they aim to encompass elements that would be common to a variety of denominational definitions of evangelism.[7] An inclusive definition of evangelism might look like this: evangelism is the work of the church trying to embody the kingdom of God in action through word and deed so as to spread the good news of the gospel of Christ through works of justice, service, teaching, and the creation of disciples.[8] Inclusive definitions of evangelism are beneficial when examining evangelism in a diverse context, because they provide

---

5. Ngursangzeli Behera, "Education and Formation," 227.
6. Adeney, *Graceful Evangelism*, 2–5.
7. Ibid., 2.
8. Ibid.

flexibility for the way that evangelism can be practiced in a variety of church contexts.

In contrast, ideological definitions are generally more specific because they highlight what is most important to a particular group of people and focus on particular goals or outcomes that are perceived to be important for that group.[9] These types of definitions can be very useful in determining where a church's vision of evangelism lies. For example, to say that one's church is "justice oriented" or that another is "proclamation oriented" is an ideological way of defining their vision of evangelism. In the former case, evangelism is best understood as doing things that bring greater equity to the world, while in the latter, it is the cognitive understanding of the Christian faith that leads to belief that is most important.

Lifestyle definitions, which comprise the third type of definition, arise out of what people do evangelistically. A lifestyle definition of evangelism can include many different actions but is rooted in the idea that living the Christian life and doing good deeds is the essence of evangelism. At its heart, a lifestyle definition of evangelism borrows the old adage "Preach the gospel; use words if necessary." The gospel is preached primarily through service and worship.[10]

Of these three types of definitions of evangelism, the one that is most appropriate for the conversation concerning the post-everything cultural realities of the present North American context is an inclusive definition. This is because it does not require a specific list of all the activities that must be included for the definition of evangelism to be properly fulfilled. Furthermore, it allows for a multifaceted understanding of cultural and contextual variance in application. This is precisely how evangelism needs to be understood and practiced in a post-Christendom context. Therefore, in this chapter, evangelism will be inclusively defined as the act of inviting people through word and deed to share in Jesus' call to a life of abundance (John 10:10) and of illuminating the action of God in the world by ushering in a taste of the reality of God's kingdom.

In moving forward from definitional categories of evangelism, it is now necessary to consider the various ways in which this definition of evangelism may be applied in practice. Within Christian tradition there is a broad understanding of evangelistic methodology. Adeney helpfully

9. Ibid., 4.
10. Ibid., 5.

outlines a number of theologies of evangelism that address the question of what evangelism looks like. Here we will adapt Adeney's categories while changing some of the terminology and will add two further categories that will make an important contribution to the understanding of evangelism. These eight approaches to evangelism will help us to consider how the twenty-first-century North American church can best understand how it may continue the proclamation of the good news in our particular time and context.

The first theology of evangelism that Adeney identifies is what she calls "discipleship in context." It postulates that evangelism is participation in the mission of God (the *Missio Dei*).[11] In this sense the church is a witness to God's reign as he restores humanity. The church most clearly bears witness to God's reign through love for God and for others. Thus, evangelism is understood as something that is interwoven into everything that the church does. Evangelism is not a program of the church but is the very nature of it. Its orientation and identity is missional, and its call is to go into all the world and participate in God's mission in all that it does and says.[12]

The second theology of evangelism is "fulfilling needs." This focuses on following Christ by obeying Jesus' commandment to love God and one another by meeting people's needs (Luke 10:27).[13] The question that the church, as a witness, has to answer is "What are people's needs, and how can we help to meet them in a way that reflects God's care and love?"

A third theology of evangelism is "community practices." This theology of evangelism views the communal life of the church as faithful witness.[14] The church is a sign and a witness to the gospel through its life together. Evangelism is primarily defined as the formation of an alternative community where people are invited to see the kingdom demonstrated in the life of the church and are invited to participate in this life. As people come into the community, they are exposed to hope

---

11. Ibid., 80.

12. For an overview of missional theology, see Goheen, *A Light to the Nations*; Hastings, *Missional God, Missional Church*.

13. Adeney, *Graceful Evangelism*, 81; Ngursangzeli Behera, "Education and Formation," 281.

14. Adeney, *Graceful Evangelism*, 82; Ngursangzeli Behera, "Education and Formation," 279.

and are made aware of the salvation that is available to them through Jesus Christ. They are accepted before they make any kind of a faith commitment and are encouraged to contribute to the life of the church regardless of their faith commitment.[15]

The fourth theology of evangelism is "transforming worldview." This is shaped around the logic of the Christian worldview and offering an apologetic for its veracity. It is rooted in verbal engagement and the exchange of ideas with the belief that a humble yet confident presentation of Christian truth can bring others to see the amazing beauty of who God is and what he can do for each one of us.[16]

"Lifestyle evangelism" is another theology of evangelism that Adeney offers, and it is perhaps the one that people most commonly associate with the term "evangelism." It encompasses the notion that talking about Jesus and his ministry with those whom we have an ongoing relationship with is the most natural way to do evangelism. This kind of personal, relational ministry is an essential part of Christian witness in the world.[17]

The sixth theology of evangelism that we will draw from Adeney's work is "church planting." Church planting is a theology of evangelism that views faith sharing as a by-product of small-group creation that develops into the growth of churches.[18] The foundational idea is that by proliferating new churches in every region, a critical mass can be reached that will enable the mass proclamation of the gospel in every community.

"Social justice" is another theology of evangelism that deserves to be considered in this overview. This approach seeks to direct people's attention to God's longing for justice in the world.[19] It emphasizes God's desire for justice and calls for people to embrace, proclaim, and live out God's desire for justice to prevail in the world. Through justice the kingdom is revealed, and people are drawn into it.

---

15. Adeney, *Graceful Evangelism*, 82. See also Stone, *Evangelism After Christendom*, for a similar but distinct perspective on this ideology.

16. Adeney, *Graceful Evangelism*, 85–87. Also see Hiebert, *Transforming Worldviews*.

17. Adeney, *Graceful Evangelism*, 90; Ngursangzeli Behera, "Education and Formation," 279.

18. Adeney, *Graceful Evangelism*, 91; Rainer, *The Book of Church Growth*, 205–14.

19. Sider, "Evangelism, Salvation and Social Justice," 185–204. See also Keller, *Generous Justice*.

An eighth theology of evangelism that needs to be considered is the practice of "power evangelism." This theology of evangelism offers that the verbal proclamation of the message of the gospel needs to be accompanied by "signs and wonders" that demonstrate the reality of God's presence and the truth of the message. Evangelism is both word and wonder in that the miraculous affirms the content of the gospel message and provides a sign that tangibly demonstrates the in-breaking of God's kingdom.[20]

The vital concept to be understood concerning these theologies of evangelism is that none of them are exclusively complete. Each of these theologies is somehow connected to biblical models of evangelism, but none of them by themselves fully captures the fullness of evangelism as it is portrayed in Scripture. We raise each of them here because they remind us that, perhaps now more than ever, we need a multifaceted understanding of gospel proclamation if the church in the Western world is going to be effective in declaring and demonstrating the message of Jesus Christ and its truth for people today. As our previously mentioned inclusive definition suggests, a holistic view of evangelism recognizes that a combination of several, or even all, of these theologies will need to be at work in any particular congregation or denomination in order to proclaim the wide-ranging, all-encompassing nature of the good news. Obviously, there are interconnected themes among these theologies, and there are also areas of difference.[21] The point is that each of these theologies is in some way concerned with presenting the abundant life to which Jesus calls his followers; they just differ in the mechanics of how that is to be expressed.

At their heart, each of these theologies sees the gospel as "good news" for the world. They emphasize themes of love, care, community, truth, relationship, justice, and healing. The goal of gospel proclamation is to present the "good news" of abundant life that Jesus came to bring through his life, death, and resurrection. In order for the church to do this, it requires a theology of evangelism that encompasses both philosophical and methodological ideals that contribute to the promotion of these themes. Further, evangelism and mission must be directed toward bringing out the best in humanity; it must have as its goal the possibil-

---

20. A classic example of this perspective on evangelism is articulated by Charles H. Kraft in *Christianity with Power*. See also Wimber and Springer, *Power Evangelism*.

21. Adeney, *Graceful Evangelism*, 94.

ity that humanity can be redeemed and that the gospel is the message that offers this possibility. This assuredly affects how the good news is presented. Methodology must regard and treat each person with dignity and respect in its approach if it is to reflect the essence of the message.[22] Evangelistic actions need to lead people to encounter the humanity of others and see faith sharing as an act of hospitality.[23]

Perhaps the essence of this is captured in 1 Pet 3:15, where Peter writes, "Always be prepared to give an answer to everyone who asks you to give the reason for the hope that you have. But do this with gentleness and respect." The intention of this verse is not to instruct people to have a pre-rehearsed defense of their faith; rather, it is an instruction for people to know what they believe and be ready to dialogue gracefully with others about the source of their hope. This instruction comes in the broader context of an epistle where the author also instructs his audience to "live such good lives among the pagans that, though they accuse you of doing wrong, they may see your good deeds and glorify God on the day he visits us" (1 Pet 2:12). This is the apostle's advice on how to do evangelism when the church finds itself on the margins. It requires alertness, graciousness, verbal sharing, and a distinctive lifestyle that all provide a clear witness to the good news of Jesus Christ.

If we define evangelism as an act that invites people through word and deed to share in Jesus' call to a life of abundance that embodies the new reality of God's kingdom, then it can be seen as a reflection of 1 Peter's approach to faith sharing and the multifaceted way in which it must take place.

When the message of Jesus is presented in a way that captures these realities, it really is "good news" for those to whom it is being offered.

IS EVANGELISM RELEVANT?

In light of this description of evangelism and its various definitions and theologies, the question "Is evangelism relevant?" is ultimately a rhetorical question. When we accept a broad and multifaceted understanding of evangelism with the message of the abundant life of Jesus Christ and the invitation God is issuing to enter into that life at its core, then

---

22. Ngursangzeli Behera, "Education and Formation," 277; Ross, "Old Church and New Evangelism," 517.

23. Root, "Tourists or Missionaries," 25.

we understand that evangelism must be a part of the church's mission. Further, we must also see that the message itself is one of great relevance to human beings in today's world and that its proclamation is at the very heart of God's purposes for his church. From God's movement toward Adam and Eve in the garden after the fall, moving through the great narrative of redemption (the call of Abraham, the establishment of Israel, etc.) all the way to the salvific victory of the incarnate Christ, his giving of the Great Commission, and the subsequent activity of the church, we see that the question is not "Is the gospel good news?" or "Is evangelism relevant?" These may be helpful rhetorical devices, but they are not legitimate questions. The questions are "*How* is the gospel good news for people?" and "*How* do we proclaim the gospel in a relevant way so as to make it good news for our particular context, whatever it may be?" To do any less than this is to fail in our calling to join God in his mission and the church's mandate to make disciples. This is intrinsic to the church's existence, and it is at the very heart of God's character as the God of mission.

WHAT DOES FAITHFUL EVANGELISM LOOK LIKE IN A POST-EVERYTHING WORLD?

The following five ideas are by no means intended to be thought of as an exhaustive response to the question posed by the heading of this section. They are intended to offer some key concepts that provide a trajectory for the direction that the Western church must continue to trace if it is to be a vital instrument of witness to God's good news.

Proclaiming a Complete Gospel

The good news of the gospel is that it is much more than a message about the forgiveness of sins. While that may be at the core of our message, we know that the "gospel" is more multilayered than that. The gospel includes the reality of Christ's identification with humanity at its deepest level, and it includes the possibility of the redemption of all creation and our responsibility to participate in what God is doing to that end. It addresses not only the spiritual realities of our broken relationship with God but also the human realities of our broken relationships with each other. It speaks to all of life and offers the potential of holistic transformation for the individual and the community. This is the whole gospel, and it is the good news that the world is waiting for.

As is explored in other chapters in this volume, the "gospel" has often been truncated in previous decades of evangelicalism. It has been reduced to "four laws" that offer a simplified version of the doctrine of penal substitutionary atonement, where Jesus' death is a payment for sin and acceptance of it provides forgiveness from sin, escape from God's wrath, and assurance of going to heaven when this life ends. This is *not* the gospel. It is a part of the gospel. It falls far short of capturing the fullness of the good news that God offers his creation in the final work of Christ on our behalf.[24]

Forgiveness for sin is essential for each of us. Having our relationship with God repaired and understanding our need to come to repentance and acceptance of God's gift is extremely important. But these ideas are not the primary questions on the minds of post-Christendom people. Moralistic therapeutic deists do not see themselves as sinners in need of saving, and whether *we* think they are or not is irrelevant. That is why we need a wider gospel with a more comprehensive message, one that starts at a different place than sin and engages a wider range of possibilities than simply personal forgiveness for sins and the promise of heaven.

One of the key issues in gospel proclamation is always about finding an appropriate starting point. This is central to helping the good news find a hearing, and it involves determining what matters to the audience. A wider understanding of the gospel helps us to consider the way that the good news connects to people in a post-everything culture. It allows us to understand that there are many ways to talk about the multifaceted truth of the gospel. Categories like relationship with God, spirituality, human relationships, peace, and creation care are all categories that the gospel speaks to and are far better starting places than "sin" in today's world.

Further, the gospel we proclaim must offer people purpose for their lives. It must transcend purely "spiritual" categories. It must answer the question "What difference does this make to my day-to-day life?" The gospel must provide a way to frame one's life in the context of the wider world, particularly in a day when the world seems to grow inexorably

---

24. Frost, *The Road to Missional*, 41–62.

in its complexity. Our proclamation and demonstration of the gospel must provide a vision for how the gospel makes sense of things. It must be a gospel that fully acknowledges that Jesus came to redeem all of the world and that invites us to be participants in God's redemptive purposes—through our work, our family life, and our relationships with others. Gospel proclamation that appreciates the need for the message of the good news to intersect with these kinds of realities says that your life has meaning, your work has purpose, and you are needed to fulfill God's purposes in this world. This is the message that we proclaim when we proclaim the gospel in all of its breadth.

Discerning the Spirit for Effective Contextualization

Perhaps the greatest need in the church today is the cultivation of the life of the Spirit in our midst. In times of change and uncertainty, it is easy for the church to become tentative and perhaps even fearful when it comes time decisively to forge the pathway forward. It was at a time like this that Jesus promised the church that he would be with them through the presence of his Spirit (John 14:16-18). Further, he promised to guide his followers and direct the way that they should go (John 14:26; 16:12-15). The early church took this promise seriously and, while they may have stumbled at certain places, depended deeply on the Spirit to guide their cause as they sought to discern what shape their life and mission should take.

The story of Peter and the Roman centurion Cornelius in Acts 10-11 is a vivid depiction of this reality. After receiving a vision that challenges his traditional ideas of clean and unclean food, Peter is led to the house of a Gentile named Cornelius, who was directed by the Spirit to bring Peter to his home. When Peter arrives at Cornelius's house, he is clear that it is against his religious tradition to enter the house of a Gentile (10:28). However, it appears that Peter sees that God is up to something in Cornelius's house, and he is inspired to cross the threshold and enter the house. There he preaches the gospel to those who are gathered, and it becomes obvious that God is at work in this context (10:34-35, 44-45) and that old ideals and practices need to be revised in order to accommodate what God is doing.[25]

---

25. Van Gelder, *The Ministry of the Missional Church*, 159.

In Acts 15 the early church debates what circumcision means now in light of the influx of Gentile believers into the church. Should they be made to be circumcised, or should they not? After a thorough discussion, they reach a decision that recognizes that something new is happening and that the tradition of circumcision is no longer necessary as a sign of faithfulness. This significant decision is expressed as having come about as a result of the Spirit's leading (15:28).

How do we know when to walk across the threshold and enter into ministry in certain contexts? How do we know when to depart from our doctrinal traditions and move in bold, new missional directions? The answer is "when we are being led by the Spirit to do so." Of course, this demands that we are able to discern the Spirit's voice and movements in our midst. This is an art in itself, but it is an art at which congregations and their leaders must become effective if we are going to bear the good news effectively in this day and age.

Our context demands new Spirit-led approaches to proclamation not only methodologically, but also in terms of the practice of the faith. It must be made clear, however, that this is not just an issue of "success." That is, it is not about trying to keep the numbers up or stave off extinction. Adapting to the reality of our times by changing our approach to ministry or reshaping traditional ways of thinking is not to be done in the name of trying to be successful. It is an issue of faithfulness. It is an issue of contextualization. Learning to follow the lead of the ever-creative Spirit of God is what the church has done for two thousand years when it has been at its best. It is ever evolving, ever changing, ever adapting to the place in which it is planted. Following the lead of the Spirit so that we can faithfully and effectively proclaim the good news of the gospel is what it means for the church to be faithful to God. At this time in Western history, it has never been more necessary for the church to act faithfully in this area of its calling.

Understanding the Mutuality of Faith Sharing

Andrew Root makes the point that believers must enter into evangelistic encounters with the assumption that the other person has something to offer us as well.[26] This assumption is based on an ontological knowledge that there is intrinsic value in the other person and that, because of

---

26. Root, "Tourists or Missionaries," 25.

that value, they have something to bring to the table in the encounter. This also plays on the assumption that God's Spirit is already at work in people found outside of the church walls.[27]

This is why listening is intrinsic to gospel proclamation today. In fact, listening can be the most evangelistic thing that we can do. Historically, faithful proclamation was about me doing the talking. That is, evangelism has been cast around the idea that "I am faithful when I have delivered certain content and ideas to the person I am sharing with." That is, evangelism was me getting the message out to as many hearers as possible. While verbally sharing the message of Jesus Christ certainly is important and even essential to evangelism in the context of the post-Christian West, it is equally as essential to listen so that faith sharing is a mutual experience, not a one-sided "I've got the answer" conversation.

In their book, *The Shaping of Things to Come*, Michael Frost and Alan Hirsch tell the story of Monte Roberts who is better known as "the horse whisperer." Roberts became known for his ability to tame wild horses by "listening" to them. He is not aggressive toward the horse; instead, he gets in the corral and remains present with the horse for an extended period, avoiding eye contact and keeping his distance from it. His approach is largely passive but hugely successful in taking the most spirited wild horse and bringing it to a place where it is willing to be saddled and ridden. Roberts's approach, which is effective despite being counterintuitive by every standard of traditional horse training, is informative to the post-everything practice of evangelism, where learning to listen to the stories, hopes, dreams, and ideas of others has far more potential for creating genuine, fruitful faith-sharing conversations that may help to draw people to Christ than does the approach outlined in the previous paragraph.[28]

When we see evangelism in this way, we are respecting that God is already at work in people's lives long before we ever show up and that they have a legitimate spiritual journey that deserves to be respected and understood. When we make listening a priority in how we approach gospel proclamation, we also give ourselves a chance to discern where God is already at work in someone's life and how we can join him in what he has already begun. While this kind of understanding of evange-

27. Adeney, *Graceful Evangelism*, 175.
28. Frost and Hirsch, *The Shaping of Things to Come*, 97–98.

lism is in contradiction to much of the way we have thought about and been trained to do evangelism in the past, it is a crucial way for us to think and act if we are to proclaim the good news effectively in this day.

Being a Missional Community

The message of the gospel is culture-forming and identity-shaping for the people of God. As we have already noted, it is not just a message of individual salvation; it is a message that invites people to enter into a worldview that orients them to life in a way that is different from the other narratives declared by the culture or cultures in which they operate. In this sense, the gospel calls people into community, a community with a distinct identity. The church is summoned by the very content of its message to be an alternative community—a people who present a different way of life to the world. At its heart as a gospel community, the church embodies the ideals of the gospel and offers those ideals tangibly through its life together. This means that gospel proclamation is not an individual endeavor; it is deeply communal. It also means that because of the narrative in which the church is rooted, it is by its very nature a missional community. That is, its very identity is shaped by its message of salvation for the world.

In the epistle of 1 Peter we read the words of an author who is shaping the identity of a marginalized community. He identifies them as people who are "aliens" and "exiles" (1:1; 2:11). They are a people, much like Christians in the Western context today, whose belief system is outside the mainstream. This language alone is powerful identity language in that it establishes the church in the same plotline of God's story as the nation of Israel, which was also a nation of exiles and aliens. Further, in 1 Pet 2:4–10 the author casts a clear vision of who his churches are, and among the things he tells them is that they are a "holy priesthood" (2:4) and a "royal priesthood" (2:9). The church is given this priestly distinction so that it may "declare the praises of him who called you out of darkness and into his wonderful light" (2:9). This is a vivid recognition of their missional identity, for Peter's audience would have understood that the function of the priest was to mediate between God and the people. Thus, Christians are to function as ones who offer themselves to the world as a witness to God and his work and are there to help bring people into God's presence. Their life together will function as the foundation of God's mission in the world. Together they declare the good news to the world, and their "holiness," or the alternative way of living that they offer, will bear clear witness to the message that they seek to offer to the world. This kind of communal witness is necessary in gospel proclamation today. As Brian Stone says in his book *Evangelism after Christendom*,

> The most evangelistic thing the church can do today is to be the church—to be formed imaginatively by the Holy Spirit through core practices such as worship, forgiveness, hospitality and economic sharing into a distinctive people in the world, a new social option, the body of Christ.[29]

The good news must be proclaimed through the life of the church. It is not enough that people see a difference within the life of individual believers. They must see how the gospel forms community and shapes those communities in specific ways that are deeply distinct from other communities that they frequent. As Stone reminds us, this is more than being nice people. It is being people who practice costly grace through inclusive practices, the free flow of forgiveness, generous hospitality, sharing resources freely, and worshiping God in a way that demonstrates that our allegiance is ultimately to him, as peculiar as that may look to those around us.

Without the body as a whole, evangelistic practice is significantly thwarted. But with it comes the possibility of demonstrating the good news as a convincing alternative narrative to the narratives of consumerism, individualism, and moralistic therapeutic deism that often prevail in Western culture today.

The Role of Signs and Wonders

In the first century, the church was faced with the monumental task of preaching the good news to a culture for whom that message was a completely foreign concept. For the Jews who heard it, it smacked of heresy and blasphemy. For gentiles, it was a message that defied their own categories of "true" religion and sound philosophy. How could the church help the gospel to make sense to its first-century hearers? Part of the answer to that question was the critical role that signs and wonders played in gospel proclamation. The apostles relied on the miraculous work of God as a way of confirming the message that they were pro-

---

29. Stone, *Evangelism after Christendom*, 15.

claiming (Acts 14:20; Mark 16:20). Signs and wonders such as healings and exorcisms were part of the demonstration of the in-breaking kingdom that was at the center of the apostles' proclamation. This was, of course, a continuation of the ministry of Jesus, who announced the good news and demonstrated it with powerful works of healing, casting out demons, and raising the dead.

Gospel proclamation in the ministry of Jesus and the early apostles was a matter of both good words and good deeds. The verbal proclamation of good news needed to be accompanied by physical demonstrations of that good news in action. This does not mean that the miraculous is the only way that the good news is demonstrated. As mentioned earlier in this chapter, the gospel is demonstrated in a multitude of ways as it transforms lives and affects communities. However, a full-orbed theology of evangelism should include the fullness of the gospel as it functions in both word and deed. These "deeds" should be both ethical transformation and miraculous demonstrations of God's power.

The need for this kind of orientation to evangelism is perhaps as great a need in the Western world today as it was in the ancient world when the church was in its infancy. While it is true that many may be skeptical of audacious displays put on by televangelists and faith healers, it is also true that demonstrations of God's power in physical healing or deliverance from chronic harmful behaviors can speak to people in ways that range beyond the intellectual realm and can connect with people in ways that an intellectual message never can. It could be that the proclamation of the gospel must be accompanied by the kind of signs and wonders that confirm its uniqueness and divine origin if it is to make a significant impact in local communities in a post-Christian society. Of course, this is not something that we can simply make happen or drum up whenever we want to. There is mystery in God's power that can never be fully harnessed or predicted, but the church needs to be attentive to this aspect of the gospel and prayerfully seek God for accompanying signs and wonders to go along with its verbal and behavioral proclamation of the good news. This must be done if the church is to offer a whole gospel and provide the kind of authentication of the message that some people need in order to come to faith or have their experience of faith confirmed.[30]

---

30. Wimber and Springer, *Power Evangelism*, 45–48.

CONCLUSION: PROCLAIMING THE GOOD NEWS BOLDLY

The apostle Paul's courageous assertion "I am not ashamed of the gospel ... " (Rom 1:16) remains for us as a testimony to be emulated. The gospel, in all of its multifaceted glory, as it has been considered in this book, is a message that we need not be ashamed of; it truly is the "good news" that God wants to offer to the world. Of course, he makes that offer to humanity primarily through his church. Living in a post-everything culture is intimidating to those of us who once were part of the establishment and whose message was a primary shaper of that culture. We now find ourselves not only with less power, but often viewed not as part of the solution but a part of the problem. This can discourage faith and diminish our courage for proclamation. However, we have a message that truly is good news. What we need is the boldness to proclaim it, despite the opposition and apathy that it inevitably provokes, and the sensitivity to do so in a voice that reaches the hearts of our hearers. We must also recognize the need to adopt a multifaceted approach to proclaiming the "good news" that reflects the depth and richness of the news itself. Perhaps this time for the church in the Western world, time spent on the margins, is forcing us to rethink both our message and our approach to sharing it. This is important work for us to enter into. We must engage these questions honestly and vigorously. Then may our deliberations ultimately bring about a new confidence that the message of Jesus Christ is the message that our world desperately needs, and may it embolden us to go into all the world and make disciples as we invite people to embrace the good news that we ourselves have discovered and have been given the task to share, even in a post-everything world like ours!

BIBLIOGRAPHY

Adeney, Francis S. *Graceful Evangelism: Christian Witness in a Complex World*. Grand Rapids: Baker, 2010.

Frost, Michael. *The Road to Missional: Journey to the Center of the Church*. Grand Rapids: Baker, 2011.

Frost, Michael, and Alan Hirsch. *The Shaping of Things to Come: Innovation and Mission in the 21st-Century Church*. Peabody, MA: Hendrickson, 2003.

Goheen, Michael W. *A Light to the Nations: The Missional Church and the Biblical Story*. Grand Rapids: Baker, 2011.

Hastings, Ross. *Missional God, Missional Church: Hope for Re-evangelizing the West*. Downers Grove, IL: IVP, 2012.

Hiebert, Paul G. *Transforming Worldviews: An Anthropological Understanding of How People Change*. Grand Rapids: Baker, 2008.

Keller, Timothy. *Generous Justice: How God's Grace Makes Us Just*. New York: Dutton, 2010.

Kraft, Charles H. *Christianity with Power: Your Worldview and Your Experience of the Supernatural*. Ann Arbor, MI: Vine, 1989.

Ngursangzeli Behera, Marina. "Education and Formation for Evangelism: Evangelism and Youth." *International Review of Mission* 96 (2007) 277–87.

Rainer, Thomas. *The Book of Church Growth: History, Theology and Principle*. Nashville: Broadman and Holman, 1993.

Root, Andrew. "Tourists or Missionaries? Theological Questions You Need to Answer Before Your Group's Next Missions Trip." *Youth Worker* March/April (2013) 24–25.

Ross, Kenneth R. "Old Church and New Evangelism: A Scottish Perspective on Christian Mission in Today's Europe." *Missiology* 37 (2009) 511–25.

Sider, Ronald J. "Evangelism, Salvation, and Social Justice: Definitions and Interrelationships." In *The Study of Evangelism: Exploring a Missional Practice of the Church*, edited by Paul W. Chilcote and Laceye C. Warner, 185–204. Grand Rapids: Eerdmans, 2008.

Smith, Christian, and Patricia Snell. *Souls in Transition: The Religious and Spiritual Lives of Emerging Adults*. Oxford: Oxford University Press, 2009.

Stone, Bryan. *Evangelism after Christendom: The Theology and Practice of Christian Witness*. Grand Rapids: Brazos, 2007.

Van Gelder, Craig. *The Ministry of the Missional Church: A Community Led by the Spirit*. Grand Rapids: Baker, 2007.

Wimber, John, and Kevin Springer. *Power Evangelism*. San Francisco: Harper & Row, 1986.

Crucial Topics

12

Baptism in the Holy Spirit
A Circumcised Heart, A New Disposition

RONALD D. PETERS

INTRODUCTION

THE TOPIC OF THIS chapter stands at the confluence of two separate yet related works. The first is an article in a recent volume of *Bible Translator*, "The Holy Spirit and a Holy Spirit: Some Observations and a Proposal," by Clint Tibbs. In his introduction, Tibbs presents the following problem:

> Is "the Holy Spirit" of Trinitarian thinking, proposed by the fourth-century fathers Athanasius of Alexandria, the Cappadocians, and Didymus the Blind, the same "holy spirit" expressed by first-century writers of the text of the Greek New Testament?[1]

Tibbs believes this Trinitarian reading is indeed incorrect. Therefore he proposes the following solution:

> I will propose that the New Testament provides evidence for "a spiritual world" populated with a multiplicity of holy spirits. The evidence for this argument is as follows: the anarthrous "a holy

---

1. Tibbs, "Holy Spirit," 153. See also Tibbs's follow up article, "PNEUMA," 172–84. For further discussion on the topic, see also Swartz, "Holy Spirit," 124–38; and Levinsohn, "Anarthrous References," 138–44.

spirit"; the anaphoric use of the articular "the spirit" to mean "a spirit"; the generic singular "the spirit of God" as an inclusive rubric for many spirits of God; and the plural "spirits" in the context of divinity.[2]

I was intrigued by the problem that Tibbs had identified, not so much because I was persuaded by his argument or proposed solution, but by the nature of the evidence he cited and the methodology he employed for its interpretation. As we see, one of the primary pieces of evidence has to do with the presence and absence of the article with regard to the head term *spirit*, πνεῦμα. He notes that both the presence and the absence of the article are significant, yet he fails to ask, in my opinion, a very important question: how does the presence or absence of the article affect the sense of the head term πνεῦμα? Tibbs's treatment of the articular and anarthrous constructions reflects the standard approach to the article that has been employed by Greek scholars for centuries.[3] When affixed to nouns, the article is viewed as a marker of syntax, specifically of particularities involving structure. It is not viewed as a modifier, as something that enters into a meaningful relationship with the head term so as to have an effect on the sense of the head term, in this case πνεῦμα.

This question that Tibbs leaves unasked is a question that is uppermost in my own mind, which brings us to the second aforementioned work, that is, my own research on the Greek article.[4] To summarize, my central thesis is that the function of the article is to characterize the head term as *concrete*, "as belonging to immediate experience as an actual thing or event."[5] By contrast, parts of speech that routinely take the article, particularly nouns, when anarthrous are characterized as *abstract*, "as not belonging to immediate experience as an actual thing or event."[6] After reading Tibbs's article, I could not help but wonder how his argument might look if the theory I propose was taken into account, particularly with regard to its implications for our understanding

---

2. Tibbs, "Holy Spirit," 153.

3. This is essentially the approach employed by Gordon Fee in his analysis of articular and anarthrous constructions of "the Holy Spirit" in the Greek New Testament (*God's Empowering Presence*, 15–24). Fee concludes that, with regard to Pauline usage specifically, "[Paul] only and always means the Spirit of the living God, the Holy Spirit himself" (24).

4. Peters, *Greek Article*.

5. Ibid., 227.

6. Ibid.

of the function of the Holy Spirit in the life of both the individual and the corporate community of believers; thus began the investigation that resulted in the present chapter.

In the following presentation, I will first provide a brief description of the general function of the Greek article. Next, I will examine several articular and non-articular constructions of "Holy Spirit" in Greek in order to determine how the variations in characterization may be interpreted. Lastly, I will apply the conclusions drawn in this investigation to the question of what it means to be baptized in the Holy Spirit and of its implication for whether or not the gospel delivers good news to a bad-news world. It is my argument that the use or non-use of the article represents a meaningful choice on the part of the speaker or writer. Thus, its presence or absence with "Holy Spirit" reflects a difference in characterization that must be explained. The resulting explanation has significant exegetical value. To this point, I will argue that, at least in certain instances, non-articular instances of "Holy Spirit" may be interpreted as reference to a "holy disposition." This understanding should inform our understanding of the work of the Holy Spirit. Specifically, the function of the Holy Spirit, the third person of the Trinity, is to transform the fundamental disposition of the individual and bring it into conformity with God's own disposition; this is the essence of a circumcised heart. In a world characterized by corruption and violence, the only solution is a transformative work that can only be accomplished by baptism in the Holy Spirit.

THE FUNCTION OF THE GREEK ARTICLE

Before I begin my analysis of the meaning of πνεῦμα ἅγιον in the New Testament, it is necessary for me to present a brief summary of my theory regarding the usage of the article in the Greek of the New Testament. As stated in the introduction above, when a speaker or writer employs the article, the head term to which it is attached is characterized as concrete, as belonging to experience as an actual thing or specific instance. By contrast, elements that may or may not take the article, primarily nouns, are characterized as abstract when the article is absent. An example of this contrast is found in Rom 8:24:

> τῇ γὰρ ἐλπίδι ἐσώθημεν· ἐλπὶς δὲ βλεπομένη οὐκ ἔστιν ἐλπίς
> For in hope we were saved; but hope being seen is not hope.

In the first occurrence, "hope," ἐλπίς, is articular. In the second and third, it is anarthrous. These constructions represent Paul's subjective view on the lexical item and how he chooses to characterize it. In the first instance, ἐλπίς is articular because Paul associates it with something concrete. In accordance with the definition above, we may say that it is associated with a specific instance. In this case, the specific instance of hope is found in the immediately preceding verse. It is hope that is based on the expectation of our adoption, the redemption of our bodies. In the second and third instances, Paul's presentation shifts. He moves from hope that is associated with a specific instance to hope in a more general or abstract sense, "hope being seen is not hope."

It is important to recognize that the characterization achieved by the article is not synonymous with notions of definiteness. Elements so characterized may or may not correspond with reality. In certain situations they are characterized as such a thing that exists without necessarily indicating real-world correspondence. In such instances, the item is so characterized so as to hold it out for inspection or consideration. This usage may be observed in 1 Cor 7:1, 3. First, we note v. 1:

> καλὸν ἀνθρώπῳ γυναικὸς μὴ ἅπτεσθαι
> [It is] good for man not to touch woman.

In this instance, ἄνθρωπος and γυνή are characterized as abstract, disassociated from any particular instance. If, as many commentators suggest, Paul is quoting a Corinthian slogan, "man" and "woman" are employed quite generically in service of the aphorism. It is also possible that the characterization serves to provide background for this particular element, as it sets up what the apostle is about to say next.[7] We note that the characterization changes in v. 3:

> τῇ γυναικὶ ὁ ἀνὴρ τὴν ὀφειλὴν ἀποδιδότω, ὁμοίως δὲ καὶ ἡ γυνὴ τῷ ἀνδρί.
> A man must give the obligation to the woman, and likewise also a woman to the man.

Here, γυνή and ἀνήρ are articular. Though both are characterized as concrete, it is not required that we conclude Paul is thinking in terms of a specific man or woman, identifiable by name and face. Rather, by char-

---

7. Regarding the article and its relation to grounding and salience, see Peters, *Greek Article*, 188–91.

acterizing them as concrete, he presents woman and man as elements that belong to the immediate realm of experience, as such elements that exist so that they may be held out for consideration. Additionally, the characterization may indicate greater salience at a discourse level.

Having presented a working definition of the function of the Greek article and illustrations supporting it, I will now move to an application regarding the matter of πνεῦμα ἅγιον.

THE HOLY SPIRIT OR HOLY SPIRIT?

Articular Constructions

The words πνεῦμα and ἅγιον appear together over eighty times throughout the New Testament. The most common construction, occurring forty-three times, is πνεῦμα ἅγιον. Second is the second attributive construction, τὸ πνεῦμα τὸ ἅγιον, occurring thirty times. In distant third is the first attributive structure, τὸ ἅγιον πνεῦμα, with a meager twelve occurrences. Irrespective of the construction, nearly every occurrence is translated in the modern English versions as "the Holy Spirit." Translation of such diverse forms by a single English form is indicative of an underlying assumption that there is little or no significance to the construction itself, in particular the presence or absence of the article. This is consistent with both historical and contemporary approaches that do not recognize that a meaningful relationship exists between the article and its head term. I wish to challenge this assumption by arguing that the article does indeed enter into a meaningful relationship with its head term, such that the sense of the head term is altered by its presence. If this is true, the implications for translation and exegesis are significant.

Based on the description of the article's function presented above, I will employ the following working proposal, which will be used as a guideline for translation and exegesis of passages incorporating the various forms of πνεῦμα ἅγιον:

> When a New Testament writer employs the article with πνεῦμα, the head term is characterized as concrete, that is, as reference to a specific instance of "spirit." When a New Testament writer employs πνεῦμα without the article, it is characterized as abstract, as disassociated from a specific instance.

In addition, I propose that in certain non-articular instances, it is arguable that the speaker or writer employs πνεῦμα in the sense other than that of a person. In such instances, πνεῦμα is used in the sense of "an attitude or disposition reflecting the way in which a person thinks or deals with some matter—'disposition, attitude, way of thinking.'"[8] Based on this proposal, we would expect that, when a speaker or writer has in view the Holy Spirit as it is historically construed, that is, the third person of the Trinity, the preferred construction will employ the article. Conversely, non-articular constructions allow for the possibility of another interpretation. It must be admitted that there are a number of factors that influence the use or non-use of the article, such as considerations of discourse grounding. However, simple recognition that the presence or absence of the article represents a meaningful choice in characterization provides a point at which to begin an investigation into the possibility of alternative interpretations.

With regard to the eight occurrences (seven of which are found in Luke-Acts) of the first attributive, τὸ ἅγιον πνεῦμα, at least five may be argued as certainly referring to the Holy Spirit in a personal sense. For example, in Luke 12:10, the Holy Spirit is presented in parallel with Jesus (the Son of Man):

> Καὶ πᾶς ὃς ἐρεῖ λόγον εἰς τὸν υἱὸν τοῦ ἀνθρώπου, ἀφεθήσεται αὐτῷ· τῷ δὲ εἰς τὸ ἅγιον πνεῦμα βλασφημήσαντι οὐκ ἀφεθήσεται.
>
> Each one who speaks a word against the Son of Man will be forgiven, but the one who blasphemes against the Holy Spirit will not be forgiven.

In this example, since both the Son of Man and the Holy Spirit are spoken against (εἰς), it is natural to understand the Holy Spirit as a person just as Jesus is a person. Similarly, two verses later, the Holy Spirit is presented as an agent who will teach the disciples what they should say:

> τὸ γὰρ ἅγιον πνεῦμα διδάξει ὑμᾶς ἐν αὐτῇ τῇ ὥρᾳ ἃ δεῖ εἰπεῖν.
>
> For in that hour the Holy Spirit will teach you regarding what you must say.

While inanimate objects, such as Scripture, may be said to teach, in this instance the Holy Spirit is better understood as having the sense of a person, that is, an active agent who teaches.

---

8. See L&N, 350, under Domain 30: "Think"; Sub-Domain A: "To Think, Thought"; 30.6: πνεῦμα.

In Acts 13:4 the Holy Spirit is again an active personal agent directing the course of Paul and Barnabas:

> Αὐτοὶ μὲν οὖν ἐκπεμφθέντες ὑπὸ τοῦ ἁγίου πνεύματος κατῆλθον εἰς Σελεύκειαν, ἐκεῖθέν τε ἀπέπλευσαν εἰς Κύπρον.
>
> Then, being sent by the Holy Spirit, they went down to Seleucia, and from there sailed to Cyprus.

In this example, the Holy Spirit is the one who sends Paul and Barnabas. This strongly suggests the Holy Spirit is characterized as a person. The only other instance of this lexical item is Acts 17:10, where the brothers in Thessalonica send Paul and Silas to Berea.

Similarly, in Acts 16:6, the Holy Spirit is an active personal agent who prevents Paul from speaking the word in Asia:

> Διῆλθον δὲ τὴν Φρυγίαν καὶ Γαλατικὴν χώραν κωλυθέντες ὑπὸ τοῦ ἁγίου πνεύματος λαλῆσαι τὸν λόγον ἐν τῇ Ἀσίᾳ.
>
> They traveled through the regions of Phrygia and Galatia, being prevented by the Holy Spirit from speaking the word in Asia.

While the hindering or preventing work of the Holy Spirit in this instance does not require that the Holy Spirit be understood as a person, it would seem to be strongly suggested.

In two instances, the Holy Spirit is grouped with the Father and the Son. The first is in Matt 28:19:

> βαπτίζοντες αὐτοὺς εἰς τὸ ὄνομα τοῦ πατρὸς καὶ τοῦ υἱοῦ καὶ τοῦ ἁγίου πνεύματος
>
> Baptizing them in the name of the Father and of the Son and of the Holy Spirit

The next is found in 2 Cor 13:13:

> Ἡ χάρις τοῦ κυρίου Ἰησοῦ Χριστοῦ καὶ ἡ ἀγάπη τοῦ θεοῦ καὶ ἡ κοινωνία τοῦ ἁγίου πνεύματος μετὰ πάντων ὑμῶν.
>
> The grace of the lord Jesus Christ and the love of God and the fellowship of the Holy Spirit be with you all.

Based on these examples, we may conclude that the construction τὸ ἅγιον πνεῦμα may be reasonably understood as a reference to the Holy Spirit.

Of the thirty occurrences of the second attributive, τὸ πνεῦμα τὸ ἅγιον, twenty-three are found in the Gospels (seven occurrences) and

Acts (sixteen occurrences). The numbers indicate an overwhelming preference for this articular construction. This may be explained by discourse considerations. The second attributive construction represents a marked construction. In addition, rhetorically, the construction gives elements that present a more "lofty" versus "concise" feel.[9] The preference for this construction for "the Holy Spirit" may reflect multiple motivations operating simultaneously: (1) to characterize the Holy Spirit as concrete in the sense of a personal agent, (2) to foreground the Holy Spirit through the use of a marked form, and (3) to elevate the Holy Spirit through the use of a "lofty" sounding structure. This may also explain the shift to the first attributive when the Holy Spirit is grouped with the Father and the Son (see above, Matt 28:19; 2 Cor 13:13), as the speaker or writer does not want to foreground or elevate the Holy Spirit at the expense of the Father and the Son.

Numerous examples suggest that this construction is used when the Holy Spirit is characterized as a living being, a person, and especially as an active personal agent. Of the thirty New Testament occurrences, nearly two-thirds (nineteen in total) are found in Luke-Acts. This is not surprising, considering Luke's emphasis on the Holy Spirit's agency in the lives of Jesus and his followers. His preference for this construction may be explained by the discourse considerations outlined above.

There are numerous examples where this construction is employed in instances in which the action performed by the Holy Spirit is consistent with a person. The only occurrence in John's Gospel is found in 14:26, where the Holy Spirit, the "paraclete," is presented as an active personal agent who will teach the apostles:

> ὁ δὲ παράκλητος, τὸ πνεῦμα τὸ ἅγιον, ὃ πέμψει ὁ πατὴρ ἐν τῷ ὀνόματί μου, ἐκεῖνος ὑμᾶς διδάξει πάντα καὶ ὑπομνήσει ὑμᾶς πάντα ἃ εἶπον ὑμῖν.
>
> But the paraclete, the Holy Spirit, whom the Father will send in my name, he will teach you all things and will bring to your memory all that I said to you.

In Eph 4:30 the Holy Spirit is presented as a person who may experience the emotion of grief:

> καὶ μὴ λυπεῖτε τὸ πνεῦμα τὸ ἅγιον τοῦ θεοῦ

---

9. Peters, *Greek Article*, 256–59.

And do not grieve the Holy Spirit of God

In Heb 3:7, the Holy Spirit speaks:

Διό, καθὼς λέγει τὸ πνεῦμα τὸ ἅγιον

Therefore, just as the Holy Spirit says

In Heb 9:8 he reveals:

τοῦτο δηλοῦντος τοῦ πνεύματος τοῦ ἁγίου

The Holy Spirit, revealing this

In Heb 10:15 he testifies:

Μαρτυρεῖ δὲ ἡμῖν καὶ τὸ πνεῦμα τὸ ἅγιον·

But the Holy Spirit also testifies to you.

Each of these examples strongly suggests that the Holy Spirit is characterized as a person.

In conclusion, based on these examples, we may propose that when πνεῦμα is articular, in both first and second attributive structures, in the vast majority of instances the context suggests that "the Holy Spirit" is presented as something or someone that is concrete, belonging to immediate experience as an actual person or thing.

Non-Articular Constructions

We now turn our attention to the non-articular construction πνεῦμα ἅγιον. If my proposed definition of the function of the article and its specific application to the current question holds true, we should expect that this construction represents a meaningful choice on the part of the speaker or writer with regard to the characterization of the Holy Spirit. This, of course, forces the question of what the speaker or writer does mean when they use this term. I propose that in many or the majority, if not all, of these instances, the non-articular (thus abstract) term πνεῦμα may be understood in terms of the definition proposed above: "an attitude or disposition reflecting the way in which a person thinks about or deals with some matter—'disposition, attitude, way of thinking.'"[10] Several instances suggest that this may well be the case.

In Acts 4:8, most translations interpret Τότε Πέτρος πλησθεὶς πνεύματος ἁγίου εἶπεν πρὸς αὐτούς· ἄρχοντες τοῦ λαοῦ καὶ πρεσβύτεροι

---

10. L&N, 350.

as a statement indicating that Peter was filled with the Holy Spirit, the personal agent who empowered, inspired, and directed his words in response to the Jewish leadership. I in no way suggest that this was not the case. However, this may not be Luke's point or may not capture his entire interpretation of the matter. Instead, the author might have wished to emphasize that the motivation behind the words Peter spoke was a "holy disposition." This interpretation would be consistent with an overarching pattern in Acts in that Luke routinely contrasts the noble motives of the heroes with the ignoble motives of the antagonists. Peter does not speak out of pride or arrogance, but out of a holy disposition. This places Peter in stark contrast with the Sadducees, who ignore the sign of the man who was healed (vv. 16, 22) and who threatened Peter and John (v. 21). We observe a similar situation when Paul rebukes Elymus in Acts 13. Paul does so not out of anger or pride, but out of πλησθεὶς πνεύματος ἁγίου, "being filled with a holy disposition," that is, a motivation based on holiness (13:9). One might even characterize Paul's response as righteous indignation. This contrasts the apostle with Elymus, who is "full of all deceit and villainy."

For Luke, a holy disposition is one of the chief character traits of the heroes of Acts. In 6:5, Stephen is ἄνδρα πλήρης πίστεως καὶ πνεύματος ἁγίου, "a man full of faith and a holy disposition." This disposition does not change, even in the face of rabid opposition (7:55). Jesus was anointed by God with πνεύματι ἁγίῳ καὶ δυνάμει, "a holy disposition and power" (10:38). Like Stephen, Luke describes Barnabas as a ἀνὴρ ἀγαθὸς καὶ πλήρης πνεύματος ἁγίου καὶ πίστεως, "good man filled with a holy disposition and faith" (11:24). This is certainly a characteristic of God's people in general. Notice that a holy disposition is presented in parallel to joy in Luke 13:52: οἵ τε μαθηταὶ ἐπληροῦντο χαρᾶς καὶ πνεύματος ἁγίου. Even when not explicitly connected to the Holy Spirit, Luke routinely makes a point of highlighting the general disposition of believers (e.g., 4:43–47; 4:32–37).

This understanding of πνεύματος ἁγίου presents an interesting interpretation of Paul's statement in 1 Cor 12:3:

> καὶ οὐδεὶς δύναται εἰπεῖν· Κύριος Ἰησοῦς, εἰ μὴ ἐν πνεύματι ἁγίῳ.
>
> And no one can say, "Jesus is Lord," except by the Holy Spirit (NRSV).

If πνεῦμα is interpreted as a disposition, then Paul is not saying that a person is unable to declare that Jesus is Lord apart from the work of the Holy Spirit. Rather, the declaration itself reflects the disposition of the speaker. If a believer does not have a holy disposition, he or she would not declare Jesus as Lord. Likewise, "no one speaking in God's disposition," οὐδεὶς ἐν πνεύματι θεοῦ λαλῶν, would ever say, "Curse Jesus." One's words are a reflection of one's heart, that is, one's disposition. Anything else is a contradiction. It is noteworthy that, when addressing the Spirit as the agent operating through the various gifts in vv. 4–11, πνεῦμα is articular. In chs. 12–14, Paul is interested in the Spirit as a personal agent and in the motives that influence the individual through whom the Spirit works. Such people should operate in love (ch. 13) and πνεῦμα ἅγιον, a holy disposition.

In Rom 5:5, the love of God is the result of a holy disposition:

ἡ ἀγάπη τοῦ θεοῦ ἐκκέχυται ἐν ταῖς καρδίαις ἡμῶν διὰ πνεύματος ἁγίου τοῦ δοθέντος ἡμῖν.

The love of God has been poured out in our hearts through the Holy Spirit given to us.

Likewise, righteousness, peace, and joy are the products of, and thus characterize, a holy disposition, δικαιοσύνη καὶ εἰρήνη καὶ χαρὰ ἐν πνεύματι ἁγίῳ (Rom 14:17). In Rom 9:1, when Paul defends the truthfulness of his words, he calls upon the testimony of his conscience, whose prevailing tendency is based on a "holy disposition" as evidence of this truthfulness:

Ἀλήθειαν λέγω ἐν Χριστῷ, οὐ ψεύδομαι, συμμαρτυρούσης μοι τῆς συνειδήσεώς μου ἐν πνεύματι ἁγίῳ

Truthfully I speak in Christ, I do not lie, my conscience bearing witness with me in the Holy Spirit.

Again, in his own defense, Paul commends himself and his associates based on the content of their character as evidenced in their "purity, knowledge, patience, kindness, holiness of spirit [ἐν πνεύματι ἁγίῳ], genuine love" (2 Cor 6:6 NRSV). In this list, "holiness of spirit" is listed among character or dispositional traits.

As these examples demonstrate, there is reason to consider that the use or non-use of the article with πνεῦμα ἅγιον represents a meaningful choice on the part of the speaker or writer. While the presence or absence of the article alone is not the only decisive factor to consider, it should prompt the interpreter to explore the possibility of alternative meanings. At the very least, we must resist the assumption that there is no substantive difference in the characterization produced by these structures. For our current purpose, it is arguable that, in certain instances, New Testament usage of the non-articular form, πνεῦμα ἅγιον, may indeed reflect an emphasis on "spirit" as "disposition." In the next section we will examine the implications of this interpretation.

SPIRIT BAPTISM AND A NEW DISPOSITION: THE GOOD NEWS FOR A BAD-NEWS WORLD

Historically, at least in terms of recent history, conversations regarding the nature of baptism in the Holy Spirit have been dominated by the question of a second work of the Spirit subsequent to salvation. For Wesley and some of his followers, including members of the nineteenth-century Holiness Movement, this work brought about the full sanctification of the believer, resulting in a life characterized by complete holiness. For Pentecostals, baptism in the Spirit brings power for service and, in particular, the endowment of charismatic gifts. One might argue that these views may be summarized by two terms: "purity" and "power."[11] Though we may debate the validity of a second work of the Spirit, neither of these outcomes, in the general sense of the work of the Spirit producing purity and power, is in dispute. Rather, I wish to add to our understanding of the work of the Spirit, particularly with regard to baptism in the Holy Spirit.

From the beginning, it was God's expectation that his people would be characterized by a different disposition. Though circumcision of the body served as an outward sign that made Israel different from the surrounding nations, God instructed Israel to "circumcise the foreskins of your heart" (Deut 10:16). It was this characteristic heart condition, this disposition, that God truly wanted from Israel to distinguish her from other nations. Israel's disposition would be one that was characterized by fear of the Lord, obedience, and fidelity of worship. They would also be characterized by love for their neighbors, manifested in generosity and justice. God gave the Israelites instructions, the torah, so that they would understand what such a kingdom should look like. These instructions

---

11. Here I obviously appropriate Keener, *The Spirit in the Gospels and Acts*.

were not merely a matter of codified behavior; they revealed the heart of God. Understanding the torah should bring about an understanding of God's disposition, that is, his very heart.

The Old Testament bears witness to the fact that Israel did not live up to this ideal. Their failure on both fronts, fidelity to God and generosity and justice for their neighbors, incited God's wrath, resulting in captivity and exile. Nevertheless, God was not finished with Israel. Following his judgment, God declared that he would give his people a "new spirit" in the sense of a new heart or "disposition, attitude, way of thinking." In Ezek 11:19–20 we read:

> I will give them one heart, and put a new spirit within them; I will remove the heart of stone from their flesh and give them a heart of flesh, so that they may follow my statutes and keep my ordinances and obey them. Then they shall be my people, and I will be their God (NRSV).

Again Ezekiel prophesies in 36:26–27:

> A new heart I will give you, and a new spirit I will put within you; and I will remove from your body the heart of stone and give you a heart of flesh. I will put my spirit within you, and make you follow my statutes and be careful to observe my ordinances (NRSV).

Despite Israel's failure, it remained God's intention to change the heart of his people.[12] The plan for his kingdom was to create a people for himself whose hearts were like his own, who shared his values and his priorities. God's people and his kingdom will be characterized by a new disposition. In the past, God gave Israel his instructions, but these instructions, on the whole, failed to produce the disposition God desired in his people. Therefore, in the future, this dispositional change will come about by the active agency of God working through his Spirit.

It is arguable that the New Testament writers interpreted the outpouring of the Holy Spirit as fulfillment of this expectation. John the Baptist proclaimed that the one coming after him would baptize "in the Holy Spirit and fire," as recorded in all three of the Synoptic Gospels:

> ἐγὼ ἐβάπτισα ὑμᾶς ὕδατι, αὐτὸς δὲ βαπτίσει ὑμᾶς ἐν πνεύματι ἁγίῳ.
>
> I baptized you in water, but he will baptize you in the Holy Spirit.

---

12. See also Isa 29:13; 59:21; 66:2; Jer 24:7.

The Baptist's words are our primary source for the phrase "baptism in the Holy Spirit." The expression itself is evocative. On the one hand, if we employ the general sense of βαπτίζω as "dip, immerse," we may infer an image of total immersion in the Holy Spirit; we are immersed in God's disposition. However, John contrasts this experience with the baptism he performed, which was a cleansing act, a necessary first step for Israel that prepared her to complete her task of preparing the way of the Lord. Baptism in the Holy Spirit, as performed by Jesus, may thus be seen as a necessary first step that is also cleansing and transformative in nature. It performs the necessary first work that prepares one for entrance into and participation in God's kingdom, with its corresponding work. The function of the Holy Spirit is to give God's people a holy spirit, that is, a holy disposition or attitude, a *prevailing tendency* of holiness, which is the defining characteristic of God's kingdom.[13] Without this dispositional change, there is no kingdom.

If indeed the Ezekiel prophecies, particularly the one found in ch. 36, stand behind the New Testament writer's interpretation of John the Baptist's words, we may find further reinforcement in the words of Ezek 36:25: "I will sprinkle clean water upon you, and you shall be clean from all your uncleanness." Of crucial importance is the nature of these cleansing works. John's baptism was one of ritual bathing, a symbolic act of cleansing, performed on the outer body. By contrast, the baptism performed by Jesus, baptism in the Holy Spirit, is more than cleansing; it is transformative. The human heart is not only cleansed, but is also transformed into a new heart, as Ezekiel proclaimed. God's people are no longer characterized by adherence to a codified system of behavior. This is where Spirit baptism may be understood in conversation with heart circumcision. As noted above, God instructed Israel to "circumcise the foreskin of your heart." Paul echoes this in Rom 2:28-29:

> For a person is not a Jew who is one outwardly, nor is true circumcision something external and physical. Rather, a person is a Jew who is one inwardly, and real circumcision is a matter of the heart—it is spiritual and not literal (NRSV).

While physical circumcision makes the body different, spiritual circumcision makes the heart different. Baptism in the Holy Spirit is a transformative work that "circumcises" the heart. The hearts of God's people

---

13. Thank you to one of my students, Aaron Woods, for this particular definition.

are different from the hearts of the world. The result is love for God, manifest in obedience and fidelity, and love for one's neighbor, manifest in generosity and justice.

The promise of the Holy Spirit is certainly good news not only for Israel, but also for the world. Genesis 6:5 and 11 record God's assessment of humanity: "The Lord saw that the wickedness of humankind was great in the earth, and the every inclination of the thoughts of their hearts was only evil continually . . . Now the earth was corrupt in God's sight, and the earth was filled with violence" (NRSV). The same assessment is reflected in the New Testament writers (Rom 1:18–32; Jas 4:4–5; 1 Pet 4:3–4). Thus, God's ongoing plan has been to create a people for himself, a kingdom characterized by holiness of spirit, that is, circumcision of the heart. The New Testament writers testify that the work of the Holy Spirit is a necessary first step of preparation for entrance into and participation in the kingdom. Jesus himself is baptized and filled with the Spirit before beginning his ministry. In Acts 1, the disciples are instructed to wait in Jerusalem until they receive the promise of the Holy Spirit. Paul states in Eph 1:14 that the Spirit is the "first installment" of the kingdom.[14] Apart from the work of the Spirit, there is no kingdom, no people who are characterized by God's disposition. If, as Thiselton concludes, "*the anointing and equipping of Jesus by the Holy Spirit* is a vital and indisputable starting point" for Jesus' own ministry, how much more so is this necessary for all people?[15] This outpouring of the Spirit is often interpreted, rightly, as a matter of purification and empowerment. I would like to add to this interpretation its necessity for transforming, that is, for circumcising, the human heart, which is the necessary prerequisite for purity and power.

CONCLUSION

In conclusion, I wish to draw attention to several important points. First, it is not my intention to challenge traditional views on the Trinitarian nature of God. It is my hope that I have adequately illustrated that there are numerous instances where the Holy Spirit is presented as a personal agent. It should be noted that these situations are marked by regularly

---

14. See Dunn, "Spirit and Kingdom," 133–41. Dunn goes so far as to see Jesus' reception of the Spirit as the beginning or the initiation of the messianic age (*Baptism in the Holy Spirit*, 24–25).

15. Thiselton, *The Holy Spirit*, 46–47. Italics his.

occurring features. First, πνεῦμα is typically articular in these instances. Based on my theory of the article's function, this is what we should generally expect. Second, in each instance where πνεῦμα is so employed, it is an agent who engages in speaking, directing, or otherwise acting in a personal manner. After Jesus ascended into heaven, he sent the paraclete, the Holy Spirit, to carry on his work as his personal representative who would guide, direct, purify, and empower the church as it carries out its commission to bear witness to God's kingdom.

Second, I do indeed wish to begin a dialogue concerning the nonarticular use of πνεῦμα in the New Testament. The use of the article was not a matter of personal idiom or style. It was not an optional part of speech. Instead, speakers and writers employed it deliberately as a part of speech that entered into a meaningful relationship with its head term in such a way that the sense of the head term was altered. The implication of this must be taken seriously. Specifically, we must accept that, when πνεῦμα is presented without the article, the writer or speaker means something different than when the article is present. Thus, πνεῦμα ἅγιον means something different than τὸ πνεῦμα τὸ ἅγιον or τὸ ἅγιον πνεῦμα. In most, if not all, instances, πνεῦμα ἅγιον may be understood in terms of a "holy disposition," and contextually, this understanding is consistent with the writer's overarching point or argument.

Third, "the Holy Spirit" and "holy disposition" should not be viewed as mutually exclusive. Implicit in the presence of a holy disposition is the presence and influence of the Holy Spirit, who acts as the agent by which the heart is circumcised and transformed into a holy disposition that is manifested in the life of the believer. There is no holy disposition without the Holy Spirit. For the New Testament writers, the presence of one presumes the presence of the other.

Fourth, the implications of this interpretation are not merely a matter of translation or pneumatology; there is an equally important application for the life of the church and the individual believer. God's desire is for a people who share his heart and his values and priorities, that is, his disposition. This desire lies behind the prophecies of Ezek 11 and 36. God has poured out his Spirit so that his people will be characterized by a disposition, a prevailing tendency, of holiness. Rather than circumcised bodies, we have circumcised hearts. It is our heart condition, our disposition that differentiates us from the world. In our natural state, being influenced only by the flesh, we do not have this disposition. At the resurrection, this will be our natural disposition (1 Cor 15:42–49). In the meantime, we have the Spirit as a first installment, a guarantee of what is to come (Rom 8:23; 2 Cor 5:5). The Spirit provides us with that which we do not have by nature and that which we look forward to someday having by nature: a holy spirit. In a bad-news world that is corrupt in God's sight and filled with violence, where the wickedness of humankind is great, where every inclination of their hearts is only evil continually, this is indeed good news.

BIBLIOGRAPHY

Dunn, James D. G. *Baptism in the Holy Spirit*. SBT 15. London: SCM, 1970.

―――. "Spirit and Kingdom." In *Pneumatology*, vol. 2 of *The Christ and the Spirit*, 133–41. Grand Rapids: Eerdmans, 1998.

Fee, Gordon. *God's Empowering Presence: The Holy Spirit in the Letters of Paul*. Peabody, MA: Hendrickson, 1994.

Keener, Craig S. *The Spirit in the Gospels and Acts: Divine Purity and Power*. Peabody, MA: Hendrickson, 1997.

Levinsohn, Stephen H. "Anarthrous References to the Holy Spirit: Another Factor." *BT* 44 (1993) 138–44.

Peters, Ronald D. *The Greek Article: A Functional Grammar of ὁ-Items in the Greek New Testament with Special Emphasis on the Greek Article*. LBS 9. Leiden: Brill, 2014.

Swartz, Steve. "The Holy Spirit: Person and Power. The Greek Article and *PNEUMA*." *BT* 44 (1993) 124–38.

Thiselton, Anthony C. *The Holy Spirit—In Biblical Teaching, Through the Centuries, and Today*. Grand Rapids: Eerdmans, 2013.

Tibbs, Clint. "The Holy Spirit and a Holy Spirit: Some Observations and a Proposal." *BT* 61 (2010) 152–63.

―――. "ΠΝΕΥΜΑ as 'Spirit World' in Translation of the New Testament." *BT* 62 (2011) 172–84.

13

The Gospel as Good News to the Poor

God as the King of Justice and Reconciliation

Beth M. Stovell

This chapter began with two simple questions: How is the gospel good news for the poor? What is the relationship between God's kingdom and God's care for the poor? These questions arose in part as a response to a quotation I found while doing research for another article on hermeneutics. The quotation resounded in my head: "Justice *is* the Kingdom of God . . . There is a new economy, a new system of justice that begins when we breathe the air of a new environment: the Kingdom of God . . . To paraphrase Ron Sider, we are not social activists, we are followers of Jesus."[1] These words were written by Kathy Maskell, the U.S. Advocacy Director for Love 146, a non-profit organization dedicated to the abolition of child sex slavery and exploitation, member of the board for Vineyard USA, and director of the Vineyard Justice Network.

This quotation has resonated with me for several reasons. In 2014, as part of my work for Ambrose University, I began working with their Canadian Poverty Institute.[2] At the same time that I was researching the causes and impact of poverty in Canada, I was teaching an Old Testament theology course where I spent an extensive amount of time talking about the depiction of God as Creator, Redeemer, and King in

---

1. Maskell, "What is the Aroma of Justice?"
2. While I began my work with the emerging Canadian Poverty Institute in 2014, I became an official Associate of the CPI in 2015.

the Old Testament. My own past research has been on the metaphor of Jesus as king in the New Testament. This intersection of poverty research and biblical research became the initial steps to thinking carefully about what it means to describe the gospel as good news to the poor in light of God's kingship.

Recent research on evangelicalism has demonstrated how some evangelicals have struggled to align themselves against some of the reigning social-gospel traditions.[3] In contrast, other evangelicals have located themselves within the broader history of evangelicalism, focusing on advocacy and care for the poor.[4] At times, this tension among evangelicals has caused some to ask the question "Is the gospel good news for the poor?" or, alternatively, "in what way is the gospel good news for the poor?"

This chapter will provide an initial exploration into a biblical theology that explains how the conceptions of God as King in the Old Testament and of the kingdom of God in the New Testament can provide a framework for understanding the gospel as good news to the poor. This chapter will suggest that the gospel message threaded throughout the Old and New Testaments addresses three kinds of poverty: spiritual poverty, economic poverty, and relational poverty. I will contend that the solution to all three kinds of poverty is found in the depiction of God as King.

Using Conceptual Metaphor Theory, this chapter will extend my previous research in the metaphor of kingship and will explore the implications of these notions of kingship and the kingdom of God in relation to the redemptive actions of restoring God's people to him, removing injustice, and reconciling God's people to one another.[5] The

---

3. Suttle points to this issue in his book *An Evangelical Social Gospel?* To see further explication of the history of the social gospel in relation to evangelicalism, see Tseng and Furness, "Reawakening of the Evangelical Social Consciousness," 114–25.

4. This chapter arises out of what some have called an increased "Evangelical Social Consciousness." Recently, many evangelicals have harkened back to their roots and returned to an emphasis on advocacy for the poor as part of their definition of being "evangelical." See, for example, Gasaway, *Progressive Evangelicals and the Pursuit of Social Justice*; Gushee, ed., *New Evangelical Manifesto*; and organizations such as New Evangelical Partnership for the Common Good (http://www.newevangelicalpartnership.org) and Evangelicals for Social Action (http://www.evangelicalsforsocialaction.org).

5. This chapter will not engage directly with social-gospel theories such as those famously put forward by Walter Rauschenbusch, but will instead focus on how a bibli-

chapter will conclude with suggestions for ways that a biblical theology of kingship as the remedy for poverty impacts practical actions in the modern world.

RECENT TRENDS AND NEW THEORIES

This chapter builds on my past work on mapping metaphors using the conceptual metaphor theories of Gilles Fauconnier and Mark Turner.[6] Conceptual blending theories provide a helpful means to explore conceptions of poverty and kingship and their mutual blending in particular biblical passages with greater depth and clarity. In order to establish the grounding for these conceptions, we will look at both modern and ancient conceptions of poverty in this initial section.

Conceptions of Poverty: Modern and Ancient

Many people think of poverty as primarily an economic issue. This is often reinforced by the way policy makers in North America focus on economic situations as the means of establishing the boundaries of who is considered impoverished.[7] Recent research on poverty has shown that poverty is more than an economic situation and includes relational and spiritual aspects as well. This is true in terms of both causes of poverty and the impact of poverty.[8] The Oxford Poverty & Human

---

cal theology of kingship and kingdom in light of recent research on inaugurated eschatology and on notions of poverty in the Old Testament and the New Testament can provide grounding for new reflection. However, it is worth noting that the explanation of the "kingdom of God" present in this chapter will follow the trajectories of biblical studies with scholars such as George Eldon Ladd and N. T. Wright rather than Rauschenbusch's definitions of the kingdom of God. Key to this difference in understanding the kingdom of God is the eschatological content of the kingdom of God. For further discussion of Rauschenbusch's approach, see Nelson, "Walter Rauschenbusch and the Social Gospel," 442–56. Wright provides an explication of his approach to the kingdom of God in *Jesus and the Victory of God*.

6. For further discussion of my approach to metaphor, see Stovell, *Mapping Metaphorical Discourse*, 29–70. I have used this approach extensively in many of my other works. See Stovell, "'I Will Make Her Like a Desert,'" 37–61; Stovell, "Yahweh as Shepherd-King in Ezekiel 34," 200–30.

7. Martin Greeley points out the problem of using income as an indicator of wellbeing, noting that policy makers should be looking at the broader factors of development and wellbeing than simply economic ones. See Greeley, "Measurement of Poverty."

8. For example, with regard to child poverty, in 1989, the United Nations General

Development Initiative (OPHI) has been working on a multidimensional definition of poverty that includes dimensions often overlooked by previous approaches, including quality of work, empowerment, physical safety, social connectedness, and psychological wellbeing.[9]

Some theologians and missiologists have long pointed to a need for a holistic understanding of poverty. In 1995, Donald Brandt, the Senior Researcher for World Vision International, suggested the need for a holistic understanding of poverty that included both physical and spiritual aspects.[10] David Williams explores how a more integrated approach to both the understanding of poverty and its remedy could help change the situation in southern Africa specifically, but also impact poverty globally.[11]

Within Christian churches, the gospel message is sometimes not seen as something linked to questions of poverty. Yet if one looks closely at the biblical account, one finds that dealing with the multidimensional aspects of poverty is an important part of the gospel message. In fact, the message of God as the great King in the Old Testament and Jesus as King of all kings in the New Testament implicitly (and explicitly) includes a message of good news proclaimed to the poor and marginalized.

Ancient Poverty and the Conception of Kingship

One need not look to modern poverty research to find holistic discussions of poverty. In fact, ancient conceptions of poverty included this triad of relational, spiritual, and economic poverty and related this to the role of the king and the gods. The development of descriptions addressing poverty, including law codes in ancient Mesopotamia as well as Egyptian and Canaanite writings, demonstrates not only the links between the roles of kings and social justice for the impoverished, but also the links between divine and human rule in these areas. To understand

---

Assembly ratified the *Convention on the Rights of the Child*, which includes a commitment to the "physical, mental, spiritual, moral and social development" of children (Section 27). Paul Spicker has identified as many as twelve different definitions of poverty in recent research, which he classifies under the three categories of "Material Conditions, Economic Circumstances, and Social Positions." See Spicker, "Definitions of Poverty," 150–62.

9. Oxford Poverty & Human Development Initiative, "Research."
10. Brandt, "The Poor and the Lost," 259–66.
11. Williams, "Poverty," 45–57.

the conceptual frameworks present in the Old Testament, it is helpful to explore these ancient Near Eastern texts.

Lohfink points to the reflection of the kings' responsibility to the poor in Egyptian and Canaanite writings. Egyptian tomb inscriptions describe how "I gave bread to the hungry, water to the thirsty, clothing to the naked, and a passage to those who had no ship."[12] Similarly, a Caananite king's main duty was to go to the city gates, and there "he helped the widow to obtain her rights, and spoke just judgment for the orphan."[13]

One early Mesopotamian text, describing the Lagashite ruler Urukagina, who lived before 2300 BCE, records that he "restored justice and freedom to the longsuffering citizens, did away with ubiquitous and oppressive officials, put a stop to injustice and exploitation, protected the widow and the orphan."[14] The Code of Ur-Nammu (Ur-Nammu was the first king of the Ur dynasty) speaks not only of establishing standard measures and re-enacting rituals to restore social order, but also of "reestablishing justice and protection for the weak": "The orphan was not handed over to the rich man, the widow was not handed over to the mighty man. I banished there evil, violence, and any cause for complaint. I established justice in the land."[15]

While the above quotations demonstrate a level of relational poverty by pointing to social imbalance between the rich and mighty and the poor and vulnerable, other aspects of the laws point to fixing economic imbalances as well as regulating prices and remitting debts and unpaid taxes.[16] The Code of Ur-Nammu describes the relationship between the gods and the king in terms of the gods' will over these matters. Justice ultimately is traced back to the gods' will and the king functions as administrator of the gods' will, specifically, for Ur-Nammu, the god Nanna, who, together with other deities, inspired the king's promulgation "in

---

12. See *The Book of the Dead*, 125, cited in Lohfink "Poverty in the Laws," 34.

13. Ugarit: *CTA* 17:V: 7–8. Herdner, *Corpus des tablettes en cunéiformes*, 82, cited in Lohfink, "Poverty in the Laws," 35.

14. Kramer, "Sumerian Theology and Ethics," 56. Kramer is citing his previous work, translating these documents and commenting on them. See Kramer, "Sumerian Historiography," 227.

15. RIME 3/2: 49; Yildiz, "A Tablet of Codex Ur-Nammu from Sipper," 95; Roth, *Law Collections from Mesopotamia and Asia Minor*, 15–21.

16. Darling, *History of Social Justice and Political Power*, 20–21.

accordance with his [i.e., Nanna's] principles of justice and equity."[17] In the hymn honoring his kingship, Shulgi, the son of Ur-Nammu, echoes this notion of the gods as the ones who empower the king to maintain justice. "Utu, the god of justice, imbued [the king] with a deep regard for law and order."[18] Further, Shulgi is described as "the faithful shepherd," and the goddess Inanna decrees Shulgi's "shepherdship of the lands."[19]

Similar notions of divine and human rule over situations of poverty can be seen in the codes of Lipit-Ishtar (1934–1924 BCE). Notably, according to these codes, Lipit-Ishtar is called "wise shepherd" by the gods and is given rulership over the lands "in order to establish justice in the land."[20] This justice includes "banishing complaints" and the protection of the weak. Several gods and goddesses among the Sumerian and Akkadian pantheon were known for their care for justice and concern for the most vulnerable in society. This concern informed the gods' and goddesses' will to see matters well taken care of by their rulers. For example, Sumerian goddess Nanshe is described as one

> Who knows the orphan, who knows the widow,
> Knows the oppression of man over man, is the orphan's mother,
> Nanshe, who cares for the widow,
> Who seeks out (?) justice (?) for the poorest (?).
> The queen brings the refugee to her lap,
> Finds shelter for the weak . . .[21]

Besides a concern for the oppressed and marginalized, Nanshe seeks to establish a new rule that changes these imbalances:

> To comfort the orphan, to make disappear the widow,
> To set up a place of destruction for the mighty,
> To turn (?) over (?) the mighty to the weak . . .
> Nanshe searches the heart of the people.[22]

These descriptions suggest a more complex view of poverty than is sometimes described in theological dictionaries when one looks up the

17. Finkelstein, "The Laws of Ur-nammu," 67, lines 41–42.
18. Kramer, "Shulgi of Ur," 376.
19. Ibid., 379.
20. ANET, 159; also Sollberger and Kupper, *Inscriptions royales sumériennes et akkadiennes*, 175–77. Lipit-Ishtar's titles: RIME 4: 48, 49, 54, 56, 60.
21. Kramer, "Sumerian Theology and Ethics," 57–58.
22. Ibid.

word "poverty." This description of poverty points to specific figures of poverty—the orphan, the widow, the poor, and the refugee—and describes their social and relational situation of oppression ("man over man") and their economic situation ("finds shelter for the weak"). The goddess seeks to fix these situations by re-establishing a spiritual connection that has been lost. Thus, Nanshe "cares" and "knows" the orphans and widows, puts refugees on her lap (a sign of intimacy), and "searches the heart of the people," suggesting an internal component to this justice alongside the external corrections both legal and relational.

The Code of Hammurabi similarly describes the divine will as the reason for the king maintaining justice. The prologue of the Code of Hammurabi states that the gods made Hammurabi king "to make good the flesh of the people . . . to cause justice to prevail in the land, to destroy the wicked and the evil, that the strong might not oppress the weak, to rise like the sun over the black-headed (people), and to light up the land."[23]

Hammurabi also describes the purpose of the Code itself; it is a means to aid the oppressed.

> In order that *the strong might not oppress the weak, that justice might be dealt the orphan (and) the widow,* in Babylon, the city whose head Anu and Enlil raised aloft, in Esagila, the temple whose foundations stand firm like heaven and earth, I wrote my precious words on my stela, and in the presence of the statue of me, the king of justice, I set (it) up in order to administer the law of the land, to prescribe the ordinances of the land, to give *justice to the oppressed.*[24]

Thus, Hammurabi fashions himself as a "king of justice," whose chief concern with the laws is to "give justice to the oppressed." However, Lohfink has helpfully pointed out that, while these ancient Near Eastern kings described themselves as (and even prided themselves on being) defenders of the weak, the actual laws did little to address societal issues of poverty. As Lohfink explains,

> The prologues and the epilogues outline a world in which everything aims at caring for the poor. But the laws proper do not even mention the poor. The laws simply pass over poverty in silence— and that in spite of the fact that by their prologues and epilogues,

---

23. ANET, 164, cited in Lohfink, "Poverty in the Laws," 36.
24. ANET, 178, cited in Lohfink, "Poverty in the Laws," 36. Italics in original.

at least in the case of Hammurabi, these very laws are proclaimed as a reason why the oppressed can set their minds at ease.[25]

Yet what these depictions provide us with is a window into the conception of how kings *should* relate to those experiencing poverty and into the conception of the facets of poverty itself. As we will see in our study of the Old and New Testaments, these ancient Near Eastern backgrounds to understandings of poverty show striking similarities to the biblical account on the issue of poverty, the king's role in justice, and the divine concern for it. Our study will examine how these notions of kings as shepherds and kings in relation to divinity and the multivalent picture of poverty provide insight into how the gospel is good news for the poor.

POVERTY AND KINGSHIP IN THE OLD TESTAMENT

This section will explore the conception of poverty in the Old Testament as it relates to the theme of kingship. By examining the interrelationship between poverty and God's kingship in the Pentateuch, Psalms, and prophetic literature, this section will establish the groundwork for how divine kingship was seen as intricately linked to the areas of spiritual, societal, and relational poverty.

Poverty and Kingship in the Pentateuch

While the Pentateuch comes chronologically before the development of the monarchy in terms of its story, scholars have long discussed the impact of the monarchy on the redaction of the Pentateuch. However, it is perhaps more important to know that conceptions of the kingship of God predate the monarchy and its perceptions of human kingship. The Pentateuch provides the foundations for understanding conceptions of God's kingship and its impact on notions of poverty. The Pentateuch also provides a foundation for how the Israelite society was encouraged to view poverty in its different dimensions. This section will explore how the picture of God as King developed in Genesis provides the framework for understanding poverty and its solutions. It will then explore how the poverty laws in Leviticus and Deuteronomy demonstrate early ways the Hebrew people tried to ameliorate the effects of poverty in their midst.

25. Ibid., 37.

Crucial Topics

Genesis: God as Creator King and the Impact of the Fall on Poverty[26]

The metaphor of God as King is conceived through understandings of how kings related to their people in the ancient Near Eastern context and in the story of Creation. The conception of the king's responsibility for justice and provision for the poor was built into the depictions of kingship in the ancient Near Eastern law codes. By extension, if God were the great Creator King, he would be deemed responsible for the entirety of human existence, including those experiencing various kinds of poverty. Thus, the entailments of God's kingship often overlap with these notions of justice and provision for the poor in depictions of God as King.

Many biblical theologians have explored the theme of God as Creator as one of the central tenets of the story of Genesis and subsequent Old Testament theology. However, it is only sometimes noted that conceptions of God as Creator are frequently blended with conceptions of God as King. Examples of this blending are found throughout the book of Genesis and in other creation accounts in the Psalter. Bernard Batto has explored in some detail the emphasis on the kingship of God as part of the image of God displayed in the priestly creation accounts.[27] Batto argues that Gen 1-2 provides us with echoes of the *Chaoskampf* tradition, pointing to God's sovereignty and kingship in the action of creation. Creation psalms in the Psalter also emphasize the connection between God's kingship and the action of creation. For example, Ps 8 emphasizes the glory and majesty of God (vv. 1-2, 9), two characteristics associated with God's kingship in the action of creation, and points to God "crowning" human beings "with honor and glory" derived from his honor and glory and his crown (v. 5). Similarly, in creation, God makes humans "rule" over the works of his hands, suggesting a passing down of authority that links back to conceptions of God's rule (v. 6).[28]

---

26. Besides the areas explored below, the kingship of God is also key to another major theme of Old Testament theology explicit in Genesis in the act of covenant making with Abraham. Historically, scholars have noted that, while covenants could be made by persons of varying status, the covenants found in Genesis most closely resemble covenants between kings. For further exploration of this, see Carroll R., "Wealth and Poverty," 882-87.

27. Batto, "The Divine Sovereign," 143-86.

28. Batto explores Ps 8 in more detail as it relates to the broader traditions of the priestly creation account. See Batto, "The Divine Sovereign," 143-86.

Goldingay also points to conceptual links between God's kingship and creation in psalms such as Ps 93. Yahweh is established as king in the act of creation, and proof of this kingship is demonstrated in God's actions in the exodus event.[29]

The value of understanding the conceptual links between Creator and King comes when we explore the concept of poverty. The notion of poverty by its very nature emphasizes the lack of something. In order to understand how this sense of lacking should be conceived, it is valuable first to establish what the original expectations of wholeness were intended to be. Genesis provides a helpful picture of this by establishing the relation of humanity to God in the *imago Dei*, the need for human beings to be in relationship with others (as demonstrated by God's judgment that Adam being alone was not good), and the dependence of human beings on the earth for provision alongside their dependence on God. What we commonly refer to as the "fall"[30] demonstrates the breaking of several links forged in the creation event that need reconstituting in the remainder of the story of Scripture. Several biblical theologians have noted the breakdown of three core relationships depicted in the fall: (1) the relationship of human beings to God, (2) the relationship of human beings to one another, and (3) the relationship of human beings to the earth. Christopher Wright explores these three aspects in terms of the theological angle (relationship to God), the social angle (relationship to human beings/Israel), and the economic angle (relationship to the land).[31] Poverty impacts all three angles of this triangle discussed by Wright, impacting spiritual relationships both for the oppressed and for the oppressors, social relationships of person to person, and economic relationships of person to the land.

Exodus: God as Exodus King and Poverty

The exodus event is demonstrative of both God's power and authority as the great King and his concern for the cries of his people in distress. The exodus, uniting, as it does, these two themes, shows how a theology

---

29. Goldingay, *Psalms*, 63–72.

30. Despite Goldingay's compelling arguments for the struggles in using the term "fall," I use the term here as a shared shorthand for the event in Genesis rather than assuming all of the soteriological implications at times implicit with such a use. See Goldingay, *Psalms*, 144–48.

31. See Wright, *Old Testament Ethics for the People of God*, 17–20.

of God's kingship is related to the good news of the gospel. The exodus event becomes a linchpin to the story of the Israelites that is told and retold throughout their history. God's concern for the people in the exodus is often linked to his role as king and to his concern for those in need. The Song of the Sea in Exod 15 emphasizes the *Chaoskampf* tradition in a manner similar to Gen 1-2, but links this to the protection of Israel from its enemy who threatened to overtake and impoverish them. Elsewhere I have explored how the blending of God as Warrior and God as King in Exod 15 provides the groundwork for later allusions such as the divine Warrior and Shepherd imagery of Isa 40:10-11. As noted above, the King as Shepherd is one of the common associations between ancient Near Eastern kings and their care for the needy. As a faithful shepherd, the human king does the work of the divine will in caring for the poor and needy. For Isa 40, the depiction of God as Warrior King becomes essential for God's treatment of the poor and needy. The exodus God continues to provide freedom for his people.[32]

In the case of the exodus event itself, the people of Israel were among the poor and marginalized in Egypt. This provides a foundation for the centrality of the exodus event in the Covenant Code in Exod 22-23 and in Levitical and Deuteronomic laws. The concern for the poor in Exod 23 is conditioned by Israel's experience earlier in the exodus story. Similarly, several times Leviticus and Deuteronomy point to the experience of the exodus as the reason why the Israelites should treat the marginalized with love and care. As Lohfink explains,

> [In the Covenant Code,] the framing and repeated prohibition not to oppress the stranger uses the word *lähas* which is not traditional in law or wisdom admonition, but is used for the oppression of the Israelities in Egypt in Exod 3:9 and in the historical Creed in Deut 26:7. Furthermore, the same motivation is added to both prohibitions: "for you were strangers in the land of Egypt . . ."[33]

Israel as a whole experienced what it was like to be slaves, sojourners, and poor. But God released them; thus, they should treat the people in their midst who are slaves, sojourners, and poor with special attention. Those studying poverty have noted that one key element of poverty awareness, prevention, and elimination is not simply alerting people to

32. See Stovell, "Divine Warrior and Shepherd."
33. Lohfink, "Poverty in the Laws," 42.

the situations of poverty in the world, but finding ways to help non-impoverished people see that those who are impoverished are not a distant "other" but are like the non-impoverished.[34] This is the rhetorical effect that God's reminder about the exodus experience is intended to have on the Israelites: The poor and marginalized are not "them." They are not some distant "other" whom the Israelites can neglect. The poor and marginalized are "us" because the Israelites were once like them. This notion of "us" is embedded not in an abstract ethical statute, but in the historical experience and narrative retelling of Israel's own identity story.[35]

Leviticus: Statutes for the Poor and Our Exodus God

The poverty laws described in Leviticus and Deuteronomy provide further exploration of the relationship between kingship and poverty. Leviticus 19 and 25–26 provide a link between the religious institutions, the government, and the poor by way of laws protecting the poor and marginalized in the midst of the Israelites. The grouping of those associated with the poor is telling of their relative situation and conceptualization. Whereas in modern culture we often remove the spiritual-religious aspect from our discussion of the poor, Leviticus embeds the poor in the sacrificial system.

Leviticus 19 provides a series of laws associated with both the Ten Commandments and with dealing justly with the poor and marginalized. The laws in Lev 19:9–10 relate to providing the opportunity for "gleaning," a practice explicitly intended to protect and provide for the poor and foreigner. This law is repeated in Lev 23:22, which suggests a level of redactional emphasis. In Lev 19, laws against stealing, dealing falsely, and lying (vv. 11–12) are placed sequentially prior to statements against oppressive behavior and stipulations about treatment of the deaf and the blind (vv. 13–14). Immediately following is a discussion of the need for justice in the courts, with righteousness being upheld over against partiality (vv. 15–16). This demonstrates the ancient Near Eastern link between justice and righteousness that also helps to fill out

---

34. Paul Cloke explores "self-other" relationships as part of the reason for rural poverty in "Rurality and Otherness," 447–56, esp. 448–49.

35. Lohfink suggests a similar point, but his emphasis is more on history than on identity-forming narrative or the self-other relationship of this assertion. See Lohfink, "Poverty in the Laws," 41–42.

our broader definition of poverty as relational, spiritual, and economic. The relational aspect of these laws is shown in the next verses, as vv. 17–18 speak of not hating and instead loving neighbors and not holding grudges. This love and righteousness involves keeping the Lord's statutes. Unsurprisingly, what follows in Leviticus is a series of statutes.

Leviticus 19:33–34 returns to the theme of the poor and marginalized by speaking of how the stranger/sojourner should be treated. Notably, the exodus experience provides the groundwork for Israel's kind treatment of the sojourner. Because Israel experienced being a foreigner in Egypt, Israel should treat foreigners in their midst with kindness. This is a means of identification that draws Israel into a union of experience with the "other" in their midst, such that the "other" is no longer seen as "other," but as like Israel. Leviticus 19:35–37 continues this theme by pointing to the reality of God as an exodus God as the reason for just measures and scales.

Leviticus 25, in speaking of the Year of Jubilee, returns to the theme of the treatment of the poor and marginalized. It is valuable to note that the conceptual basis for much of the Year of Jubilee is the fact that the Israelites themselves are not owners of their land: "The land shall not be sold in perpetuity, for the land is mine. For you are strangers and sojourners with me" (Lev 25:23). Since the Israelites are themselves strangers and sojourners, they have no right to mistreat the strangers and sojourners among them. The treatment of the poor brother in Israel's midst (vv. 25–28, 35–37) is also linked to the exodus event (v. 38). The theme of Israel's slavery in Egypt conceptually grounds vv. 39–43. In these verses, the poor among the Israelites are barred from being put into slavery by other Israelites. The reason for this barring is that God redeemed all of the Israelites from their enslavement and does not want to see them enslaved again by their own people. The Year of Jubilee and its release of slaves ultimately point to the Israelites as no longer being slaves to Egypt but instead being servants to Yahweh who belong to him (Lev 25:55). Leviticus 26 lays out the rewards for obedience and the penalties and curses for disobedience to these laws. This section provides a helpful grounding for understanding the prophets' response to the experience of Assyrian and Babylonian rule. The people in the prophet's time were being cursed for not following the law as Leviticus describes.

This exploration demonstrates that Leviticus locates Israel's relationship with the poor and marginalized in the larger story of Israel's exodus experience. The poor and marginalized groups, such as foreigners, are linked to Israel's own story as a way of reminding Israel to care for them justly. Such poverty laws impact the land, the religious systems, and the court systems alongside relational treatment of others. While these passages in Leviticus do not directly link kingship itself with poverty, they do explore the theme of the exodus event, which, as we have already noted above, is linked to God's kingship in several distinct ways. It is to this exodus God-King that Israel belongs as servants (Lev 25:55), and their actions toward those in poverty extend from this awareness.

Deuteronomy: A Receptive Heart and Open Hands

In exploring Deuteronomy, themes similar to those in Leviticus arise, such as the contextualization of Israel's laws in relation to their experience of the exodus event, while the role of the king becomes more of a focus. Deuteronomy 4 relates submission to the statutes of God to the exodus event as well, but rather than focusing on the release from slavery, the emphasis is on the experience of God's presence in the wilderness and the giving of the law to Moses. Alongside these focuses, there is a strong emphasis on the power of God—"with a mighty hand and an outstretched arm." Like Lev 26, Deut 4:25–31 points to the promise of the covenant alongside its curses and the potential for the loss of the land if the covenant is forgotten.

Deuteronomy 10:17–19 combines the ultimate kingship of God with the treatment of the poor and marginalized:

> For the LORD your God is God of gods and Lord of lords, the great, the mighty, and the awesome God, who is not partial and takes no bribe. He executes justice for the fatherless and the widow, and loves the sojourner, giving him food and clothing. Love the sojourner, therefore, for you were sojourners in the land of Egypt.

Verse 17 demonstrates that it is God's role as almighty God and all-powerful king that provides the groundwork for the treatment of the poor and marginalized. The characteristics described in vv. 17–19 give insight into conceptions of God's character as king and conceptions of poverty. As with ancient Near Eastern kings, who serve the will of the gods, Israel's great God King is defined by his execution of justice (v. 18). The categories for this justice also echo the ancient Near Eastern descriptions of orphans, widows, and sojourners. God's behavior in relation to these poor and marginalized people is specific: just and equal treatment (v. 17) characterized by justice for the fatherless and widow (v. 18). God shows love to the sojourners via action: giving food and clothing (v. 18). As in Leviticus, the grounding for Israel's response to the sojourners is based on their Egypt experience as sojourners (v. 19).

Deuteronomy 14:28–29 returns to the fatherless, the widow, and sojourners, this time including the Levites in the group, and shows how to provide for them:

> At the end of every three years you shall bring out all the tithe of your produce in the same year and lay it up within your towns. And the Levite, because he has no portion or inheritance with you, and the sojourner, the fatherless, and the widow, who are within your towns, shall come and eat and be filled, that the LORD your God may bless you in all the work of your hands that you do.

This triad of "come," "eat," and "be filled" needs some unpacking. "Come" implies reconnection with the community if distant, demonstrating a relational need. "Eat and be filled" suggests that the food provided would not be minimal, but sufficient to the point of "filling."

Deuteronomy 15:1–3 continues the discussion of the poor by looking at debt (note here the link between debt and poverty). Deuteronomy 15:4–5 makes clear the ultimate point of all this:

> But there will be no poor among you; for the LORD will bless you in the land that the LORD your God is giving you for an inheritance to possess—if only you will strictly obey the voice of the LORD your God, being careful to do all this commandment that I command you today.

Thus, the removal of poverty is based on obeying all of what the Lord commands. As the prophets show us, the Israelites did not succeed in this. No wonder Micah and Amos rail with such fury against Israel's injustice: the great God King gave them means to *end* poverty, and they ruined it! Yet Deut 15:7–11 moves from the ideal world (no-poor world) to the practical world (where the poor are always with us) and again shows that poverty is not simply about finances, but about heart and relationship. It is not simply the case that someone should give to their poor brother; their heart should be turned to this person. This is because poverty impacts relationships, and it can lead to a spiritual situation (e.g., crying out to God about sin in Deut 15:9).

Poverty and Kingship in the Prophets and Psalms

While an extensive explanation of poverty within prophetic literature and the Psalms is beyond the scope of this chapter, we will use two passages as anchor points for how poverty is conceptualized in these corpora: Ezek 34 and Ps 72. These two passages have been chosen in part because they represent aspects found more broadly in their respective corpora and also because they form the basis for portrayals of the kingship of Jesus in the New Testament and are thus helpful for broader movements of biblical theology.

PROPHETS' CALLS, GOD'S KINGSHIP, AND THE NOTION OF POVERTY

Ezekiel's call in Ezek 1, 3, 10, and 33 is articulated as a call to minister to a rebellious people who have hardened themselves. Ezekiel's exploration of theodicy points to this rebellion as the cause of the people's punishment through the siege of Jerusalem, the destruction of the temple, and their exile in Babylon. Ezekiel is placed as a watchman to warn the people of the results of their actions in God's judgment upon them. Throughout Ezekiel, the themes of spiritual reawakening, relationship reconciliation, and dealing with injustice become interwoven. One locus of these interwoven themes is Ezek 34.[36]

In setting out a depiction of the wicked shepherds (likely Israelite kings) in contrast to Yahweh's kingship, Ezek 34 links aspects of socioeconomic poverty with relational poverty: the mistreatment of one another in terms of relational poverty leads to socioeconomic poverty. As Ezek 34 shows, injustice of socioeconomic poverty often has roots in spiritual poverty (in other words, injustice is often linked to spiritual abuses). This is true in the depiction of the leaders' treatment of the people, as they act in injustice against the people on the socioeconomic level, which disrupts their relational ties with one another, and, on the spiritual level, disconnects them from God. Similarly, the treatment of the weak sheep by the powerful sheep shows similar dynamics of relational, spiritual, and socioeconomic devolution. The contrast with Yahweh's kingship is striking. Not only does Yahweh remove injustice and restore justice on

36. I have explored similar themes in Stovell, "Yahweh as Shepherd-King in Ezekiel 34," 200–230; Stovell, *Mapping Metaphorical Discourse*, 122–27.

the socioeconomic level, but he also draws his people back to himself, restoring the spiritual resources the people desperately need, and draws the people back into relationship with one another.

PSALM 72: KING YHWH AND THE DAVIDIC KING AS "KING OF THE DISADVANTAGED"

As with Hammurabi and other ancient Near Eastern kings, in Ezek 34, Yahweh claims that he is the "king of justice" who will restore his will under a Davidic king who will echo his justice. This notion is also found throughout the Psalter in psalms like Ps 72. A unique facet of Ps 72 is its focus on the desire for a king to be like Yahweh in his justice and righteousness.[37] In similar fashion to the way in which links occur in Ps 8 between creation and justice, in Ps 72 the elements of creation become, through the blending of natural metaphors with kingship metaphors, part of the depiction of the justice and righteousness brought by the king.[38] Much in these depictions links the land and economic provision to the king and what he provides, touching upon aspects of the economic angle of poverty. For example, the mountains and hills give provision to the people (v. 3), the king's life endures forever like the sun and moon (v. 5),[39] the king is compared to beneficial waters showering the land (v. 6), and the people themselves are compared to the grassy fields receiving these bountiful provisions (v. 16).[40] These natural metaphors use the language of creation to emphasize the relationship between Yahweh as Creator and the human king and also the link between cosmic and social order.[41] Scholars have noted that this use of all of creation makes the

---

37. Houston points to the unique centrality of social justice in Ps 72 in comparison to the other royal psalms and the implications of this psalm for understanding the depiction of God and social justice. See Houston, "The King's Preferential Option for the Poor," 341–67.

38. I have explored the blending of other forms of metaphors in relationship to kingship metaphors in Stovell, *Mapping Metaphorical Discourse*, 103.

39. Scholars have noted that solar imagery is frequently used to describe the king. See Brown, *Seeing the Psalms*, 238.

40. Talmon has noted that Ps 72:6 and 16 depict the blessings of the king through metaphors from the plant world. However, Talmon argues that the king rather than the people is compared to the grassy growth on the mountains. Talmon, *King, Cult, and Calendar in Ancient Israel*, 111. Many scholars instead see v. 16 to be referring to the people. See Weiser, *The Psalms*, 500–504.

41. Hayes, *Earth Mourns*, 61; Mowinkel, *The Psalms in Israel's Worship*, 1, 164.

claims of Ps 72 for the ideal Davidic king some of the grandest in the Psalter.[42]

Alongside these universal and economic claims, Ps 72 depicts the connection between the great King Yahweh and the human king concerning social/relational and spiritual aspects of poverty. The social and relational aspects are highlighted in the language of justice and judging (v. 2); defending the afflicted, saving the children of the needy, and crushing the oppressor (v. 4); the deliverance of the needy who cry out with no one to help (suggesting a loss of social connection) (v. 12); and rescue from oppression and violence (v. 14). The spiritual contours of justice are also present in the discussions of righteousness and the preciousness of the blood of the weak and needy in the king's sight (v. 14).

Further, our earlier comparisons between the ancient Near Eastern kings who only *claim* justice as their work and do not actually show justice for the poor in their laws remain true in Ps 72. This psalm points to the differences between, on the one hand, Yahweh's kingship and the Davidic king's form of kingship and, on the other hand, the kingship of the neighbouring kings. Elsewhere I have argued for Ps 72's place in the conceptual network of God's kingship, which gives an alternative vision of kingship from those represented in the neighboring ancient Near Eastern cultures.[43] Psalm 72:8–11 points to the kings of the nations (who are potentially the enemies and oppressors depicted as being put down by Yahweh in the previous verses) bowing before the king. While this psalm provides a grand picture of the extent of the Davidic rule, this rule is ultimately derived from the great divine King.[44] The psalm highlights the difference that having Yahweh as the great King makes when his just, righteous, and merciful character is mirrored in his chosen king. Rather than seeking his own wealth and fame, the king is to seek the wellbeing of God's people. Psalm 72's description of the king as full of justice and righteousness, seeking the wellbeing of his people and caring

---

42. Creach describes Ps 72 as "presenting the grandest hopes for the Davidic king." Creach, *The Destiny of the Righteous in the Psalms*, 102.

43. Much of my discussion on Ps 72 here derives from my previous research in Stovell, *Mapping Metaphorical Discourse*, 102–4.

44. Roberts highlights the fact that the human king is participating in the work of the divine king as the "regent of the divine sovereign, participating in what is ultimately divine rule." See Roberts, *The Bible and the Ancient Near East*, 353.

for the poor and needy among them, echoes the conception of Yahweh's kingship, challenging the oppressive visions of kingship of their time.[45]

Moore has described the tradition of Yahweh as "the King of the disadvantaged" as one of the key conceptions in the metaphor "God is King" found throughout the Hebrew Bible;[46] Ps 72 uses the conception of interdependence between Yahweh as King and the human king to describe the human king as the "king of the disadvantaged" as well. As Ellen Davis helpfully expresses it, "the poet of Ps 72 shows what 'the system' could look like: justice flowing from God, through the Israelite king and out into a land prospering under the hand of a people free to work it and committed to its care, generation after generation."[47]

POVERTY AND KINGSHIP IN THE NEW TESTAMENT

This section will examine the kingship and kingdom of God described in the New Testament in terms of its continuity with Old Testament kingship/kingdom and in relation to the conceptions of poverty discussed in the Old Testament section above. Rather than trying to encompass the entire New Testament, this section will focus on the Gospels. The reason for this choice of the Gospels is twofold: first, they provide narrative accounts of Jesus as King in the New Testament, which continue the trajectory of God as king through the Second Temple period and into the New Testament context; and second, as the overall theme of this paper is how the "gospel" is good news for the poor, it would be appropriate to use the genre of "gospel" to discuss the implications of the gospel as good news.[48]

---

45. Roberts notes the link between this vision in Ps 72 and the vision depicted in Isaiah, esp. chs. 9 and 11. In both cases, the great King Yahweh equips the human king for his task, and both texts focus on the judicial function of kingship while providing a vision of an age of justice and salvation. See Roberts, *The Bible and the Ancient Near East*, 350–53.

46. Moore argues that the *Bildfeld* of the metaphor "God is King" "contains three relational spheres: (1) God as the universal/cosmic suzerain, (2) Yahweh as the covenantal sovereign over Israel, and (3) Yahweh as the compassionate and just monarch upon whom the disadvantaged and the oppressed may depend for their needs and for the resolution of their situation." Moore, *Moving Beyond Symbol and Myth*, 270. Moore presents not only Ps 72 but also Pss 5, 22, 68, 102, 103, 145, and 146 as psalms that contain the image of Yahweh as "compassionate monarch of the disadvantaged," including Ps 72. Moore, *Moving Beyond Symbol and Myth*, 268.

47. Davis, "Two Psalms," 23. See also Miller, "Ruler in Zion and the Hope of the Poor," 187–98.

48. Elsewhere in this volume, several scholars have discussed in more detail the

This section will focus on allusions to the Old Testament passages on poverty and will show how they are used in the New Testament and what this says about Jesus' discussion of the kingdom of God and Jesus' kingship.

Markan Jesus, the Kingdom of God, and Poverty: Exploring Mark 9–12

Mark 9–12 provides an interwoven picture of figures associated with poverty and marginalization (chs. 9–10, 12) with the promise of Jesus as King and his overturning of injustice (ch. 11). Aspects of Mark's portrayal of these events echo with elements of the Deuteronomic and Levitical poverty laws as well as with portrayals of God as King in relation to the human king. These passages are drawn together both conceptually and linguistically through lexical cohesion and metaphorical coherence. They emphasize situations of spiritual possession in relation to physical ailments, Jesus' resolution of these problematic situations through the power of his kingdom, and the linkage between these spiritual and physical realities and social marginalization and economic poverty.

Children, the Blind, and Widows in the Kingdom of God in Mark

Mark 9–10 and 11 are linked through the imagery of kingship and kingdom and through discussion of the least being the first in the kingdom of God. Mark 9 begins with the healing of a boy from demon possession and leads into a picture of children being placed on Jesus' lap and described as those who will be part of his kingdom. Jesus models welcome to these "least." In modern society it is hard to think of children being classed among the "least of these," but in ancient society the constructs of the rights of children did not exist, leaving them among the most vulnerable in society. In ancient society, children were conceptually linked to "the poor" due to their lack of social and political status, their lack of financial security, and their vulnerability to oppression from others.

---

intricate relationship between the "gospel" as a message of good news related to Jesus and the "gospel" as a specific genre (including the history of the development of this term and this genre). My chapter is not primarily concerned with these generic questions, but in a sense assumes a relationship between the genre/form of literary type called "gospel" and the content of the Gospels. See Pang's and Porter's contributions to this book for more discussion on this topic.

One type of cohesion in Mark 9–10 is lexical cohesion, which in this case involves accumulating a series of words that are within the semantic range of "child": *paidion*, "child" (9:24, 36–37; 10:13–15); *mikron*, "little one" (9:42); *tekna*, "children" (10:24, 29–30); *huios*, "son" (9:7, 9, 12, 17, 31); and *neotēs*, "youth" (10:20). Mark 9–10 is cohesively framed through the repeated phrase "first will be last" and "the last shall be first/the servant of all" (9:35; 10:31). Repeated reference to the kingdom of God and David's kingship in relation to the "least" and children (9:1, 47; 10:14, 23–25, 47–48; 11:10) also creates cohesive linking between kingship and poverty. These passages further interweave the Son of Man figure, who is associated with kingship in Dan 7, with these larger narratives through Son of Man discourses (9:9, 12, 31; 10:33, 45).

Yet surprisingly, in Mark 9–11, Jesus links the blessings of the kingdom of God to "little ones" like these. The demon-harassed boy in Mark 9 represents the height of poverty in several directions. He has been exiled from the community due to this demonic situation. Jesus' healing restores the boy to his family and his community. The children of Mark 9:33–42 and 10:13–16 are described as being linked to the kingdom. The blind man in Mark 10:48–52 and the widow in Mark 12:41–44 are also each linked to the kingdom.

By contrast, Mark 10–12 also provides a series of figures who are against the kingdom through their practices: (1) those who are sending away the children in Mark 10:13–14, (2) the rich man who ultimately rejects Jesus' call for his wealth in Mark 10:17–31, (3) the people who rebuke the blind in Mark 10:48, and (4) the leaders stealing from the widows in Mark 12:40.[49] These passages echo the poverty laws in the Pentateuch and the consequences of breaking these laws in both the Pentateuch and the prophets. The children, the blind, and widows are the vulnerable, marginalized, and "least" and yet are greatest in Jesus' kingdom.

What can be observed on this lexical and linguistic level can further be explored in terms of the framing of the overall structure of

---

49. Several scholars have noted that the widow giving everything she has is directly linked to the injustice against widows by violating Levitical laws. See Horsley's reading of this passage in light of political indictments against the temple in *Hearing the Whole Story*, 216–17. Compare this to Second Temple Judaism's views on widows and poverty in Mathews, *Riches, Poverty, and the Faithful*, 92–96. For an exploration of this topic in relation to popular culture, see also Kotrosits and Taussig, *Re-Reading the Gospel of Mark*.

Mark's Gospel. The passage on children in Mark 9 is followed, in Mark 10:17–31, by the struggles of the rich man deciding whether or not to follow Jesus. These passages (10:13–16 and the rich-man passage) are linguistically linked via the use of the word "children" in v. 24. Mark 10:17–31 highlights the struggles of the rich in following Jesus.[50]

In the midst of these poverty-linked passages enters Mark 11, in which Jesus as King (vv. 1–11) overturns the tables at the temple (vv. 12–26), echoing the cry of the blind man for the Son of David to show mercy to him. Jesus' authority as king is linked to his authority to replace the practices of the temple, which is exercised in his overturning the situation in the temple courts that is unfavorable to the poor. Jesus is depicted not only as the great King who exhibits power (vv. 27–33), but the king who will show mercy. Elsewhere I have discussed the kingship dimensions of "Son of Man" and "Son of David" in the Old Testament and Second Temple conceptual matrix.[51] The accumulation of these references climaxes in the Jerusalem entry scene of Mark 11, with the explicit reference to Ps 118, the allusion to Zech 9, and the phrase "Blessed is the coming kingdom of our father David!" (Mark 11:10). This reference to the kingdom of David links Mark 11 to Mark 10's Son of David references. While it is unclear among scholars how many allusions are to be read in Mark 11, many would argue that an allusion to Zech 9 echoes in the temple tables being overturned. This is particularly true of the theme of God as the divine Warrior King seeking justice for his people against oppressive forces. Judgment against the fig tree alongside the discourse appears to echo this.

Mark and the Other Gospels

Mark's conceptualization of kingship in relation to poverty and marginalization shows notable links to the other Gospels. For example, "Son of David" language in Mark 10:47–48 is linked to the blind man being given sight as an act of mercy. Notably, John 9–10 also places Jesus' act of mercy to a blind man prior to a discourse regarding his kingship, leading up to the Jerusalem entry and its focus on kingship in ch.12. Elsewhere I have demonstrated the linguistic cohesion between John 9

---

50. For more on this passage and its links to the preceding passage, see Donahue and Harrington, *Gospel of Mark*, 302–9.

51. See Stovell, *Mapping Metaphorical Discourse*, 152–69.

and 10.⁵² As noted here, Mark 9–11 shows many striking elements of similar linguistic cohesion.

Similarly, Matt 20–21 links the healing of the blind with the Jerusalem entrance. In Luke, the widow's justice in 18:1–8 leads to a passage on children in 18:15–17. In all three Synoptics the tale of the rich man is placed after this along with the Son of Man discourse and the healing of the blind man (Matt 19:16–26; 20:29–34; Mark 10:17–27, 46–52; Luke 18:31–34; 18:35–43). Luke includes two stories after this material and before the Jerusalem entry (19:28–40): the story of Zacchaeus (19:1–10) and the parable of the talents (19:11–27). This parable ends with a reference to the unfaithful not wanting the Lord to reign over them (v. 27) and the penalty for not accepting this reign. This theme of reign and kingdom leads naturally into Jesus' triumphal entry into Jerusalem.⁵³

John's Gospel addresses the marginalized in several ways that both echo aspects of the Synoptics and, at times, tell stories unique to John's Gospel. For example, the story of the Samaritan woman in John 4 provides a unique view of the social and religious contexts of marginalization in Jesus' time and Jesus' response of mercy as the Messiah (God's chosen one), who will bring in God's kingdom and true worship. In John 9–10, John links the story of the blind man who receives his sight to the story of Jesus as the Good Shepherd who cares for his sheep.

My past research has demonstrated the pervasive quality of the kingship metaphor within John's Gospel and has connected this notion with the concept of Jesus as a king of justice.⁵⁴ As with Luke 4's appropriation of Isa 61, which demonstrates a consistency in the picture of Jesus' continuity with the Old Testament, John's picture of Jesus as the Good Shepherd in John 10 (which links to ch. 9 and the story of the blind man) points to a link with Ezek 34 that is also telling in terms of the blending of the picture of Jesus' kingship with conceptions of justice for the poor and restoration of relationship with God and one another. The cohesive links between chs. 9 and 10 point to John's desire to join

---

52. See Stovell, *Mapping Metaphorical Discourse*, 221–56.

53. Others have noted similar links between children and the poor in Matthew and Luke and have compared these two groups with Mark's discussion of children and the kingdom. See Gundry, "Children in the Gospel of Mark," 143–76.

54. This discussion is based on the research provided in Stovell, *Mapping Metaphorical Discourse*, 221–56.

the story of injustice against the blind man and Jesus' restoration of his sight to Jesus' role as the Shepherd King who restores justice in Ezek 34. Through the experiences of the blind man at the temple in ch. 9 and the mistreatment of the sheep in ch. 10, the section of John 9–10 highlights further conceptual links between the injustice in relational, economic, and spiritual aspects of marginalization. Yet in both cases Jesus' kingdom becomes the means of wholeness and healing. In John 9, it is Jesus' healing of the blind man that gives him the confidence to face the unjust practices of his local leaders; in John 10, it is Jesus' authority as King (like Yahweh the Shepherd King) that promotes goodness and a re-creation of right order among his sheep as well as a stance against the injustice of the current leaders who have been wicked shepherds of their people.

TOWARDS A BIBLICAL THEOLOGY OF KINGDOM AS GOOD NEWS FOR THE POOR

Exploring the role of God as king in relation to poverty in the Old and New Testaments points us to the idea that, essentially, a biblical theology of kingdom as good news for the poor is missional. Missiologists have grasped this point, often aligning the *missio Dei* with the kingdom of God and a heart and mission for the poor.[55] An approach to poverty that incorporates this biblical theology of the kingdom highlights certain aspects of poverty when set alongside the modern three levels of poverty engagement, which will be introduced below. This approach suggests three outcomes that interweave with the levels of engagement: restoration of God's people to God, removal of injustice, and reconciliation of God's people to one another.

Developing a Biblical Model

A biblical model for engagement with the issues intrinsic in poverty forces us to ask new questions with a set of ancient lenses as a starting point. I begin with a list of some of these questions. If Deuteronomy suggests that God's kingship gives us a place where no one is poor, how can we creatively make poverty guidelines that enact elements of Leviticus and Deuteronomy? What would "gleaning" look like today? How do we deal with debt? How do we provide for the vulnerable such that they "come,"

---

55. See particularly the work of Christopher Wright in *Old Testament Ethics for the People of God*; *Mission of God*; *The Mission of God's People*.

"eat," and are "filled"?[56] How do we treat immigrants (our sojourners) and poverty? How do we make just laws that show equality to the poor?

THREE LEVELS OF POVERTY ENGAGEMENT

Recent approaches to poverty have highlighted three levels of poverty engagement: poverty alleviation, poverty prevention, and poverty eradication.[57] The first level, poverty alleviation, is similar to Christian concepts of charity. These practices seek to alleviate the symptoms that poverty creates. This can include creative responses that lead to restoration, as with the work of Compassion, World Vision, and other charity organizations.

Poverty prevention moves to a new level of action in relation to poverty. It seeks to prevent poverty by addressing the relational, spiritual, and economic needs of persons at risk of poverty before they reach that stage. This can mean addressing not only the symptoms of poverty, but acknowledging the systems that lead to poverty. This means building an awareness of the poor in our midst and those who are struggling on the margins and are approaching poverty. Several organizations currently work toward creating plans to access the best strategies for poverty prevention. For example, the Charis Project in Thailand rejects the usual strategies of creating orphanages to alleviate the *symptoms* of poverty in Thailand and instead aims to prevent the causes that create the need for orphanages. Through this they have been able to restore families to situations where they can keep their children rather than abandon them.[58]

Poverty eradication is the third level of poverty engagement. It seeks to eliminate poverty entirely, not only dealing with symptoms and causes, but undoing the entire system that leads to poverty in the first place. Current poverty eradication plans do not go far enough. To

---

56. Poverty prevention is in action here, because if they have never entered the system, they will not become impoverished.

57. For example, the Canadian Council on Social Development's "Poverty Reduction Policies and Programs" speaks of "current federal, provincial, and territorial approaches to poverty reduction, alleviation and eradication." Similarly, the United Nations has, as part of its sustainable development programs, a program for poverty eradication as the next level in poverty strategies. See "Poverty Eradication." Recent work at the Canadian Poverty Institute housed at Ambrose University has focused on these measures in relation to a definition of child poverty. See Canadian Poverty Institute, "The Influence of Policy on Childhood Poverty in Selected Provinces in Canada."

58. For more information, see http://thecharisproject.org.

eradicate poverty, we need to become warriors, like our Warrior King, against injustice. Jesus models for us resistance against unjust practices, speaking against the mistreatment of the poor. While Jesus did not overturn the Roman government, his treatment of the poor brought restoration and healing and led to social change. Echoing Deut 15, Jesus modeled a responsive heart and open hands, which should be a model for Christians involved in poverty eradication. Jesus' approach was more than simply social and economic, but also relational and spiritual. The gospel needs to be a part of the good news to the poor because the story of Jesus as king is very good news!

So what might this look like in light of our study of a biblical theology of kingdom in relation to poverty in the Scriptures? I will conclude this chapter with three key realms where poverty exists according to the Scriptures and three key responses that convey the good news of the Scriptures to the poor: restoring God's people to God, removing injustice, and reconciling people to one another.

Restoring God's People to God

While the gospel is not only about evangelism, nonetheless, the restoration of God's people to God is one of the essential means by which the spiritual aspects of poverty are remedied. Yet, we should be careful not to locate *all* of the solutions to poverty in restoring people in their relationship with God or assume that economic poverty is the same as spiritual poverty. The poor are neither holier nor more sinful than anyone else. Rather, it is more helpful to say that the experience of poverty has spiritual impact alongside the other impacts of poverty. Jesus' approach to remedying this problem was an integrated approach that connected to a variety of aspects of people's lives. He saved their souls, their physical lives, and their relational and social experiences, and he addressed societal injustice. When we view the "good news" of the gospel as primarily a message for the soul, we see only one part of the holistic vision of how the good news functions for all people, those experiencing poverty included.

Another spiritual aspect to poverty that is often overlooked—yet repeated again and again in Scripture—is that the treatment of the poor by the non-poor has a potential impact on the non-poor's spiritual wellbeing. Far more frequently than discussing the spiritual wellbeing of the poor, Scripture speaks of the spiritual downfall of the rich when they resent, overlook, oppress, or mistreat the poor. A response to poverty based on kingship must be with open hands and hearts, not with begrudgingly tight fists. Deuteronomy 15:9 speaks of any other response as a sin. Thus, responding to poverty must involve pricking people's consciences. As with God's reminder to the Israelites—"you were slaves and sojourners"—we must remind others that the person in poverty is not a distant "other," but is one of us. Abolition in the United Kingdom began by connecting people first to the children at home and then to the slaves. Perhaps a move toward child poverty may help in this way, awakening people's hearts to seeing the impoverished as "us."

Removing Injustice

Just as we should not bypass the soul in our considerations of poverty, in the same way it is not enough only to seek for justice; we must also remove injustice. Removing injustice is one of the key steps in a holistic understanding of the good news of the gospel. Removal of injustice is key for all three levels of poverty engagement: prevention of poverty occurs when unjust practices are removed, allowing those who are on the borders of poverty to be cared for justly.

Alleviation of poverty can also occur more consistently if laws do not inhibit the ability to provide for those in need. Recent research has shown how some large NGOs at times siphon funds in ways that allow very little money to go to those most in need.[59] Similarly, unjust political systems can create massive problems for poverty alleviation. As Ezek 34 points out, this is an issue not only for leaders, but for individuals as well.

All routes to poverty elimination require the removal of injustice. Injustice stands directly at odds with eliminating poverty, and this is often the reason that many point to passages like Deut 14, which Jesus echoes, reminding us that "you will always have the poor among you" (John 12:8; see also Matt 26:11; Mark 14:7) because unjust systems are always at play. As Christians, we may live in the already-but-not-yet tension of working towards more just systems today while having the awareness that such systems can only go part of the way to absolute change.

Reconciling People to One Another

The breakdown of relationships impacts poverty intensely, as shown by our study of the Old and New Testaments. Ezekiel 34 has demonstrated

---

59. Examples include Routley, *Negotiating Corruption*.

that it is not only the leaders' responsibility to build just systems, but the responsibility of the people to care for and not oppress the weak among them. This means that in order to be "good news" and to preach the "good news" to the poor, we must seek not only spiritual or socioeconomic fixes, but also locate ourselves within our local communities as people who seek reconciliation for these communities. In their book, *An Other Kingdom*, Peter Block, Walter Brueggemann, and John McKnight have argued that one way of restoring justice and rejecting the pull of consumerism is to reconnect with our local communities.[60] The message of the good news in Scripture provides a picture of wholeness and reconciliation that reconnects people to their God, to justice, and to their neighbor.

BIBLIOGRAPHY

Batto, Bernard. "The Divine Sovereign: The Image of God in the Priestly Creation Account." In *David and Zion: Biblical Studies in Honor of J. J. M. Roberts*, edited by Bernard F. Batto and Kathryn L. Roberts, 143–86. Winona Lake, IN: Eisenbrauns, 2004.

Block, Peter, et al. *An Other Kingdom: Departing the Consumer Culture*. Hoboken, NJ: Wiley, 2016.

Brandt, Donald P. "The Poor and the Lost: A Holistic View of Poverty." *Missiology: An International Review* 23 (1995) 259–66.

Brown, William P. *Seeing the Psalms: A Theology of Metaphor*. Louisville: Westminster John Knox, 2002.

Canadian Poverty Institute. "The Influence of Policy on Childhood Poverty in Selected Provinces in Canada." https://static1.squarespace.com/static/595d068b5016e12979fb11af/t/595d6e6ed2b8577ba0a0156d/1499295346865/cpi_influence_doc.pdf

Carroll R., M. Daniel. "Wealth and Poverty." In *Pentateuch*, Vol. 1 of *Dictionary of the Old Testament*, edited by T. Desmond Alexander and David W. Baker, 882–87. Downers Grove, IL: InterVarsity, 2003.

Cloke, Paul. "Rurality and Otherness." In *Handbook of Rural Studies*, edited by Paul Cloke et al., 447–56. London: Sage, 2006.

Creach, Jerome F. D. *The Destiny of the Righteous in the Psalms*. Danvers, MA: Chalice, 2008.

Darling, Linda. *A History of Social Justice and Political Power in the Middle East: The Circle of Justice from Mesopotamia to Globalization*. New York: Routledge, 2013.

Davis, Ellen F. "Two Psalms." In *Justice and Rights*, edited by Michael Ipgrave, 21–26. Washington, DC: Georgetown University Press, 2009.

Donahue, John R., and Daniel J. Harrington. *The Gospel of Mark*. SP. Collegeville, MN: Liturgical, 2005.

Finkelstein, J. J. "The Laws of Ur-nammu." *JCS* 22 (1969) 67.

---

60. Block et al., *An Other Kingdom*.

Gasaway, Brantley W. *Progressive Evangelicals and the Pursuit of Social Justice.* Durham, NC: UNC Press, 2014.

Goldingay, John. *Psalms* 90–150, Vol. 3 of *Psalms*. BCOTWP. Grand Rapids: Baker, 2008.

Greeley, Martin. "Measurement of Poverty and Poverty of Measurement." *IDS Bulletin* 25 (1994). No Pages.

Gundry, Judith M. "Children in the Gospel of Mark, with Special Attention to Jesus' Blessing of the Children (Mark 10:13–16) and the Purpose of Mark." In *The Child in the Bible*, edited by Marcia J. Bunge et al., 143–76. Grand Rapids: Eerdmans, 2008.

Gushee, David, ed. *A New Evangelical Manifesto: A Kingdom Vision for the Common Good.* Atlanta: Chalice, 2012.

Hayes, Katherine M. *"The Earth Mourns": Prophetic Metaphor and Oral Aesthetic.* AcBib 8. Atlanta: SBL, 2002.

Herdner, A. *Corpus des tablettes en cunéiforms alphabétiques découvertes à Ras Shamra-Ugarit de 1929 à 1939.* MRS 10. Paris: Geuthner, 1963.

Horsley, Richard A. *Hearing the Whole Story: The Politics of Plot in Mark's Gospel.* Louisville: Westminster John Knox, 2001.

Houston, Walter J. "The King's Preferential Option for the Poor: Rhetoric, Ideology and Ethics in Psalm 72." *BibInt* 7 (1999) 341–67.

Kotrosits, Maia, and Hal Taussig. *Re-Reading the Gospel of Mark Amidst Loss and Trauma.* Basingstoke, UK: Palgrave Macmillan, 2013.

Kramer, Samuel Noah. "Shulgi of Ur: A Royal Hymn and a Divine Blessing." *JQR* 57 (1967) 369–80.

———. "Sumerian Historiography." *IEJ* 3 (1953) 227–32.

———. "Sumerian Theology and Ethics." *HTR* 49 (1956) 45–62.

Lohfink, Norbert. "Poverty in the Laws of the Ancient Near East and of the Bible. " *TS* 52 (1991) 34–50.

Maskell, Kathy. "What is the Aroma of Justice?" Vineyard USA. https://web.archive.org/web/20160313061701/http://www.vineyardusa.org/site/about/article/what-aroma-justice.

Mathews, Mark D. *Riches, Poverty, and the Faithful: Perspectives on Wealth in the Second Temple Period and the Apocalypse of John.* Cambridge: Cambridge University Press, 2013.

Miller, Patrick D. "Ruler in Zion and Hope for the Poor: Psalms 9–10 in the Context of the Psalter." In *David and Zion: Biblical Studies in Honor of J. J. M. Roberts*, edited by Bernard F. Batto and Kathryn L. Roberts, 187–98. Winona Lake, IN: Eisenbrauns, 2004.

Moore, Anne. *Moving Beyond Symbol and Myth: Understanding the Kingship of God of the Hebrew Bible through Metaphor.* Studies in Biblical Literature 99. New York: Peter Lang, 2009.

Mowinckel, Sigmund. *The Psalms in Israel's Worship.* 2 vols. New York: Abingdon, 1962.

Nelson, Janet R. "Walter Rauschenbusch and the Social Gospel: A Hopeful Theology for the Twenty-First Century Economy." *Cross Currents* 59 (2009) 442–56.

Oxford Poverty & Human Development Initiative. "Research." http://www.ophi.org.uk/research.

"Poverty Eradication." Sustainable Development Knowledge Platform. https://sustainabledevelopment.un.org/topics/povertyeradication.

"Poverty Reduction Policies and Programs: Social Development Report Series, 2009." Canadian Council on Social Development. http://www.ccsd.ca/index.php/research/social-reports.

Roberts, J. J. M. *The Bible and the Ancient Near East: Selected Essays*. Winona Lake, IN: Eisenbrauns, 2002.

Roth, M. T. *Law Collections from Mesopotamia and Asia Minor*. 2nd ed. WAW 6. Atlanta: Scholars Press, 1997.

Routley, Laura. *Negotiating Corruption: NGOs, Governance and Hybridity in West Africa*. New York: Routledge, 2015.

Sollberger, E., and J.-R. Kupper. *Inscriptions royales sumériennes et akkadiennes*. LAPO. Paris: Cerf, 1971.

Spicker, Paul. "Definitions of Poverty: Eleven Clusters of Meaning." In *An International Glossary of Poverty*, edited by Paul Spicker et al., 150–62. London: Zed Books, 1999.

Stovell, Beth. "Divine Warrior and Shepherd as an Echo of Exodus in Isaiah 40:10–11: Contributing Voice." In *Isaiah*, edited by Carol Dempsey. Collegeville, MN: Liturgical. Forthcoming.

———. "'I Will Make Her Like a Desert': Intertextual Allusion and Feminine and Agricultural Metaphors in the Book of the Twelve." In *The New Form Criticism and the Book of the Twelve*, edited by Mark J. Boda et al., 37–61. ANEM 10. Atlanta: SBL, 2015.

———. *Mapping Metaphorical Discourse in the Fourth Gospel: John's Eternal King*. LBS 6. Leiden: Brill, 2012.

———. "Yahweh as Shepherd-King in Ezekiel 34: Linguistic-Literary Analysis of Metaphors of Shepherding." In *Modeling Biblical Language: Papers from the McMaster Divinity College Linguistics Circle*, edited by Stanley E. Porter et al., 200–30. LBS 13. Leiden: Brill, 2016.

Suttle, Tim. *An Evangelical Social Gospel? Finding God's Story in the Midst of Extremes*. Eugene, OR: Wipf and Stock, 2011.

Talmon, Shemaryahu. *King, Cult, and Calendar in Ancient Israel: Collected Studies*. Jerusalem: Magnes Press, Hebrew University, 1986.

Tseng, Timothy, and Janet Furness. "The Reawakening of the Evangelical Social Consciousness." In *The Social Gospel Today*, edited by Christopher Hodge Evans, 114–25. Louisville: Westminster John Knox, 2001.

United Nations General Assembly. *Convention on the Rights of the Child*. http://www.ohchr.org/en/professionalinterest/pages/crc.aspx.

Weiser, Artur. *The Psalms: A Commentary*. Translated by Herbert Hartwell. Philadelphia: Westminster, 1962.

Williams, David T. "Poverty: An Integrated Christian Approach." *JTSA* 77 (1991) 47–57.

Wright, Christopher J. H. *The Mission of God's People: A Biblical Theology of the Church's Mission*. Grand Rapids: Zondervan, 2010.

———. *The Mission of God: Unlocking the Bible's Grand Narrative*. Downers Grove, IL: InterVarsity, 2008.

———. *Old Testament Ethics for the People of God*. Downers Grove, IL: InterVarsity, 2004.

Wright, N. T. *Jesus and the Victory of God*. Minneapolis: Fortress, 1996.

Yildiz, F. "A Tablet of Codex Ur-Nammu from Sipper." *Or* 50 (1981) 95.

14

Is the Gospel Good News for Women?

Cynthia Long Westfall

INTRODUCTION

THE IMPACT OF THE gospel on women is a topic that is relevant in North America, in Christian circles, and in popular media, but it also extends to the plight of women in the Majority World. The question is "Is the gospel good news for women?" The answer to the question is largely determined by the values, presuppositions, and agenda of the one who asks the question. How do we understand "good news"? What is the gospel? The understanding is crucial, but the criteria are often left undefined. In order to be good news, what must be the gospel's impact on women? Are the doctrinal aspects of the gospel adequate benefits for the gospel to be considered good news for women? Are realities such as salvation, forgiveness of sins, regeneration, indwelling of and power through the Holy Spirit, reconciliation with God, personal relationship with Christ, membership in the family of God, sanctification in Christ, participation in the corporate mission, and eschatological status as an equal heir of the kingdom enough to be considered good news for women? Or must the gospel have a discernable positive impact on women's wellbeing within the culture, such as the direct advancement of equal rights between the genders, the raising of women's status, the reversing of patterns of oppression, and the addressing of women's self-actualization (e.g., control over meeting their own needs, setting priorities, and fulfilling goals and aspirations), to be deemed good news?

The answer to these questions can be quite complex, in part due to the nature of the gospel, the relationship between the gospel and a target culture, theological inconsistencies within particular groups, systemic abuses and contractions in the Christian traditions in regards to gender, and failure to realize theological doctrines that are shared in the way they are pragmatically realized and experienced by women in churches, homes, and their spiritual lives.

WHAT IS "GOOD"?

For the purposes of this essay, I propose that the gospel is "good" if it positively addresses and impacts women's real lives lived in the real world. However, some assume that to be "good" means that the equality of women must be explicitly acknowledged, the value of women's culture and women's historical heritage must be revealed and affirmed, and the self-actualization of women must be promoted.[1] This would essentially mean that women in the vast majority of cultures that existed before the rise of technology could never have received good news because those cultures were androcentric. The gospel was forged within androcentric cultures in a way that accommodated, adapted, and sought to be relevant in order to communicate the message to that worldview. We should rather take the position that the gospel is communicated through Scripture, which is God's word to humanity, in the context of real lives that had to be lived in the real world using real language.[2] The effec-

---

1. For example, Schüssler Fiorenza states that she "set out to explore the problem of women's historical agency in ancient Christianity in light of the theological and historical questions raised by the feminist movements in society and church and to do so in terms of critical biblical studies" (*In Memory of Her*, xiv). The feminist critique is primarily the product of the twentieth century and is embedded in the culture of that time.

2. This includes the issue of grammatical gender in the biblical languages. Hebrew, Aramaic, and Greek are highly gendered, and masculine is the default gender. As such, the masculine gender is characteristically used for both male and female. In order to communicate to the respective cultures, the only option for the biblical writers was to use heavily gendered language—and where there is no choice, there is no meaning. When it is inaccurately assumed that a grammatically masculine referent must be male, it incorrectly renders women to be all but invisible in the text. For a technical linguistic discussion of gender systems, see Corbet, *Gender*. Translators and interpreters who speak English (which has a minimal amount of grammatical gender) have tended to project androcentric language and construct an androcentric theology on the basis of

tiveness of God's word was dependent on its relevance and its ability to communicate through specific languages, which were social semiotics shaped by the ideologies and social interests of the culture.[3] To demand otherwise would be to insist that the message could not be given in human language.

Therefore, the gospel can be described as "good" if it has positively addressed and met real women's real needs in the times and places where they have lived. Maslow's hierarchy of needs[4] orders human needs from the most basic to the most complex: physiology, safety, love/belonging, esteem, and self-actualization. While the first three are quite helpful, the need for esteem and self-actualization can be problematic. The issue of esteem for a woman within a hierarchical honor-shame culture was complex, just as it was for others with low status such as the poor and slaves. However, the gospel promotes reversals of status for these groups without changing their status within the dominant culture.[5] In addition, the category of "self-actualization" is ethnocentric and reflects the Western individualistic secular society rather than those that are collectivist and communal, which was the worldview of the Bible's cultures. Instead of self-actualization, perhaps a more general definition of "good" would be to thrive within the standard of the culture and to be equipped to fulfill one's spiritual, moral, and social obligations.

---

misunderstandings of grammatical gender, confusing the system of the language with the meaning of the message (e.g., Poythress and Grudem, *The Gender-Neutral Bible Controversy*). For a description of how Bible translations have distorted the Greek of the New Testament, see Miller, "Defense of Gender-Accurate Bible Translation"; Strauss, *Distorting Scripture?*

3. For a technical linguistic explanation of how the social reality of a culture is encoded in the language that it uses, see Halliday, *Language as Social Semiotic*. That is, meanings are created within a social system, and language represents the set of semantic options that are available to a speaker within a given cultural context. This is a reason why words have meaning in context rather than having an abstract meaning.

4. Fully expressed in 1954 in *Motivation and Personality*, Maslow's theory of the hierarchy of needs is one of the best-known theories of motivation and directly influences any discussion about human needs. It has been criticized as ethnocentric, individualistic, and insensitive to context and circumstances (see, e.g., Kendrick et al., "Renovating the Pyramid," 292–314).

5. Two places that dramatically illustrate the reversals that occur as a result of preaching the gospel are Mary's Magnificat (Luke 1:51–53) and Jesus' announcement of his ministry (Luke 4:18–19). This is consistent with the reversal of the rich and poor among believers in Jas 1:9–11.

I will maintain that the needs that the gospel meets should generally be the same for both genders—the needs of women are, for the most part, undifferentiated from the needs of men. We should resist or at least question doctrines or applications of Scripture that make good news for men one thing and good news for women something completely different, opposite, or distinct in a way that is essentially complementary in some sense of yin and yang. That tends to create a context in which the news is not good and women cease to be human. If having life "abundantly" (John 10:10) is understood as some form of freedom and self-actualization for men (Gal 5:1), it should not be understood as subjugation for women.[6]

WHAT IS THE GOSPEL?

While the gospel is often understood in terms of its content as certain truths, principles, or propositions, which are included in the doctrine of salvation (soteriology), it should instead be understood as a narrative.[7] In the Greco-Roman world, a "gospel" (εὐαγγέλιον) was good news about a significant event such as a victory in battle or the birth of a ruler that heralded a new era. The reports were communicated as a story, just as it is in most newspaper articles. We might describe the news with reference to its topic, but it is a story. According to Kenneth Schenk, the gospel refers primarily to "the announcement of 'good news' associated with the arrival of God's kingdom, particularly in association with Jesus' mission and identity as the Messiah."[8] It is no coincidence that the four Gospels came to be called "Gospels"—they are, in fact, the early church's stories that were the default form of that announcement. Scholars may argue about their genre, but everyone agrees that they are narratives.

---

6. Galatians 5:2 states, "For freedom Christ has set us free. Stand firm, therefore, and do not submit again to a yoke of slavery" (NRSV). Yet, the conservative evangelical teaching generally follows Piper in emphasizing the male's "good God-given sense of responsibility and leadership," which requires a woman's subjugation to that authority (Piper, "A Vision," 42).

7. Note that in the introduction I distinguished between a summary of the doctrinal aspects or spiritual components of the gospel and pragmatic aspects of social justice for women that some claim must be biblically understood as a legitimate and integral part of that gospel, while others claim they are openly denied or contradicted in the Bible and are not addressed by the gospel.

8. Schenck, "Gospel," 342.

CRUCIAL TOPICS

WAS THE CONTENT OF THE GOSPEL GOOD NEWS FOR WOMEN?

The narratives of the New Testament depict women as key participants and models whose needs are addressed, whose actions are honored, and who are included, recognized, or invited to be full participants in the ministry of the gospel in ways that transcended the standards of the Greco-Roman culture. In the Gospel stories, women appear as major participants in dialogues with Jesus and in his teaching. In a culture in which women were rendered invisible, the Gospels mention women over forty times, not counting parallel references, and women play key roles in which they are often anything but silent, weak, and passive.[9] As Dorothy Sayers has said, "Women were first at the Cradle and last at the Cross."[10] The Samaritan woman evangelizes her hometown (John 4:39), women are the first to witness Jesus' resurrection, and women are the first commissioned to announce it (Matt 28:8–10; Mark 16:6–8; Luke 24:6–10; John 20:11–18).

But for our purposes, the most notable case is the woman who anoints Jesus on the head with an alabaster jar of very expensive perfume in the home of Simon the Leper in Bethany. The disciples are indignant because they believe she is wasting money that could be given to the poor. Jesus responds:

> Why do you trouble the woman? She has performed a good service for me. For you always have the poor with you, but you will not always have me. By pouring this ointment on my body she has prepared me for burial. Truly I tell you, wherever this good news is proclaimed in the whole world, what she has done will be told in remembrance of her. (Matt 26:10–13//Mark 14:6–9)[11]

The words of Jesus indicate that this woman's action is specifically highlighted by Jesus as significant: it is a ministry that Jesus associates with priestly preparation for sacrifice. It is prophetic both by its nature and by its reference, and she is supposed to be commemorated for it perpetually in the gospel. The context of Jesus' words in this story places the woman in a consummate positive contrast with the priestly and lay leadership of Palestine and even more starkly in contrast with the disciples.

---

9. Tucker and Liefeld, *Daughters of the Church*, 25.
10. Sayers, *Are Women Human?* 47.
11. Unless otherwise indicated, Scripture quotations are taken from the NRSV.

Jesus' statement that the woman "performed a good service" (ἔργον ... καλὸν ἠργάσατο) for him, his statement that she prepared him for burial, and the honor he shows her indicate that her action certainly places her in the category of significant ministry—and that ministry was rendered directly to Jesus. It is possible that the action of the woman is being associated with priestly sacrifice, because Jesus' words and the description of her action collocate with the Levitical sacrifice of the grain offering (cf. Lev 2:2; Num 5:25–26) but have other significant cultic associations with the LXX as well. In seven references to the grain offering in Leviticus and Numbers, the wording is consistently τὸ μνημόσυνον αὐτῆς (in memory of "her"), which in the Old Testament context refers to the feminine noun θυσία (sacrifice), but Jesus' words "in remembrance of her" most naturally refer to the woman.[12] The grain offering is composed of flour, oil, and frankincense. The woman's action involves oil and wordplay concerning myrrh,[13] which is associated with frankincense in the role and identity of Jesus in Matt 2:11 and is used for embalming. The grain offering was a voluntary act of worship/love and devotion by the worshipper, which is exactly what commentators suggest was the woman's intent. The woman is not only the one who presents the offering as an act of devotion to Jesus, but also the one who is performing the sacrifice, which fills the role of the priest. In the story, the woman is accused of wrongdoing and harshly rebuked.[14] An association between Jesus' death and the cleansing of sin would be understood—in this case, the woman is not only vindicated, but commemorated, which is a dramatic reversal in which the woman is transformed from being an accused woman who is out of place to being a new prototype. This prototype represents the priesthood of the believer, who has been cleansed for service, including the child, the gentile, the slave, and the woman.

The woman's action is prophetic according to the Old Testament tradition. The prophets not only made predictions, but were directed to

---

12. But see Greenlee, who takes this to be a subjective genitive translated "her memorial for Jesus" (Greenlee, "For Her Memorial," 245).

13. There is suggested wordplay between σμύρνα (Matt 2:11), which is myrrh from the balsam tree in Greek, and μύρον, which is ointment or perfume that has its origin in myrrh and balsam in Semitic languages, in the anointing of Jesus.

14. In Num 5:25–26, the grain offering forms part of a test given to a woman accused of unfaithfulness by her husband. If she passes the test, then she is not only innocent, but clean, cleansed of guilt, and healed—she will be able to have children (Num 5:28).

enact metaphors that represented God's message to his people. In the case of the woman who anointed Jesus, she enacted a metaphor that had significance beyond her intent as well as constituted a prediction of a future event.[15] The anointing of the head with oil has a long tradition as a customary treatment of an honored guest at a banquet (cf. Ps 23:5). In a similar or parallel account in Luke 7:36–50, where a woman with a bad reputation pours oil on Jesus' feet and wipes it off with her hair, Jesus points out that her action indirectly rebukes the host of the banquet (Simon the Pharisee) by saying, "You did not anoint my head with oil, but she has anointed my feet with ointment" (Luke 7:46), so that in both cases the action exceeded what would be expected in hospitality on several levels. In addition, priests were anointed (Exod 29:1, 7; Lev 8:12), prophets were anointed (1 Kgs 19:16; Ps 105:15), kings were anointed by prophets and/or priests (1 Sam 10:1; 16:1, 13; 19:16), and the word "messiah" or "Christ" means "the anointed one." Both the extravagance of the act and Jesus' words tell us that the significance of the action goes far beyond the surface, so that the woman's action is saying something more than honoring him as a guest or her own intention. She is proclaiming Jesus' messianic destiny, in which his death is directly connected to his roles, which are prophet, king, and eventually priest.[16] Furthermore, according to Jesus, her action is a prophecy in that it prepares him for his death—that is where the wordplay between myrrh and ointment/perfume becomes explicit, because myrrh is used for embalming the dead.

The word "memorial" stands out because it occurs only in this pericope and in the story of Cornelius in Acts in the New Testament. However, it is more common in the LXX, associated primarily with a symbol that serves as a memorial, such as a grain offering or a concrete object, but it is also associated with names and records (memorandums) that preserve the memory of a person or an event, including the name of Yahweh, which was to be a memorial from generation to generation (Exod 3:15 LXX). According to Matthew, telling this story throughout the world would be such a memorial to the woman (εἰς μνημόσυνον αὐτῆς

---

15. The early church believed that someone could unknowingly predict an event, as in cases of the Old Testament prophets and Caiaphas the high priest (1 Pet 1:12; John 11:50–52).

16. Those that argue the early church saw a royal anointing include Dibelius, *Jesus*, 96; Hooker, *Mark*, 98.

[Matt 26:13]).[17] That is, the gospel is a story, and it should include this story. It is significant that in Matthew and Mark, the Eucharist occurs in the very next passage (Matt 26:17–27; Mark 14:12–22). As Luke and Paul indicate, the Eucharist was understood by the early church as a memorial or reminder of Christ (εἰς τὴν ἐμὴν ἀνάμνησιν, Luke 22:19; 1 Cor 11:25; cf. Heb 10:3).[18] Apart from Jesus, the woman who anointed him is the only person in the New Testament who is honored in this way. What is significant about this is that Jesus directly confronts Greco-Roman gender roles and values, in which women were held to have no honor. It was said that a woman's honor was her shame. So, in some sense, the woman receives protection, love, belonging, esteem, and confirmation of ministry from Jesus himself. This was good news for women.

Of course, this is not just a story about the woman's action, but is also presented by Matthew as part of the record of Jesus' teaching that should be taught to all disciples in all nations according to Matt 28:20, just as Jesus says it is supposed to be preached throughout the world in Matt 26:13. Furthermore, the story is told in a context in which the woman's action is superimposed against the actions of men who are priests, leaders, and in Jesus' inner circle. In Matt 26:1–5, the chief priests and elders plot to kill Jesus.[19] In 26:1–9, the disciples are indignant and rebuke the woman for honoring Jesus. In 26:14–26, in direct response to what happened with the woman, Judas Iscariot betrays Jesus to the chief priests. After the Last Supper, in 26:31–35, Jesus predicts that all the disciples will fall away and that Peter will deny him. So instead of presenting the priests, leaders, prophets, and disciples as the ones who recognize him, minister to him, and keep watch with him, the gospel story tells of them plotting, dishonoring, abandoning, and betraying. Only the woman

17. Outside of this pericope, the only other place that this construction occurs in Scripture is in Acts 10:4, where Cornelius is told, "Your prayers and your alms have ascended as a memorial (εἰς μνημόσυνον) before God." This passage has intertextual ties with the sacrifice of the grain offering that was burned on the altar (τὸ μνημόσυνον αὐτῆς [Lev 2:2 LXX]), so that Cornelius's prayers are parallel to the smoke that rises up from the offering.

18. It is interesting that the Greek word that is used for the remembrance or reminder of the Eucharist is in the same semantic domain as μνημόσυνον, but the word is far less common in the LXX, and the cultic associations are not as powerful (Lev 24:7; Num 10:10; 37:1; Ps 69:1; Wis 16:6).

19. Keener states, "In Matthew's view, the Jerusalem aristocracy (21:46) as well as Pilate (27:24) concern themselves more with political prudence and crowd control than with justice (26:5)" (Keener, *Commentary*, 612).

ministers to Jesus in the place of the priests, leaders, and prophets who should be doing it. The church has taught that a woman should not hold a traditional office in the church in part because Jesus did not select a woman to be one of the twelve apostles. However, in this pericope, the twelve apostles fail to lead in honoring Jesus and to stand with him in the passion narrative.[20] The church has taught that a woman should not hold a traditional office in the church because women were not priests, but in the context of the Gospels, it is the priests who are plotting to kill Jesus. The unnamed woman steps out of an obscure role and performs the functions of ministry and leadership that the men either refused to do or simply miss.

Women play other parts in the story of the gospel that have similar significance. For example, the roles of Mary as the mother of Jesus in Luke and as the ideal disciple in John, along with her actions and her speech, have all the ramifications of reversal that she preaches in her Magnificat (Luke 1:46–55). In John, it is Martha who receives one of Jesus' most profound statements about his identity and who, in response, makes the first full messianic confession in John's Gospel (John 11:25–26). This is to say that the content of the gospel in the oral traditions of the early church and in the first written documents that preserved these traditions was profoundly affirming to women in terms of their value, their potential role, and their significance, and it gives concrete examples that model women's full participation in the ministry and spread of the gospel—it could even be said that the Gospels show that women can do more than men in some situations.[21] Jesus' affirmation of what women did in worship and ministry is often in direct opposition to the androcentric culture in the narrative. Men in the Gospels, including the disciples in Jesus' inner circle, often respond to women's actions with rejection ranging from indignation to rebuke. On the other hand, the

---

20. Keener writes, "We disciples who are grieved by the failure of every single one of our male spiritual predecessors to stand with our Lord in his time of testing (vv. 40–56) can at least find some solace in the love shown by the women disciples (v. 7; 27:61; 28:1; cf. Mark 15:40–41). Although the threat to their safety may have been less grave, they nevertheless put us men to shame in the passion narrative" (Keener, *Commentary*, 365–66).

21. The presence of male followers of Jesus at the cross would have constituted a political threat that indicated resistance, but the presence of women did not communicate a threat to the officials—which explains the presence of the women and the absence of all the disciples but John (John 19:26). Similarly, the gospel could more easily spread through women in the domestic sphere.

women are often able to function in situations in which men would be a threat, such as at the foot of the cross or at the tomb.

The preservation of the Gospel narratives as Scripture, their authority over the church, and particularly the Protestant doctrine of *sola scriptura* ensured that the Gospel narratives would continue to be great news for women, as long as the narrative was interpreted correctly.[22] The perception of the gospel stories as good news for women has increased as the literacy rates of women have risen and the education of women has equipped them to interpret the stories. Even though the practice of preaching the gospel and the description of its content resulted in its nature being understood as doctrinal, confessional, and abstract in a way that obviated much of the theology in the story that is relevant to women, the postmodern shift from the abstract to the narrative sets the table for more insight into what the Gospels have to offer.

WAS THE SPREAD OF THE GOSPEL GOOD NEWS FOR WOMEN?

As stated above, the culture of Palestine that is represented in the Gospel narratives was an androcentric culture that was part of Hellenistic culture and belonged to the Roman Empire. Yet the impact of the Jews' sacred Scriptures historically provided a perpetual witness to, impact on, and corrective of the influence of the Greco-Roman culture of the Jews in Palestine and the dispersion. While the Hebrew Bible and the LXX translation were also forged in androcentric cultures, the stories,

---

22. Central foundational biblical truths are conveyed by narrative—the gospel itself is a narrative as well as the creation account and the exodus. However, the interpretation of narrative suffered during the modern period, in which it was often denied that one could find theology in a biblical narrative or history and in which it was commonly claimed that truth was propositional and that theology was conveyed in the biblical propositions. Consequently, the Pauline epistles were prioritized over the Gospel narratives in the study, teaching, and preaching of the New Testament, and the Old Testament narratives have often been neglected. In practice, restrictive interpretations of Paul's instructions to women have tended to override the positive models of women in the Old and New Testaments, which contradict the restrictive interpretations' dismissal of basing theology on history/narrative. Through the twentieth century, it was difficult for lay people to find any guidance in interpreting narrative other than moralistic guidance: they were instructed to look for an example to follow or avoid. In the postmodern period, narrative has gained a more central and biblical role, and various methodologies have been developed to interpret narrative, such as narrative criticism. For an overview, see Westfall, "Narrative Criticism." For helpful exercises in interpreting narrative, see Rhoads, *Mark as Story*, 151–59.

poetry, and laws reflected a significantly higher view of the ontological nature of women, their roles, their character, and their treatment. Of course, the influence went both ways, and we can see Jews such as Philo interpret and apply the Old Testament with a hermeneutic that incorporated much of the oppressive Greek philosophy about women.[23]

As the gospel spread through the Jewish communities from Palestine to the diaspora and then to gentiles, non-Jewish women in the Greco-Roman world who responded to the gospel were impacted not only by the arguably subversive nature of the Gospel narratives for women and others with low status, but also by the contents of the LXX, which was the sacred Scripture of the early church. Therefore, I am going to argue that the gospel was good news for women in the first century and that this continues to be the trajectory of the impact of the gospel on the lives of individual women and cultures.

The Spread of the Gospel Was Good News for Women in the First Century

The spread of the gospel in the first century was good news for both men and women in a brutal culture that was characterized by cruelty and deceit.[24] The apostle Paul's ministry and theology promoted salvation for everyone: every class, race, and gender. While it is true that no woman was one of the twelve apostles, no gentile or slave could be one of the twelve either, but Paul called people on his ministry team 'apostles,' including the woman Junia![25] In addition, during Jesus' ministry, preaching, teaching, and exercising spiritual authority were by no means restricted to the Twelve, but were given by Jesus to a group that he explicitly described as unqualified according to the culture's standards

---

23. See Philo, *Spec.* 3.171, where Philo follows the Greek classical ideal in stating that women should live lives of seclusion, even to the extent of going to the temple after people have gone home.

24. Evaluation of the Roman Empire and the Greco-Roman culture has shifted from an historically positive evaluation.

25. Paul lists "apostle" as one of the spiritual gifts, which is a separate category from the apostles who were Jesus' twelve disciples, but still indicative of a foundational function of leadership (1 Cor 12:28–29; Eph 4:11). In Rom 16:7, he names the woman Junia as an apostle, which has been predictably challenged, though the arguments that she was a man (medieval) or that the grammar indicates her reputation among the apostles (twentieth to twenty-first century) are weak and transparently driven by presuppositions that it would be unbiblical for a woman to be an apostle. See Epp, *Junia*.

(Luke 10:1–22).²⁶ Christianity was particularly attractive in contrast with pagan religions because it offered intimacy with God (divinity) through Christ and membership for all in the family of God.

Rodney Stark points out that Christianity dealt more effectively than pagan religions with the ever-present reality of crises, danger, and the threat of death.²⁷ There were theological explanations for death and suffering, together with a call to suffer for a godly purpose. People were therefore willing to suffer with Christ or on behalf of Christ. It was a high price, but the price indicated the value of the benefits—you get what you pay for, and converts were motivated to make extraordinary sacrifices due to a powerful belief in life after death. Consequently, the worst events, such as urban plagues, became opportunities for the faithful. The central value of love/charity created an effective system of mutual support. Christians sacrificed to care for the sick, give aid, and support those in trouble and received the same care from the Christian community, which provided an attractive ethical and moral contrast to the dominant culture. Needless to say, the hands-on day-to-day care for the sick, the giving of practical aid, such as provisions of clothing and preparation of food for the poor, primarily required women's work.

In the second century, Origen quoted Celsus, who accused Christian teachers of targeting "the foolish . . . slaves, women and children" for conversion (Origen, *Contra Celsum* 3:59). Though Origen denied it, the gospel clearly had additional attractions for women in the Greco-Roman world beyond the general draw. Women were better treated in the stories of Jesus and the writings of Paul than in the dominant Greco-Roman culture. Furthermore, women tended to have a higher status and more safety in Christian homes for a number of specific reasons.²⁸ The

---

26. The seventy that were sent out in twos in Luke 10:1–22 cannot be grammatically restricted to males, and they were characterized by Jesus as "lambs" among wolves (10:3) and "little children" or "infants" as opposed to "the wise and the intelligent" (10:21). Jesus' point is that those he appointed to preach, teach, and exercise spiritual authority are the very ones who were not qualified in the eyes of the world. As Peter says, the success of his ministry (in this case healing) was not due to his own power or piety (Acts 3:12), nor was it successful because he was a male who had authority. It is ironic that the Twelve, who are characterized by Israel's qualified leaders as "uneducated and ordinary" (Acts 4:13), have been used as a standard to disqualify people from ministry.

27. Stark, *Rise of Christianity*, 73–94, 163–90.

28. See Stark, "The Role of Women," 229–44. The higher status of women in Christianity is one of Stark's primary arguments in the article.

culture had a definite double standard in which women were required to be faithful to their husbands, but men had no external restrictions. Christianity not only required faithfulness in marriage for husbands, but it also favored monogamy. Greco-Roman husbands exercised control over the size of the family through ordering infanticides (which were done far more often to females than males)[29] and demanding abortions for their wives (which often resulted in death or infertility).[30] Christians prohibited both infanticide and abortions, so that women who did not want to kill their infants or have unsafe abortions were drawn to Christianity. In other words, unlike the surrounding culture, Christians raised their baby girls and prevented the deaths of women from unsafe abortions. The pragmatic result was that the churches and Christian families would not only attract women, but would literally produce a higher ratio of women to men than the dominant culture would because Christian females were much less likely to be killed at birth or through botched abortions. Finally, the woman's traditional gender roles became missional in practice and motivation: her role in the home was to be an apologetic for the word of God to the culture (Titus 3:3–5), and her submission to her husband was practical evangelism (1 Pet 3:1–7). Jesus', Paul's, and Peter's teachings made women's submission equivalent to the general instructions to all believers who followed Christ in humility and who qualified for leadership and won people to Christ by becoming a slave (Phil 2:1–11; Eph 5:25–33; Luke 22:25–27; 1 Cor 9:19). This was in contrast to the dominant culture and subverted the culture's hierarchy, the obligation for a woman to adopt her husband's beliefs and religion(s), and the metanarratives about women's inferiority and moral culpability.

Women had a special significance and role in the foundation and growth of the early church (Rom 16). While Jewish Christianity most likely spread through the synagogues in the diaspora, the Pauline mission spread through house churches, which placed most of the activity of the gentile mission's churches in the domestic sphere, and the domestic sphere was women's domain in the Greco-Roman culture. Consequently, in early Christianity, women were vitally important in the spread of the gospel. They created community through meals and practical care, evangelized around the hearth and through their community

---

29. Harris, "Child Exposure in the Roman Empire," 1–22; Harris, "Extensive Infanticide in the Graeco-Roman World," 114–16.

30. Stark, *Rise of Christianity*, 95–128.

network, practiced hospitality, and hosted prayer and worship. Serving communal meals in the home, such as the love feast, was significantly different than religion that was primarily practiced in the public sphere.[31] Furthermore, according to 1 Cor 11:5 and 14:26–32, the house-church services were participatory and interactive occasions in which women prayed and, more importantly, prophesied, which was Paul's most valued ministry (1 Cor 14). As Stark argues, Christianity spread effectively through the network of women's roles and culture.[32]

The result is that women had basic needs of belonging, esteem, and significance met through their calling and their involvement in significant ministry. Paul did not hesitate to suggest and model the sacrifice of power, love, and safety on various levels for women as well as men, but it was always with the strategic purpose of advancing the gospel.

The Spread of the Gospel Continues to Be Good News for Women

The spread of the gospel continued to be good news for women, and it remains good news. When the gospel results in reconciliation and a relationship with God, the gospel is good news for women. When women find a church community in which they can worship and serve with their Spirit-given gifts and their God-given competencies, the gospel is good news for women.[33] If there is no Judeo-Christian heritage, the gospel

---

31. As Osiek and MacDonald say, one of their assumptions is that "women participated in all the activities of the house church in the first generations of the Christian era and that the house church was the center for worship, hospitality, patronage, education, communication, social services, evangelism and mission" (*A Woman's Place*, 9).

32. Stark, "The Role of Women," 229–44.

33. However, the role of women's experience in their gifting, calling, and areas of strength is a major issue in many evangelical churches. For example, the Danvers Statement states, "In both men and women a heartfelt sense of call to ministry should never be used to set aside Biblical criteria for particular ministries (1 Tim 2:11–15, 3:1–13; Tit 1:5–9). Rather, Biblical teaching should remain the authority for testing our subjective discernment of God's will" (Council on Biblical Manhood and Womanhood, "Danvers Statement," 3). However, experience is the only criterion for gifting and calling. The statement is misleading because it does not mean the same thing for men as it does for women. For men, the qualifications are ethical and developmental so that "anyone" or "whoever" can aspire to be a bishop (1 Tim 3:1). But regardless of the inclusive language/grammar, 1 Tim 3:1 is only applied to men in the outworking of the Danvers Statement. For women, the experience of a call or the possession of spiritual gifts, let alone any aspiration to serve the church in areas of leadership, is simply prohibited as unbiblical regardless of qualifications of ethical piety or maturity. In fact, a woman's experience of a call, gifting, or aspiration to serve as a church leader is treated

rightly preached will be good news for women. If the gospel places the Bible in the hands of women and proclaims its authority, and if women are taught to read and to interpret it, the gospel is very good news for women. If survival is at issue, if there is a state of crisis and/or the threat of death, the gospel rightly preached is good news for women—that was the same context in which much of the New Testament was written. If the core biblical values of servanthood, love, and service are primary in the preaching of a given context, the gospel is good news for women. If the gospel scatters the proud, brings down the rulers, and lifts up the humble, the gospel is good news for women. If the gospel is preached to the poor, proclaims freedom to prisoners and healing for the blind, and releases the oppressed, the gospel is good news for women.

WHEN IS THE GOSPEL NOT GOOD NEWS FOR WOMEN?

While the gospels themselves are very good news for women, the historical preaching of the gospel to women has not always gone well in church history, the traditions of various churches and denominations, or the history of interpretation.[34] There are crucial tipping points in which preaching, teaching, and traditions concerning women have invalidated the word of God as it applies to women, in the same way that, according to Jesus in Mark 7:9–13, the Pharisees made void God's word:

> Then [Jesus] said to them, "You have a fine way of rejecting the commandment of God in order to keep your tradition! For

---

as an ethical problem, because according to the Danvers Statement, those experiences cannot come from God or the Holy Spirit, because they contradict how Scripture is interpreted—in essence, a woman who is gifted and called to be a teacher within the church as a whole would be a false teacher by definition. But biblically, our calling, gifting, and accomplishing the good works that we are created to do (Eph 2:10) can only be a matter of experience. Therefore, the spiritual experiences of men are validated and lauded, but the spiritual experiences of women must be treated as suspect by definition. See Westfall, *Paul and Gender*, 205–7, for a more detailed discussion of the inconsistencies in the interpretation of male and female experience according to biblical teaching.

34. See Westfall, *Paul and Gender*, 179–80, for a brief summary of how Pauline teaching on celibacy was interpreted by men with Platonic philosophy, resulting in a disgust for women's bodies and the projection of their own sexual attraction and lust onto the ontological nature of women. Consequently, women were viewed as "temptresses like Eve, obsessed by sex, and worldly and wicked by nature and inclination." The Reformation elevated the role of the family over celibacy, but the traditional interpretation of passages on women perpetuated hostility towards women (thus continuing the practice of the inquisition against women) and the body shaming of women.

Moses said, 'Honor your father and your mother'; and, 'Whoever speaks evil of father or mother must surely die.' But you say that if anyone tells father or mother, 'Whatever support you might have had from me is Corban' (that is, an offering to God)—then you no longer permit doing anything for a father or mother, thus making void the word of God through your tradition that you have handed on. And you do many things like this."

I will identify four general areas in which serious abuses have occurred and still occur that work against the biblical wellbeing of women, consequently causing God's name to be blasphemed among unbelievers (Rom 2:24).

When the Church Exhibits a Culture of Hostility and Suspicion towards Women

Many conservative evangelical scholars and probably an even greater percentage of laypeople in evangelical churches strongly uphold the authority of men over society, the church, and the home.[35] However, when they promote the restriction of women in society, the church, and the home to varying degrees with what I call "the theology of drawing the line," it creates a culture of hostility and suspicion towards women. "Drawing the line" is based on the belief that the Bible teaches that women should be restricted in some way, and each church, ministry, and husband has the biblical obligation to decide to what extent they will restrict women.[36] They assume that the restriction of women in and of itself indicates a high view of Scripture and a defense of its authority and even the authority of God himself. However, this understanding of the Bible has been robustly challenged among evangelical scholars with a high view of Scripture. Legitimate, alternate interpretations have

---

35. The promotion of what is often called "biblical manhood and womanhood" has been the primary mission of the Council of Biblical Manhood and Womanhood, expressed in the Danvers Statement, which was first published in November 1988 (see Council on Biblical Manhood and Womanhood, "Danvers Statement"). The Gospel Coalition shares overlapping participants and takes the same stand on gender roles.

36. See, for example, Grudem, "What Should Women Do?" where he lists eighty-three activities in the church (3), then determines which activities he believes "the Danvers statement would definitely prohibit" women from doing (5). He suggests that women should be prohibited from at least twenty of the activities, but encourages and supports churches that may wish to be more restrictive. Note that his guiding authority quickly shifts from what Scripture prohibits or allows to what he believes the Danvers Statement prohibits, virtually treating the two as equivalent in authority.

been given of the passages that are used to support the restriction and subjugation of women.[37] But those who restrict women assume that they have the high ground and therefore encourage those who take the Bible seriously to consider how to "draw the line" on the ways that they will restrict women.[38] There is often a confusion as to whom exactly women are supposed to submit: to their husbands alone, to all men in the congregation, or to all males who are purported to be created with a God-given responsibility to protect and lead all women? Greater submission creates greater levels of vulnerability. One teaching that is clear to most is that, on the basis of 1 Tim 2:12, women cannot exercise any kind of authority in the church if men are present. However, that is not the clear meaning of the verse in the Greek text, even though it appears to be so in most English translations.[39] And on the basis of those English translations, the churches are called to make up their minds carefully about exactly what women can do and what they cannot do. Prohibitions have included activities such as playing the organ, giving announcements (or women are coached on how to give an announcement with non-authoritative language and demeanors and using the imperative "Let's worship God together!" when singing a solo), and so on. In this climate

---

37. See Westfall, *Paul and Gender*, 205–315, to see examples in which the restrictions of women's call and authority in the church are inconsistent with the Bible's clear teaching in Pauline passages that are used to restrict women and with the contexts of situation, text, and canon in which they occur.

38. Grudem's express goal in "What Should Women Do?" 7, is to help "many churches in coming to their own understanding of where to 'draw the line'" in restricting women. The issue has progressively been given such gravitas that, predictably, the tendency of some is to tend toward being more restrictive, in order to make sure that God is obeyed. Of course, this is the essence of Jesus' problems with the legalism of the Pharisees.

39. The prohibition of women from the exercise of any authority is primarily due to the translation of the word αὐθεντεῖν as "authority" in 1 Tim 2:12: "I do not permit a woman to teach or to exercise authority over a man" (ESV). However, the Greek word is never used to refer to legitimate ministry in the church (whether by men or by women)—and a word cannot mean now what it did not mean then. Apart from other interpretive issues, this word is by no means a generic word for all authority, but is rather used for ultimate authority such as the power over life and death, and that is why the referent action is sometimes murder, execution, or judgment. In every case of its occurrence in which it is transitive with a personal direct object (a sentient being), it is destructive even when the action is evaluated positively (such as God's action against the inhabitants of Sodom and Gomorrah). See Westfall, "The Meaning of αὐθεντέω," 138–73.

it is very easy to cross "the line" and be rebuked by virtually anyone in the congregation.

Even though George Knight III rightly points out that all biblical submission is voluntary,[40] the church and certain evangelical leaders are responsible for the environment that has been created through theology, teaching, and practice—and though they may suggest caution and personally treat individual women with respect, they do not establish defendable boundaries or require accountability for extreme practices, abusive enforcement, and derogatory language, even in their own churches.[41] Meanwhile, sermons, organizations, and conferences are held to encourage men to strengthen their authority and move forward in their potential for leadership.[42] The pragmatic results of these dynamics are that, while men in general (without qualification) are given encouragement, authority, and motivation to serve, women may be treated by individuals in the church with varying degrees of hostility, suspicion, condescension, and even disgust, and they are rebuked or disciplined for aspiring to serve the church in leadership roles.[43] Leaders and pas-

---

40. Knight, "Husbands and Wives as Analogues," 167.

41. Grudem actually encourages churches to set stricter boundaries than he himself sets in "What Should Women Do?" 7, without setting limits.

42. I do not mean to suggest that men are benefitting from the aggressive propagation of essential gender roles. The statistics may suggest that men suffer more than women from the (crushing?) pressure and expectations of traditional responsibilities and roles. They appear to suffer most from the over-corrective practice and pushback against feminism: in the evangelical church, there is a positive perception of all that is "male" versus a disgust, hostility, and suspicion towards women and the "feminization of the church." The Danvers Statement appears to believe that restoring women to their proper role and promoting essential manhood and womanhood will address issues such as homosexuality and transgender identity. However, the statistics indicate that increasingly more males are sexually attracted to males. This makes sense in a culture where women are denigrated. In a culture in which disgust, suspicion, hostility, and condescension towards women flourishes, an attraction toward men for both genders is quite logical. We saw this in same-gender sex in the Greek culture, in which essential gender roles were firmly in place. In a culture in which the male form was promoted as ideal, attraction to the male form would seem to be a foregone conclusion, even as the supposedly fatal attraction of women was muted by veiling. More importantly, 3:1 or 4:1 of those who are born with male genitals self-identify as female in contrast to those born with female genitals who identify as male. Essential gender roles directly contribute to the perception that one does not or cannot identify with one's gender—the traits become so restrictive that one cannot account for ways in which one deviates from the standard norm.

43. Thus, women are shamed if they interpret 1 Tim 3:1 literally: "The saying is

tors are often unaware of what is actually said and done to women in the churches and fellowships and of its cumulative effect.⁴⁴ Much of the teaching and the restrictions render obedience to clear biblical commands to serve in the area of a woman's gifting virtually impossible, and the negativity can be crippling. Though this is not the experience of every woman in the evangelical church, it is unquestionable that numerous women who are gifted in areas other than "helps," giving, and mercy are being intimidated into immobility, changing denominations or leaving the church altogether.

"Why are you bothering this woman? She has performed a good service for me" (Matt 26:10). This same scenario is being played out over and over again in our evangelical churches. Women who teach and become pastors predictably come under various forms of criticism and obstacles when they believe that they have the same experience of being called to vocation or ministry as men. But sadly, harassment is being experienced by women in the church who are simply committed to learning Scripture or theology or who volunteer for ministries that do not involve authority or teaching and yet exercise influence or who innocently violate some other, often arbitrary line that has been drawn. Women in the evangelical church are often treated with suspicion, discouragement, and dark warnings by leadership and/or church members, and the gospel is not good news when it subjects women to that environment or fails to protect them when many have been rendered powerless and vulnerable to routine attacks and criticisms.⁴⁵

---

sure: whoever aspires to the office of bishop desires a noble task." In fact, the practice of restricting and subjugating women under the authority of men sets up numerous contradictions in Scripture for women, when they seek to read and apply Scripture critically according to the best traditions of the Reformation.

44. The "strange, sexist, abusive and toxic" things that are said to Christian women (usually in church) have been the subject of a Twitter conversation that went viral in April 2017: #ThingsOnlyChistianWomenHear. A record of the conversation may be found in Asproth, "55 Things Only Christian Women Hear." The list reveals a widespread experience of women within a specific culture of hostility that is found only in the church.

45. See Zimbrick-Rogers, "A Question Mark," for how the dynamics of discomfort and a lack of welcome have been documented among women scholars in the Evangelical Theological Society, which she correctly claims "has broader implications for the wider evangelical academy and the evangelical church" (11).

When Gender Roles Are More Important than a Woman's Safety or Life

When Christians are committed to the priority of establishing essential roles for men and women, they may neglect to protect vulnerable women and speak out for those who suffer oppression and harm as a direct result of male entitlement and power.[46] This is a problem not only in North America and within the churches, but even more so worldwide: domestic violence against women is an acute problem (according to one statistic, accounting for 64 percent of murdered women),[47] but the scale and significance of "femicide" (the murder of women by men) and male violence against women is an overwhelmingly one-sided issue.[48] When the gospel is preached together with the perpetuation of patriarchy, it sometimes is even used to counter the protection and support of women and the family. When the church and Christian scholars and leaders fail to take measures to do whatever is in their power effectively to protect women and children from deprivation, domestic abuse, and violence, the gospel is not good news for women.

When a woman who is suffering from domestic abuse or violence seeks counselling from a pastor who supports "essential roles for men and women," instead of protecting the woman, the pastor's first priorities are too often the "protection of the marriage," the prevention of divorce at all costs, and the support of the husband's ultimate authority in the home within a culture that challenges it. Often the woman's story is questioned, and even more often, the first assumption will be that the primary problem is her lack of submission. There are variations on this scenario, but it involves partiality for the one who holds the power in the relationship and in the church and a failure effectively to detect, address,

---

46. For issues and examples of abuse and violence in the church, see Kroeger and Beck, *Women, Abuse and the Bible*; Kroeger and Beck, *Healing the Hurting*; and Kroeger and Nason-Clark, *No Place for Abuse*.

47. In statistics of domestic violence, Christians mirror the society. In the U.S., according to the report of the Center of Disease Control and Prevention issued July 21, 2017, in 2003 to 2013, 55.3 percent of all homicides for women were IVP (intimate partner violence) related. However, that does not account for all domestic violence in the U.S. perpetrated by men against women, because it excludes fathers, sons, other male relatives, and males that are closely connected in some other way to the home environment. The official report concluded that "homicide is one of the leading causes of death for women aged <44 years."

48. "Femicide," the murder of women/females by men, is not being tracked as a category at this time, so hard statistics are not available. This should be rectified.

and oppose sin, violence, and oppression against women within church membership.[49] The culture described above that tends to support men and suspect women doubly victimizes a woman who suffers from domestic abuse or violence.

The evangelical teaching on the submission of women throws Christian wives and professional Christian counselors into a quandary. The problem is that the teaching not only subjects women to godly and loving men who attempt to read and obey the Bible (the minority), but it also uncritically subjects women to men who will range from entitled narcissists or men who are addicted to pornography to addicts, sociopaths, pedophiles, and those addicted to other forms of sexual perversion. When such individuals are in the church or have come under the influence of Christianity, they will often cite the Bible to support their exercise of unlimited authority and physical domination over their wife and family. Their exercise of power endangers the life and safety of women and children while also enabling and perpetuating dysfunctional patterns of generational sin. The abused woman is often caught in a double bind between the perceived spiritual obligation voluntarily to submit/obey and the necessity to take personal responsibility to protect herself and her children and/or to refuse to enable and perpetuate sinful behavior. Christian counselors often help women to take responsibility and will help them to place restraining orders on their husbands, which creates a tension between the counselors' theology on women and marriage and their obligations to their clients as counselors and also creates a tension between the Bible and the practice of counseling because of the way that the Bible has been (wrongly) interpreted.

---

49. In the U.S., women in the church are generally encouraged or forced to seek protection from the law and law enforcement rather than their spiritual authority ("Call the police!"). Generally, American evangelical churches/pastors will support and uphold the law and the decision of the courts in favor of women. However, there are two problems with this scenario: first, essential male and female roles assume that a Christian woman is dependent on and protected by government and legal systems that have laws that protect women against violence and a court that will enforce the laws. Legal protection of women has only developed over time in the Western world (some of it is a result of the maligned feminist movement), and the safeguards are definitely not in place in the Majority World—women and girls have varying or no legal protection. Second, there is a serious problem when the church depends on the law of the land to ensure the safety of Christian women because it will not take responsibility for the ethical behavior of its membership.

These dilemmas and abuses should raise questions about our theology of power, authority, and leadership as well as our interpretation of the biblical texts. The dilemmas suggest that the church has confused divine authority (rooted in God and originating in the Spirit) with the hierarchical system of worldly rulers, authorities, and powers of this age that Jesus is in the process of confronting and dismantling (1 Cor 2:6–8; Eph 3:10; 6:12; Col 2:15). While we continue that conversation, let me issue this challenge to those who support the authority of men and the submission of women as biblical teaching: If a church preaches and teaches that husbands should have authority in the home and wives should submit, let that church also hold husbands accountable for the mistreatment of their wives and family. If evangelicals promote their theological views about the submission of women along with the spread of the gospel in the Majority World, let them be informed about the impact of their theology and Bible translations on the real lives of women in other cultures as well. Let the evangelical church teach biblical social justice in gender relationships just as strongly as it teaches essential roles for men and women in which everyone is encouraged to speak out on behalf of women who are defenseless or have been rendered theologically and psychologically defenseless by the teaching of the church. Let the evangelical church be at the forefront of global initiatives that protect women as well as children and promote their economic and social wellbeing. In summary, all of us need to take responsibility for how the gospel that we teach and the accompanying process of discipleship impacts people. Above all, let us strive to make the church a source of safety and refuge for women and for other broken people.

When the Gospel Is Redefined for Women

In the history of interpretation, some of the essentials of the gospel have been qualified in their application to women to mean something different than they do for men, due to interpretations of a couple of verses in the Pauline corpus. I will provide three of the more glaring qualifications of the core of the gospel, noting that there are many clear passages that are thrown into contradiction in regard to women by the alleged teachings on gender roles, prohibitions, and subjugation in these few Pauline texts. The first two examples are drawn from 1 Tim 2:9–15, which is arguably the central passage that is used to determine women's roles in the church. The third example touches at the heart of grace.

Crucial Topics

Qualification of the Redemptive Death of Christ

The redemptive death of Jesus Christ is central to all Christian confessions. We believe that Christ has died for our sins and that his act removes sin, so that guilt may be removed and the sinner may be pardoned and justified by his blood. While there is disagreement on whether original sin is transmitted or imputed, it is agreed that humans can be released from the bondage of sin through Christ's redemption. Furthermore, Christ is in the process of rolling back the consequences of the fall, with the effect that "the curse will be no more" and the last enemy to be destroyed will be death. However, the traditional interpretation of 1 Tim 2:12–14 holds that women are prohibited from teaching and having authority in the church, in part because women are being penalized for Eve's sin at the fall.[50] The weight of the logical connection between the prohibition in v. 12 and the narrative in vv. 13–14 rests on the meaning of the Greek conjunction γάρ, which interpreters have taught means "because," even though the conjunction cannot be shown to indicate more than the signal that the content of these verses is support material. The logical relationship must be inferred, and that inference should be consistent with Pauline and biblical teaching elsewhere.

However, within patriarchal contexts in which the subordination of women was assumed on the basis of women's inferiority, the idea that women were paying and should pay the consequences for Eve's action made sense—all women were required to expiate the sin of their gender, so that the work of Christ was not sufficient for women. In the second century, Tertullian wrote,

> [A woman should be] walking about as Eve mourning and repentant, in order that by every garb of penitence she might the more fully expiate that which she derives from Eve,—the ignominy, I mean, of the first sin, and the odium (attaching to her as the cause) of human perdition . . . And do you not know that you are (each) an Eve? The sentence of God on this sex of yours lives in this age: the guilt must of necessity live too. *You* are the devil's gateway: *you* are the unsealer of that (forbidden) tree: *you* are the first deserter of the divine law: *you* are she who persuaded him whom the devil was not valiant enough to attack. *You* destroyed

---

50. *Decretum Gratiani* causa 2, question 7.

so easily God's image, man. On account of *your* desert—that is, death—even the Son of God had to die.[51]

In the sixteenth century, John Knox expressed the same understanding of women's continued culpability.

> But after her fall and rebellion committed against God, there was put upon her a new necessity, and she was made subject to man by the irrevocable sentence of God, pronounced in these words: "I will greatly multiply thy sorrow and thy conception. With sorrow shalt thou bear thy children, and thy will shall be subject to thy man; and he shall bear dominion over thee" (Gen. 3:16). Hereby may such as altogether be not blinded plainly see, that God by his sentence has dejected all women from empire and dominion above man. For two punishments are laid upon her: to wit, a dolour, anguish, and pain, as oft as ever she shall be mother; and a subjection of her self, her appetites, and will, to her husband, and to his will. From the former part of this malediction can neither art, nobility, policy, nor law made by man deliver womankind . . . I am not ignorant, that the most part of men do understand this malediction of the subjection of the wife to her husband, and of the dominion which he bears above her. But the Holy Ghost gives to us another interpretation of this place, taking from all women all kinds of superiority, authority, and power over man, speaking as follows, by the mouth of St. Paul: "I suffer not a woman to teach, neither yet to usurp authority above man" (1 Tim 2:12). Here he names women in general, excepting none; affirming that she may usurp authority above no man.[52]

The traditional assumption that women are restricted because of Eve's culpability in the fall has been taken to indicate that the church should take serious responsibility for ensuring and enforcing the consequences of the fall on women within the church and Christendom, as shown in the case of Knox.[53] The above quotation was taken from a polemic

---

51. Tertullian, *On the Apparel of Women* 1.1 (Thelwall; *Ante-Nicene Fathers* 4:14). Emphasis and parentheses are original.

52. Knox, *Monstrous Regiment of Women*.

53. The consequent fear or disgust toward women was expressed in a genocide of women by both the Catholic Inquisition and the Protestants (advocates include Luther, Calvin, King James I, and the Puritans) from the fifteenth to the seventeenth century. In 1484, at the instigation of Innocent III, Heinrich Kramer and James Sprenger published *Malleus Maleficarum* (Hammer of Witches), which is a handbook on how to identify, torture, place on trial, and execute witches. The book touched off a widespread persecution of women throughout Europe, often focusing on midwives and the vulnerable

against the women rulers of his time (Mary Tudor in England and Mary Stuart in Scotland). On the other hand, biblical scholars, theologians, and pastors have not suggested that the "judgment" against men should be enforced by the church. Similar enforcement should include penalties for (1) weeding gardens and fields, (2) wiping or washing sweat off the body (particularly the face) before eating, (3) the invention or use of labor-saving devices, and (4) the practice or utilization of any form of healing that would ward off death.[54] On the contrary, the New Testament and the work of Christ have been understood to say that God is in the process of fully rolling back the consequences of the fall for men, but most have not seen that God is rolling back the consequences of the fall for women. Contemporary interpreters who understand Eve's sin as a reason or grounds for the prohibition in 1 Tim 2:12 have the same exegetical and theological problem of inconsistency even if they do not explicitly state that women must continue to expiate for Eve's sin. This assumption of culpability has contributed to the culture of hostility toward women. As in the examples of Tertullian and Knox, justifications for this reading have included various lists of women's genetic flaws or weaknesses, and such lists have reflected and fed the negative stereotyping of women and have cultivated misogyny and shaming.

Qualification of Salvation by Faith

There is evidence that in 1 Tim 2:15, the conclusion of 2:9–15, Paul directly addresses the reversal of the consequences of the fall for women. Following a brief narrative on creation and the fall, the Greek reads as a promise for women that they have hope in God when they face the threat

---

or undesirable. By the most conservative estimates, 50,000 were killed (though it was more likely many more), of which 85 percent were women. Most of them were burned at the stake.

54. Archaeological excavations of monasteries confirm contemporary accounts that they practiced herbal medicine and used painkillers for everything from hangovers to mortal injuries. However, women were forbidden to use painkillers while giving birth because the churches and the powers of Christendom believed that God desired women to be punished with severe pain as a consequence of the fall. Consequently, midwives as well as their patients were put to death for witchcraft if they used painkillers. The prohibition was eventually lifted due to the advent of modern medicine, when men replaced women as healthcare providers and began to deliver babies. James Young Simpson became the father of obstetric anesthesia in 1847 and was able to promote its use, though it spawned a lively theological debate, and devout Christians resisted the practice through the nineteenth century.

of childbirth and maternal mortality, which is one of the primary consequences of the fall for women and was the primary cause of death for women before modern medicine.[55] It may be translated, "A woman will be brought safely through childbirth if they both (the husband and wife)[56] continue in faith, love and holiness together with self-control" (CEB). That is, the language and content reads consistently with the multitude of promises in the Old Testament/LXX and the New Testament for the healing and rescue of God's people, together with practical and spiritual actions that promote safety, health, and spiritual perseverance in the face of danger (cf. Jas 5:15).[57] However, 1 Tim 2:15 is most often translated as something like "Yet she will be saved through childbearing, provided they (the plural referent is taken to be women) continue in faith and love and holiness, with modesty" (NRSV). That is, the verse has been interpreted and translated by scholars and theologians in a way that qualifies or contradicts salvation by faith for women because it indicates that a woman's salvation is contingent on giving birth, but only provided that the women also practice good behavior such as modesty![58] In fact,

---

55. See Hubbard, "Kept Safe through Childbearing," 743–62; Westfall, *Paul and Gender*, 129–40.

56. The verb "continue" (μείνωσιν) is plural rather than singular, as is the verb "will be saved" (σωθήσεται). Therefore, it is necessary to look for the closest referents/participants, which would be the woman and man in v. 12. A connection between the verb and the woman and man is likely if this passage is understood as addressing the relationship between a wife and a husband, and it is most likely, since the support material deals with the passage on marriage and childbirth. Most often the context of this passage is interpreted as instructions on church order, which is not warranted by the context and which becomes virtually incomprehensible given the reference to childbirth. See Westfall, *Paul and Gender*, for a more comprehensive critique of the assumed context of church order.

57. Most scholars reject 1 Tim 2:15 as a promise of divine help for women because they say that women continued to die in childbirth. However, we have exactly the same dilemma inherent in any promise for healing or rescue for men who place their trust in God. See, for example, Old Testament promises of the rescue of men in battle (e.g., Pss 6:2–4; 7:11; 67:21), and note how the experience of childbirth is used as a metaphor for soldiers' mortal fear (Ps 48:4–6). Sometimes godly men died from sickness, warfare, and attack, but that does not negate God's promises. Insisting otherwise involves a failure to understand the comprehensive nature of God's help—Paul's instructions would increase the likelihood of a woman's survival, but sometimes rescue in the face of death means that one is able to persevere in faith. As articulated in Dan 3:16–18, God is able to save us from death, but even if he does not, our godly response rescues us from a worse fate: serving other gods, worshipping idols, or generally losing our faith.

58. Schreiner, "Interpretation of 1 Timothy 2:9–15," 120, suggests that the phrase

the verse is interpreted as a double-edged threat. The pervasive double standards for gender thus receive authoritative affirmation from English translations and interpreters. However, the doctrine that salvation is by faith alone through grace, not works (e.g., Eph 2:8–9), is a central doctrine for Protestants, and the Reformation in part consisted in scrutinizing and rejecting traditions and translations and even questioning canonical material that compromised or contradicted salvation by faith. Furthermore, it directly contradicts Paul's teaching in 1 Cor 7:8, 34, in which he urges the Corinthian women to consider being single and says that the unmarried woman may be holy in body and spirit because she is concerned about God's concerns in contrast with the married woman, who is concerned with the world's concerns because she pleases her husband. The glaring contradiction in the translations has contributed to many contemporary scholars rejecting the Pastoral Epistles as Pauline. For those who accept the Pastoral Epistles as Pauline and authoritative, it produces serious theological tensions. Most evangelical scholars have preferred to live with tensions and be in denial about the contradictions instead of recognizing it as a promise to women that reverses the consequences of the fall for the godly.[59] There are multiple negative effects of such interpretations and translations on women in the church—a passage that should give counsel and hope is turned into a one-sided threatening list of legalistic obligations and raises a very real question for women about their eternal security when they attempt to interpret the Scripture—if a woman's salvation is contingent on not only her ability to bear children, but her good behavior, then her case is hopeless according to Paul's teaching.

"a woman will be saved through childbirth" indicates that women will experience eschatological salvation by functioning in their God-given role of wife and mother. While this may take away the offense of a woman's salvation being contingent on giving birth (which excludes the unmarried and the barren), the dependence of salvation upon functioning in a role still compromises the doctrine of salvation by grace through faith.

59. Many scholars insist that "salvation" (σώζω) and its cognates are a technical term for Paul, which he uses only to refer to salvation in a spiritual sense. However, this is not true (cf. 1 Cor. 3:15); it incorrectly restricts the meaning of spiritual salvation because it misunderstands the pragmatic nature of salvation in the present (such as receiving mercy [1 Tim 1:15] or being moved from darkness to light [Eph 5:8]), and it assumes that Paul would never use a word in a way that is most commonly used in the LXX and the Christian community. Rolling back the fall is the central way that salvation as a "technical term" is understood.

Redefinition of Grace

A third way in which the gospel has been qualified for women is to directly contradict Paul's statements about a woman's freedom from the law. In Galatians, Paul makes a major point about gentiles being free from the law and other restrictions placed on them by people such as Judaizers, lest they nullify the grace of God (Gal 2:21; 5:1). However, Jewish women under the law had fewer restrictions placed on their authority than women in the traditional church, which has been explicitly recognized and stated in the historical development of those restrictions:

> In the Old Testament much was permitted which today [i.e., in the New Testament] is abolished, through the perfection of grace. So if [in the Old Testament] women were permitted to judge the people, today because of sin, which woman brought into the world, women are admonished by the Apostle to be careful to practice a modest restraint, to be subject to men and to veil themselves as a sign of subjugation.[60]

That is to say, the same grace that brought male gentiles freedom came to be interpreted in such a way that it brought women greater subjugation once the significance of the role of Eve in the fall was clarified by Paul. Again, even where this theology is not explicitly articulated, it is an inference that can be drawn from the actual practice of the churches, and particularly so in the Western churches. It is always interesting to hear justifications and explanations of how women truly benefit more from increasing their subjugation, so that it is grace, and how male entitlement of authority and privilege is really servanthood. This only comes close to working for the wellbeing of women in the minority of specific cases where men are seriously pursuing godliness and try to understand how to promote the welfare of their wives, particularly in learning how to recognize and avoid exploitation, which is very difficult in a context in which women's voices are silenced. The general submission of women to the leadership of males has not historically promoted their welfare—the boundaries of the Western legal system may foster the pretense that women are not seriously harmed by male power, but global as well as local statistics indicate that male dominance fully manifests the sinful effects of the fall. There seems to be little recognition or responsibility for the majority of the cases in which this teaching supports and represents

---

60. *Decretum Gratiani* causa 2, question 7, cols 750–51, princ.

God as supporting an increased oppression of women while promoting increased freedom for men.

These interpretations invalidate the central doctrines of the good news of the gospel for women. They turn the Bible into a Gordian's knot for women that is hermeneutically inscrutable and incoherent in content. In summary, they indicate that women are not fully saved by faith, their sins are not fully cleansed, and grace brought greater subjugation instead of freedom. The problematic theology of gender and the hermeneutical inconsistencies between how passages are applied to men and how they are applied to women need far greater attention from the Christian community that holds the Bible to be authoritative. Perhaps the incoherence and logical inconsistencies resulting from these contradictions have not been resolved because as long as biblical scholarship was the domain of men, there was a lack of theological empathy with the theological tensions and double binds that are placed on women who attempt to apply Scripture.

When the Gospel Is Used to Subordinate Women in Western Democratic Societies

In North America, there continues to be a largely unquestioned commitment among evangelical leadership to the control and reformation of Western society. For many, this would include the reestablishment of Christendom in countries such as the United States. Part of that agenda is the maintenance of "traditional" gender roles and the restrictions of women, because those roles are purported to be synonymous with keeping God's standards for sexuality, the practice of biblical sexual ethics, and a biblical understanding of associated practices such as marriage, divorce, and abortion.[61] If an essential cause-and-effect relationship between the erosion of the purported "essential gender roles" and sexual misconduct could be established, perhaps Wayne Grudem may be justified in the claim that essential gender roles are an "ethical is-

---

61. See Council on Biblical Manhood and Womanhood, "Danvers Statement," for an expression of the assumed connection between maintaining specific gender roles and protecting the institution of marriage, promoting the value of parenting (motherhood), and the prevention of "illicit and perverse sexual relationships," including pornography. See also Piper, "A Vision," 26: "The consequence of this confusion [of gender roles] is not a free and happy harmony among more homosexuality, more sexual abuse, more promiscuity, more social awkwardness, and more emotional distress and suicide that come with the loss of God-given identity."

sue." However, "illicit and perverse sexual relationships," promiscuity, pornography, and sexual abuse were arguably far more prevalent in the Greco-Roman culture, which held a very explicit distinction of gender roles that are virtually the same as what is being called "essential manhood and essential womanhood."[62] Divorce was also a common problem, as seen in both Roman law and the Bible, *even when women were not allowed to initiate divorce*. The first-century culture did not regulate sexual behavior for men beyond forbidding access to the wives and daughters of Roman citizens. However, below the status of aristocrat, women were allowed no sexual freedom, whether they were chaste matrons, cloistered daughters, or slaves and prostitutes who were forced to be sexually available. If nothing else, a history of sexual behavior should teach us that essential gender roles and the subjugation and restriction of women cannot logically be the solution for the problems of sexual conduct in our culture.

On the other hand, one thing that has significantly changed in the last fifty years is the issue of transgender identity, but that is a problem that has been created by the capabilities of modern medicine, which claims the godlike ability to create a male or a female.[63] Furthermore, an individual's perceived need for the self-identification of gender is clearly based on the assumption of essential gender identity and roles. That is, if male and female characteristics and roles were not understood as essential to one's identity, then there would be no reason to have sex-change operations or hormonal "therapy" to change genders, and the claim that one "feels" like they are a certain gender would not make sense. Rather, it is vital as believers to ground our identity and sexual ethics in Jesus Christ rather than in essential gender roles. Whether male or female, we should "put on the Lord Jesus Christ, and make no provision for the flesh, to gratify its desires" (Rom 13:14).

62. Loader, *Sexuality*, 87, observes that the Roman male's "sexual capacity was one of their weapons of subjugation." He also notes that Christianity required a more radical change to men's behavior than it did to women's in the Greco-Roman culture (361). As for pornography, any tourist in Pompeii may see the casual graphic use of male genitals as street signs.

63. But it is males who have dominated the practice of modern medicine and all its complications. Furthermore, the lopsided ratio of those who are born male who identify as female versus those who are born as female but identify as male (3:1 or 4:1) may have some significance for the discussion. Women, women's issues, and the feminist movement appear to be scapegoated for contemporary issues that are both caused by men and plague men to a far greater degree than women.

The aggressive commitment of Christian leadership and the churches to the restriction of women is biblically problematic in and of itself (Rom 14:4), and the understanding and application of gender roles within cultures that practice democracy is idiosyncratic, departing from Christian tradition in a number of ways that even further compromise the coherence of Christian teaching and practice.[64] Ideas about hierarchy and society have changed significantly since the first century. The North American culture supports freedom and equality for all. In this volume, theologian Ross Hastings claims that Christianity was the seedbed of science. It can be similarly claimed that Christianity was the seedbed for democratic republics or parliamentary democracies as well as human rights. The understanding of women's intelligence and other capacities has also changed significantly. Women now have equal access to education, and they achieve higher levels of physical training and achievement. Our culture has been redefined by the Industrial Revolution and the age of technology, so women can perform most jobs that men can do. The access to safe birth control allows women to join the workforce in greater numbers and gives them control of their progress in a vocation. Statistics have reversed myths about the greater depravity of women's spiritual and moral behavior. When women are given education and opportunity, they are shown to be capable of various activities and vocations for which they were formerly declared unfit. Though the churches have historically taught the ontological inferiority of women, after approximately 1985, few Christian theologians and biblical scholars have taught that women are inferior to men.[65] The cultural justifications of the past for the restriction of women in society and the church, which were based on assumptions about ontology and aptitude, have evaporated in the face of statistical studies. While there are measurable biological and physiological differences between males

---

64. I have argued against the restrictions of women in service, calling it inconsistent with the Bible's clear teaching, in *Paul and Gender*, 205–42.

65. 1985 marks the publication of Knight's book, *Role Relationship*, 32–36, which shifted the rationale and focus underlying the subordination of women from the assumed ontological inferiority to equality with a distinction in role, based on a parallel with an anti-Nicene view of the Trinity: the subordination of Christ within the equality of the Godhead. While there appears to be a lack of consensus among the evangelical public as to whether the Bible teaches the ontological inferiority of women, most evangelical scholars who uphold the inspiration of Scripture and the subordination of women now follow Knight in maintaining separate roles/authority but equal ontology.

and females, they cannot be shown to warrant the kinds of restrictions on women that conservative Christians wish to impose. When we are able to observe and quantify aptitude, achievement, and moral behavior, creation itself teaches us. Without a creational rationale based on the world that God created, the restrictions on women are rather a legalistic set of regulations that are the products of inference and human tradition embedded in past cultures rather than principles drawn from the Bible.

Our worldview, our culture, and our lifestyles are radically different from those of Christians in the first century, but in many ways our worldview emerged from the influence of Christianity. The men are freed from the rigid hierarchy and terrorism of the Roman Empire, a rigid role in a patron-client relationship, submission to their paterfamilias, being bonded to the family occupation, and the threat of slavery. Though Scripture taught men to submit to their authorities in the culture, they are no longer bound to the Greco-Roman culture or the specific practices and systemic humiliation of its hierarchical system. Rather, they enjoy a share in the government, a system of checks and balances, and a legal system that limit the power of other men over them—initially these safeguards were put in place because there was a belief in the depravity of humanity and the principle that power corrupts. Therefore, in places such as the United States, men enjoy freedoms as privileges protected by law that were undreamt of in the first-century Roman Empire, so that the male gender role has been completely transformed. The rigid hierarchies of the Roman Empire have been systematically deconstructed politically, socially, economically, and within the family. It would seem that the gospel has been very good news for the wellbeing of men, though the last enemy to be destroyed is inequality due to race.[66]

Nevertheless, many who hold the Bible as inspired and authoritative believe that the Bible teaches that women are still supposed to be ethically bound by the hierarchy and gender roles of the first century. Interestingly, the asserted absolute power of a husband over his wife exceeds the authority and control that the average first-century man would have in many ways. As brutal as the Greco-Roman society was, there were still safeguards for a woman within the extended household through the power of a paterfamilias, who had the responsibility to check abuse within the extended family, and through the right of protection by

---

66. Nevertheless, see James, *Malestrom*, for the destructive impact of patriarchy on men.

her family—safeguards that are virtually removed in Western society. The ideas promoted by influential leaders such as John Piper on how women should be restricted in interaction and occupations far exceed Greco-Roman restrictions.[67] Even though the stereotypical women in the first century had a great deal of authority in the domestic sphere, it is sometimes assumed by interpreters of the Bible that a woman could not exercise any legitimate power, so that when a Greek noun or adjective that indicates authority or power modifies a woman, many translations use a non-authoritative word as a gloss.[68]

On the other hand, women in contemporary Western democratic societies are neither legally nor pragmatically vulnerable like the first-century women. Instead, they are now told by influential leaders such as John Piper that they have a moral obligation to act according to "mature femininity." Women are expected to subject themselves voluntarily to their husbands as if he were Jesus Christ and never through their demeanor and conversation violate any man's God-given responsibility to protect and lead.[69]

---

67. For example, businesswomen as well as women in the home were slave-owners of male slaves in the Roman Empire, which was never prohibited in the New Testament. The regulations for the masters of slaves have no gender qualifications, though the masculine plural is often wrongly understood as gender specific. However, Piper, in "Should Women Be Police Officers," states that women are unsuited to any job in which a woman has "influence over a man, guidance of a man, leadership of a man," as female authority that "is personal and directive . . . will generally offend a man's good, God-given sense of responsibility and leadership, and thus controvert God's created order." He concludes that a woman should not be a police officer, and though he does not wish to follow Grudem's example and make a list of jobs and "draw the line," his principles are more restrictive than Grudem's guidelines and would mean that women are not suited for most jobs. The Greco-Roman culture had a lower view of the ontology of women, but was pragmatic about the areas in which women could exercise authority due to status, circumstances, or wealth.

68. For the various ways in which women exercised authority in the Greco-Roman culture and the words and roles in the New Testament that show women held authority, see Westfall, *Paul and Gender*, 260–68.

69. Piper teaches that "mature femininity" will not "strain the personhood of [any] man" by personal influence or guidance, saying women should show "culturally appropriate expressions of respect for his kind of strength, and glad acceptance of his gentlemanly courtesies. Her demeanor—the tone and style and disposition and discourse of her ranking position—can signal clearly her affirmation of the unique role that men should play in relationship to women owing to their sense of responsibility to protect and lead" (Piper, "A Vision," 41).

If the church is committed to the development and application of a coherent theology and praxis, if it is dedicated to the mission of God's kingdom as prayed in the Lord's Prayer, if it is dedicated to reversing the fall and standing against oppression, then these gender issues constitute a call for new wineskins. They call for a fresh look at Scripture, as was the case with the inclusion of the gentiles in the people of God and the abolition of slavery. I believe that the contemporary subjugation of women is highly destructive of Christianity's reputation in the culture. It does not make the gospel attractive, and it causes people to disrespect and reject the word of God.

CONCLUSION: THE GOSPEL REMAINS GOOD NEWS FOR WOMEN

The good news for women is that the priorities and goals of any disciple of Jesus Christ are not to pursue personal status, personal power, or happiness. The goal of every Christian is to be conformed to the image of Christ. If faithful women are persecuted, punished, pressured, accused, undervalued, criticized, or unpaid for their resources and gifts and/or their ministries, that experience may be transformed into the development of cruciformity and maturity (Jas 1:2–8; Rom 5:3–5), given that the treatment is truly persecution and not a result of enablement or self-martyrdom. Cruciformity is the primary qualification for serving the church according to Jesus and Paul, and they both were treated the same way. But a primary concern must be that women are being misled by false teaching to voluntarily become people-pleasers (contra 1 Thess 2:4; Eph 6:6), to abdicate the exercise of self-control (contra Gal 5:23), to avoid conflict (contra John 16:33), and voluntarily to serve men (literally) rather than God (contra Luke 14:26), all the while wrongly believing that they are honoring God in the highest way possible. A woman's personal loss can be her gain if she understands Scripture correctly by walking in the footsteps of Jesus and Paul—which is to obey God, follow Jesus, and answer his call, regardless of the price or the objections of family or authority (Matt 10:37; Mark 10:29; Luke 14:26). This understanding is what I hold to be central to what is known as the egalitarian position,[70] and it brings pragmatic hope and dignity to women in all

---

70. The call of women to servanthood was clear in one of the early egalitarian books (1998): Hull, *Equal to Serve*.

contexts, whether cultural or historical. The road to dignity and hope is exactly the same for women as it is for men, both in general principle and in the outworking of each individual as God's workmanship (Eph 2:10), in which the times, places, and people groups in which God places us play a vital role (Acts 17:26–27), as well as our physical design and capacities, which are customized by God (Ps 139).[71] The gospel has always been good news, but it has never been a safe gospel.[72] True mission entails risk and sacrifice, and neither men nor women should confuse the call to discipleship with maintaining their comfort zones or personal advancement in the world system.[73]

On the other hand, the Bible consistently calls believers to social justice.[74] We are called to hunger and thirst for righteousness (Matt 5:6) and to confront error such as systemic neglect, abuse, and favoritism among God's people. Again, this is following in the footsteps of Jesus (confronting the legalistic restrictions of the Pharisees) and Paul (fighting for the spiritual status/rights of gentile men). The biblical practice

---

71. Paul urges the Corinthian church to avoid recognizing, judging, or evaluating its members according to human standards, but rather to recognize new possibilities and potential for ministry in the new creation (2 Cor 5:16–21). While society and culture may restrict an individual's potential, the church should never limit a man's gifting or ministry potential because of social, economic, or racial reasons; no more should the church restrict a woman to gender roles that prevent her from fulfilling her "good God-given" potential or her spiritual gifting! But this is what is happening in areas that are permissible for women within the Western culture!

72. In the first century, it was relatively more unsafe for men when they had more to lose than women within a rigid patriarchal system and where their participation in the counter-culture of the Christian movement could constitute a political and military threat to the Empire.

73. It is far more spiritually dangerous to be an oppressor who subjugates others, which may well explain the malaise of men in the church and Western society. The problem is that many men have unexamined mindsets of personal entitlement and presuppositions and assumptions that are consistent with a colonial worldview in which they are created by God to occupy the dominant role in a sort of manifest destiny. Every male is understood to have "good God-given sense of responsibility and leadership" (Piper, "A Vision," 42), and that authority is often understood as parallel to the ascendant position of Jesus Christ in heaven (Knight, "Husbands and Wives as Analogues," 164–65). See Westfall, "This Is a Great Metaphor!" 561–98 for a corrective understanding of the metaphor of the husband as head. These assumptions' potential destruction of the spiritual transformation of men and how much it compromises faithful service cannot be over-emphasized.

74. For a discussion of the believer's call to biblical social justice, see Westfall and Dyer, eds. *The Bible and Social Justice*.

of addressing and speaking against oppression may consist of fighting for the rights of an oppressed minority. It is in the best interest of the Christian tradition to use one's resources and power to redress a wrong.

However, if a Christian woman confronts any systemic abuse against women in the church, home, or society, it is easily confused with and dismissed as the pursuit of her own personal rights, status, power, or happiness. Anything that smacks of a power struggle seems problematic and unbiblical by definition, and the subjective personal relevance of the woman's story, gifting, or calling may be perceived as ungodly rank ambition if it is not rejected as overtly unbiblical and disobedient from the start. This is compounded by the navigation of the unavoidable issue of anger, which may well be prophetically righteous, but is probably more often a mixed bag. Of course, no anger is seen as justifiable in a context in which women are supposed to be subordinate. Therefore, many women are immobilized or diverted from speaking or acting by the controversial nature of the discussion in which this article is engaged, or they may appear to be disqualified by ambition or anger. For example, an evangelical woman biblical scholar typically finds herself choosing between following her own passion in her research, on the one hand, and becoming embroiled in an ongoing self-defense of the legitimacy of a woman being a biblical scholar, teaching men in academic courses, etc., on the other.[75] Therefore, the egalitarian position has come under criticism because it appears to be enmeshed in a power struggle for rights, status, and position, and women scholars may appear to be focused only on the women's passages and gender issues.

I would like to suggest a nuancing of terminology that may help us navigate the gender conversation more accurately.[76] I have persistently resisted the label "feminist" for the arguments that are presented in this chapter, because I suggest that the gospel is good news for women in the same way that it is for men, but our response to the good news is servanthood, not the pursuit of status, power, or rights. Every believer is called to follow Jesus, to lay down their prerogatives, and to conduct themselves in the spirit of servanthood and cruciformity, which is *the*

---

75. Most female evangelical biblical scholars who teach Old Testament or New Testament courses in conservative Bible schools and seminaries must work very hard at developing a thorough understanding of the gender issues and their interpretation of key passages at one point or another, whether or not they take a public position verbally.

76. The discussion of the use of terminology addresses some of Lee-Barnewall's issues with the label "Egalitarian" in *Neither Complementarian nor Egalitarian*.

qualification for ministry. Regardless of social status, race, or gender, everyone is equally qualified to be a slave at the foot of the cross, and that certainly may be called a "right."[77] Add to that a thorough understanding of the sovereignty of God and the Lordship of Christ. The Spirit sovereignly distributes spiritual gifts that enable individuals to serve and equip the church, which by definition can never be predetermined by gender roles, social roles, race, or where a church chooses to "draw the line." With regard to any trappings of status within the church (which are arguably culturally based), biblically, there can be no partiality with Christ (Jas 2:1–12). This has been my theological framework and reference, and this has been the central framework and reference of the position of "egalitarianism" since I became aware of it in 1989. However, when one takes an active role in the pursuit of biblical social justice in gender relationships in the society, church, and home and engages in the fight for the global wellbeing of women, it clearly involves issues of status, position, and control of resources.[78] I suggest that the egalitarian theological position and the individual engagement of women in servanthood/service and ministry should not be confused or confounded with the specific call of individuals to pursue biblical social justice by promoting egalitarian theology, participating in theological debates, and taking political action. That is, I suggest that we may comfortably refer to evangelical individuals who actively defend women and pursue biblical social justice for women locally and globally as "feminists," but that a feminist is by no means the same thing as an egalitarian.

BIBLIOGRAPHY

Asproth, Rachel. "55 Things Only Christian Women Hear." *Arise*, 19 April 2017. https://www.cbeinternational.org/blogs/55-things-only-christian-women-hear.

Corbett, Greville. *Gender*. CTL. Cambridge: Cambridge University Press, 1991.

The Council on Biblical Manhood and Womanhood. "The Danvers Statement." http://www.churchcouncil.org/iccp_org/Documents_ICCP/English/17_Male_Female_Distinctives_A&D.pdf.

---

77. In Westfall, *Paul and Gender*, 244: "Paul relativized the authority structure in the church by casting every leader as a slave of both God and the community, while he still advocated conventional reciprocity for benefits received among those functioning as clients, who received benefits from others."

78. I want to restate that I believe that men are also victimized and experiencing worse consequences to their wellbeing because they are being misled to see their primary role as taking control instead of serving, which is far more dangerous to one's citizenship in the kingdom of heaven.

Dibelius, Martin. *Jesus*. Translated by Charles B. Hebrick and Frederick C. Grant. Philadelphia: Westminster, 1949.
Epp, Eldon Jay. *Junia: The First Woman Apostle*. Minneapolis: Fortress, 2005.
Friedberg, Emil Albert, ed. *Corpus Iuris Canonici: Decretum magistri Gratiani*. Vol I. 1879–1881. Reprint, Graz: Akademische Druck- und Verlaganstalt, 1955.
Greenlee, J. Harold. "Εἰς μνημόσθνον αὐτῆς, 'For her Memorial': Mt xxvi.13, Mk xiv.9." *ExpTim* 71 (1960) 245.
Grudem, Wayne. "But What Should Women Do in the Church?" *CBMW News* 1 (1995) 1, 3–7.
Halliday, M. A. K. *Language as Social Semiotic*. London: Edward Arnold, 1978.
Harris, William V. "Child Exposure in the Roman Empire." *JRS* 84 (1994) 1–22.
———. "The Theoretical Possibility of Extensive Infanticide in the Graeco-Roman World." *ClQ* 32 (1982) 114–16.
Hooker, Morna D. *The Message of Mark*. London: Epworth, 1983.
Hubbard, Moyer. "Kept Safe through Childbearing: Maternal Mortality, Justification by Faith, and the Social Setting of 1 Timothy 2:15." *JETS* 55 (2012) 743–62.
Hull, Gretchen Gaebelein. *Equal to Serve: Women and Men Working Together Revealing the Gospel*. Grand Rapids: Baker, 1998.
James, Carolyn Custis. *Malestrom: Manhood Swept into the Currents of a Changing World*. Grand Rapids: Zondervan, 2015.
Keener, Craig S. *A Commentary on the Gospel of Matthew*. Grand Rapids: Eeerdmans, 1999.
———. *Matthew*. IVPNTC. Downers Grove, IL: IVP, 1997.
Kendrick, D. T., et al. "Renovating the Pyramid of Needs: Contemporary Extensions Built upon Ancient Foundations." *Perspectives on Psychological Science* 5 (2010) 292–314.
Knight, George W., III. "Husbands and Wives as Analogues of Christ and the Church: Ephesians 5:21–33 and Colossians 3:18–19." In *Recovering Biblical Manhood and Womanhood: A Response to Evangelical Feminism*, edited by John Piper and Wayne Grudem, 165–78. 1991. Reprint, Wheaton, IL: Crossway, 2006.
———. *The Role Relationship of Men and Women: New Testament Teaching*. Rev. ed. Grand Rapids: Baker, 1985.
Knox, John. *The First Blast of the Trumpet Against the Monstrous Regiment of Women (Annotated)*. Edited by Edward Arber. Nottingham: DB Publishing House, 2011.
Kramer, Heinrich, and James Sprenger. *The Malleus Maleficarum*. Edited and translated by Montague Summers. London: John Rodker, 1928.
Kroeger, Catherine Clark, and James R. Beck, eds. *Women, Abuse and the Bible: How Scripture Can Be Used to Hurt or Heal*. Grand Rapids: Baker, 1996.
———. *Healing the Hurting: Giving Hope and Help to Abused Women*. Grand Rapids: Baker, 1998.
Kroeger, Catherine Clark, and Nancy Nason-Clark. *No Place for Abuse: Biblical and Practical Resources to Counteract Domestic Violence*. Downers Grove, IL: IVP, 2010.
Lee-Barnewall, Michelle. *Neither Complementarian nor Egalitarian: A Kingdom Corrective to the Evangelical Gender Debate*. Grand Rapids: Baker, 2016.
Loader, William. *The New Testament on Sexuality*. Grand Rapids: Eerdmans, 2012.
Maslow, Abraham H. *Motivation and Personality*. 3rd ed. Revised by Robert Frager et al. London: Longman, 1987.

Miller, Jeffrey. "A Defense of Gender-Accurate Bible Translation." In *Discovering Biblical Equality*, edited by Ronald W. Pierce and Cynthia Long Westfall. 3rd ed. Downers Grove, IL: IVP, forthcoming.

Osiek, Carolyn, and Margaret Y. MacDonald. *A Woman's Place: House Churches in Earliest Christianity*. Minneapolis: Fortress, 2006.

Piper, John. "Should Women Be Police Officers?" *Ask Pastor John*, 13 August 2015. https://www.desiringgod.org/interviews/should-women-be-police-officers.

———. "A Vision of Biblical Complementarity: Manhood and Womanhood Defined According to the Bible." In *Recovering Biblical Manhood and Womanhood: A Response to Evangelical Feminism*, edited by John Piper and Wayne Grudem, 25–55. 1991. Reprint, Wheaton, IL: Crossway, 2006.

Poythress, Vern, and Wayne Grudem. *The Gender-Neutral Bible Controversy: Muting the Masculinity of God's Words*. Nashville: Broadman and Holman, 2000.

Rhoads, David, et al. *Mark as Story: An Introduction to the Narrative of a Gospel*. 2nd ed. Minneapolis: Fortress, 1999.

Sayers, Dorothy L. *Are Women Human?* Grand Rapids: Eerdmans, 1971.

Schenck, K. "Gospel: Good News." In *Dictionary of Jesus and the Gospels*, edited by Joel Green et al., 342–45. Rev. ed. Downers Grove, IL: IVP, 2013.

Schüssler Fiorenza, Elisabeth. *In Memory of Her: A Feminist Theological Reconstruction of Christian Origins*. New York: Crossroad, 1994.

Schreiner, Thomas R. "An Interpretation of 1 Timothy 2:9–15: A Dialogue with Scholarship." In *Women in the Church: A Fresh Analysis of 1 Timothy 2:9–15*, edited by Andreas J. Köstenberger et al., 105–54. Grand Rapids: Baker, 1995.

Stark, Rodney. "Reconstructing the Rise of Christianity: The Role of Women." *Sociology of Religion* 56 (1995) 229–44.

———. *The Rise of Christianity: A Sociologist Reconsiders History*. New York: Harper Collins, 1996.

Strauss, Mark. *Distorting Scripture? The Challenge of Bible Translation and Gender Accuracy*. Eugene, OR: Wipf & Stock, 2010.

Tertullian. *On the Apparel of Women*. In *The Ante-Nicene Fathers: The Writings of the Fathers Down to A.D. 325*, edited by Alexander Roberts and James Donaldson, revised by A. Cleveland Coxe, 4:14–26. Translated by S. Thelwall. Edinburgh: T. & T. Clark, 1986. Reprint, Grand Rapids: Eerdmans, 1989.

Tucker, Ruth A., and Walter Liefeld. *Daughters of the Church: Women and Ministry from New Testament Times to the Present*. Grand Rapids: Zondervan, 1987.

Westfall, Cynthia Long. "The Meaning of αὐθεντέω in 1 Timothy 2:12." *JGRChJ* 10 (2014) 138–73.

———. "Narrative Criticism." in *Dictionary of Biblical Criticism and Interpretation*, edited by Stanley E. Porter, 237–39. London: Routledge, 2006.

———. *Paul and Gender*. Grand Rapids: Baker, 2016.

———. "'This Is a Great Metaphor!': Reciprocity in the Ephesians Household Code." In *Christian Origins and Greco-Roman Culture: Social and Literary Context for the New Testament*, edited by Stanley E. Porter and Andrew W. Pitts, 561–98. ECHC 1. Leiden: Brill, 2013.

Westfall, Cynthia Long, and Bryan R. Dyer, eds. *The Bible and Social Justice: Old Testament and New Testament Foundations for the Church's Urgent Call*. MNTS 14. Eugene, OR: Pickwick, 2015.

Zimbrick-Rogers, Emily Louise. "'A Question Mark Over My Head': Experiences of Women ETS Members at the 2014 ETS Annual Meeting." https://www.cbeinternational.org/sites/default/files/A%20Question%20Mark%20Over%20My%20Head.pdf.

Index of Modern Authors

Ackroyd, Peter R., 33, 44
Adeney, Francis S., 246, 248-52, 258, 262
Alexander, T. D., 137, 151
Anderson, Bernard W., 228, 242
Anderson, Gary A., 167, 174
Aquinas, Thomas, 200
Arnold, Bill, 16, 20, 24, 28
Arnold, Clinton E., 159-60, 172, 174
Asproth, Rachel, 350
Assisi, Francis of, 200
Auld, A. Graeme, 21, 28
Autenrieth, Georg, 49, 56
Avioz, Michael, 15, 28

Baik, Chung-Hyun, 182, 220
Balthasar, Hans Urs von, 216
Barbour, Ian, 186, 220
Barclay, John M. G., 161-71, 173-74
Barnes, J. A., 86, 95
Barrett, C. K., 145, 151
Barth, Karl, 99, 100, 102-4, 109, 118, 182-83, 189, 191-96, 200-201, 205-6, 211, 220-21, 225, 242
Batto, Bernard, 292, 311
Beach, Lee, 5, 83
Beck, James R., 333, 351
Bell, Richard H., 170, 174
Bergen, Robert D., 13, 25, 28
Black, Peter, 311
Block, Daniel I., 229, 242
Block, Peter, 311
Bloomquist, L. Gregory, 99, 118

Bockmuehl, Markus, 101, 118
Boda, Mark, 3, 313
Boersma, Hans, 239, 242
Boone, R. Jerome, 229, 242
Bourdieu, Pierre, 173
Brahe, Tycho, 188
Brandt, Donald P., 287, 311
Briggs, Charles A., 23, 28
Briggs, Emilie G., 23, 28
Bright, John, 24, 26, 28
Brodie, Louis T., 35, 44
Brodie, Thomas L., 225, 242
Brown, Alexandra, 122, 151
Brown, William P., 300, 311
Bruce, F. F., 160, 174
Brueggemann, W., 12-15, 19, 26, 27, 28, 30, 37, 44, 311
Bruno, Giordano, 180-81
Buchanan, G. W., 136, 151
Budde, Karl, 42, 44
Bulb, Jeffrey, 204

Calderone, Philip J., 18, 28
Calvin, John, 191, 221, 238, 242, 337
Campbell, Douglas, 4, 120-150, 155, 170, 172, 174
Carroll R., M. Daniel, 152, 292, 311
Carson, D. A., 143, 151
Cayzer, Jeffrey F., 122, 151
Childs, Brevard, 21, 28, 38
Clements, Ronald E., 17, 18, 28, 33, 35, 42, 43, 44
Cloke, Paul, 295, 311

355

Index of Modern Authors

Coe, Douglas E., 185
Cohick, Lynn, 4, 103, 118
Collins, Adela Yarbro, 63, 81
Collins, Francis, 185
Copernicus, Nicholaus, 180, 188
Corbett, Greville, 315, 350
Cousar, Charles B., 151
Creach, Jerome F. D., 301, 311
Cross, F. M., 11, 12, 28
Cruse, Alan, 47, 57

Dabney, D. Lyle, 229, 242
Danker, Frederick W., 60, 82
Darling, Linda, 288, 311
Darwin, Charles, 184
Davis, Ellen F., 302, 311
Davis, Martin M., 215, 221
Dawson, Zachary, 54, 57
Day, John, 35, 45
De Boar, Martinus, 122, 151
Del Colle, Ralph, 231, 242
Descartes, Rene, 212-13
deSilva, David, 110, 118
Dibelius, Martin, 320, 351
Dickau, Tim, 115, 118
Dietrich, Walter, 11, 28
Dobzhansky, T., 185
Donahue, John R., 305, 311
Donfried, Karl, 109, 111, 112, 118
Dooyeweerd, Herman, 211, 221
Draper, John Wilson, 197
Dumbrell, W. J., 136, 139, 151
Dunn, James D. G., 158, 174, 233, 242, 281, 283
Dyer, Bryan R., 348, 352

Edwards, Jonathan, 216
Ehrenberg, Victor H., 60, 82
Eichrodt, Walter, 228, 243
Einstein, Albert, 204
Ellul, Jacques, 117, 118
Epp, Eldon Jay, 324, 351
Erasmus, Desiderius, 181
Eslinger, Lyle M., 15, 28
Evans, Craig A., 51, 57
Evans, Paul S., 2, 3, 11, 22, 28

Fabry, H.-J., 229, 243

Fatehi, Mehrdad, 237, 243
Fauconnier, Gilles, 286
Fee, Gordon, 105, 118, 223, 243, 268, 283
Fensham, F. Charles, 16, 28
Fiddes, Paul S., 189, 221
Finkelstein, J. J., 289, 311
Fiore, Benjamin, 122, 151
Fishman, Joshua A., 87, 95
Foster, Michael, 197-98
Foster, Paul, 170-72, 174-75
Fowl, Stephen, 99, 100, 102-4, 118
Fredriksen, Paula, 160, 175
Freedman, D. L., 136-37, 152
Freedman, Tuvia, 225, 243
Friedberg, Emil, 351
Frost, Michael, 255, 258, 262
Furness, Janet, 285, 313

Gadamer, Hans-Georg, 211, 221
Gager, John G., 159, 175
Galilei, Galileo, 180-81, 188
Garlington, Don, 149, 152
Gasaway, Brantley W., 285, 312
Gaventa, B. R., 122, 152
Goheen, Michael W., 250, 262
Goldingay, John, 293, 312
Goodwin, Mark J., 110, 118
Gordon, R. P., 17, 28
Gorman, Michael, 98, 113, 118, 122, 152, 155, 175
Gould, Stephen Jay, 184-85, 202, 221
Grayson, Albert Kirk, 229, 243
Greely, Martin, 286, 312
Greenlee, J. Harold, 319, 351
Grenz, Stanley, 100, 118, 200, 221
Grudem, Wayne, 238, 243, 316, 329-31, 342, 346, 351-52
Guelich, Robert A., 63, 82
Gundry, Judith M., 306, 312
Gushee, David, 285, 312

Habel, Norman C., 224, 243
Habets, Myk, 231, 243
Halliday, Michael, 53, 54, 57, 351
Harrington, Daniel J., 305, 311
Harris, William V., 326, 351
Harrison, James R., 162-63, 175

Index of Modern Authors

Hasenfratz, Hans-Peter, 229, 243
Hastings, Ross, 4, 211, 250, 262, 344
Hayes, Katherine M., 300, 312
Hayhoe, Katherine, 192
Hays, Richard, 103, 110, 118, 173, 175
Hegerman, H., 137, 152
Henderson, Jim, 85, 95
Herdner, A., 288, 312
Herion, Gary A., 16, 17, 25, 29, 135, 152
Hezser, Catherine, 90, 95
Hiebert, Paul G., 251, 262
Hilborn, D., 140, 152
Hildebrandt, Wilf, 225, 243
Hirsch, Alan, 258, 262
Ho, C. Y. S., 21, 29
Hodge, Charles, 185, 221
Holmes, Janet, 86, 95
Hood, Jason, 98, 118
Hooker, Morna D., 320, 351
Hopkins, Gerard Manley, 218, 221
Hoppe, Leslie J., 229, 244
Horgan, John, 202, 221
Horsley, Richard A., 304, 312
Hossfeld, F.-L., 23, 29
Houston, Jim, 206
Houston, Walter J., 300, 312
Hubbard, Moyer, 339, 351
Hull, Gretchen Gaebelein, 347, 351
Hurowitz, Victor, 15, 29
Huxley, Julian, 184–85, 221

James, Carolyn Custis, 344, 351
Jervis, L. Ann, 108, 118
Jewett, R., 152, 233, 237, 243
Jipp, J. W., 122, 152
Jones, A. H. M., 60, 82
Joyce, Paul M., 229, 243
Judge, Edwin, 207–8, 221

Kahn, Charles H., 133, 152
Kákosy, László, 229, 243
Kalluveettil, Paul, 16, 29
Keener, Craig S., 278, 283, 351
Keller, Timothy, 251, 263
Kendrick, D. T., 316, 351
Kidwell, Jeremy, 190, 221
Kilpatrick, G. D., 102, 119

Kim, Seyoon, 143, 152
Kline, Meredith G., 228, 243
Knight, George, W., III, 331, 344, 348, 351
Knoppers, Gary N., 13, 18, 20, 24, 25, 29
Knox, John, 337–38, 351
Koester, Helmut, 58, 60–62, 69, 78, 82
Kotrosits, Maia, 304, 312
Kraft, Charles H., 252, 263
Kramer, Heinrich, 337, 351
Kramer, Samuel Noah, 288–89, 312
Kraus, Hans-Joachim, 23, 29
Kroeger, Catherine Clark, 333, 351
Kruse, C. G., 144, 152
Kruse, Heinze, 13, 18, 29
Kupper, J.-R., 289, 313

Ladd, G. E., 186
Laato, Antti, 23, 29
Lamb, David A., 54, 57
Lamoureux, Denis, 180
Lee, Jae Hyun, 4, 138, 139, 143–44, 147, 149, 152
Lee-Barnewell, Michelle, 349, 351
Levinsohn, Stephen H., 267, 283
Levison, John R., 226, 243
Lewis, C. S., 188, 221
Liefeld, Walter, 318, 352
Linebaugh, Jonathan, 165–66, 175
Lloyd-Jones, M., 27, 29
Loader, William, 343, 351
Lohfink, Norbert, 288, 290, 294–95, 312
Longenecker, Bruce, 109, 119
Lossky, Vladimir, 217, 221
Lowe, Matthew, 3, 97, 98, 111, 119
Luther, Martin, 103, 161, 337

Macaskill, Grant, 122, 152
Macchia, Frank D., 230, 243
MacDonald, Margaret Y., 327, 352
MacMurray, John, 209
Malina, B. J., 53, 54, 57
Matlock, R. B., 122, 135, 140, 152, 169, 175
Martin, Craig, 227, 243
Martin, Ralph, 102–4, 119

357

Index of Modern Authors

Martyn, J. Louis, 171
Maskell, Kathy, 284, 312
Maslow, Abraham H., 316, 351
Mathews, Mark D., 304, 312
McCarter, P. Kyle, 13, 29
McCarthy, Dennis J., 12, 16, 19, 29
McConville, G. J., 136, 152
McDonald, Lee, 144, 152
McIntyre, Alasdair, 211
McKnight, John, 311
McLaren, Brian, 85, 96
Meeks, Wayne, 53, 57
Melanchthon, P., 104
Mendenall, George E., 16, 17, 25, 29, 135, 152
Merton, Thomas, 209–10, 221
Miano, D., 136–37, 152
Michaelis, Wilhelm, 109, 119
Middleton, J. Richard, 113, 119
Miller, Jeffrey, 316, 352
Miller, Patrick D., 302, 312
Milligan, George, 50, 57
Milroy, Leslie, 87, 96
Mitchell, J. C., 86, 96
Montague, George T., 226, 230, 243
Moo, D. J., 122, 137, 140, 152
Moore, Anne, 302, 312
Mott, Stephen Charles, 162, 175
Moulton, James, 50, 57
Mowinckel, Sigmund, 300, 312

Nanos, Mark D., 105, 119
Nason-Clark, Nancy, 333, 351
Nelson, Janet, 286, 312
Newbigin, Leslie, 212–14, 221
Neyrey, Jerome, 53, 57
Ngursangzeli Behera, Marina, 248, 250–51, 253, 263
Noth, Martin, 10–12, 29

Oakes, Peter, 99, 100, 119
O'Brien, Peter, 172, 175
Ockham, William, 180–81
O'Donovan, Oliver, 190, 221
Olson, Roger E., 100, 118
Ong, Hughson T., 3, 85, 86, 94, 96
Osborne, Grant R., 137, 152, 233, 243
Osiek, Carolyn, 327, 352

Osteen, Joel, 84, 96
Oswalt, John N., 33, 34, 36, 41, 45

Padgett, Alan, 186, 206, 221
Pang, Francis, 3, 303
Park, Young-Ho, 101, 108, 111, 119
Patton, Corinne L., 23, 29
Pavlou, Pavlos, 47, 57
Perry, Peter S., 122, 152
Peters, Ronald, 5, 268, 270, 274, 283
Peterson, Eugene, 104
Peterson, Norman R., 53, 57
Phillips, Peter M., 54, 57
Piper, John, 317, 342, 346, 348, 351–52
Polanyi, Michael, 209, 211, 214–15
Polkinghorne, John, 181, 202–4, 215, 218, 221–22
Popper, Karl, 207–8
Porter, Calvin L., 129, 152
Porter, Stanley E., 3, 49, 52, 62, 66, 74, 82, 84, 144, 149, 152, 303
Poythress, Vern, 316, 352
Provan, Iain W., 25, 29
Puhalo, Lazar, 180–81, 216–18, 222
Punt, Jeremy, 106, 119

Rabens, Volker, 112–14, 119
Rad, Gerhard von, 11–13, 24, 29, 230, 243
Rainer, Thomas, 251, 263
Rauschenbusch, Walter, 285–86
Reeves, Rodney, 98, 119
Reid, Nicole, 5, 83
Rensberger, David, 53, 57
Rhoads, David, 323, 352
Riesner, Rainer, 90, 96
Roberts, J. J. M., 35–38, 45, 301–2, 313
Robertson, A. T., 102, 119
Robinson, John A. T., 65, 82
Robson, James, 229, 243
Rohrbaugh, Richard L., 53, 57
Römer, Thomas, 13, 29
Root, Andrew, 253, 257, 263
Ross, Kenneth R., 246, 253, 263
Roth, M. T., 288, 313
Routley, Laura, 310, 313
Russell, Bertrand, 197

Index of Modern Authors

Sailhamer, John H., 225, 243
Sanders, E. P., 158, 169, 175
Sawyer, John F. A., 31, 45
Sayers, Dorothy L., 318, 352
Schenk, K., 317, 352
Schmemann, Alexander, 218-22
Schreiner, T. R., 122, 140, 145, 152, 153, 339, 352
Schultz, Richard L., 33, 45
Schüssler Fiorenza, Elisabeth, 315, 352
Schwartz, Seth, 155, 175
Scott, J. M., 135, 153
Scotus, Duns, 180, 200, 201
Seifrid, M., 122, 135, 153
Seitz, Christopher, 33, 35, 38, 40, 42, 43, 45
Sider, Ronald J., 251, 284, 263
Simpson, G. G., 185
Smend, Rudof, 11, 30
Smit, Peter-Ben, 100, 104, 119
Smith, Christian, 247, 263
Smith, J. Warren, 135, 153
Smith, James K., 200, 211, 222
Snell, Patricia, 247, 263
Sollberger, E., 289, 313
Sophocles, E. A., 49, 57
Spicker, Paul, 287, 313
Sprenger, James, 337, 351
Springer, Kevin, 252, 261, 263
Stambaugh, John E., 119
Stark, Rodney, 325-27, 352
Stone, Brian, 246, 251, 260, 263
Stovell, Beth, 6, 109, 286, 294, 299-301, 305-6, 313
Strauss, Mark, 316, 352
Studebaker, Steven, 4, 224-25, 230-31, 239, 243-44
Stuhlmacher, Peter, 233, 244
Suttle, Tim, 285, 313
Swartz, David L., 173, 175
Swartz, Steve, 267, 283

Talmon, Shemaryahu, 300, 313
Taussig, Hal, 304, 312
Thiselton, Anthony C., 281, 283
Tibbs, Clint, 267-68, 283
Tilling, Chris, 122, 135, 153
Tomlin, Graham, 103, 104, 119

Torrance, J. B., 123, 135, 153
Torrance, T. F., 183, 206-7, 215, 222
Tseng, Timothy, 285, 313
Tsumura, David Toshio, 224, 244
Tucker, Ruth A., 318, 352
Tull, Patricia K., 33, 45
Turner, Mark, 286

Van Gelder, Craig, 256, 263
Van Seters, John, 13, 30
Vaux, Ronald de, 18, 30
Vawter, Bruce, 229, 244
Veijola, Timo, 13, 23, 30
Vetter, Eva, 86, 96

Waltke, Bruce, 225, 244
Walton, John H., 226, 244
Warren, Rick, 240, 244
Watson, Francis, 173, 175
Watts, John D., 42, 45
Webb, Barry G., 33, 45
Weber, Robert, 31, 45
Weinfeld, Moshe, 16-18, 30, 135, 153
Weippert, Helga, 13, 30
Weiser, Artur, 300, 313
Wellhausen, Julius, 10, 30
Westerholm, Stephen, 143, 153
Westfall, Cynthia, 6, 103, 323, 328, 330, 339, 344, 346, 348, 352
Wieringen, A. L. H. M. van, 39, 43, 45
Wilckens, Ulrich, 145, 153
Wilkinson, Loren, 197-98, 200, 222
Williams, David T., 287, 313
Williamson, H. G. M., 42, 45
Williamson, Paul R., 16, 17, 30, 42, 137, 153
Wilson, Brittany E., 125
Wimber, John, 252, 261, 263
Witherington, Ben, 100-103, 109, 110, 119, 149, 153
Wolff, Hans Walter, 11, 12, 30
Wolters, Al, 228, 244
Woodhouse, Susanne, 229, 244
Wright, Christopher J. H., 293, 307, 313
Wright, John T., 229, 244
Wright, N. T., 98, 101, 112, 119, 120, 155, 158, 175, 286, 313

Index of Modern Authors

Yates, John W., 229-30, 237, 244
Yildiz, F., 313
Yinger, Kent L., 158, 175
Yong, Amos, 230, 244

Zeilinger, Anton, 204

Zenger, E., 23, 28
Zerbe, Gordon Mark, 100-102, 104-6, 120
Zimbrick-Rogers, Emily L., 332, 353
Zizioula, John, 204

Index of Ancient Sources

ANCIENT NEAR EASTERN DOCUMENTS

The Book of the Dead

125	288

OLD TESTAMENT

Genesis

1	191, 196, 198, 224–25, 230–31, 237
1–2	292, 294
1:2	224–25, 228–29
1:3	225
1:27	190
2	191, 237
2:7	226–27, 229, 231, 242
2:17	139
4	191
6:5	281
6:11	281
6:18	136
9:8–17	136
12	17, 18
12:2	17
15	18, 137
15:6	18, 136
15:18	136
17	137
17:1	18
17:6	17
17:7	17
17:10–14	18
17:16	17
22:17	17

Exodus

3:9	294
3:14	209
3:15	320
14:21	227
15	294
15:8	227–28
15:10	227–28
20:1–3	139
22–33	294
23	294
29:1	320
29:7	320

Leviticus

2:2	319, 321
8:12	320
19	295
19:9–10	295
19:13–14	295
19:15–16	295
19:17–18	296
19:33–34	296
19:35–37	296
23:22	295

Index of Ancient Sources

Leviticus (continued)

24:7	321
25	296
25–26	295
25:23	296
25:25–28	296
25:35–37	296
25:38	296
25:39–43	296
25:55	296–97
26	296–97

Numbers

5:25–26	319
5:28	319

Deuteronomy

4	297
4:25–31	297
10:17	297–98
10:17–19	297
10:18	297–98
10:19	298
14	310
14:28–29	298
15	309
15:9	310
15:1–3	298
15:4–5	298
15:7–11	298
15:9	299
26:7	294
28:15–68	137
29–30	136
31	11
32:10	228
34	12

Joshua

1:11–15	11
1:23	11
12	11
21:45	13
23:14–15	13
24:1–28	136

Judges

2:11–23	11

1 Samuel

4–5	14
6–7	14
10:1	320
12	11, 137
13:13–14	12
16:1	320
16:13	320
16:14	19
19:16	320
25:28	12

2 Samuel

3:2–5	14
3:18	12
4:10	52, 56
5:1–3	14
5:6–9	14
5:11	14
5:13–16	14
5:17–25	14
6:1–11	14
6:17	14
7	2, 9, 12–14, 17–24, 26, 27
7:1	12
7:2–4	15
7:6–7	15
7:8–9	15
7:9	17
7:11	15, 17
7:14	16, 17, 20, 27
7:14–15	21
7:14–16	19
7:15	16
7:16	19, 23
7:28	9, 13
10:16	278
18:20	52
23:5	16

1 Kings

2:3–4	13

Index of Ancient Sources

8:14–61	11	8:6	292, 300
8:17	13	8:9	292
8:56	13	8:16	300
8:57	13	18:50	9
11:13	25	22	302
11:32	25	23:5	320
11:34–36	25	32:12	137
12:15	25	33:6–7	225
15:11–14	19	34:19	85
19:16	320	48:4–6	339
		67:21	339
		68	302
2 Kings		72	9, 299–302
17:7–23	11	72:2	301
18:3–5	19	72:4	301
21:11–15	23	72:8–11	301
22:2	19	72:12	301
23:1–3	137	72:14	301
23:25	12	72:17	27
24–25	20	74:12–17	224, 226
24:19–20	23	84:9	9
24:20	25	89	21–24, 137
		89:3	16
		89:3–4	9, 16
1 Chronicles		89:28	16
17	21, 24	89:31–34	22
17:13–14	21	89:34	16
		89:38–39	22
		89:39	16
2 Chronicles		89:46–51	9, 22
13:5	16	102	302
21:7	16	103	302
		105:15	320
		118	305
Job		132	21–24, 26
26:12–13	224	132:10	9
		132:11–12	22, 23
		132:13–14	23
Psalms		132:17	9
2	9, 38	132:17–18	23
2:7	27	139	348
5	302	145	302
6:2–4	339	146	302
7:11	339		
8	292, 300		
8:1–2	292	**Isaiah**	
8:3	300	5:8–25	42
8:5	292, 300	6	35, 39, 42, 43

363

Index of Ancient Sources

Isaiah (continued)

Reference	Pages
6–12	3, 31, 44
6:3	43
6:5	43
6:8–9	42
6:11–13	43
6:13	43
7	31, 32, 35, 36
7–8	35, 38
7–10	39
7–12	31–35, 39–43
7–39	33
7:1–2	39
7:2	32, 34, 35
7:3	35
7:4	41
7:6	32
7:8	32
7:9	32, 36
7:11	34, 35
7:13	32
7:14	35
7:15–16	36
7:17	32, 36
7:23	39
7:23–24	34
7:24	39
8:4	35
8:6	32
8:7	35, 36
8:7–8	33
8:8	36
8:11	32
8:12	32
8:16	34
8:17	36
8:18	34–36, 39
8:20	34
8:22	34
8:23—9:1	34
9	38, 302
9–10	38
9–11	38
9–12	37, 38
9:2–7	9
9:3	34, 35
9:5–6	38
9:6	38
9:8	32
9:9	40
9:11	9, 32, 34, 35, 39
9:13	40
9:16	34, 35, 39
9:17	34, 35, 39–41
9:18	39
9:20	34, 39
9:21	32, 35
10:1	34, 42
10:1–2	37
10:1–4	38
10:4	34, 35, 39
10:5	34, 42
10:5–6	38
10:8–14	33
10:15	40
10:15–16	33
10:16–18	41
10:17	34, 39
10:18	34, 35, 40
10:19	34, 35, 40
10:20	37
10:21	37
10:22	37
10:24–26	33
10:26	34, 35
10:32	33
10:33–34	40, 41
10:34	34, 35, 39
11	38, 302
11–12	39, 43
11:1	40, 41, 43
11:1–5	38
11:1–9	231
11:4	231–32
11:8	41, 43
11:10	34, 40
11:11	33, 37
11:11—12:6	33
11:12	34
11:13–14	32, 33
11:16	33, 37
12:1	34, 35
12:1–2	38
29:13	279
32	228
32:14–18	229

Index of Ancient Sources

32:15	226	37:9	229
35:5–6	72	37:14	229
36	33	37:23	16
36–39	33, 36		
39–40	43	### Daniel	
40	294		
40–46	33	3:16–18	339
40:9	56, 62	7	304
40:10–11	294		
42	23	### Joel	
42:1	231, 233		
42:3–4	233	2	233, 239
42:18	72	2:28	239
52:7	55, 56, 62	2:28–32	233
52–53	31		
54:5–10	16	### Amos	
55:3–4	137		
58:6	74	4:13	55
59:21	279		
61	306	### Zechariah	
61:1	55, 56, 62, 72		
61:1–2	74	9	305
61:1–3	54	11:4–17	137
61:1–9	232		
63:11–14	228	## APOCRYPHA	
66:2	279		
		### Tobit	
### Jeremiah			
		4:11	167
24:7	279		
30:8–33	25	### Sirach	
31:33	16		
33:14	25	18.1	201
		### Wisdom of Solomon	
### Ezekiel			
		1–16	129
1	299	8:21	166
3	299	11:23	145
10	299	16:6	321
11	282		
11:19–20	279	## PSEUDEPIGRAPHA	
33	299		
34	9, 299, 306–7, 310	### 1 Enoch	
36	280, 282		
36–37	229	89:42	102
36:25	280		
36:26–27	279		
37:1–4	229, 231		

Index of Ancient Sources

NEW TESTAMENT

Matthew

Reference	Page(s)
1:20	231–32
1:21	44
2:11	319
3	44
3:7	91
3:10–12	44
3:11	233
4:12–13	70
4:12–14	69
4:12–17	69
4:17	70, 83
4:23	69–71
4:23–25	69
5–7	87, 93
5:1	93
5:3	73
5:6	348
5:13	73
5:20	91, 92
6:20–21	167
6:24	143
7:28	93
8:1	93
8:14–15	89
9:9–13	89
9:11	91
9:18–19	89
9:20–22	89
9:23	93
9:22–26	89
9:25	93
9:27–31	87
9:34	91
9:35	71
10	71
10:37	347
11:5	55, 56, 72, 76
12	92
12:1–8	91
12:2	91
12:14	91
12:15	93
12:18	233
12:24	91
12:27	241
12:28	233
12:38	91
13:1–3	93
13:2	93
14:5	93
14:21	94
15:10	93
15:12	91
15:21–28	89
15:30	93
15:35	93
15:39	91
16:21	91
16:27	146
17:1–9	89
19:2	93
19:16–26	306
20–21	306
20:18	91
20:29–34	306
21:15	91
21:23	91, 92
21:26	93
21:46	93, 321
22:15	91
22:23	91
22:34	91
22:41	91
22:41–46	92
22:46	92
23	92
23:2	91
23:3	92
23:13	91
23:13–14	92
23:15	91
24:14	71
25:31–33	146
26:1–5	321
26:1–9	321
26:5	93, 321
26:6–13	89
26:10	332
26:11	310
26:13	72, 321
26:14–26	321
26:17–27	321
26:31–35	321

26:37-38	89	9-10	303-4
26:40-56	232	9-11	304, 306
26:55	90	9-12	303
27:1	91	9:1	304
27:3	91	9:2-9	89
27:7	232	9:7	304
27:12	91	9:9	304
27:20	91, 93	9:12	304
27:22	93	9:17	304
27:24	321	9:24	304
27:41	91	9:31	304
27:55-56	89	9:33-42	304
27:61	89, 232	9:35	304
28:1	232	9:36-37	304
28:1-8	89	9:42	304
28:8-10	318	9:47	304
28:9-10	89	10	94, 305
28:19	273-74	10-12	304
28:20	321	10:1	93
		10:13-14	304
		10:13-15	304
Mark		10:13-16	304-5
1:1	59, 62-64, 67, 83	10:14	304
1:8	63, 233	10:17-27	306
1:9	63	10:17-31	304-5
1:13	63, 64	10:20	304
1:14	63-65, 69	10:23-25	304
1:14-15	83	10:24	304-5
1:15	64, 65, 69, 70	10:28	85
1:29-31	89	10:29	67, 347
2:4	93	10:29-30	304
2:14-17	89	10:31	304
2:23-28	91	10:33	91, 304
3:9	93	10:35	94
5:21-24	89	10:35-45	94
5:25-34	89	10:36	94
5:25-43	89	10:37-34	94
5:37-43	89	10:45	304
6:3	203	10:46-52	306
6:34	93	10:47-48	304-5
6:44	94	10:48	304
7:9-13	328	10:48-52	304
7:24-30	89	10:50	94
8:11-21	91	10:51	94
8:31	91	10:51-52	94
8:31-33	66	11	303, 305
8:35	66, 67, 85	11:1-11	305
9	304-5	11:10	304-5

Mark (continued)

11:12–26	305
11:18	91, 93
11:27	91
11:27–33	305
11:28	92
11:32	93
12	303
12:34	92
12:40	304
12:41–44	304
13:10	68, 69, 71
13:26–27	146
14:1	91
14:7	310
14:3–9	89
14:9	68, 71, 72
14:12–22	321
14:25	93
14:33–34	89
14:43	91
14:53	91
15:1	91
15:31	91
15:40–41	89, 322
15:47	89
16:1–8	89
16:6–8	318
16:9–11	89
16:15	62
16:20	261

Luke

1:19	73
1:35	231–32, 234
1:46–55	322
1:51–53	316
2:10	73
3:16	233
3:18	74
4	306
4:1	235
4:1–13	233
4:14	235
4:14–19	232
4:17–19	234
4:18	54, 56, 74
4:18–19	316
4:19	55
4:31—5:26	232
4:32–37	276
4:38–39	89
4:43	75, 76, 83
4:43–47	276
5:1	93
5:15	93
5:27–32	89
6:1–5	91
6:1–49	93
7:22	76
7:36–50	89
7:46	320
8:1	76
8:40–42	89
8:43–48	89
8:49–56	89
8:51–57	89
9:2	76
9:6	76
9:14	94
9:22	91
9:28–36	89
10:1–22	325
10:3	325
10:21	325
10:27	250
11:13	234
12:10	272
13:52	276
14:26	346
16:16	77
18:1–8	306
18:15–17	306
18:31–34	306
18:35–43	306
19:1–10	306
19:11–27	306
19:27	306
19:28–40	306
19:47	90
20:1	77, 91
20:2	92
20:19	91
20:40	92
21:37	90

Index of Ancient Sources

22:2	91	11:25–26	322
22:19	321	11:27	90
22:20	138	11:28–30	91
22:25–27	326	11:32	90
22:66	91	11:33–36	90
23:10	91	11:50–52	320
23:49	89	12	305
23:55–56	89	12:1–8	89
24:1–11	89	12:4–8	90
24:6–10	318	12:8	310
24:10–11	89	12:37–43	92
24:49	234	14:10	182
		14:6	210
		14:16–18	256
		14:20	182

John

		14:23	182
1	187–88	14:26	256, 274
1:1	187, 232	16:12–15	256
1:1–3	196, 203	17:5	187
1:1–4	189	17:24	187
1:1–14	187	17:26	237
1:3	187, 196, 199	19:25–27	89
1:4–13	205	19:26	322
1:12–13	235	20:1–2	89
1:14	182, 196, 212–13, 216, 232	20:11–13	89
1:18	181–82	20:11–18	318
1:33	233	20:14–18	89
3:1–8	235		
3:1–21	87		
3:16	85		

Acts

4	306		
5:13	93	1	234, 281
5:22	146	1:4–5	234
5:26–27	146	2	234
6:22	93	2:17	234
7:49	93	2:33	234
8:19	182	2:38–39	240
9	305–7	3:12	325
9–10	305–7	4:8	275
10	306–7	4:13	325
10:10	317	4:16	276
10:38	182	4:21	276
11:1–44	90	4:22	276
11:5	90	6:5	276
11:8–16	90	7:55	276
11:16	90	9:5–9	103
11:20	91	10:4	321
11:21–22	90	10–11	256
11:24	91	10:28	256

369

Acts (continued)

10:34–35	256
10:38	276
10:42	146
10:44–45	256
11:24	276
13	276
13:4	273
13:9	276
14:20	261
15	257
15:28	257
16:6	273
16:33	347
17:10	273
17:26–27	348
23:8	91

Romans

1–3	129, 133, 145
1–4	125, 133, 137
1:4	233
1:5	112
1:6–17	126
1:16	143, 262
1:18	129, 137–39, 143–44
1:18–23	138
1:18–32	122, 126–30, 132–33, 141–45, 149, 281
1:18—2:8	126, 141
1:18—3:20	121–28, 132–33, 137–38, 141, 143, 148–50
1:18—3:30	130
1:18—4:25	123, 137–38, 141–42
1:19–20	138, 143–44
1:19–32	129, 144
1:20–23	138
1:21–22	138–39
1:21–23	142–44
1:23	133, 138
1:23–27	129
1:24–27	129, 144
1:24–32	144
1:26–27	133
1:28	139, 142–43, 145
1:28–31	133, 139
1:28–32	144
1:29–31	129, 139, 143
1:32	129–30, 133, 145
2	130
2:1	130, 142–43, 145, 149
2:1–5	126–28, 133, 145, 149
2:1–8	128, 133
2:1—3:9	141
2:1—3:20	122
2:2	145
2:4–5	130–31, 145
2:5–6	128
2:6	126
2:6–8	126
2:6–10	131, 145–46
2:6–11	139, 146–47
2:7–10	128
2:8	139
2:9—3:9	126, 141
2:9–16	126, 134
2:9–29	133–34
2:14	143, 147
2:14–15	126
2:14–16	132, 147, 150
2:15–16	147
2:16	131
2:17–24	126, 128
2:17–29	134
2:21–22	128, 147
2:21–23	132, 147
2:23–26	147
2:24	329
2:25–29	126, 132, 147
2:28–29	280
3:1–8	137
3:1–9	126, 128, 134
3:1–20	133–34
3:4	168
3:9	148
3:9–18	134
3:9–20	126, 140–41
3:10–18	128
3:19–20	134
3:21	130
3:21–26	138
3:21–31	126, 128
3:21—4:25	124, 127
3:22	155

3:26	155	10:13	161, 237
4:1–25	126	10:15–16	55, 56
4:23–25	126	12:13	109
5–8	123–25, 139–41, 148	12:14	105
5:3–5	85, 347	13:14	343
5:5	277	14:4	344
5:6	167	14:7	277
5:9	140	15:11	112
5:12	139–40	16	326
5:12–14	142	16:3	114
5:12–21	124, 148	16:7	324
5:12—8:39	150	16:9	114
5:14	140	16:21	114
5:15–21	142		
5:16	140		
6:1	27, 149	**1 Corinthians**	
6:1–12	148	1	106
6:1–14	236	1:18	161
6:1–23	148	1:21	161
6:1—7:25	149	1:26–28	168
6:13–23	148	2:4	111
6:15	27, 140, 149	2:6–8	335
6:15–23	148–49	3:6	114
6:23	149	3:15	340
7:1	149	4:13	105
7:1–4	148–49	6:3	101
7:7	148–49	6:20	85
7:7–13	148	7:8	340
7:7–25	148	7:34	340
7:13	148–49	8	110
7:14	148	9:19	326
7:14–24	148	9:22	112
7:25	148	11:5	327
8:1–11	236	11:25	138, 321
8:1–13	148	12	114
8:10	236	12–14	277
8:11	231, 233, 236, 241	12:3	276
8:14–16	345	12:4–11	277
8:19–22	84	12:28–29	324
8:21	241	13	277
8:23	283	14	327
8:24	269	14:26–32	327
8:32	172	15:3	91
9:6	168	15:42–49	283
9:25–26	110		
10:2–3	162	**2 Corinthians**	
10:8–10	85		
10:10–11	161	3:3	110

371

2 Corinthians (continued)

4:5	114
4:10–14	241
4:18	241
5:5	283
5:10	146
5:16–21	348
6:6	277
6:16	110
7:1	270
7:3	270
8:9	172
8:23	114
9:15	172
11:3–4	102
11:13–15	102
11:23–29	154
12:14–15	114
13:13	273–74

Galatians

1:4	172
1:6–7	50
2:16	155
2:21	341
3:20	155
3:22	155
3:26–28	235
5:1	317, 341
5:2	317
5:23	347
6:7	140

Ephesians

1:1—3:12	4
1:7	157, 160, 171
1:7–10	156
1:7–13	157
1:8	157
1:9–10	131
1:10	169, 171
1:11	158
1:11–12	157
1:11—2:22	158
1:13	158, 172
1:14	281
1:15	172
1:22–23	131
2	156, 159, 172
2:1	156, 159
2:1–10	156
2:2	159
2:4	159
2:5	156, 159
2:5–9	169
2:5–10	159, 173
2:7	156, 167, 171–72
2:8	155–56, 159, 167, 170–72
2:8–9	155, 167, 340
2:8–10	4, 26, 155–56, 160, 173
2:9	162, 172
2:10	159, 168, 328, 348
2:11	159
2:11–22	159
2:13	171
2:14	159
2:16	171
3	172
3:1–12	156–57
3:1–13	171
3:3–5	157
3:4	170
3:6	157, 160, 170–71
3:6–12	168
3:7	157, 167
3:8	157, 170–72
3:9	171
3:10	157, 160, 170, 335
3:11	170
3:12	157, 170, 172
4	160
4:1	172
4:4	172
4:7	167
4:11	324
4:24	160
4:30	274
5:8	340
5:25–33	326
6:6	347
6:12	335

Index of Ancient Sources

Philippians

1:8	99
1:12	99, 109
1:12–26	100
1:13	99, 107
1:14	99
1:15–18	99
1:27	98, 100, 101
1:28	140
1:29–30	85
1:30	116
2:1–5	99
2:1–11	326
2:6–8	101
2:9–11	101
2:12	85
2:17–18	108
3	102
3:1	102, 104
3:2	103, 106, 116
3:2–11	102, 105
3:4	104
3:5–6	162
3:8	103
3:8–9	104
3:9	155
3:10–11	107
3:12–17	107
3:17	99
3:17—4:1	103
3:18	107
3:20	100, 101, 107
4:4–7	107
4:21–22	107

Colossians

1:15	192
1:15–17	196
1:25	114
2:14	167
2:15	335

1 Thessalonians

1	109, 112
1:1–10	112
1:2–10	109
1:3	112
1:5	111
1:6	108, 112
1:6–7	108
1:8	109, 112
1:9	98
1:9–10	109, 140
1:10	111, 112
2:4	347
2:16	140
2:19	112
3:13	112
5:3	104
5:8	112

2 Thessalonians

1:6–10	131

1 Timothy

1:15	340
2:4	85
2:9–15	335, 338
2:11–15	327
2:12	330, 336, 338–39
2:12–14	336
2:13–14	336
2:15	318, 339
3:1	327, 331
3:1–13	327
6:15	181

Titus

1:5–9	327
3:3–5	326

Hebrews

3:7	275
9:8	275
9:15	138
10:3	321
10:15	275
12:24	138
13:14	241

James

1:2–4	85
1:2–8	347
1:9–11	316
2:1–12	350
2:23	26
4:4–5	281
5:15	339

1 Peter

1:1	259
1:6–7	85
1:12	320
2:4	259
2:4–10	259
2:9	259
2:11	259
2:12	253
3:1–7	326
3:15	253
4:3–4	281

1 John

1:1	214

Revelation

21–22	241
21:1–4	241

GRECO-ROMAN WRITINGS

Aristophanes, *Eq.*

643–56	53

Aristotle, *Eth. nic.*

1157b7–8	165

Chariton, *Chaer.*

2.1.3	53

Diodorus Siculus, *Library of History*

15.74	51

Josephus, *War*

4.618	51

Philo

Abr. 268	164
Conf. 123–27	164
Ebr. 73, 75	164
Leg. 3.161–165	164
Legat. 2.44–48	164
Legat. 3.77, 79, 83, 95	165
Migr. 77	165
Mos. 2.242	165
Post. 142–47	162
Sacr. 54–57	165
Spec. 3.171	324
Virt. 41	52

Plutarch, *Ages.*

17.3.6	52
33.5	51

Seneca, *Ben.*

1.1.1–2	164
1.15.6	163–64
3.1.1	163
3.6.1–2	165
3.29.1–38.3	164
4.6.4–5	164
4.18.1	163

Xenophon, *Hell.*

1.6.37	51
4.3.14	52

Index of Ancient Sources

EARLY CHRISTIAN WRITINGS

2 Clement

8.5	78

Chrysostom, *Hom. Phil.*

89 (Homily 5)	116

Didache

9.5	102

Eusebius, *Hist. eccl.*

3.39.15	65

Gregory Nyssen, *Contra Eunom.*

3	217

Ignatius, *Eph.*

7:1	102

Origen, *Cels.*

3:59	325

Tertullian, *Cult. fem.*

1.1	337